D0777981

Paul, Thessalonica, *and* Early Christianity

Karl Paul Donfried

William B. Eerdmans Publishing Company
Grand Rapids, Michigan / Cambridge, U.K.

Copyright © 2002 by T&T Clark
All rights reserved

Originally published 2002 in the United Kingdom by
T&T Clark Ltd
The Continuum International Publishing Group Ltd
The Tower Building, 11 York Road
London SE1 7NX *and*

370 Lexington Avenue
New York 10017-6503, USA

This edition published 2002 in the United States of America by
Wm. B. Eerdmans Publishing Company
255 Jefferson Ave. S.E., Grand Rapids, Michigan 49503 /
P.O. Box 163 Cambridge CB3 9PU U.K.
www.eerdmans.com

Manufactured in Bodmin, Cornwall, UK

07   06   05   04   03   02   5   4   3   2   1

ISBN 0-8028-0509-4

BS
2725.52
.D660
2002

JESUIT - KRAUSS - McCORMICK - LIBRARY
1100 EAST 55th STREET
CHICAGO, ILLINOIS 60615

THIS BOOK IS RESPECTFULLY DEDICATED TO

SHEMARYAHU TALMON
J. L. Magnes Professor Emeritus of Biblical Studies
The Hebrew University of Jerusalem

JOSEPH A. FITZMYER, S. J.
Professor Emeritus of Biblical Studies
The Catholic University of America

KARL KERTELGE
Professor Emeritus für Exegese des Neuen Testaments
Katholisch-theologische Fakultät der Westfälischen Wilhems-
Universität Münster

GENEROUS FRIENDS, MAGNIFICENT HUMAN BEINGS
AND MODELS OF OUTSTANDING SCHOLARSHIP

Contents

Preface

This volume contains a selection of fifteen essays written between 1974 and the present; they are offered here in their original form with the exception of minor corrections. The introduction is intended to place these essays in a context and, to a limited degree, respond to my dialogue partners. The only exception to this has been my article on 'Justification and Last Judgment in Paul', which has required a more detailed reply both in light of recent ecumenical developments and the publication of additional texts from the Dead Sea Scrolls.

Also published for the first time is my essay entitled 'Shifting Paradigms: Paul, Jesus and Judaism', which was given as the inaugural lecture for the Elizabeth A. Woodson Chair in Religion and Biblical Literature at Smith College in April 2001. The article published in the Festschrift for Otto Knoch in German appears for the first time in English as 'Was Timothy in Athens? Some Exegetical Reflections on 1 Thessalonians 3. 1–3'. 'Chronology: the Apostolic and Pauline Period' is an abbreviated version of a longer entry in *ABD*, the section on Jesus having been omitted given the primary intention of this collection.

Articles in this volume are arranged in the following manner. 'Shifting Paradigms: Paul, Jesus and Judaism' is placed in the opening position since it is the most recent and situates my understanding of Paul and 1 Thessalonians in the context of the Judaisms of the Second Temple Period. This essay is followed by general articles on 1 and 2 Thessalonians, then articles on 1 Thessalonians according to their sequence in the letter and, finally, more general articles dealing with Paul but having specific relevance to 1 Thessalonians. The discussion of these essays follows this order except in those cases where it seemed more helpful to cluster the conversation around common themes.

I am especially grateful for a number of opportunities that have helped sharpen, expand and mature my thinking with regard to the Thessalonian correspondence:

- the opportunity to serve as visiting professor at Yale Divinity School during the 1993–4 academic year which allowed me to explore the theme of the apocalyptic in Paul with some very fine students and to deepen my already high regard for Abraham Malherbe and Leander Keck;
- the enriching experiences in Jerusalem during 1997 as Fulbright Visiting Professor at Hebrew University. Not only am I indebted to the splendid students in my graduate seminar on 'Paul and the Dead Sea Scrolls', but also to a number of superb colleagues in Jerusalem from whom I learned so much as a result of their generous sharing and kind hospitality: Magen Broshi, David Flusser, Kevin McCaffrey, Jerome Murphy-O'Connor, Stephen Pfann, Bargil Pixner, David Satran, Shemaryahu Talmon and Justin Taylor;
- the co-chairmanship with Johannes Beutler of the 'The Thessalonian Correspondence Seminar' of the *Studiorum Novi Testamenti Societas* (SNTS) from 1995–2000 and the superb collaboration with the outstanding members of that seminar which helped produce *The Thessalonians Debate: Methodological Discord or Methodological Synthesis?*

Finally, a word about the dedication of this book to three exceptional biblical scholars. I first met *Shemaryahu Talmon* during his first visit to Smith College in the early 1970s, where, subsequently, he has been a frequent lecturer, most recently in the year 2000. His friendship, incredible support and generous hospitality during our time in Jerusalem will never be forgotten and his life story has forever deepened my solidarity with my Jewish brothers and sisters. Since the beginning of our common work in 1971 on the national Lutheran–Roman Catholic Dialogue's project on Peter in the New Testament and, subsequently, on Mary in the New Testament, I have benefited greatly from *Joseph Fitzmyer*'s enormous learning and generosity of spirit. His pioneering work on the Dead Sea Scrolls and his commentary on Romans, one of the most outstanding commentaries of the twentieth century, have profoundly influenced my own scholarship. *Karl Kertelge* and I had the privilege of co-chairing the Seminar on Pauline Theology of the *Studiorum Novi Testamenti Societas* (SNTS) from 1976–79, an attempt by a German Roman Catholic scholar and an American Lutheran scholar to bridge both cultural and confessional boundaries in the study of Paul. His magnificent study, *'Rechtfertigung' bei Paulus*, ushered in a new era in the study of this controversial Pauline theme and has significantly shaped my own exegesis. A friendship of mutual respect and admiration has continued ever since our initial, successful collaborative SNTS efforts.

There is yet one other significant person to whom I owe an enormous debt of gratitude: Kathy, my wife and friend for over forty years. Her generous assistance throughout my academic career has been invaluable and her assistance in the critical reading of this manuscript and in compiling the Index of Modern Authors and the Index of Ancient Texts has been indispensable. How appropriate are the words written by Ben Sira in Sirach 26:1–3, especially his insight that a 'good wife is a great blessing'!

Karl P. Donfried
Elizabeth A. Woodson Professor of Religion
    and Biblical Literature
Smith College
Northampton, MA 01063

꧁꧂

Acknowledgments and Original Locations

I am grateful to the original publishers for permission to republish the following essays in this book.

'The Cults of Thessalonica and the Thessalonian Correspondence', *NTS* 31 (1985) pp. 336–56.

'2 Thessalonians and the Church of Thessalonica', in *Origins and Method: Towards a New Understanding of Judaism and Christianity. Essays in Honour of John C. Hurd*, ed. Bradley H. McLean (Sheffield: Sheffield Academic Press, 1993), pp. 128–44.

'1 Thessalonians, Acts and the Early Paul', in *The Thessalonian Correspondence*, ed. R. F. Collins, BETL 87 (Leuven: University Press–Peeters, 1990), pp. 3–26.

'Chronology: the Apostolic and Pauline Period', is an abbreviated form of 'Chronology, New Testament' in *The Anchor Bible Dictionary* (6 vols), ed. David Noel Freedman (New York: Doubleday, 1992), pp. 1:1011–22.

'The Theology of 1 Thessalonians as a Reflection of Its Purpose', in *To Touch the Text: Biblical and Related Studies in Honor of Joseph A. Fitzmyer, SJ*, ed. Maurya P. Horgan and Paul J. Kobelski (New York: Crossroad, 1989), pp. 243–60.

'The Assembly of the Thessalonians: Reflections on the Ecclesiology of the Earliest Christian Letter', in *Ekklesiologie des Neuen Testaments* (Festschrift K. Kertelge; ed. Rainer Kampling and Thomas Söding; Freiburg, Basel, Wien: Herder, 1996), pp. 390–408.

'The Epistolary and Rhetorical Context of 1 Thess. 2.1–12', in *The Thessalonian Correspondence: Methodological Discord or*

Methodological Synthesis?, ed. Karl P. Donfried and Johannes Beutler (Grand Rapids: Eerdmans, 2000), pp. 31–60.

'Paul and Judaism: 1 Thessalonians 2.13–16 as a Test Case', *Int* 38 (1984), pp. 242–53.

'Was Timothy in Athens? Some Exegetical Reflections on 1 Thess. 3.1–3'. Appeared originally as 'War Timotheus in Athen? Exegetische Überlegungen zu 1 Thess 3,1–3', in *Die Freude an Gott – unsere Kraft: Festschrift für Otto Bernhard Knoch zum 65. Geburtstag*, ed. J. J. Degenhardt (Stuttgart: Verlag Katholisches Bibelwerk, 1991), pp. 189–96. This translation into English appears in print for the first time.

'Paul and Qumran: The Possible Influence of סרך on 1 Thessalonians', in *The Dead Sea Scrolls Fifty Years After Their Discovery* (Jersusalem: The Magnes Press, 2000), 1–9.

'The Kingdom of God in Paul', in *The Kingdom of God in 20th Century Interpretation*, ed. Wendell Willis (Peabody, MA.: Hendrickson, 1987), pp. 175–90.

'Justification and Last Judgment in Paul', in *La Notion biblique de Dieu*, ed. J. Coppens; BETL 41 (Gembloux: J. Duculot, 1976), pp. 293–313.

'Paul as Σκηνοποιός and the Use of the Codex in Early Christianity', in *Christus Bezeugen* (Festschrift für Wolfgang Trilling; ed. Karl Kertelge, Traugott Holtz and Claus-Peter März; Leipzig: St. Benno Verlag, 1990), pp. 249–56.

Acronyms and Abbreviations for Journals and Book Series

BKP	Beitrage zur klassischen Philologie
BNTC	Black's New Testament Commentaries
BPAA	Bibliotheca Pontificii Athenaei Antoniani
BZNW	Beihefte der Zeitschrift für die neutestamentliche Wissenschaft
CBQ	*Catholic Biblical Quarterly*
DBAT	Dielheimer Blätter zum Alten Testament
EDNT	*Exegetical Dictionary of the New Testament*, ed. Horst Balz and Gerhard Schneider 3 vols (Grand Rapids: Eerdmans, 1990–93)
EKK	Evangelische-katholischer Kommentar zum Neuen Testament
ExpTim	*Expository Times*
EtB	Études bibliques
EThSt	Erfurter theologische Studien
ETL	*Ephemerides Theologicae Lovanienses*
EvTh	*Evangelische Theologie*
FB	Forschung zur Bibel
FFNT	Foundations and Facets, New Testament
FRLANT	Forschungen zur Religion und Literatur des Alten und Neuen Testaments
GNT	Grundrisse zum Neuen Testament
GTA	Göttinger theologische Arbeiten
HNT	Handbuch zum Neuen Testament
HNTC	Harper's New Testament Commentaries
HTKNT	Herders theologischer Kommentar zum Neuen Testament
HTR	*Harvard Theological Review*
HUTh	Hermeneutische Untersuchungen zur Theologie
IBS	*Irish Biblical Studies*
ICC	International Critical Commentary
IDB	*The Interpreter's Dictionary of the Bible*, ed. G. A. Buttrick, 4 vols (Nashville, 1962)
Int	*Interpretation*
JBL	*Journal of Biblical Literature*
JJS	*Journal of Jewish Studies*
JSNT	*Journal for the Study of New Testament*

JSNTSup	Journal for the Study of the New Testament, Supplement Series
JSOT	*Journal for the Study of the Old Testament*
JTS	*Journal of Theological Studies*
KEK	Kritisch-exegetischer kommentar über das Neuen Testament
KNT	Kommentar zum Neuen Testament
LD	Lectio Divino
LEC	Library of Early Christianity
LW	*Living Word*
NAC	New American Commentary
NCB	New Century Bible
NICNT	New International Commentary on the New Testament
NIGTC	New International Greek Testament Commentary
NovT	*Novum Testamentum*
NovTSup	Novum Testamentum, Leiden – Supplements
NTAbh	Neutestamentliche Abhandlungen
NTD	Das Neue Testament Deutsch
NTOA	Novum Testamentum et Orbis Antiquus
NTS	*New Testament Studies*
PBA	Proceedings of the British Academy
ProEccl	*Pro Ecclesia*
PRSt	*Perspectives in Religious Studies*
PVTG	Pseudepigrapha Veteris Testamenti Graece
RechBib	Recherches bibliques
RB	*Revue biblique*
RGG	*Religion in Geschichte und Gegenwart*, ed. K. Galling, 6 vols, 3rd ed. (Tübingen: J. C. B. Mohr, 1957–62)
RTR	*Reformed Theological Review*
SBLDS	SBL Dissertation Series
SBLSBS	SBL Sources for Biblical Literature
SBS	Stuttgarter Bibelstudien
SBT	Studies in Biblical Theology
SHCT	Studies in the History of Christian Thought
SJT	*Scottish Journal of Theology*
SJTOP	Scottish Journal of Theology Occasional Papers

SNTSMS	Society for New Testament Studies Monograph Series
SP	Sacra Pagina
SVTP	Studia in Veteris Testamenti Pseudepigraphica
TBT	*The Bible Today*
TDNT	*Theological Dictionary of the New Testament*, ed. G. Kittel and G. Friedrich, 10 vols (Grand Rapids: Eerdmans, 1964–76)
TGI	*Theologie und Glaube*
ThF	Theologische Forschung
ThH	Théologie Historique
ThR	*Theologische Rundschau*
ThStKr	*Theologische Studien und Kritiken*
ThZ	Theological Zeitschrift, Basel
TLZ	*Theologische Literaturzeitung*
TThR	Tübinger theologische Reihe
TU	Texte und Untersuchungen
UNT	Untersuchungen zum Neuen Testament
WBC	*Word Biblical Commentary*
VF	*Verkündigung und Forschung*
WMANT	Wissenschaftliche Monographien zum Alten und Neuen Testament
WUNT	*Wissenschaftliche Untersuchungen zum Neuen Testament*
ZBK.NT	Züricher Bibelkommentar, NT
ZNW	*Zeitschrift für die Neutestamentliche Wissenschaft*
ZTK	*Zeitschrift für Theologie und Kirche*
ZWKB	Zürcher Werkkommentar zur Bibel

The Scope and Nature of the Essays: An Introduction and Some Responses

'The Cults of Thessalonica and the Thessalonian Correspondence',[1] an essay originally presented as an invited main paper at the 1984 annual conference of the *Studiorum Novi Testamenti Societas* meeting at the University of Basel, has as its primary goal to place the Thessalonian correspondence within the broader Greco-Roman culture of the city of Thessalonica, particularly its cultic background, and to urge that such an analysis was essential for an informed interpretation of the letters. Caution was urged both with regard to the explanation of often fragmentary evidence as well as to its application. By making possible suggestions with regard to specific exegetical matters it was intended to raise levels of awareness rather than advocating definitive answers to controverted issues. A wide range of monographs, commentaries and articles now recognize such an analysis as being essential, even if the evaluations of the evidence differ.[2] Holland Hendrix urges that without 'a thorough knowledge of the material evidence for

---

[1] K. P. Donfried, 'The Cults of Thessalonica and the Thessalonian Correspondence', *NTS* 31 (1985), pp. 336–56; pp. 21–48 in this volume.

[2] A few examples must suffice: M. Adinolfi, *La prima lettera ai Tessalonicesi nel mondo greco-romano* (BPAA 31; Roma: Editrice 'Antonianum', 1990); R. F. Collins, *The Birth of the New Testament: The Origin and Development of the First Christian Generation* (New York: Crossroad, 1993); H. L. Hendrix, 'Archaeology and Eschatology at Thessalonica', in *The Future of Christianity* (Festschrift Helmut Koester; ed. B. A. Pearson; Minneapolis: Fortress Press, 1991), pp. 107–18; H. L. Hendrix 'Thessalonica', *ABD* VI, pp. 523–27; Robert Jewett, *The Thessalonian Correspondence: Pauline Rhetoric and Millenarian Piety* (FFNT;

circumstances addressed by Paul, we would miss what might be a critical and provocative dimension of his indictment of the times'.[3]

The first of two principal issues that have been raised with regard to this essay is concerned with the degree to which an understanding of the broader Graeco-Roman backgrounds, including material evidence, can be helpful in understanding the Thessalonian correspondence and, in particular, 1 Thessalonians. Especially critical have been Helmut Koester[4] and Simon Légasse.[5] The former argued that there 'is no evidence whatsover that the beliefs of the community in Thessalonica are in any way influenced by the pagan background of the converts',[6] and the latter is dismissive of the relevance of the archeological and textual evidence that we possess with regard to our knowledge of the Christian community in Thessalonica. 'Entre les cultes de Thessalonique, dans la mesure où l'on peut s'en faire une idée, et la lettre de Paul aux néochrétiens de la ville certain auteurs relèvent des contacts qui, à leurs yeux, ne sauraient être fortuits. En réalité tous font une grande part à l'imagination et aucun ne résiste à un examen critique.'[7]

Koester's skepticism appears to be generated in large part by his negative reaction to Robert Jewett's, *The Thessalonian*

Philadelphia: Fortress Press, 1986); S. Légasse, *Les Épîtres de Paul aux Thessaloniciens* (LD 7; Paris: Cerf, 1999); P. Perkins, '1 Thessalonians and Hellenistic Religious Practices', in *To Touch the Text, Festschrift J. A. Fitzmyer*, ed. M. P. Horgan and P. J. Kobelski; (New York: Crossroad, 1989), pp. 325–34; Rainer Riesner, *Die Frühzeit des Apostels Paulus. Studien zur Chronologie, Missionsstrategie und Theologie* (WUNT 71; Tübingen: Mohr, 1994) [ET: *Paul's Early Period: Chronology, Mission Strategy, Theology* (Grand Rapids: Eerdmans, 1998)]; T. D. Still, *Conflict at Thessalonica: A Pauline Church and Its Neighbours*, JSNTSup 183; (Sheffield: Sheffield Academic Press, 1999); C. A. Wanamaker, *The Epistle to the Thessalonians. A Commentary on the Greek Text* (NIGTC; Grand Rapids: Eerdmans, Exeter, UK: Paternoster, 1990).

[3] Hendrix, 'Archaeology and Eschatology', p. 118

[4] H. Koester, 'Archäologie und Paulus in Thessalonike', in *Religious Propaganda and Missionary Competition in the New Testament World. Essays Honoring Dieter Georgi*, ed. L. Bormann, K. Del Tredici and A. Standhartinger (NovTSup 74; Leiden: Brill, 1994), pp. 393–424; H. Koesler, 'From Paul's Eschatology to the Apocalyptic Schemata of 2 Thessalonians', in *The Thessalonian Correspondence*, ed. R. F. Collins (BETL 87; Leuven: University Press–Peeters, 1990), pp. 441–58.

[5] See n. 2 above.

[6] Koester, 'From Paul's Eschatology', p. 457.

[7] Légasse, *Les Épîtres de Paul aux Thessaloniciens*, p. 31. [ET: 'Some authors detect points of commonality between the cults at Thessaloniki – at least to the extent that we can figure them out – and Paul's letter to the new Christians of the city. These, they claim, can hardly be fortuitous. In fact, all of these suggestions owe a lot to imagination and not one can resist serious critical examination.']

Correspondence: Pauline Rhetoric and Millenarian Peity.[8] Jewett's monograph was among the first to take seriously the proposals made in the 'Cults' essay but, in the judgment of many, had the unfortunate tendency to convert the tentative suggestions made there into highly speculative conclusions. While I had urged that attention be given to the centrality of the Cabirus cult in Thessalonica, Jewett made this cult the lynchpin for a far broader argument and Helmut Koester, in particular, has been sharply critical of Jewett's overstatement of the evidence. As a result, Koester has only been able to distinguish with difficulty my own cautious, tentative approach from that of Jewett's. In fact, Koester's two articles subsequent to the 'Cults' essay agree far more with my approach and conclusions than he seems willing to admit.[9] For him to state, as I noted above, that there 'is no evidence whatsoever that the beliefs of the community in Thessalonica are in any way influenced by the pagan background of the converts'[10] and then to conclude that 'Paul envisions a role for the eschatological community that presents a utopian alternative to the prevailing eschatological ideology of Rome'[11] seems to underestimate Paul's specific interaction with the pagan context of the Christian community of Thessalonica.[12]

Both Koester and Légasse seem to have read the 'Cults' article in light of Jewett's conclusions and this may have led to a skewed reading of some of the tentative proposals that were originally made. With regard to 1 Thess. 4.4, for example, I made the following observations:

> But the sexual symbols of the cult were not mere representations of the hope of a joyous afterlife; they were also sensually provocative. The fact that the god Dionysus was the god of wine and joy often gave allowance for a strong emphasis on noisy revelry of all sorts. Already in an antici-patory way we might ask whether this emphasis on the phallus and

---

[8] See n. 2 above.

[9] Many points articulated in Koester, 'From Paul's Eschatology', affirm what had been previously stated in 'The Cults of Thessalonica'.

[10] Koester, 'From Paul's Eschatology', p. 457.

[11] Koester, 'From Paul's Eschatology', pp. 457–58.

[12] C. vom Brocke, *Thessaloniki – Stadt des Kassander und Gemeinde des Paulus* (WUNT 125; Tübingen: Mohr-Siebeck, 2001).

sensuality offers a possible background for the exhortations in 1 Thess.
4.3–8 in general and for the difficult problem of the σκεῦος in particular.[13]

These comments raise a *question* as to *possible* backgrounds for
notoriously difficult texts. For Koester[14] to state that we have
definitively explained 1 Thess. 4.4 on the basis of the Dionysos
herm, or 1 Thess. 5.7 on the basis of the presence of the god of
wine in Thessalonica, fundamentally misunderstands our intent
of creating a *broad* contextual background against which the interpreter might be able to raise more informed questions with regard
to otherwise enigmatic phrases in this first Pauline letter. Similarly,
Simon Légasse,[15] in dismissing a number of particular suggestions,
tends thereby to overlook the *broader* pagan context in which Paul's
ministry in Thessalonica was carried out. While Légasse may be
justified in challenging a number of our individual recommendations, to be so readily dismissive of the whole approach appears
to be guilty of overlooking the forest for the trees.

The 'Cults of Thessalonica' article was, in fact, instrumental in
breaking with the dominant translation of 1 Thess. 4.4 (typified
by the RSV: 'that each one of you know how to take a wife for
himself in holiness and honor') by suggesting that τὸ σκεῦος
might better be understood in the more general sense of 'to gain
control over the σκεῦος'.[16] While this proposal was prompted by
material evidence, it was not *determined* by that perspective;
rather a far broader range of considerations come into play. The
influence of our recommendation is unmistakable in the NRSV's
translation of this verse: 'that each of you know how to control
your own body in holiness and honor'. Particularly helpful is the
detailed discussion of the problem by Légasse who, in the final
analysis, follows our interpretation by citing Augustine's
interpretation of σκεῦος as referring to the 'genital organs'.[17]

---

[13] Donfried, 'The Cults of Thessalonica', p. 337; p. 24 in this volume.

[14] Koester, 'Archäologie und Paulus in Thessalonike', p. 394.

[15] Légasse, *Les Épîtres de Paul aux Thessaloniciens*, p. 31.

[16] Donfried, 'The Cults of Thessalonica', p. 342; p. 31 in this volume.

[17] *Nupt.* II.5.14. Légasse (*Les Épîtres de Paul aux Thessaloniciens*, p. 218) concludes that 'la lecture la plus vraisemblable' is 'celle qui comprend ici le mot *skeuos* au sens d' «organe génital» masculin' [ET: 'the most plausible reading is the one which interprets the word *skeuos* in this case as desig-nating the male genital organ'.] His complete discussion can be found on pp. 210–19.

To conclude this part of our discussion: while Koester and Légasse are correct in urging a careful and cautious use of sparse material evidence, I nevertheless maintain that such evidence, properly used, can be of great assistance in helping the interpreter to gain better insight into the pagan world in which the Thessalonian Christians lived, especially since Paul makes specific reference to such alien perspectives (for example, 1 Thess. 4.5, 13).

The second principal challenge that has been raised with regard to the 'Cults' essay is the question of the exact circumstances of the congregation in Thessalonica, i.e. precisely in what way were they 'afflicted'? What did Paul intend with the reference to their suffering (ἐπάθετε; 2.14), and with the phrase θλίψει πολλῇ (1.6) as well as similar references found elsewhere in the letter? I had urged for consideration that the primary 'afflictions' that the Thessalonians Christians suffered involved some degree of *non-systematic* persecution primarily by non-Christians in the city and that this situation might have led to the premature death of those Christians to whom Paul refers in 1 Thess. 4.13–18.[18] Although this has not been an uncontroversial recommendation for some, as we will observe momentarily, it will be useful to compare the translations of the relevant verses in the RSV and the NRSV, the one translation having preceded 'The Cults of Thessalonica' and the other having followed it. (The translations in question are in italics.)

1 Thess. 1.6: Καὶ ὑμεῖς μιμηταὶ ἡμῶν ἐγενήθητε καὶ τοῦ κυρίου, δεξάμενοι τὸν λόγον ἐν θλίψει πολλῇ μετὰ χαρᾶς πνεύματος ἁγίου
RSV: And you became imitators of us and of the Lord, for you received the word in much *affliction*, with joy inspired by the Holy Spirit
NRSV: And you became imitators of us and of the Lord, for in spite of *persecution* you received the word with joy inspired by the Holy Spirit

1 Thess. 3.3: τὸ μηδένα σαίνεσθαι ἐν ταῖς θλίψεσιν ταύταις
RSV: that no one be moved by these *afflictions*
NRSV: so that no one would be shaken by these *persecutions*

1 Thess. 3.4: καὶ γὰρ ὅτε πρὸς ὑμᾶς ἦμεν, προελέγομεν ὑμῖν ὅτι μέλλομεν θλίβεσθαι

---

[18] Donfried, 'The Cults of Thessalonica', p. 350; p. 43 in this volume.

RSV: For when we were with you, we told you beforehand that we were to suffer *affliction*

NRSV: In fact, when we were with you, we told you beforehand that we were to suffer *persecution*

1 Thess. 3.7: διὰ τοῦτο παρεκλήθημεν, ἀδελφοί, ἐφ᾽ ὑμῖν ἐπὶ πάσῃ τῇ ἀνάγκῃ καὶ θλίψει ἡμῶν διὰ τῆς ὑμῶν πίστεως

RSV: For this reason, brethren, in all our distress and *affliction* we have been comforted about you through your faith

NRSV: For this reason, brothers and sisters, during all our distress and *persecution* we have been encouraged about you through your faith

Even though the NRSV now interprets θλῖψις as 'persecution' in light of the way the term functions within the entire context of 1 Thessalonians, there is still considerable dissent from such a conclusion. John Barclay argues that the term is best described as 'social harassment'[19] and Abraham Malherbe moves toward a more psychological interpretation, viz. that 'it is reasonable to understand *thlipsis* in 1.6 [and 3.3–4] as the distress and anguish of heart experienced by persons who broke with their past as they received the gospel'.[20] Todd Still is convinced that θλῖψις 'is best conceived as intergroup conflict between Christians and non-Christians in Thessalonica'.[21] Although he prefers not to use the term 'persecution'[22] he is willing to acknowledge that 'on the rarest of occasions such opposition might have culminated in death'[23] and that such opposition may have been generated by 'political issues'.[24] There are others, of course, in addition to the NRSV committee itself, who agree that the problem

[19] J. M. G. Barclay, 'Conflict in Thessalonica', *CBQ* 55 (1993), pp. 512–30, here p. 514.

[20] A. J. Malherbe, *Paul and the Thessalonians. The Philosophic Tradition of Pastoral Care*, 2nd ed. (Philadelphia: Fortress Press, 1988), p. 48. See now A. J. Malherbe's, *The Letters to the Thessalonians: A New Translation with Introduction and Commentary*, AB 32B (New York: Doubleday, 2000), especially pp. 115 and 168, which appears quite non-specific on these issues. Yet in discussing 2 Thessalonians, Malherbe makes this remark in referring to the Thessalonian Christians: 'They were being persecuted as they had been when he wrote the first letter (see 1 Thess 2.14)', p. 351.

[21] Still, *Conflict at Thessalonica*, p. 17.

[22] Still, *Conflict at Thessalonica*, p. 213.

[23] Still, *Conflict at Thessalonica*, p. 216. One should also note his further comment: 'I would contend, then, that it is best to regard the Thessalonians' affliction to which Paul repeatedly refers as external (i.e. observable, verifiable), non-Christian opposition which took the forms of verbal harassment, social ostracism, political sanctions and perhaps even some sort of physical abuse, which on the rarest of occasions may have resulted in martyrdom', p. 217.

[24] Still, *Conflict at Thessalonica*, p. 266.

the Thessalonian Christians faced involved far more than 'social harassment', although that certainly was an important component of a considerably more complicated problem.[25] Finally, however, this important question of translation can only be resolved through a closer analysis of the entire letter and especially such passages as 1 Thess. 2.1–12 and 1 Thess. 2.13–16. These, and other texts, now await our further consideration.

'2 Thessalonians and the Church of Thessalonica' attempts to articulate further certain suggestions made at the conclusion of the 'Cults' article. Essential to the argument is that one of Paul's co-senders, perhaps Timothy, was the author of 2 Thessalonians. This has the advantage of recognizing a variety of cogent arguments against Pauline authorship and in taking seriously the unlikelihood that a pseudonymous author would have written such a letter about a half-century after 1 Thessalonians. Rather, the letter was written to the Thessalonian Christians within a reasonable interval after 1 Thessalonians and the stamp of the pagan cults is still very much evident. In fact, it is this later context that helps to explain a number of exegetical difficulties in the letter, not least the identification of τὸ κατέχον/ὁ κατέχων in 2 Thess. 2.6 and 7.[26] And, finally, it was urged that the rhetorical definition of belonging to the deliberative genre was both important for understanding the intention of 2 Thessalonians but also in helping us understand how it differed from 1

---

[25] See, for example, J. S. Pobee, *Persecution and Martyrdom in the Theology of Paul* (JSNTSup 6; Sheffield: JSOT Press, 1985), pp. 113–14; J. Chapa, 'Is First Thessalonians a Letter of Consolation?' *NTS* 40 (1994), pp. 150–60; Collins, *Birth of the New Testament*, p. 112; Riesner, *Paul's Early Period*, pp. 386–7.

[26] Important here is the work of C. H. Giblin, *The Threat to Faith: An Exegetical and Theological Re-examination of 2 Thessalonians 2* (AnBib 31; Rome: Pontifical Biblical Institute, 1967), p. 201. See now also Giblin's article, '2 Thessalonians 2 Re-Read as Pseudepigraphical: A Revised Reaffirmation of The Threat to Faith', in *The Thessalonian Correspondence*, ed. R. F. Collins (BETL 87; Leuven: University Press, 1990), pp. 459–69. See also G. S. Holland, *The Traditions That You Received From Us: 2 Thessalonians in the Pauline Tradition* (HUTh 24; Tübingen: Mohr-Siebeck, 1986). As we have tried to indicate, the work of Holland and Giblin can be employed in a complementary manner. Thus it is curious that Malherbe (*Thessalonians*) cites only Giblin, but not Holland, and that Still (*Conflict at Thessalonica*) cites only Holland and not Giblin.

Thessalonians which belongs, in all likelihood, to the genre of epideictic rhetoric or some form thereof.[27]

Despite the emergence of some fine scholarly efforts since 1993 toward resolving the issues surrounding 2 Thessalonians, the attempt to untie the Gordian knot of authentic or pseudonymous authorship still dominates many of these interpretations. Especially true of those studies arguing for non-Pauline authorship, is a tendency to be quite non-specific concerning the circumstances that prompted the writing. And so, Menken, who understands 2 Thessalonians to have been written between 80 and early second century CE,[28] begins quite appropriately that 'we should take seriously the circumstance that 2 Thessalonians is a letter, albeit an imitated one, written by a specific sender to a specific addressee in a situation. It is not a kind of general tract, but a writing in which two specific problems are tackled.'[29] Unfortunately, as with Trilling,[30] a known setting within early Christianity is, however, never reconstructed with any detail. So also Richard, who concludes that 2 Thessalonians is a pseudonymous letter, makes a generalized, but inadequate, reference to paulinists who are responding to some increased apocalyptic fervor.[31]

Among those recent authors who maintain Pauline authorship of 2 Thessalonians, Malherbe has emphasized the weakness of the pseudepigraphial approach with regard to defining a specific *Sitz im Leben* of this document and, further, in underestimating 'the difficulty of bringing such a letter into circulation'.[32] Yet Malherbe's observations raise more questions than they answer. 'The basic facts about the Thessalonians, however, emerge clearly from what Paul writes and are ones we have already

[27] K. P. Donfried, 'The Theology of 1 Thessalonians', in *The Theology of the Shorter Pauline Letters*, ed. K. P. Donfried and I. H. Marshall (New Testament Theology; Cambridge: Cambridge University Press, 1993), pp. 4–5, 83–84.

[28] M. J. J. Menken, *2 Thessalonians* (New Testament Readings; London: Routledge, 1994), p. 66.

[29] Menken, *2 Thessalonians*, p. 15.

[30] W. Trilling, *Der Zweite Brief an die Thessalonicher* (EKK XIV; Zürich, Einsiedeln, Köln, Neukirchen: Benziger, Neukirchener Verlag, 1980).

[31] E. J. Richard, *First and Second Thessalonians* (SP 11; Collegeville, Minnesota: Liturgical Press, 1995), p. 32.

[32] Malherbe, *Thessalonians*, p. 373.

encountered in the first letter. They were being persecuted as they had been when he wrote the first letter (see 1 Thess. 2.14), but the attention Paul now devotes to the problem (1.3–10) suggests that the persecution had increased or that his readers' consternation in face of it required more attention.'[33] Yet when we look at the reference to 1 Thess. 2.14 Malherbe comments that Paul does not say that they endured 'any persecution at all'.[34] However one is to understand Malherbe's ambiguity at this point, the factors that led to a changed situation in 2 Thessalonians are never articulated. Similarly, Todd Still, agreeing with our assertion that it 'is difficult to imagine a setting where a letter specifically addressed to the Thessalonians by Paul would be relevant and convincing to a non-Thessalonian church some thirty or more years after the Apostle's death',[35] does not provide a clearly articulated setting for 2 Thessalonians, although in some general way it is connected with that of 1 Thessalonians.

Charles Wanamaker also adheres to the Pauline authorship of 2 Thessalonians. Commenting on 2 Thess. 2.12 he notes:

> If my interpretation of this passage is correct, it has an interesting correlation with the situation at Thessalonica as I have depicted it in the Introduction. There, following the lead of Donfried and others, I sought to argue that the persecution of Christians in Thessalonica was related to the apparent sense of competition which the Christian movement engendered in some people who saw it as a threat to their own religion. What Paul says here could certainly be directed against Jewish instigators of opposition to Paul as well as those who sought to defend the civic cults of Thessalonica, including the imperial cult, against the anti-imperial religion of Paul, which promised the public manifestation of the true Lord.[36]

Although the enigma of who wrote 2 Thessalonians and for what purpose still eludes scholarship, many of Wanamaker's insights are helpful and provocative, including, along with Menken, the cautious use of rhetorical analysis.[37] The actual situation of

---

[33] Malherbe, *Thessalonians*, p. 351.

[34] Malherbe, *Thessalonians*, p. 172.

[35] Still, *Conflict at Thessalonica*, p. 58.

[36] C. A. Wanamaker, *The Epistle to the Thessalonians. A Commentary on the Greek Text* (NIGTC; Grand Rapids: Eerdmans, Exeter, UK: Paternoster 1990), pp. 263–4.

[37] Of course, not to be overlooked here is the pathbreaking publication of F. W. Hughes, *Early Christian Rhetoric and 2 Thessalonians* (JSNTSup 30; Sheffield: JSOT, 1989).

the church in Thessalonica, living in the midst of an antagonistic religious, cultic and political environment, at times leading to persecution, must stand at the center of continuing attempts to unlock the mysteries of 2 Thessalonians.

Originally delivered as a lecture at the *Colloquium Biblicum Lovaniense* in 1988,[38] the thrust of the argument of '1 Thessalonians, Acts and the Early Paul' centers on the suggestion that one needs to distinguish more clearly between the coherent and the contingent in the Pauline letters.[39] To do so one would have to take more seriously 1 Thessalonians as an indication of the theology and ethics of the early Paul and one would need to distinguish it more clearly from such later letters as Galatians and Romans. Aside from the work of Siegfried Schulz,[40] Udo Schnelle[41] and my own essays, there has been little attempt to situate the ethics of 1 Thessalonians within a pre-Pauline trajectory. Schulz places it in the context of the pre-Pauline hellenistic church found primarily in Antioch.[42] Subsequently, I have become increasingly uneasy with the 'pan-Antiochenism' that has invaded scholarship. My own study of Paul increasingly suggests a pre-Antiochian, Palestinian influence that shares similarities with the thought of the community (*yahad*) of Qumran.[43]

In order to emphasize that 1 Thessalonians may well have been representative of an early stage in Paul's missionary career, several areas requiring study were suggested, in addition to the issue of chronology, which will be referred to below. These included an examination of aspects of Paul's theology, including

[38] K. P. Donfried, '1 Thessalonians, Acts and Early Paul', in *The Thessalonian Correspondence*, ed. R. F. Collins (BETL 87; Leuven: University Press–Peeters, 1990), pp. 3–26.

[39] J. C. Beker, *Paul the Apostle: The Triumph of God in Life and Thought* (Philadelphia: Fortress Press, 1980).

[40] S. Schulz, 'Der frühe und der späte Paulus', *ThZ* 41 (1985), pp. 228–36.

[41] U. Schnelle, 'Der erste Thessalonicherbrief und die Entstehung der paulinischen Anthropologie', *NTS* 32 (1986), pp. 207–24.

[42] S. Schulz, *Neutestamentliche Ethik* (Zürich: Theologischer Verlag, 1987), pp. 137–78.

[43] For a recent critique of the role of Antioch in Paul, see M. Hengel and A. M. Schwemer, *Paul Between Damascus and Antioch: The Unknown Years* (Louisville: Westminster, 1997), esp. pp. 279–310.

an examination of 1 Thess. 1.9–10 and 4.13–18, as well as some comparisons between the early and later Pauline letters, particularly with regard to the question of 'the law' and the theme of 'justification'. Also the assertion of Vielhauer that Acts 'presents no specifically Pauline idea'[44] was challenged, including a response that Acts may well have had a keener interest in the early rather than the late Paul.

A proposal of far reaching implications is that 1 Thessalonians is to be dated to the early 40s and that Acts 18 is a conflation of two visits to that city. C. K. Barrett states the options with clarity: 'If the view is taken that the expulsion took place, and resulted in the arrival in Corinth of Aquila and Priscilla in 41 CE, we must suppose that Paul reached Corinth for the first time in that year, or soon after. This throws out the whole of Pauline chronology as this is usually understood, and also means that the order of Acts is distorted; Paul reached Corinth before the famine (11.29) and before the Council (15.6–29).'[45] The 49 CE date continues to be problematic for the expulsion of Jews from Rome since Dio Cassius refers to this anti-Jewish action as having been taken by Claudius in 41 CE and Lüdemann also understands the Suetonius text to refer to 41 CE, as do Penna, Hemer, Slingerland and Murphy-O'Connor.[46] Further, I remain convinced that Lüdemann's suggestion of a conflation of two different Pauline visits to Corinth needs to be considered more seriously. To solve the problem in the way that Jervell does, arbitrary as it is, actually lends support to Lüdemann: 'Die Lehrwirksamkeit des Paulus im Hause des Titius Justus gehört auch zum Missionsbericht, und somit auch der Bruch mit der

---

[44] Donfried, '1 Thessalonians, Acts and Early Paul', p. 19; p. 90 in this volume. Original citation is found on p. 48, P. Vielhauer, 'On the 'Paulinism' of Acts', in *Studies in Luke-Acts*, ed. L. E. Keck and J. L. Martyn (Nashville: Abingdon, 1966), pp. 33–50.

[45] C. K. Barrett, *The Acts of the Apostles* (ICC; 2 vols; Edinburgh: T&T Clark, 1994), 2:859.

[46] The references to the texts from antiquity are found in P. Orosius (*Historiae adversum Paganos* 7.6.15–16; CSEL 5.451) who quotes Suetonius' text; Dio Cassius is found in his *Roman History* 60.6.6. The modern authors cited are R. Penna, 'Les Juifs à Rome au temps de l'Apôtre Paul', *NTS* 28 (1982), pp. 321–47; C. J. Hemer, *The Book of Acts in the Setting of Hellenistic History*, ed. C. H. Gempf (WUNT 49; Tübingen: Mohr Siebeck, 1989), p. 168; D. Slingerland, 'Acts 18.1–17 and Lüdemann's Pauline Chronology', *JBL* 109 (1990), pp. 686–90; J. Murphy-O'Connor, 'Paul and Gallio', *JBL* 112 (1993), pp. 315–17.

Synagoge, V 7. Der Name des Leiters der Gemeinde ist ebensowenig von Lukas erfunden wie der Name, der den grössten Missionstriumph in Korinth aufzeigt: Krispus, V 8.'[47] All of this is not to disagree with Fitzmyer's suggestion that Gallio was proconsul of Achaia from late spring to late autumn, 52 CE, it is simply to deny that that was the apostle's first visit to Corinth. The essay 'Chronology: The Apostolic and Pauline Period', is a more detailed analysis of the issues first taken up in '1 Thessalonians, Acts and the Early Paul'. The comparison between the traditional chronology and the newer one pioneered by John Knox should prove useful.[48] Such an illustration will suggest that Pauline chronology is an issue far from settled.[49] This fact, coupled with the recognition of a remarkably early form of Pauline theology continues to persuade me that 1 Thessalonians is more appropriately dated to the early forties than to the late forties or early fifties of the first century.

'The Theology of 1 Thessalonians as a Reflection of Its Purpose' was originally delivered to the Pauline Consultation of the Society of Biblical Literature in 1986[50] and published in the Fitzmyer Festschrift in 1989.[51] This essay deepens a number of themes already touched on in 'The Cults of Thessalonica and the Thessalonian Correspondence' (1985)[52] and then further developed in the Cambridge New Testament Theology series

[47] J. Jervell, *Die Apostelgeschichte* (KEK 3; Göttingen: Vandenhoeck and Ruprecht, 1998), p. 463. [ET: 'The teaching activity of Paul in the house of Titius Justus also belongs to the missionary report and so, similarly, the rupture with the synagogue, v. 7. The name of the leader of the community is as little fabricated by Luke as is the name of the one who demonstrates the greatest missionary victory in Corinth: Crispus, v. 8.']

[48] J. Knox, *Chapters in a Life of Paul*, ed. D. A. Hare, rev. ed. (Macon, GA: Mercer University, 1987).

[49] See also my article, 'Chronology: The Apostolic and Pauline Period', *ABD* 1.1011–22; pp. 99–117 in this volume. When Johnson comments that 'the date of the edict is usually put at 49 AD, and is considered one of the key dates for establishing the possibility of an absolute chronology for Paul's career' he obscures the complexity of the issue (L. T. Johnson, *The Acts of the Apostles* (SP 5; Collegeville, MN: Liturgical, 1992), p. 322.

[50] With a most helpful and positive response by Professor Raymond E. Collins.

[51] K. P. Donfried, 'The Theology of 1 Thessalonians as a Reflection of Its Purpose', in *To Touch the Text, Festschrift J. A. Fitzmyer*, ed. M. P. Horgan and P. J. Kobelski (New York: Crossroad, 1989), pp. 243–60; pp. 119–38 in this volume.

[52] K. P. Donfried, 'The Cults of Thessalonica and the Thessalonian Correspondence', *NTS* 31 (1985), pp. 336–56; pp. 21–48 in this volume.

dealing with the theology of 1 Thessalonians.[53] A critical issue highlighted is what is meant by the term 'paraenesis' and how its application to 1 Thessalonians assists in clarifying the intent of that letter.[54] Might it not be more helpful, I asked, to speak of a 'paracletic' letter, recognizing 1 Thessalonians as sharing some of the characteristics of a *consolatio*?[55] Subsequently, H. J. Klauck and Jutta Bickmann have moved in a similar direction by referring to it as 'Trostbrief'.[56] Such a *consolatio* is required precisely because some in the Thessalonian congregation have died as a result of persecution.

Some comments are in order with regard to some more specific aspects of this article: 1) In connection with the theme of persecution, one should note the criticisms made in the literature as I responded to them in discussing 'The Cults of Thessalonica and the Thessalonian Correspondence' above. 2) In interpreting the phrase τῶν ἰδίων συμφυλετῶν in 1 Thess. 2.14, I indicated that the phrase does not exclude local Jews. This understanding receives support from Richard[57] and Reinmuth,[58] qualified support from the analysis of vom Brocke[59] and is rejected in the recent studies by Holtz, Richard, Still[60] and others. The overwhelming obstacle for many in understanding this phrase as including Jews is the gentile character of the Thessalonian

[53] K. P. Donfried and I. H. Marshall, *The Theology of the Shorter Pauline Letters* (New Testament Theology; Cambridge: Cambridge University Press, 1993).

[54] See W. Popkes, *Paränese und Neues Testament* (SBS 168; Stuttgart: Katholisches Bibelwerk, 1996).

[55] See A. Smith, *Comfort One Another. Reconstructing the Rhetoric and Audience of 1 Thessalonians* (Literary Currents in Biblical Interpretation; Louisville: Westminster/John Knox, 1995); A. Smith, 'The Social and Ethical Implications of the Pauline Rhetoric in I Thessalonians' (Unpub. PhD diss.; Vanderbilt University, 1989); and J. Chapa, 'Is First Thessalonians a Letter of Consolation?' *NTS* 40 (1994), pp. 150–60.

[56] J. Bickmann, *Kommunikation gegen den Tod. Studien zur paulinischen Briefpragmatik am Beispiel des Ersten Thessalonicherbriefes* (FB 86; Würzburg: Echter, 1998), p. 291; H. J. Klauck, *Die antike Briefliteratur und das Neue Testament* (Paderborn: Schöningh, 1998), p. 291.

[57] E. J. Richard, *First and Second Thessalonians* (SP 11; Collegeville, MN: Liturgical Press, 1995), p. 120.

[58] E. Reinmuth, 'Der erste Brief an die Thessalonicher', in *Die Briefe an die Philipper, Thesslonicher und an Philemon* (N. Walter, E. Reinmuth and P. Lampe; NTD 8/2; Göttingen: Vandenhoeck and Ruprecht, 1998), p. 129.

[59] vom Brocke, *Thessaloniki*, p. 165.

[60] Still, *Conflict at Thessalonica*, p. 225.

Christian community. First, however, one must examine carefully the profile of this church to determine the accuracy of this oft-made assertion, and then, second, ask whether, if this characterization were to be correct, the missionizing activity of the Jew Paul would not still be a disturbing factor to Jews in Thessalonica? 3) The final section, 'Paul's Defense of His Behavior', deals with 1 Thess. 2.1–12. A more extensive analysis of this text can now be found in 'The Epistolary and Rhetorical Context of 1 Thessalonians 2.1–12' in which the rhetorical nature of this pericope is developed more fully. There it is urged that this first part of the *narratio* (2.1–16) is neither apologetic nor polemical; rather, among several goals, it serves to distinguish Paul's gospel and ethos from the error and delusion surrounding the Thessalonian Christians. It is part of Paul's larger strategy in which he employs the 'insider-outsider' model, for example, in 1 Thess. 4.1–12, 4.13–18; 5.4–10, to distinguish the new Christian community from other groups who are not 'in Christ'.

The title of this essay, 'The Epistolary and Rhetorical Context of 1 Thessalonians 2.1–12', suggests that there is a question of methodology at stake, viz. the appropriateness of epistolary and/or rhetorical analysis for the analysis of 1 Thessalonians. While valuing the importance of identifying epistolary components, I remain hesitant that an epistolary analysis of 1 Thessalonians, *by itself*, can determine the intention, especially the intention of this letter as a 'speech-act',[61] because of its inability to identify with any degree of precision the parameters of the letter 'body'.[62] Since 1 Thess. 5.27 ('I solemnly command you by the Lord that this letter be read to all of them') contains a specific Pauline mandate which makes it evident that it is indeed something that must be *read* before the entire congregation, I turn to the contributions of classical rhetorical criticism for the analysis of this 'speech-act' and conclude that 1 Thessalonians has certain affinities with epideictic rhetoric. In judicial rhetoric, for example,

---

[61] I am indebted to Raymond Collins for this term.

[62] C. A. Wanamaker, 'Epistolary vs. Rhetorical Analysis: Is a Synthesis Possible', in *The Thessalonians Debate: Methodological Discord or Methodological Synthesis?*, ed. K. P. Donfried and J. Beutler (Grand Rapids: Eerdmans, 2000), pp. 268–9.

1 Thess. 2.1–2 would have been taken up in the *probatio* which is exactly what does not happen here. In the general framework of epideictic, this pericope is placed within the context of the larger *narratio* of the communication (2.1–3.10). The first part of the *narratio* (2.1–16) is neither apologetic nor polemic. Rather, it recounts the relationship of friendship established between Paul and the Thessalonians during the time of his founding visit; it serves to distinguish Paul's gospel and ethos from the error and delusion surrounding the Thessalonian Christians, specifically, from the idolatry of the pagans; and it presents characteristics of Paul's ethos about which the apostle wishes to remind his congregation about in the *probatio*, especially in 4.1, 'Finally, brothers, we ask you and urge you in the Lord Jesus that, as you learned from us how you ought to live and to please God (as, in fact, you are doing), you should do so more and more.' In light of this, the apostle's antithetical style serves not as a defense against hypothetical accusations but, rather, as in hellenistic Judaism, as an attempt to distance himself and the Thessalonians from both pagan thought and practice by using this stylistic technique. As a result, I conclude that one should neither define 1 Thess. 2.1–12 as an apology nor read this text in a mirror fashion as if Paul were countering specific charges that had been leveled against him.

In the relatively early (1984) essay, 'Paul and Judaism: 1 Thessalonians 2.13–16 as Test Case', a quite general argument was mounted for the authenticity of these verses against dominant voices to the contrary.[63] I argued that 1 Thess. 2.13–16 is not inconsistent with the structure of the letter and that the comments made about 'the Jews' in this passage do not contradict Paul's argument in Romans. It was also urged that the account of Paul's activity in Thessalonica as reported by Luke in Acts 17 contained elements of reliable information.

These proposals have subsequently been elaborated and treated in sophisticated detail by other scholars: 1) Concerning

---

[63] For example, Pearson, Boers, Koester and Schmidt. See K. P. Donfried, 'Paul and Judaism: 1 Thessalonians 2.13–16 as a Test Case', *Int* 38 (1984), pp. 242–53, notes 18–22; pp. 195–208 in this volume.

those interpreters who urged that 1 Thess. 2.13–16 was an interpolation because it did not cohere with Paul's 'thanksgiving
pattern', Jan Lambrecht comments appropriately: 'One remains
somewhat baffled at the ease with which certain scholars use the
three thanskgivings as an argument for their hypothetical
conflation of two letters or a so-called interpolation of 2.13–16.'[64]
Not only must one take into account Paul's 'redactional freedom'
and 'epistolary liberty'[65] but one must be careful not to retroject
thanksgiving patterns from the later letters onto Paul's first letter.
Lambrecht counters Schubert's influential position that 1
Thessalonians contains a 'highly complex though formally
orthodox thanksgiving'[66] with this response: 'When Paul
composed 1 Thessalonians, that "formal orthodoxy" did most
probably not yet exist.'[67] 2) While disagreeing with some of the
arguments of content used to commend the authenticity of 1
Thess. 2.13–16, Carol Schlueter agrees with regard to my major
emphasis: 'there does seem to be a central coherence to Paul's
thought' and, most significantly, that this passage is Pauline.[68]
Further, she correctly identifies certain words and phrases that
need to be explained more precisely both within a rhetorical and
eschatological context, specifically those which may have certain
connections to the Dead Sea Scrolls.[69] And, finally, Schlueter
cites a comment by Montefiore that deserves significant
attention: 'There were in the first century "several Judaisms, all
more or less fluid and growing".'[70] Exegetes need to ask who οἱ
Ἰουδαῖοι of 1 Thess. 2.14 are. Whom precisely does Paul have in
mind here? 3) With regard to the reliability of Acts, my position,
as revealed in this and other essays collected in this volume, has

---

[64] Donfried, *Thessalonians Debate*, p. 146.

[65] Both phrases from J. Lambrecht, 'Thanksgivings in 1 Thessalonians 1–3', in *The Thessalonians Debate: Methodological Discord or Methodological Synthesis?*, ed. K. P. Donfried and J. Beutler (Grand Rapids: Eerdmans, 2000), p. 147.

[66] Lambrecht, 'Thanksgivings', p. 147, n. 30.

[67] Lambrecht, 'Thanksgivings', p. 147.

[68] C. J. Schlueter, *Filling up the Measure: Polemical Hyperbole in 1 Thessalonians 2.14–16* (JSNTSup 98; Sheffield: JSOT, 1994), p. 60.

[69] Schlueter, *Filling up the Measure*, pp. 107–10.

[70] Schlueter, *Filling up the Measure*, p. 194, n. 2; see further my 'Shifting Paradigms: Paul, Jesus and Judaism', pp. 1–20 in this volume.

consistently been that Luke has a theological program that shapes his historical narrative but that within this narrative one often finds valuable and accurate pieces of specific information. And, to a significant extent, this is a valid observation with regard to Acts 17.1–9 as well and finds considerable support in the newest volume on the subject by vom Brocke. Particularly important for the student of 1 Thessalonians is his conclusion: 'Ingesamt gesehen kann mann annehmen, daß die jüdische Gemeinde Thessalonikis – zumal als Hauptstadtgemeinde Makedoniens – bereits im 1. Jh. n. Chr., wie die Apostelgeschichte berichtet (Apg 17,1), über eine Synagoge verfügte.'[71] Further, in opposition to the rather extreme position outlined by Koester that 'all the individual events of Paul's activity in this city are legendary',[72] one finds more balanced approaches to the tension between theological framework and individual facts in the newest commentaries on Acts by Fitzmyer and Barrett as well as in Malherbe's commentary on 1 Thessalonians. Unaware of the newest supporting evidence provided about Judaism in Thessalonica by vom Brocke, Malherbe nevertheless comes to a remarkably similar conclusion, viz. 'that Paul does blame the Jews for his ejection from Thessalonica . . . . Whether or not this agrees with Acts is not important for the interpretation of the letter, but it should be noted, according to Acts, Paul apparently goes into hiding and ceases his preaching when the Jews organized against him. This would seem to agree well with what he says in 2.15–16.'[73]

My preliminary and rather general work on the theme of Judaism in 'Paul and Judaism', my previous work on the early dating of 1 Thessalonians and my discussion of an 'early Paul' received new focus when my exegetical work on 1 Thessalonians

[71] vom Brocke, *Thessaloniki*, p. 231. [ET: 'Seen as a whole, one can assume that the Jewish community of Thessaloniki, particularly as a congregation in the dominant city of Macedonia, did, as Acts reports (Acts 17.1), possess a synagogue.']

[72] A. J. Malherbe, *The Letter to the Thessalonians: A New Translation with Introduction and Commentary* (AB 32B; New York: Doubleday, 2000), p. 57; H. Koester, *Introduction to the New Testament*. Volume II: *History and Literature of Early Christianity* (Philadelphia: Fortress Press, 1982), p. 108.

[73] Malherbe, *Letter to the Thessalonians*, p. 62.

kept suggesting some interesting points of similarity between 1 Thessalonians (and Paul in general) and the Dead Sea Scrolls. In one way or another these harmonies between the two are discussed in the following essays: 'Shifting Paradigms: Paul, Jesus and Judaism', [SP] 'The Assembly of the Thessalonians: Reflections on the Ecclesiology of the Earliest Christian Letter', [AT] 'Paul and Qumran: The Possible Influence of סרך on 1 Thessalonians', [PQ] and 'Justification and Last Judgment in Paul – Twenty-Five Years Later' [JL]. The following relationships between Paul and Qumran are proposed:

Election   In addition to similar eschatological/apocalyptic contexts, there are remarkable similarities between the Paul of 1 Thessalonians and the Qumran Community, including election and the calling of God, holiness/sanctification, the light/day–night/darkness contrasts, and the wrath/salvation dualism. Not unimportant is the term 'sons of light' (בני אור) 1QS 3.13 and in 1 Thess. 5.5. For example, ἐκλογή, found only in 1 Thessalonians (1.4) among the Pauline letters, shows an intimate connection with the Essenes who also regarded themselves as 'those chosen by (divine) benevolence' (1QS 8.6). This is exactly what ἐκλογή is expressing in 1 Thessalonians, supplemented by the phrase ἀδελφοὶ ἠγαπημένοι ὑπὸ [τοῦ] θεοῦ. [AT]

Church   Paul speaks τῶν ἐκκλησιῶν τοῦ θεοῦ τῶν οὐσῶν ἐν τῇ Ἰουδαίᾳ ἐν Χριστῷ Ἰησοῦ in 1 Thess. 2.14. Lying behind this plural reference to the 'churches of God' is the phrase ἐκκλησία τοῦ θεοῦ (1 Cor. 1.2; 10.32; 11.22; 15.9; 2 Cor. 1.1; Gal. 1.13) and this may well reflect the earliest Christian use and, in all likelihood, the self-designation of the early Jerusalem church itself. This formulation is likely a translation of קהל אל, signifying the eschatological company of God, found in such Qumran texts as 1QM 4.10 and 1QSa 2.4. [AT].

The disordered   Who are the ἄτακτοι in 1 Thess. 5.14, translated by many commentators as 'idlers' or 'loafers'? Arguing for the inadequacy of such a translation, I raise the question whether there is not a meaning for ἄτακτος that coheres more closely with the rhetorical, ecclesiological and theological intention of 1 Thessalonians. An examination of the Hebrew and Aramaic equivalents to the terms ἐν τάξει and ἄτακτος in the Napthali and, especially, in the Levi materials, suggests a nearness to the linguistic world of Qumran. Of particular importance is the double presence of בסרך and ἐν τάξει used equivalently in both fragments. Reviewing several meanings of סרך in the texts of the Dead Sea Scrolls, including, for example, 1QS 5.1 ('This is the rule (הסרך) for the men of the Community who freely volunteer to convert from all evil and to keep themselves steadfast in all he prescribes in compliance with his will. They should'), it is suggested that 1 Thess. 5.14 points back to the small collection of rules in 1 Thess. 4.1–12 – the סרך for the Thessalonian community – and that those who do not follow them are 'out-of-order'; they are 'disordered', not 'idlers' or 'loafers' in the normal sense of those terms [PQ].

Righteousness of God My original essay on 'Justification and Last Judgment in Paul' is accompanied by a new, lengthy response, 'Justification and Last Judgment in Paul – Twenty-Five Years Later', in which a number of further relationships with the Qumran community are established. It is noted that although the phrase 'the righteousness of God' used by Paul is not found in the Old Testament, it is found in 1 QM 4.6 as צדק אל and in 1QS 10.25; 11.12 as צדקת אל. This prior usage of the concept by the scrolls would indicate that it was not created by Paul. In addition, this response notes another critical parallel, as noted below.

Works of the law It has been correctly stated that the Pauline phrase ἔργα νόμου has no parallel in the Jewish Bible. However, the precise parallel phrase to Paul's ἔργα νόμου is found in the Qumran texts. In 4QMMT C27 one reads מקצת מעשי חתורה ('some deeds of the law'), in 4QMMT C 30–31 the emphasis falls on the correct practice of these deeds ('in your deed [בעשותך] you may be reckoned as righteous') and in 1QS 5.21 and 6.18 one finds the phrase מעשיו בתורה ('his deeds in the law'). Particularly noteworthy is that the theme of being reckoned as righteous, which is so central to Paul's argument in Gal. 3.6 and Rom. 4.3, occurs in a remarkably similar context in 4QMMT C 30–31. This new essay on 'Justification' [JL] concludes with a sharp criticism of the understanding of Judaism in the so-called 'new perspective' on Paul.

The many It is instructive that *The Community Rule* (1QS) of Qumran refers to its membership with a Hebrew word, הרבים, precisely the term that lies behind Paul's 'the many' [τῶν πλειόνων] in 2 Cor. 2.5–6. It is evident that this 'majority/assembly' referred to in 2 Corinthians was empowered with judicial functions in a manner that corresponds closely to 1 QS 6.1: 'Also, no man is to bring a charge against his fellow before the assembly [הרבים] unless he has previously rebuked that man before witnesses' [SP].

New covenant When Paul speaks of a new covenant [καινῆς διαθήκης] in 2 Cor. 3.6, such usage is also to be noted in CD 6.19: הברית החדשה. In other words, between Jeremiah's use of the term 'new covenant' in 31.31 and that of the early Jesus movement, there is at least one other group that applied this eschatological language to itself: the Community of the Renewed Covenant [SP].

Given these several harmonies between Paul and the Qumran community, was there some contact between them? In the first of these collected essays, 'Shifting Paradigms: Paul, Jesus And Judaism', the case is made for possible contacts between Paul and the Essene community in Jerusalem.

Finally, brief reference must be made to three remaining essays in this volume. 'Was Timothy in Athens? Some Exegetical Reflections to 1 Thess. 3.1–3' attempts to deal with the differing information provided by 1 Thessalonians and Acts 17 with regard to the presence of Paul's co-workers in Athens and comes to the conclusion that neither Silas/Silvanus nor Timothy were with Paul when he arrived in Athens. In fact, we have no evidence that either of these persons were ever with Paul in that city. In 'The Kingdom of God in Paul' I survey the use of the terms 'kingdom' and 'kingdom of God', in Paul and in Acts, with a particular interest in 1 Thessalonians. This may be a useful place to respond to Otto Merk's concerns with my analysis of 'kingdom' in 1 Thess. 2.11–12 in which I interpreted the term in the context of these verses and concluded that Paul 'stresses the present and continuing nature of the event in which they now participate and which will be consummated in the future'.[74] I then add that the 'newness of their [the Thessalonian Christians] life in Christ has already begun and will be completed on the last day'.[75] Merk writes 'Donfried concludes *inter alia* that 1 Thess. 2.11–12 (along with 1 Cor. 4.20 and Rom. 14.17) is not eschatological but refers to the βασιλεία as already present'[76] and then argues against his understanding of my interpretation with a reference to Ki-Seong Lee that βασιλεία and δόξα should be understood 'strictly in the future sense'.[77] First, I did not quite say what Otto Merk writes since I suggested a present *and* future sense. Second, I disagree with Lee that βασιλεία has a strictly future sense. Much closer to the overall understanding of 1 Thessalonians that I have proposed,[78] is the helpful reference that Merk makes to the work of W. Kraus.[79] He summarizes Kraus in this way:

> By emphasizing the present participle καλοῦντος and taking into consideration a primarily present understanding of βασιλεία (though not

---

[74] K. P. Donfried, 'The Kingdom of God in Paul', in *The Kingdom of God in 20th Century Interpretation*, ed. W. Willis (Peabody, MA: Hendrickson, 1987), p. 10; pp. 233–52 in this volume.

[75] Donfried, 'The Kingdom of God in Paul', p. 11.

[76] O. Merk, '1 Thessalonians 2.1–12: An Exegetical-Theological Study', in *The Thessalonians Debate: Methodological Discord or Methodological Synthesis?*, ed. K. P. Donfried and J. Beutler (Grand Rapids: Eerdmans, 2000), p. 109.

[77] Merk, '1 Thessalonians 2.1–12', p. 110.

[78] See K. P. Donfried, *The Theology of the Shorter Pauline Letters* (New Testament Theology; Cambridge: Cambridge University Press, 1993).

[79] W. Kraus, *Das Volk Gottes. Zur Grundlegung der Ekklesiologie bei Paulus* (WUNT 85; Tübingen: Mohr, 1996).

excluding eschatological aspects) found closely connected to ἡ δόξα in the Sabbath Hymns of Qumran, Kraus concludes: 'The expression "to be called to the βασιλεία" in fact means the same as "to belong to the people of the βασιλεία." By using this expression Paul places the Gentiles who have come to the faith on the same level with the members of God's people. The calling of the Gentiles who have become believers to the βασιλεία in 1 Thess. 2.12 is unmediated. It means nothing less than that the Thessalonians who have come to faith in Jesus are equated with the people of God.'[80]

It might not be inappropriate to mention that this is yet one more of the many connections that seem to link 1 Thessalonians and the *yahad* of Qumran.[81] For Merk not to take seriously this connection between the language of Paul and the Dead Sea Scrolls on the basis that it 'would hardly have been understood by the Christians in Thessalonica, who came from a Gentile environment'[82] misses the point. Paul himself was not a Gentile but a Jew. The question of how he communicated his Jewish influenced theology to his audience and how one defines that audience is a secondary question.

In 'Paul as Σκηνοποιός and the Use of the Codex in Early Christianity' I share some queries about Paul, the itinerant preacher, and his 'reference library'. The text in question is 2 Tim 4.13: 'When you come, bring the cloak that I left with Carpus at Troas, also the books [τὰ βιβλία] and above all the parchment [τὰς μεμβράνας].' Although most scholars do not regard the Pastoral Epistles as Pauline, one does need to ask whether this is perhaps an authentic Pauline fragment. If so, one might reckon with the possibility that the Latin word *membrana* is referring to parchment notebooks and that Paul the σκηνοποιός, i.e. leather-worker, produces and makes use of these proto-codices in his missionary work. By so doing he facilitates the codex to become the medium for Christian written communication. These parch-ment codices would in essence be testimony books with easy to find proof texts in addition to providing inexpensive and

---

[80] Merk, '1 Thessalonians 2.1–12', p. 110.

[81] See now also the article by B. T. Viviano, 'The Kingdom of God in the Qumran Literature', in *The Kingdom of God in 20th Century Interpretation*, ed. W. Willis (Peabody, MA: Hendrickson, 1987), pp. 97–107.

[82] Merk, '1 Thessalonians 2.1–12', p. 111.

convenient compactness for the traveling missionary since both sides of the page could be written on. As we know, Paul cites traditional formulations, sometimes even using the Jewish formula 'I delivered to you . . . what I also received. . . .' This is the case, for example, in 1 Cor. 11.23 where he cites the earliest extant words of Jesus concerning the institution of the Lord's Supper, and in 1 Cor. 15.3 where he cites a confession of faith. These kinds of pre-Pauline tradition, together with other pre-Pauline hymns (for example, Phil. 2.5–11), not to mention his correspondence, might well have been recorded in his *membranae*. If these conjectures have any plausibility, then it may well be appropriate to speak of the apostle Paul as the most instrumental factor in the shaping of the book as we know it today, that is, in the form of a codex rather than a roll.[83] If these proposals are to be rejected because of the paucity of the factual evidence, the intriguing question still remains: What kinds of materials did Paul and his co-workers have at their disposal for the citation and collection of assorted biblical texts, multiple traditions and external correspondence?

[83] See the compatible view of I. H. Marshall, *The Pastoral Epistles* (ICC; Edinburgh: T&T Clark, 1999), pp. 818–21. Quite the opposite interpretation of 2 Tim. 4.13 is given by L. Oberlinner, *Die Pastoralbriefe* (HTKNT XI/2; Freiburg: Herder, 1995), pp. 172–5.

1

❦

Shifting Paradigms: Paul, Jesus and Judaism[1]

Discoveries in the Desert

When a Bedouin shepherd threw a stone into a cave at Kirbet Qumran in 1947 our understanding of Judaism and Christianity in the first century CE changed dramatically.[2] The last half of the twentieth century was responsible for publishing the vast majority of the 800 texts found in these caves; scholarship beginning in the twenty-first century will need to rewrite the complex phenomenon known as Second Temple Judaism, the history of the early Jesus movement and the interaction of the two. No longer can we speak about Judaism and Christianity in the first century as unified religions in sharp conflict with one another; rather we must recognize the enormous diversity of Judaism, a diversity so extensive that it included the earliest followers of Jesus.

These 800 texts, which have so dramatically altered our perception of this period, were part of a broader Essene movement.[3] Shemaryahu Talmon of Hebrew University prefers

[1] This essay originally was given as the inaugural lecture for the Elizabeth A. Woodson Chair in Religion and Biblical Literature on 9 April 2001, at Smith College, Northampton, MA. It appears here in slightly revised form.
[2] For an overview see L. H. Schiffmann, *Reclaiming the Dead Sea Scrolls* (Philadelphia and Jerusalem: The Jewish Publication Society, 1994).
[3] See J. A. Fitzmyer, *The Dead Sea Scrolls and Christian Origins* (Grand Rapids: Eerdmans, 2000), pp. 249–60.

to refer to this movement in terms of their own self-description, the Community of the Renewed Covenant or simply, the *yahad*. Part of this group relocated itself from Jerusalem to Qumran in the approximate period of 150–134 BCE and remained there until 68–70 CE when they were destroyed by the Romans marching on their way to Masada, fresh from having conquered and burned Jerusalem. Josephus, the first-century Jewish historian, reminds us that some of the Essenes remained in Jerusalem and that, in fact, there was an Essene quarter in the southwest corner of the city.[4] From the Damascus Document, one of the major texts found in Cave 4, we know that the Essene movement was spread throughout the land that we now know as Israel.[5] And it was not a small movement. Josephus tells us that during his time the Pharisees numbered 6,000 and the Essenes about 4,000.[6] Since 1947, we now have original texts describing this community, thus shedding enormous light – sometimes directly and sometimes indirectly – on the entire shape of the Judaisms[7] of this period, including the Sadducees, the Pharisees, the Essenes and the early Jesus movement. Not to be overlooked is the fact that the relationships between these schools of Torah interpretation were not necessarily friendly. Just listen to the following descriptions of the Pharisees made by the Essenes: they are 'interpreters of false laws', they are 'seekers after smooth things' and they are accused of creating and following false laws; in fact, one of their leaders is referred to as the 'Man of Scoffing'.[8] What was at stake in these controversies was the correct interpretation of Torah, a consuming interest of late second-century Judaism, and one that is likely to arouse intense emotions.[9] The rebuke of the apostle Paul to those who challenge his understanding of the Torah with

---

[4] Josephus, *JW* 5.145.

[5] For example, CD 7.6–9.

[6] Josephus, *Ant.* 18.18–22.

[7] The term 'Judaisms' is used intentionally in order to indicate the diversity and non-monolithic character of Second Temple Judaism.

[8] See 4Q 169.3–4; CD 4.18–20 and Schiffman, *Reclaiming*, pp. 250–1; see also 'Justification and Last Judgment in Paul – Twenty-Five Years Later', pp. 279–92, in this volume.

[9] See Schiffman, *Reclaiming*, pp. 245–87.

regard to circumcision may not be atypical: 'I wish those who unsettle you would castrate themselves!' (Gal. 5.12).

What I should like to call attention to is that the Dead Sea Scrolls have not only made available a large quantity of hitherto unknown texts but they have also provided, as a result of these documents, a new context for comprehending 1) the complexity of Second Temple Judaism, 2) the intention of Jesus of Nazareth and his movement and 3) for understanding the great missionary of this movement, Saul of Tarsus, later to be known as Paul. By providing a fresh perspective in which to understand Paul, I will argue that this new context brings Paul not only far closer to the thought of Jesus but that Paul himself can become a major interpretative key for understanding the proclamation and activity of Jesus.

The Older Understanding of Paul

When I was a graduate student in the 1960s the dominant paradigm of the apostle Paul present in leading academic centers went something like this:

- that the major religious influences on Paul were those of the Greco-Roman culture, not Judaism;[10]
- that the center of Paul's theology was justification by faith; as a result, Christ was considered to be the end, the termination of the Torah. This emphasis, it was argued, together with Paul's use of phrases such as 'works of the law', indicated his antipathy to Judaism; Judaism, in fact had become a mere relic of his past.[11]

Further, for this long-reigning paradigm, Romans was viewed as the center and summary of Pauline theology; it became the center by which all other aspects of his thought were judged.[12]

---

[10] See R. Bultmann, 'Zur Geschichte der Paulus-Forschung', *ThR* 1 (1929), pp. 26–59.

[11] See H. Conzelmann, *An Outline of the Theology of the New Testament* (New York: Harper, 1969), pp. 155–61.

[12] G. Bornkamm, 'The Letter to the Romans as Paul's Last Will and Testament', in *The Romans Debate: Revised and Expanded Edition*, ed. K. P. Donfried (Peabody, MA: Hendrickson, 2001), pp. 16–28.

Simultaneously, the Acts of the Apostles, an admittedly secondary presentation of Paul written in the name of Luke, was viewed as flawed precisely because it presents a very Jewish Paul in which the theme of justification by faith is virtually absent.[13]

The publications and subsequent interpretations of the Dead Sea Scrolls have lead an increasing number of New Testament scholars to question this older paradigm.[14] In the same way that the Second Vatican Council's Decree on Ecumenism, issued in 1964, brought to the fore the great text on Christian unity, John 17, and permitted it to be seen with fresh insight, so too the Dead Sea Scrolls have brought renewed emphasis to Paul's long-neglected and repeated self-identification as a Jew throughout his letters. In Phil. 3.5–6 the apostle describes himself as: 'circumcised on the eighth day, a member of the people of Israel, of the tribe of Benjamin, a Hebrew born of Hebrews; as to the law, a Pharisee; as to zeal, a persecutor of the church; as to righteousness under the law, blameless'. In 2 Cor. 11.22 he asks, 'Are they Hebrews? So am I. Are they Israelites? So am I. Are they descendants of Abraham? So am I.' And in Rom. 11.1 the anguished Paul writes: 'I ask, then, has God rejected his people? By no means! I myself am an Israelite, a descendant of Abraham, a member of the tribe of Benjamin. God has not rejected his people whom he foreknew.'

Did Paul give up his Judaism once he was called – please notice that I have avoided the verb 'converted' – by the risen Lord to be an apostle to the Gentiles or does he continue to consider himself a Jew? For those who argue the former, several texts are cited, especially, Rom. 10.4, that Christ is the end of the law; and a series of texts in Galatians and Romans dealing with 'the works of the law' which allegedly support such an interpretation of Rom. 10.4. Even so noted a scholar as Hans Joachim Schoeps, himself a Jew, comments that 'Paul furnished a solution to the problem of the law which in the last resort rested on a

[13] For example, P. Vielhauer. 'On the 'Paulinism' of Acts', in *Studies in Luke-Acts* (Festschrift Paul Schubert; ed. L. E. Keck and J. L. Martyn; Nashville: Abingdon, 1966), pp. 33–50.

[14] See, for example, J. A. Fitzmyer, 'Paul and the Dead Sea Scrolls', in *The Dead Sea Scrolls After Fifty Years*, vol. 2, ed. P. W. Flint and J. C. Vanderkam (Leiden: Brill, 1999), pp. 599–621.

misunderstanding'.[15] And speaking of Paul's interpretation of the law in Gal. 3.19 he adds: 'The whole thing is, of course, pure speculation, and shows not the slightest dependence on scripture or reminiscence of rabbinical opinions.'[16] Of course, what Schoeps was largely unaware of was the huge body of literature that lies between Jewish scripture and the rabbis, that body of literature that is now so obvious to us – the Dead Sea Scrolls.

The Dead Sea Scrolls and Paul

Among the many unique contributions of the Dead Sea Scrolls is that they provide texts which illuminate aspects of late Second Temple Judaism previously unknown. Previous generations of scholars who were interested in establishing Paul's Jewishness, such as Schoeps and one of my own teachers, W. D. Davies, had to depend on the considerably later rabbinic texts.[17] These texts may or may not have represented well the pharisaic perspectives of the first century; certainly they do not represent either the rich variety or the conflicted situation of first-century Judaism, both BCE and CE. But that has all changed. As one enters into the world of the Dead Sea Scrolls, one is immediately impressed by a significant overlap between Pauline and Essene language, including such controversial terms as 'justification', the 'righteousness of God' and 'the works of the law'.[18] These and many other linguistic and conceptual parallels invite and compel the interpreter to examine more carefully the Pauline letters in light of the Essene texts. But before we engage in that exercise a word needs to be said about chronology.

The Essene community, at least during the time that it had a center in Qumran, can be dated, as I have mentioned, to the approximate period of 150–134 BCE to its destruction by the

---

[15] H. J. Schoeps, *Paul: The Theology of the Apostle in the Light of Jewish Religious History* (Philadelphia: Westminster Press, 1961), p. 200.

[16] Schoeps, *Paul*, p. 183.

[17] W. D. Davies, *Paul and Rabbinic Judaism: Some Rabbinic Elements in Pauline Theology* (Philadelphia: Fortress Press, 1980).

[18] See further the article on 'Justification and Last Judgment in Paul – Twenty-Five Years Later', pp. 279–92 in this volume.

Romans in the period 60–70 CE. Jesus of Nazareth lived from about 6 BCE until his death in 30 CE; Paul was active at least during the 30s, 40s, 50s and perhaps early 60s of the first century. All of this is relatively undisputed. What is disputed is how we date Paul's first letter, and thus the earliest extant document of Christianity, 1 Thessalonians. The old paradigm had a vested interest in pushing the date late, around 50 CE, so that it could distance Paul from Jesus and claim a virtual abyss between the two and assert that Paul was the real founder of Christianity. If, aside from the fact that the prevailing Pauline chronology which places all his writing activity between c. 50–56 is far too compressed, we find significant parallels between 1 Thessalonians and the thought world of the Dead Sea Scrolls, then we need to consider further the proposals of those scholars who wish to redate 1 Thessalonians to the earlier 40s.[19]

The old paradigm simply assumed the theological priority of Romans and, as a consequence, had little use for 1 Thessalonians; as a result it became the step-child of Pauline studies precisely because it did not employ the concept of 'justification' and for this and other reasons appeared to be insufficiently 'Christian'. Now this latter point calls for a renewed plea, viz. to continue to use the inaccurate terms 'Judaism' and 'Christianity' as descriptors for certain religious phenomena during this period of the first century CE that leads to both imprecision and distortion. We have already emphasized the rich and controversial pluriformity of late Second Temple Judaism. Yet, at the same time, one should also use with exceptional caution the term 'Christianity' for the period of its earliest beginnings since one really ought to view the followers of Jesus during his lifetime as another school of Torah interpretation, one that was as thoroughly Jewish as Jesus himself. As we move into the second half of the first century CE we can perhaps begin to use the term 'Christianities', recognizing that the theologies of James, Peter and Paul are strikingly

---

[19] See further J. Knox, *Chapters in a Life of Paul*, ed. D. A. Hare, rev. ed. (Macon, GA: Mercer University, 1987); G. Lüdemann, *Paul, Apostle to the Gentiles: Studies in Chronology* (Philadelphia: Fortress Press, 1984) and K. P. Donfried, 'Chronology, New Testament', *ABD* 1:1011–1022; modified as 'Chronology: The Apostolic and Pauline Period', pp. 99–117, in this volume.

different. In fact, one could argue that they represent different Torah schools for the post-resurrection disciples. Therefore to speak of 'Judaism' and 'Christianity' as being opposites in this pre-70 CE period conceals the complexity and intensity of these interactions both within and between these traditions.

1 Thessalonians

Let us turn now more specifically to 1 Thessalonians. A number of elements in this letter suggest affinities with the *yahad*, the prophetic movement of the Community of the Renewed Covenant at Qumran and elsewhere. Some of the similarities between the two include:[20]

1. eschatological/apocalyptic similarities in their intense expectation of the final consummation of history;
2. the election and calling of God, as when Paul writes to the Thessalonian church that 'we know, brothers and sisters beloved by God, that he has chosen [ἐκλογή] you' (1.4);
3. holiness/sanctification, as in 1 Thess. 4.3, 'For this is the will of God, your sanctification' (literally, holiness [ἁγιασμός]);
4. the light/day//night/darkness contrasts and the use of the term 'sons of light'. In 1 Thess 5.5 Paul writes: 'for you are all sons of light and sons of the day; we are not of the night or of darkness'. One of the major descriptors for the *yahad* is that they are 'sons of light'.[21]
5. the wrath/salvation dualism. 'For God has destined us not for wrath but for obtaining salvation …' are words found in 1 Thess. 5.9;
6. the phrase 'church of God' which has its direct parallel in the Qumran term קהל אל;[22]

---

[20] For further details see K. P. Donfried, 'Paul and Qumran: The Possible Influence of סרך on 1 Thessalonians', in *The Dead Sea Scrolls Fifty Years After Their Discovery* (Jersusalem: The Magnes Press, 2000), pp. 148–56, and, pp. 221–31 in this volume; 'The Assembly Of The Thessalonians: Reflections on the Ecclesiology of the Earliest Christian Letter' in *Ekklesiologie des Neuen Testaments* (Festschrift Karl Kertelge; ed. R. Kampling and T. Söding; Freiburg: Herder, 1996), pp. 390–408, and, pp. 139–62 in this volume.

[21] For example, 1QS 2.16; 1QM 1.1, 13; 13.16.

[22] See Donfried, 'The Assembly', 405–7; and, pp. 156–8 in this volume.

7. ἄτακτος and the ethical order. It is now quite likely that the 'idlers' or 'loafers' of 1 Thess. 5.14, the ἄτακτοι in Greek, should, on the basis of parallel texts related to the Dead Sea Scrolls, be translated as those 'who are out of order', namely not following the סרך, the order of the community as described in 1 Thess. 4.1–12. One of the major documents of the Qumran library is *The Community Rule* (1QS), the סרך היחד and it, too, contains admonitions and encouragements to properly follow its order.

Other Pauline Letters

The shared conceptual world between the *yahad* and Paul expands considerably as the remainder of his correspondence is examined. To illustrate I will cite three examples:

1. In 2 Cor. 2.5–6 Paul writes to the Christians in Corinth: 'But if anyone has caused pain, he has caused it not to me, but to some extent – not to exaggerate it – to all of you. This punishment by the majority [or the many; τῶν πλειόνων] is enough for such a person'. This unusual term also appears in the last supper tradition of Mark [14.24] and Matthew [26.28]: 'He said to them, "This is my blood of the covenant, which is poured out for many [πολλῶν]".' It is not uninteresting that *The Community Rule* (1QS) of Qumran refers to its membership with a Hebrew word, הרבים, precisely the term that lies behind Paul's 'the majority/the many'. In 1QS we read: 'During the session of the assembly of the congregation [הרבים] no man should say anything except by the permission of the assembly of the congregation [הרבים].' הרבים appears in this sense some twenty-six times in *The Community Rule* and another three times in the *Damascus Document* (CD). It is evident that this 'majority/assembly' referred to in 2 Corinthians was empowered with judicial functions in a manner that corresponds closely to 1QS 6.1: 'Also, no man is to bring a charge against his fellow before the assembly [הרבים] unless he has previously rebuked that man before witnesses.'

2. The phrase 'works/deeds of the law' in Gal. 2.15 and elsewhere in the Pauline letters, until recently thought to be a creation of Paul, is now verified in the newest texts from Qumran, particularly in 4QMMT where not only the phrase 'some of the deeds of the law' appears but also the relationship of this phrase to 'righteousness' can be seen anew and in a way contradictory to many of the most prestigious scholarly inter-preters of Paul.[23]

3. Paul is clearly not among the first who makes use of the term 'new covenant' in 2 Cor. 3.6. It is already used by the *yahad* several times, especially in the Damascus Document.[24] Thus it may startle, but should not really surprise, us that a colleague of mine in Jerusalem is preparing a volume of texts entitled 'The Essene New Testament'.[25] And not to be overlooked is the reference in Luke 22.20, where referring to Jesus the text reads: 'And he did the same with the cup after supper, saying, "This cup that is poured out for you is the new covenant in my blood."' In other words, between Jeremiah's use of the term 'new covenant' in 31.31 and that of the early Jesus movement, there is at least one other group that applied this eschatological language to itself: the Community of the New or Renewed Covenant.

Paul and the Essene Community: Possible Contacts

All of this would suggest the possibility that the Jew Paul may have had some contact with the Essene world of thought. How does one explain these commonalities between 1 Thessalonians and the *yahad* of Qumran? Critical is the question raised by Fitzmyer in a recent publication: 'Where and how would he [Paul] have come into contact with this non-Pharisaic Palestinian Judaism, which some of the items in his theological teaching

[23] See K. P. Donfried, 'Justification and Last Judgment in Paul – Twenty-Five Years Later', pp. 279–92, in this volume.

[24] For example, CD 6.19.

[25] Stephen Pfann.

echo?'[26] Is the specific terminology and the broader conceptual similarities between the two mediated through earliest Christianity or was the pre-Christian Paul already influenced by the prophetic movement of the *yahad*?

Pre-Damascus

Since the Community of the Renewed Covenant had a settlement in Jerusalem (by the Essene gate in the south of the city) as well as attracting followers throughout Palestine, contact between Paul and this movement is possible.[27] In my judgment the contact took place in Jerusalem when Paul studied at the Pharisaic מדרש בית. In Josephus' *Vita* he shares a desire not only to study the teachings of the Pharisees and Sadducees, but also those of the Essenes.[28] Would Paul, the inquisitive and highly intelligent 'graduate student' in Jerusalem, be any less motivated to be in dialogue with the teachings of the Community of the Renewed Covenant than Josephus? Such a question brings to the forefront the issue of the pluralistic environment of Jerusalem prior to the 'progressive "unification"'[29] of Palestinian Judaism under the guidance of the rabbinic scribes afer 70 CE.

The exploration of Paul's dialogue with a pluralistic pre-70 CE Judaism raises further questions. Paul describes himself as a Pharisee and yet at key points he breaks with that tradition. Was there a predisposition to do so even prior to his call from the risen Jesus on the road to Damascus? Could he have received encouragement for such a move as the result of his contact with the prophetic movement of the Community of the Renewed Covenant? Talmon's recent work (1994) is suggestive. He describes the Community of the Renewed Covenant as a 'third- or second-century crystallization of a major socio-religious

---

[26] J. A. Fitzmyer, *According to Paul: Studies in the Theology of the Apostle* (New York: Paulist Press, 1993), p. 35.

[27] See the discussion in B. Pixner, 'Jerusalem's Essene Gateway – Where the Community Lived in Jesus' Time', *BAR* 23 (1997), pp. 22–66 and the further literature cited there.

[28] Josephus, *Vita*, 10–11.

[29] For this phrase and a broader discussion of this theme see Martin Hengel, *The Pre-Christian Paul* (London: SCM Press, 1991), p. 44.

movement which arose in the early post-exilic Judaism ... The development of the movement runs parallel to that of the competing rationalist stream which first surfaces in the book of Ezra, and especially in the book of Nehemiah, and will ultimately crystallize in Rabbinic or normative Judaism.'[30] And, he adds, that the '*yahad*'s final dissent from the emerging brand of Pharisaic Judaism at the turn of the era constitutes the climax of the lengthy confrontation of these two streams'.[31] Does Paul's contact with the *yahad* Community of the Renewed Covenant facilitate his own dissent from the brand of Pharisaic Judaism that had shaped his own spirituality? Does this tension within Judaism predispose him toward the Jesus movement and its proposed solution to the very issues that had been and were still central to Paul's own religious struggle?

Post-Damascus

Bargil Pixner and others have drawn attention to the connection between Jesus' own family – although not Jesus himself – and the Essene movement.[32] Further, several have now argued that Jesus' last supper took place in a guest house in the Essene quarter of Jerusalem.[33] Since they had a different calendar from the rest of Judaism, a solar rather than a lunar calendar, this would help explain a discrepancy with regard to the date of Passover between the Synoptic Gospels and the Gospel of John and would suggest that it is John who has got it right.

These observations in turn raise other fascinating questions: Who were the earliest followers of Jesus and where did they

---

[30] S. Talmon, 'The Community of the Renewed Covenant', in *The Community of the Renewed Covenant: The Notre Dame Symposium on the Dead Sea Scrolls*, Christianity and Judaism in Antiquity Series, 10, ed. E. Ulrich and J. VanderKam (Notre Dame, Indiana: University of Notre Dame, 1994), pp. 3–24, here p. 22.

[31] Talmon, 'The Community of the Renewed Covenant', p. 22.

[32] B. Pixner, *With Jesus in Jerusalem: His First and Last Days in Judea* (Rosh Pina, Israel: Corazin, 1996), pp. 15–21; *With Jesus through Galilee According to the Fifth Gospel* (Rosh Pina, Israel: Corazin, 1992), pp. 14–16 and 49–53. See also the discussion in D. Flusser, *Jesus* (Jerusalem: Magnes, 1997), pp. 24–36; 180–6.

[33] For example, Pixner, *With Jesus in Jerusalem*, pp. 91–106.

reside? The common answer is that they were Jews. Jews, yes, but what kind of Jews? Sharpening the issue is the assertion made in Acts 6.7: 'The word of God continued to spread; the number of the disciples increased greatly in Jerusalem, and a great many of the priests became obedient to the faith.' What kind of priests were these?[34] They had to be either Sadducean or Essene. Given some striking similarities between the Essene's in terms of messiahship, eschatology, temple and meal with the earliest followers of Jesus, they would certainly be likely candidates. And where did these Essene priests live who were in Jerusalem? Precisely in the Essene quarter which later became the center of the Christian church in Jerusalem, with certainty, at least after 70 CE. The leader of the Jesus movement in Jerusalem after Peter was James, the brother of the Lord, and it would be quite easy to imagine that this conservative Jew and his associates may have lived in this same area well prior to 70 CE – in fact, from shortly after the time of the crucifixion of Jesus. This would also explain very nicely why the earliest followers of the resurrected Jesus adopted the typically Essene system of common property. And, if these suggestions are on the right track, then it was here on Mount Zion that Paul visited Peter and James some three years after his call on the road to Damascus and it is here that Paul might have encountered a transformed Essene intellectual and religious presence.

And, finally, we should not overlook Damascus as a possible place for Paul to have been in contact with the thinking of the Community of the Renewed Covenant. In Damascus, an afternoon's drive from Jerusalem (if that were possible), Paul would have found around 33 CE not only a strong Jewish community but also participants in the Jesus movement.[35] And if the Damascus Document found in Qumran is a real, not a

[34] See J. A. Fitzmyer, *Essays on the Semitic Background of the New Testament* (Missoula, MT: Scholars' Press, 1974), pp. 279 and 296 and É. Nodet and J. Taylor, *The Origins of Christianity: An Exploration* (Collegeville: The Liturgical Press, 1998) for a more general discussion of the earliest developments of the Jesus movement in Jerusalem.

[35] With regard to Acts 9.1–2, see C. K. Barrett, *The Acts of the Apostles*, 2 vols (ICC; Edinburgh: T&T Clark, 1994), I: 446–8 and J. A. Fitzmyer, *The Acts of the Apostles: A New Translation with Introduction and Commentary* (AB 31; New York: Doubleday, 1998), pp. 23–5.

symbolic name, then these Jews were at least partially of Essene persuasion; this might also help explain why there were followers of the risen Jesus in this location so early. Again, my point is that the partially similar apocalyptic conceptual frameworks of both would allow for an easy reciprocity in the thought and belief patterns between them.

In short, then, that Paul had been in dialogue with some form of Essenianism is probable; the conceptual cross-fertilization might have taken place in Jerusalem, Damascus or at one of the many Essene communities between the two. The evidence for a possible visit by Paul to Qumran is non-existent.

The Jewish Paul as an Interpreter of Jesus

Hardly anything is more contentious in New Testament studies today than the question of the historical Jesus. Not, of course, that he existed but, rather, what he actually taught and did. Go to your favorite bookstore and you can select whatever image of Jesus you find most satisfying: Jesus the charismatic leader; Jesus the existential religious thinker; Jesus the magician; Jesus the witty, subversive sage; Jesus the passionate social revolutionary; Jesus the prophet of the end. Each appeals to the same data and each presented with the same flourish of authority. Little wonder that one colleague has written recently, 'If this is progress, we might wish for less of it.'[36]

The present controversy concerning the interpretation of the historical Jesus is largely due to a group in the United States known as the 'Jesus Seminar'.[37] By eliminating the apocalyptic dimension of Jesus' teaching they argue that Jesus was a peasant reformer and Cynic sage strongly influenced by Greco-Roman thought. This results, for example, in their elimination of the Lord's Prayer from the authentic words of Jesus since he could never have uttered the phrase, 'thy kingdom come'. Jesus, as a

---

[36] This citation as well as some of these descriptions of Jesus come from P. Fredriksen, *Jesus of Nazareth, King of the Jews* (New York: Vintage, 2000), p. 4.

[37] See R. E. Brown, *An Introduction to the New Testament* (ABRL; New York: Doubleday, 1997), pp. 819-23.

social reformer, was simply not interested in a future consummation and fulfillment of what God had inaugurated in his ministry of word and deed. If this were indeed the case is it not odd that Paul uses the phrase 'kingdom of God' in several of his letters in remarkably similar ways?[38]

Given our suggestion of a new context in which to understand Paul, the question now arises whether Paul, as the earliest interpreter of Jesus, can give us further perspective in the midst of the present confusion?

Apocalyptic – eschatological teaching

From beginning to end Paul is an apocalypticist.[39] The term 'apocalypse' derives from the Greek word, *apocalypsis*, meaning an unveiling or a revelation. Those within Judaism who adhered to such a worldview held that God had revealed to them the future course of events, one in which the forces of evil would be annihilated and in which God would establish his kingdom on earth. From 1 Thessalonians to Romans, Paul's burning commitment is focused not on the past but rather on the immediate future; his gospel proclaims the coming or returning Christ, whose resurrection signaled the imminent redemption and transformation of the world. Now those who insist that Jesus himself was non- or even anti-apocalyptic explain such apocalyptic developments as late misrepresentations of his teachings.[40] But we need to ask: 'Why would the later tradition repeat something *already* seen not to be true? Why invent a tradition that would already be an embarrassment?'[41] And, further, we need to inquire why Paul, who stood in such immediate proximity to the Jesus tradition, makes no reference to Jesus as a Cynic sage or social reformer.

---

[38] See K. P. Donfried, 'The Kingdom of God in Paul', in *Kingdom of God in 20th Century Interpretation* ed. W. Willis (Peabody, MA: Hendrickson, 1987), pp. 175–90; in this volume, pp. 233–52.

[39] See J. J. Collins, *Apocalypticism in the Dead Sea Scrolls* (London: Routledge, 1997), pp. 1–11.

[40] See J. D. Crossan, *The Historical Jesus* (San Francisco: Harper, 1991).

[41] Fredriksen, *Jesus of Nazareth*, p. 94.

Kingdom of God

If Jesus died about 30 CE and Paul encountered the risen Jesus on the way to Damascus about 33 CE and he returns to see Peter and James in 36 CE, he does not stand very distant from the actual teaching ministry of Jesus even though we have no evidence that he had ever met Jesus. In Gal. 1.18–19 Paul specifically states that 'after three years I did go up to Jerusalem to visit Cephas and stayed with him fifteen days; but I did not see any other apostle except James the Lord's brother'. The Greek verb standing behind 'to visit', ἱστορῆσαι, can mean 'to gain information'.[42] In light of this, one should note the specificity involved in Paul's use of Jewish formulas of transmission, 'For I handed on to you as of first importance what I in turn had received' (1 Cor. 15.3), 'For I received from the Lord what I also handed on to you, that the Lord Jesus on the night when he was betrayed took a loaf of bread' (1 Cor. 11.23). The exactitude of such transmissions concerning the Jesus tradition is manifested in Paul's correspondence with the Romans: 'But thanks be to God that you have become obedient from the heart to the form of teaching [τύπον διδαχῆς] to which you were entrusted' (Rom. 6.17).[43] It is hardly likely that Paul's teaching, which included the theme of the kingdom of God, the key concept proclaimed by the historical Jesus and a term found eight times in the Pauline letters, is something that would have been created anew by social reform programs that sprung up in the years immediately following the death of Jesus. Rather consistently Paul argues, on the contrary, that the kingdom of God will come at that time when the eschatological Christ overthrows the evil and oppressive forces of this world. That Paul knows nothing of what the Jesus Seminar wishes to attribute to Jesus – a social reformer informed by Greek philosophical traditions – should give us considerable pause and

---

[42] See R. E. Brown, K. P. Donfried and J. Reumann, *Peter in the New Testament* (Minneapolis: Augsburg, 1973), p. 23 n. 52.

[43] See J. A. Fitzmyer, *Romans: A New Translation with Introduction and Commentary* (AB33; New York: Doubleday, 1993), p. 449.

critical distance before accepting some of these highly popularized perspectives too easily or too readily.

The temple

Let us examine just a few rather remarkable areas of coherence between the teachings of Jesus and the proclamation of Paul, beginning with the issue of the temple. Standing at the center of today's Jesus controversy is the interpretation of Jesus' words and actions in the cleansing of the temple scene in Mark 11.15–17 and parallels. Was he predicting the destruction of the temple or insisting on its renewal?[44] The Jesus Seminar insists on the former, for such an interpretation would provide a reason for the crucifixion of Jesus. To understand the words of Jesus about the temple as ones of prophetic renewal complicate the issue of what caused his death, particularly for those who argue that it was the cleansing of the temple that was the catalyst for Jesus' death.

The Qumran texts, harshly critical of the existing temple and the priests serving it, speak repeatedly about the hope of a future renewed temple. Their hope is not one of destruction but of renewal. In fact, the temple Scroll found in Cave 11, expects that the current temple will be replaced in the end of days (29.2–10).[45] The members of the Renewed Covenant will build the temple in the place where God shall choose to place his name, that is, the sacred place of God's presence. But until such time the *yahad* viewed its entire religious life and communal experience as a substitute for the temple, worship in which they no longer participated. They were, in fact, left with a Judaism devoid of temple and sacrifice, a Judaism in which prayer, purity and study, together with the life of the community itself, served as a replacement for the temple. And since the Qumran community saw itself as embodying the temple, it was obligated to act accordingly.

Paul, whose missionary activity falls in the period after the death of Jesus but before the destruction of the temple by the

[44] See Fredriksen, *Jesus of Nazareth*, pp. 42–50; pp. 225–34.
[45] See Schiffman, *Reclaiming*, pp. 257–71; pp. 369–94.

Romans in 70 CE, never suggests in any way that Jesus had urged its annihilation or that he advocated such a position. Rather, he specifically identifies the Christian community with the temple of God in 1 Cor. 3.16–17 and 2 Cor. 6.14–7.1.[46] In 1 Cor. 3.16 Paul writes: 'Do you not know that you are God's temple and that God's Spirit dwells in you? If anyone destroys God's temple, God will destroy that person. For God's temple is holy, and you are that temple.' These words would stand in severe tension with Jesus' temple words if their intention had, in fact, been the foretelling of the temple's ruin. Paul offers some reflections on this theme in 2 Cor. 6.14–7.1:

> Do not be mismatched with unbelievers. For what partnership is there between righteousness and lawlessness? Or what fellowship is there between light and darkness? What agreement does Christ have with Beliar? Or what does a believer share with an unbeliever? What agreement has the temple of God with idols? For we are the temple of the living God; as God said,

> 'I will live in them and walk among them,
>   and I will be their God,
>   and they shall be my people.
> Therefore come out from them,
>   and be separate from them, says the Lord,
> and touch nothing unclean;
>   then I will welcome you,
> and I will be your father,
>   and you shall be my sons and daughters,
> says the Lord Almighty.' [Lev. 26.11–12; Ezek. 37.27]

> Since we have these promises, beloved, let us cleanse ourselves from every defilement of body and of spirit, making holiness perfect in the fear of God.

This text helps us to understand why Paul, much like the piety of Qumran and the practice of Jesus, takes the matter of purity with such seriousness.[47] As the temple must remain pure, so its members, the individual members of the body of Christ, need to maintain strict standards of behavior. It becomes evident that when the action of Jesus in the temple is viewed as an apocalyptic prophecy referring to its renewal rather than to its destruction,

---

[46] See the study by Bertil Gärtner, *The Temple and the Community in Qumran and the New Testament* (SNTSMS 1; Cambridge: University Press, 1965).

[47] See Fredriksen, *Jesus of Nazareth*, pp. 197–207.

there are clear areas of correlation between such teaching and that of the *yahad* and Paul.

Divorce

Another area of such continuity is the issue of divorce. In the Damascus Document, the biblical right to divorce is interpreted so as to permit separation but not remarriage.[48] This is precisely the position of Paul in 1 Cor. 7.10–11: 'To the married I give this command – not I but the Lord – that the wife should not separate from her husband (but if she does separate, let her remain unmarried or else be reconciled to her husband), and that the husband should not divorce his wife'. And Jesus' prohibition of divorce grounds itself on the same text from Gen. 1.27 as is cited in these Qumran texts: 'Some Pharisees came to him, and to test him they asked, "Is it lawful for a man to divorce his wife for any cause?" He answered, "Have you not read that the one who made them at the beginning 'made them male and female,' and said, 'For this reason a man shall leave his father and mother and be joined to his wife, and the two shall become one flesh'? So they are no longer two, but one flesh. Therefore what God has joined together, let no one separate"' (Matt. 19.3).

Our attempt to draw a firmer and closer linkage between Paul and Jesus, could be elaborated and supported further by more detailed analysis of such items as:

- the theme of the law of love as the heart of Torah which is articulated both by Jesus in Mark 12 and Paul in Galatians 4 and Romans 13;
- the similar use of Qumran *pesher*-like interpretation of the Old Testament by both Jesus and Paul in which the earlier words of a given prophet are understood to be addressing and fulfilled in their immediate contemporary application;
- the mission to the Gentiles, while dramatically expanded in Paul, already has its origin in the teaching and action of Jesus.

[48] CD 4.20–21.

'I tell you, many will come from east and west and will eat with Abraham and Isaac and Jacob in the kingdom of heaven' (Matt. 8.11; see also Luke 13.29). And then, too, there is the story of the Syrophoenician woman in Mark 7.24–30. A not uninteresting question is whether Paul, given the proximity of his thought to that of Jesus, would have risked the well-being of the Thessalonian community, not to mention his own life, in promoting a mission to the Gentiles to turn from idols to the one true God if there had not been any firm indication that Jesus' own ministry anticipated such a mission? I think not.

The Possibility of a New Pauline Paradigm?

So we are back to 1 Thessalonians. But no longer as the step-child of Pauline studies but as an integral link to Paul's apocalyptic Jewish context. As a result this earliest extant Christian document will become decisive for a more comprehensive understanding of Pauline theology. This new paradigm, with its emphasis on Paul the Jew situated within the Judaisms of his day, stands in tension with the previously dominant paradigms that have concentrated on the Greco-Roman influence as being primary and have so exalted the letter to the Romans and the theme of justification as to distort the totality of Pauline thought. In fact, the close proximity of several themes in 1 Thessalonians to the thought world of the Community of the Renewed Covenant gives additional support for the early dating of 1 Thessalonians (c. 43 CE), urging further consideration of the relationship between the early Paul and the Judaisms of his period and prompting additional queries about the theological profile of earliest 'Christianity' in Jerusalem.

The plausibility of the new Pauline paradigm suggests that other dominant paradigms will also need to be amended. No longer can a sharp chasm of synthetic differences disconnect Paul from Jesus; rather Paul may well serve as one of Jesus' earliest interpreters. The relationship between the apocalyptic eschatology of Jesus of Nazareth and Paul will need to be probed in depth with regard to themes held in common, viz. the kingdom of God, the temple, divorce, methods of biblical interpretation and the question of openness to Gentiles. Indeed, the dominant paradigms may have shifted so substantially that scholarship in the twenty-first century will need not only to rewrite the history of Second Temple Judaism, but also the character and identity of the earliest Jesus movement as well as the interaction between the two.

2

The Cults of Thessalonica and the Thessalonian Correspondence

Introduction

Despite the relative brevity of 1 and 2 Thessalonians, there is little scholarly consensus today concerning their interpretation. Whether the issue is the integrity of 1 Thess. 2.13–16 or the authenticity of 2 Thessalonians, whether the problem involves the interpretation of the so-called 'apology' in 1 Thess. 2.1–12 or that of τὸ κατέχον of 2 Thessalonians, whether the question deals with the eschatology of 1 Thess. 4.13—5.11 or of 2 Thessalonians, or whether the query involves the form-critical analysis of either document, there is little agreement among contemporary New Testament scholars.[1]

Given this bewildering array of contradictory positions, is there any way of proceeding in the interpretation of the Thessalonian correspondence which may give us a different

---

[1] A recent commentary on 1 and 2 Thessalonians is I. H. Marshall, *1 and 2 Thessalonians* (NCB; Grand Rapids: Eerdmans, 1983). On the whole it contains a good review of the differing positions on main issues of interpretation. In addition to the bibliography in Rigaux (n. 2 below), one should consult R. F. Collins, *Studies on the First Letter to the Thessalonians* (ETL 66; Leuven: University Press, 1984). [Since the publication of this essay, one would profit from the following newer literature: T. Holtz, *Der erste Brief an die Thessalonicher*, 2nd ed. (EKKNT 13; Zürich/Neukirchen-Vluyn: Benzinger/Neukirchener Verlag, 1990); C. A. Wanamaker, *The Epistle to the Thessalonians. A Commentary on the Greek Text* (NIGTC; Grand Rapids: Eerdmans, Exeter, UK: Paternoster 1990); S. Légasse, *Les Épîtres de Paul aux Thessaloniciens* (LD Commentaires 7; Paris: Cerf, 1999); M. J. J. Menken, *2 Thessalonians* (New Testament Readings; London and New York: Routledge, 1994).]

vantage point? Our proposal is neither novel nor bold; it is the modest suggestion that the starting point for the interpretation of the Thessalonian correspondence must be the reconstruction, as best we can, of the religious and political history of Thessalonica, at least to the time of the earliest Christian community. One looks in vain to the commentaries of the last twenty-five years for any significant discussion of the cults of Thessalonica or for any extensive discussion of the history of Thessalonica and the implications of that historical survey for the understanding of the two documents.[2] The basic question we propose to ask is simply this: What was Thessalonica like when Paul first visited and established a Christian community there and what impact does this information have for understanding 1 and 2 Thessalonians?[3]

As our study will show, all the cults in Thessalonica at the time of Paul were closely interrelated and that is a fact which is important to stress. In order to outline the significant developments which bring us to this point it will be necessary to distinguish between the 'religious' and the 'political', while fully recognizing that in the first century AD they were closely interrelated.

The Religious Cults of Thessalonica

From an archeological point of view, the *cult of Serapis* stands at the center of interest. Shortly after the 1917 fire in Thessaloniki a Serapeion was found in the sacred cult area of the city, some 250–300 meters west/northwest of the *agora*, and in 1939 a small temple of the Roman period was also discovered under the narthex.[4] Following the excavations by Pelekides and Makarona,

---

[2] B. Rigaux, *Saint Paul: Les Épîtres aux Thessaloniciens (EtB*; Paris: Gembloux, 1956) is the last commentary to deal, even though briefly, with the religious cults of Thessalonica.

[3] For a fuller treatment of the importance of audience criticism, see K. P. Donfried, *The Dynamic Word* (New York: Harper & Row, 1981).

[4] C. Edson, 'Cults of Thessalonica', *HTR* 41 (1948), p. 182; see also M. Vickers, 'Towards Reconstruction of the Town Planning of Roman Thessaloniki', in *Ancient Macedonia I: Papers Read at the First International Symposium Held in Thessaloniki, 26–29 August 1968*, ed. B. Laourdas and C. I. Makaronas, 2 vols (Thessaloniki: Institute for Balkan Studies, 1970), 1.239–51.

Edson concluded that this *serapeum* 'is the source of a body of evidence, archaeological and epigraphical, second only to that of Delos and covering a much longer period of time.'[5] Of the thirty-six inscriptions found, most refer to Serapis and Isis. Additionally, a small fragment of the 'Hymn to Isis' has also come to light.[6] From all that can be determined the *cult of Isis* was particularly anxious to extend her catholic claims of salvation and eternal life. Humility, confession of sin and repentance were urged prior to nocturnal initiation. Although we know that Isis is invoked as μύστις,[7] the exact nature of the mystic rites carried out in her name remain unknown.

The rich evidence now at our disposal suggests that not only were the rites of the Nile performed diligently in this temple by a board of some fourteen priests who were referred to as the 'priest of the gods',[8] but if Pelekides' conjecture is correct, the Cabiri (and perhaps others) also practiced their secret rites in this temple.

The *cult of Dionysus* is epigraphically attested to beginning in 187 BC;[9] included in the epigraphic evidence is the famous 'testament of a Thessalonicean priestess'.[10] As one looks at the Dionysiac mysteries in general, there are several components which are of particular interest for this study. The hope of a joyous afterlife is central and appears to be symbolized by the phallus. Whereas the prominent place of the phallus in the liknon, the basket sacred to Dionysus and carried on the head at festivals, symbolized fertility to an old agricultural people, we might ask with Nilsson whether for an urban people the phallus did not rather symbolize life-giving power.[11] It is common for

---

[5] R. Witt, 'The Egyptian Cults in Ancient Macedonia', in *Ancient Macedonia II: Papers Read at the Second International Symposium Held in Thessaloniki, 19–24 August 1973*, ed. B. Laourdas and C. I. Makaronas, 2 vols (Thessaloniki: Institute for Balkan Studies, 1977), 1.324–33.

[6] Edson, 'Cults of Thessalonica', p. 181.

[7] *P.Ox.* 1380; Witt, 'The Egyptian Cults', p. 332.

[8] Edson, 'Cults of Thessalonica', p. 135.

[9] Edson, 'Cults of Thessalonica', p. 165.

[10] For a discussion and reconstruction of this testament see Edson, 'Cults of Thessalonica', pp. 165–70.

[11] M. P. Nilsson, *The Dionysiac Mysteries of the Hellenistic Age* (Lund: Gleerup, 1957), pp. 44–5.

phalli to be erected on their tombs and there is evidence for this in Macedonia.[12] Nilsson understands such a use of the phallus as a 'life-giving power, like eggs and seeds which were laid down in the tomb' and suggests that 'initiation consisted in revealing just this symbol'.[13]

But the sexual symbols of the cult were not mere representations of the hope of a joyous afterlife; they were also sensually provocative. The fact that the god Dionysus was the god of wine and joy often gave allowance for a strong emphasis on noisy revelry of all sorts. Already in an anticipatory way we might ask whether this emphasis on the phallus and sensuality offers a possible background for the exhortations in 1 Thess. 4.3–8 in general and for the difficult problem of the σκεῦος in particular.

In the Homeric 'Hymn to Dionysos'[14] we read how the infant Dionysus was cuddled and nursed by the nymphs of Nysa, who eventually take on the role of the divine women so central to Dionysiac mysteries.[15] Homer refers to these female attendants as 'nurses'. According to Otto these women, these nurses, represent archetypal femininity so that 'all beauty, sweetness, and charm must combine their rays into the sun of motherliness that warms and nurtures the most delicate life for all eternity'.[16] Thus the nurse is linked to the loved one by a delicate bond. Is there any relationship between this language and imagery and the words of the apostle in 1 Thess. 2.7–8: 'So, being affectionately desirous (ὁμείρομαι) of you, we were ready to share with you not only the gospel of God but also our own selves, because you had become very dear to us'? Not to be overlooked is that ὁμείρομαι is a *hapax legomenon* in the New Testament. For what reason does Paul use it here? Hesychius, the first century CE lexicographer, equates the term with ἐπιθυμέω and Heidland defines it as 'to feel oneself drawn to something, with strong intensification of the

---

[12] Strymon.

[13] Nilsson, *The Dionysiac Mysteries*, p. 45.

[14] Number 26; we have used the edition by A. N. Athanassakis, *The Homeric Hymns* (Baltimore: The Johns Hopkins University Press, 1976).

[15] W. F. Otto, *Dionysus: Myth and Cult* (Bloomington: Indiana University Press, 1965), p. 81.

[16] Otto, *Dionysus: Myth and Cult*, p. 178.

feeling'.[17] The possibility that the Dionysiac background, together with the information we have in connection with the mysteries of Samothrace to be discussed below, might illuminate the verses just cited, as well as the obvious reference to the term 'nurse' in 1 Thess. 2.7, deserves further reflection.[18]

Of the other divinities worshiped at Thessalonica we know that Zeus played an important role; additionally there are references to Asclepius, Aphrodite, Demeter and others.[19] But since the information is so sparse, we will move on to what may have been the most important religious cult of Thessalonica at the time of Paul, the *cult of Cabirus*. This cult is often referred to in the plural as the cult of the Cabiri; this is in general a correct way to refer to the cult but not for the city of Thessalonica since there was only one Cabirus in the cult, a fact attested to in both the literary and numismatic evidence.

The most complete literary reference to the cult of Cabirus in Thessalonica is that of Clement of Alexandria.[20] Here we learn that two brothers kill the third, wrap his head in a purple cloth, place a crown on it and bury it at the foot of Mount Olympos; henceforth he becomes the focal point of the cult. To explain the origin of the name Cabirus, Clement recounts a myth in which this pair of murderers took the phallus of Dionysus in a small box to Tyrrhenus. This myth attests not only to the antiquity of the name Cabirus but also to the centrality of the phallic symbolism in it.[21]

The uniqueness of the Cabirus cult in Thessalonica is not only apparent by its stress on Cabirus as an unbearded young man,[22] but especially by its emphasis on a single figure. This is attested

---

[17] H. W. Heidland, ὁμείρομαι, *TDNT* 5.176. [See now also N. Baumert, 'ὁμείρομαι in 1 Thess 2,8' *Bib* 68 (1987): pp. 552–63.]

[18] On the whole we find the cultic background more persuasive than the example cited by Malherbe from the Cynic-Stoic philosophers. See A. Malherbe, ' "Gentle as a Nurse": The Cynic Background to I Thess ii', *NovT* 12 (1970), pp. 203–17, esp. p. 211. [Reprinted in A. Malherbe, *Paul and the Popular Philosophers* (Minneapolis: Fortress Press, 1989), pp. 35–48.]

[19] For further details see Edson, 'Cults of Thessalonica', and Witt, 'The Egyptian Cults'.

[20] B. Hemberg, *Die Kabiren* (Uppsala: Almqvist and Wiksells, 1950), p. 207.

[21] For other literary references see Hemberg, *Die Kabiren*, p. 205.

[22] Hemberg, *Die Kabiren*, p. 208.

to by numismatic evidence and the fact that 'from the Flavian period at the latest, Cabirus was the chief, the tutelary deity of Thessalonica'.[23] This point would be dramatically underscored if we could assume the identification of the Dioscuri with that of Cabirus as does Edson in his statement that 'by the Roman period the conflation of the Dioscuri with the Cabiri was general'.[24] The importance of this matter follows from the fact that there is a second-century CE relief on the Vardar gate, the western entrance to Thessalonica, which represents the Dioscuri. However, Hemberg denies the validity of Edson's identification of the two cults, especially in Macedonia, where we have already noted the unusually bloody dimension of the Cabirus cult.[25] Additionally, we would add, in agreement with Hemberg, that there is the further awkwardness of blending the plural dimension of the Dioscuri with the unique singular emphasis of the Cabirus cult in Thessalonica. However this may be decided, at the time Paul founded a Christian congregation in Thessalonica, there is little doubt about the prominence of this Cabirus cult, whose god promoted fertility and protected sailors.

This disagreement between Hemberg and Edson underscores the great difficulties surrounding any precise understanding of the Cabirus cult, in terms of both practice and origin. Edson argues that the Cabirus cult is not indigenous to Macedonia and was introduced from the nearby island of Samothrace.[26] From where the cult ultimately derives is a matter of scholarly debate, although there is some evidence pointing towards a Phrygian origin. That the cult finds its way to Thessalonica from Samothrace is unlikely for reasons given by Hemberg:

> Da die Kabiren wenigstens seit etwa 200 v.Chr. in Larisa bekannt waren, ist die Vermutung kaum abzuweisen, daß ihr Name in jener Zeit auch in der Hafenstadt Thessalonike im Gebrauche war. Beachtenswert ist indessen auch, daß die Samothrakes Theoi, obwohl sie in dem nicht weit von Thessalonike gelegenen Amphipolis verehrt wurden, – soviel wir bisher wissen – nicht in den thermaischen Meerbusen Eingang gefunden

---

[23] Edson, 'Cults of Thessalonica', p. 192.
[24] Edson, 'Cults of Thessalonica', p. 192.
[25] Hemberg, *Die Kabiren*, p. 210.
[26] Edson, 'Cults of Thessalonica', pp. 188–9.

THE CULTS OF THESSALONICA

haben. Das Wahrscheinlichste ist deshalb, daß der Kabirenname schon vor der samothrakischen Diaspora (etwa 260–100 v.Chr.) in Makedonien allgemein angenommen war.[27]

These observations cohere with Hemberg's earlier conclusions regarding the cult of the Cabiri and its relationship to Samothrace: 'Eine genaue Analyse der Texte und Inschriften zeigt m.E., daß der Kabirenname auf Samothrake nicht heimisch war.'[28] The fact of the matter is that to date no inscription has been found on Samothrace bearing the name of the Cabiri, thus throwing into question Herodotus' account.[29] It appears as if the cult of the Cabiri was loosely attached to the Megaloi Theoi in Samothrace at some point after its introduction in Macedonia.

Even though the Cabirus cult was in all likelihood not introduced in Thessalonica by way of Samothrace and even though the Cabiri worshiped on Samothrace were significantly different from the worship of Cabirus in Thessalonica, we cannot overlook the close connection between the city and the island and the probable influence of the Samothracian mysteries in general on Thessalonica.

The evidence for intercourse between the city and the island is clear.[30] The earliest preserved record linking the cult of Samothrace with Thessalonica is an inscription listing the names of individuals who visited the island between about 37 BCE and 43 CE. In this catalogue a certain Θεσσαλονικεὺς Ἀρχέπολι[ς] Νικοπόλεως appears among the μύσται εὐσεβεις. According to Edson the 'name of this person can be restored with great probability as that of the priest and agonothete of Augustus in a list of priests and magistrates of Thessalonica which is to be dated

---

[27] Hemberg, *Die Kabiren*, pp. 209–10. [ET: 'It is difficult to challenge the assumption that since the Cabiri were known in Larisa since about 200 BC that their name was also in use in the port city of Thessaloniki at about the same time. Still it is noteworthy that the Samothracian Great Gods, although they were honored in the not very distant Amphipolis, did not, as far as we know, gain entry in the Thermaikos Gulf. Therefore the most probable explanation is that the name of the Cabiri had in general already been accepted in Macedonia prior to the Samothracian diaspora (c. 260–100 BC).']

[28] Hemberg, *Die Kabiren*, pp. 73–74. [ET: 'An exact analysis of the text demonstrates, in my opinion, that name of the Cabiri was not indigenous to Samothrace.']

[29] Hemberg, *Die Kabiren*, p. 75.

[30] Edson, 'Cults of Thessalonica', pp. 180–90.

to that emperor's reign'.[31] In 1925 F. Chapouthier found an inscription in Samothrace which also lists some initiates from Thessalonica.[32] It is Edson's conclusion that 'by the reign of Augustus at the latest members of the city's upper classes were showing interest in the cult of the Samothracian gods'.[33] When we read in Acts 17.4 that Paul's preaching attracted 'not a few of the leading women' to his movement, it is likely that, at a minimum, they were familiar with the mysteries of Samothrace, not to mention their acquaintance and possible participation in the other cults of the city.

Samothrace unveils a number of interesting phenomena. Among these is the Hieron, a hall for the performance of religious rites, which externally has the appearance of a temple but inwardly is remarkably similar to an early Christian assembly room: the religious rites are enacted before a seated congregation. Also closely related to early Christianity is the rite of confession.[34]

A basic emphasis in Samothrace is on the 'benign nurturing of life'.[35] In her interpretation of one of the extant pedimental sculptures, Phyllis Lehmann notes that it fits the formal requirements of a certain divinity by the name of Okeanos. As his name suggests, he is the father of all rivers, brooks and streams and together with his spouse Tethys, is described as the primordial source of life. Plutarch refers to Tethys as 'the kindly nurse and provider of all things',[36] language reminiscent of what we heard in the cult of Dionysus and again suggesting that when Paul uses the term 'nurse' in 1 Thess. 2.7 he is using a word that has definite connotations for the citizens of Thessalonica.

---

[31] Edson, 'Cults of Thessalonica', pp. 189–90.

[32] P. M. Fraser, *Samothrace: The Inscriptions on Stone* (Bollingen Series 60.2.1; New York: Pantheon, 1960), p. 58.

[33] Edson, 'Cults of Thessalonica', p. 190.

[34] From the Archaic period onward, admission to the *epopteia* was preceded by an obligatory confession of sins'. P. W. Lehmann, *Samothrace: The Heiron* (Bollingen Series 60.3; Princeton: Princeton University, 1969), p. 54.

[35] P. W. Lehmann, *The Pedimental Sculptures of the Hieron in Samothrace* (Locust Valley, New York: J. J. Augustin, 1962), pp. 17–18.

[36] Lehmann, *Pedimental*, p. 18; Plutarch, *Zeus and Osiris*, 364 D.

As with some of the other cults in Thessalonica, so the mysteries of Samothrace are 'subject to Bacchic frenzy'.[37] Also, for the initiates there is an implied hope for a blessed afterlife and according to Lehmann 'we may assume that such promise was indeed offered by the *epopteia* in Samothrace'.[38] Additionally, the theme of the *hieros gamos* is present as well as the fertility symbol of the male genitals.[39] Finally, a comment must be made about Lehmann's interpretation of the frieze of the dancing maidens. 'Each of the maidens and the musicians wear a polos, the headgear reserved for divinity, especially the Great Goddess in her many forms. In profane life, mortal women are never shown wearing a polos but, as participants in ritual actions, they become assimilated to divinity by wearing a garb that otherwise is restricted to the gods.'[40] This concern with special headgear is widespread: in Thessalonica we know of a series of coins with the helmeted head of Roma on the obverse and on the reverse the inscription ΘΕΣΣΑΛΟΝΙΚΕΩΝ.[41] Another series depicts Cabirus wearing a laurel crown. Also, Macedonia was famous for its crowns made from roses, crowns which were used in the commemoratory sacrifice of the cult of Dionysus. So when Paul urges his hearers to put on for 'a helmet the hope of salvation' (1 Thess. 5.8) he himself may well have been influenced by Isa. 59.17, but the use of the term 'crown' would have signaled some very different associations for his audience.

Before turning our attention to the important role of the civic cult in Thessalonica, let us pause briefly to suggest a few further relationships between the Thessalonian correspondence and the material just reviewed. Since we do not wish at this point to enter into detailed exegesis, our comments will be cursory.

Certainly a knowledge of the cults in Thessalonica allows us to understand with more precision such references as 1 Thess. 1.9,

---

[37] N. Lewis, *Samothrace: The Ancient Literary Sources* (Bollingen Series 60.1; New York: Pantheon, 1958), p. 97; Strabo, 10.3.7.

[38] Lehmann, *Hieron*, p. 42.

[39] Lehmann, *Hieron*, p. 40.

[40] P. W. Lehmann and D. Spittle, *Samothrace: The Temenos* (Bollingen Series 60.5; Princeton: Princeton University, 1982), 221.

[41] H. L. Hendrix, *Thessalonicans Honor Romans* (ThD diss., Harvard 1984), p. 141.

'you turned to God from idols', and 1 Thess. 4.5, 'not in the passion of lust like heathen who do not know God'. In addition, the more detailed knowledge that we can ascertain about the Christian community's pagan past, the more likely we will be to interpret certain problematic passages such as 1 Thess. 4.1–9 against the broader background.

1 Thess. 4.1–9 is filled with what we might refer to as 'high density' paraenetic language. The most frequent use of περιπατέω in Paul is in the Corinthian letters (1 Cor. 3.3; 7.17; 2 Cor. 4.2; 5.7; 10.2; 12.18). The specific reference 'to please God' (ἀρέσκειν Θεῷ) is only found in Rom. 8.8. The reference to 'instructions' (παρεγγελίας) is found only here in the Pauline letters and the verbal form, other than the Thessalonian letters themselves, only in 1 Cor. 7.10 and 11.1. The only other reference to 'the will of God' (θέλημα τοῦ Θεοῦ) in a specific ethical context of 'doing the will of God' is in Rom. 12.2. To 'disregard' (ἀθετῶν) God who gives you the Holy Spirit has no exact parallel in Paul, with the possible exception of Gal. 2.21 where he talks about setting aside the grace of God. Further, Paul does not often use the full title 'the Holy Spirit' (τὸ πνεῦμα αὐτοῦ τὸ ἅγιον) except for the most solemn occasions such as in Rom. 5.5; 9.1; 14.17; 15.13, 16 and 19, or when he uses the term in a catalogue (2 Cor. 6.4) or in a benediction (2 Cor. 13.14). Finally, the reference to 'unchastity' (πορνεία) is again found only in the Corinthian correspondence (1 Cor. 5:1; 6.13, 18; 2 Cor. 12.21), except for its use in the catalogue of vices in Gal. 5.19. All of this suggests that Paul is very deliberately dealing with a situation of grave immorality, not too dissimilar to the cultic temptations of Corinth. Thus, Paul's severe warnings in this section, using the weightiest authorities he possibly can, is intended to distinguish the behavior of the Thessalonian Christians from that of their former heathen and pagan life which is still much alive in the various cults of the city.

Given this background and context, what is the meaning of τὸ σκεῦος in 1 Thess. 4.4? Given the ambiguity of the reference and the intensity of the scholarly discussion,[42] as well as the cultic

[42] See Marshall, *Thessalonians*, pp. 107–9.

backgrounds just discussed, it is difficult to agree with John Eadie's conclusion: 'One may dismiss at once the more special meanings assigned to it, as *membrum virile*'[43] Hardly! Both Antistius Vetus[44] and Aelianus[45] use the term σκεῦος as referring to the *membrum virile* and given the strong phallic symbolism in the cults of Dionysus, Cabirus and Samothrace such a reference is hardly surprising. The additional verb κτάομαι which Paul uses would suggest a meaning for the phrase something like 'to gain control over the σκεῦος'. The specific meaning of this term would surely not be lost on the Thessalonian audience nor its wider meaning of 'gaining control over the body with regard to sexual matters'. The reference to πράγματι in 4.6 would certainly refer back to this intended meaning.

Finally, one should not overlook the obvious parallels between the following texts and the mystery cults: 1 Thess. 5.5–7 with its reference to darkness and drunkenness; 1 Thess. 5.19–22 where Paul explicitly urges his hearers not 'to quench' the Spirit but 'to test' it. Quite clearly the apostle does not wish the gift of the Spirit to be confused with the excesses of the Dionysiac mysteries; for Paul the Spirit does not lead to 'Bacchic frenzies' but to joy precisely in the context of suffering. Discussion of those texts dealing with hope will be reserved for a fuller discussion in a later context.

The Civic Cults of Thessalonica

In Acts 17 we learn that the Jews together with some persons from the *agora* in Thessalonica attacked the home of Paul's sponsor, Jason. Then we read in verses 6 and 7 that 'when they could not find them, they dragged Jason and some of the brethren before the city authorities, crying, "These men who

---

[43] J. Eadie, *Commentary on the Greek Text of the Epistles of Paul to the Thessalonians* (New York: Macmillan, 1877), p. 127.

[44] 1 CE in *Anth. plan.* 4.243; W. F. Arndt and F. Wilbur Gingrich, *A Greek-English Lexicon of the New Testament and Other Early Christian Literature* (Chicago: University of Chicago, 1979), p. 754.

[45] 170–235 CE; *Nat. an.* xvii.11; Arndt-Gingrich, *A Greek-English Lexicon*, p. 754.

have turned the whole world upside down have come here also, and Jason has received them; and they are all acting against the decrees of Caesar [τῶν δογμάτων Καίσαρος], saying that there is another king, Jesus."' What are these δογμάτα Καίσαρος which Paul and his associates violated? Is Luke here spinning an entertaining story or is he faithfully describing the reality of the Thessalonian situation? As we have argued elsewhere, our predisposition is to take much of the detailed material of Acts seriously as a possibly credible source of information.[46] One cannot help but be favorably impressed with the reliability of certain details in Acts when, for example, such a unique term as 'city authorities' (τοὺς πολιτάρχας), used in Acts only with regard to Thessalonian authorities (17.8), has been archaeologically verified.[47] Neither the unjustified extreme skepticism of recent years nor an uncritical fundamentalism is justified with regard to the interpretation of Acts.

To return to the issue of the 'decrees of Caesar': A. N. Sherwin-White regards Acts 17.7 as 'the most confused of the various descriptions of charges in Acts'.[48] He correctly recognizes – over against many commentaries – that Acts cannot be referring to a breach of the Roman law of treason (*maiestas*) since at this time the concept of treason, although centering 'upon the *maiestas* of the Caesarian succession was founded upon public law, not Caesarian decree'.[49] To what type of situation the Acts accounts might be referring is left unanswered by Sherwin-White.

In his important study E. A. Judge cites a number of imperial decrees which might have been referred to as 'decrees of Caesar' in Thessalonica. Among them is the following intensified ban on prediction from Tiberius in CE 16:

> But as for all the other astrologers and magicians and such as practised divination in anyway whatsoever, he put to death those who were foreigners and banished all the citizens that were accused of still

[46] K. P. Donfried, 'Paul and Judaism: I Thessalonians 2.13–16 as a Test Case', *Int* 38 (1984), p. 247.
[47] J. Finegan, *The Archeology of the New Testament* (Boulder: Westview, 1981), p. 108.
[48] A. N. Sherwin-White, *Roman Society and Roman Law in the New Testament* (Oxford: Oxford University, 1963), p. 103.
[49] E. A. Judge, 'The Decrees of Caesar at Thessalonica', *RTR* 30 (1971), p. 2.

employing the art at this time after the previous decree (*dogma*) by which it had been forbidden to engage in any such business in the city. ...[50]

While this reference is helpful the question still remains why the Thessalonian politarchs rather than the proconsul of Macedonia would have been asked to enforce a ban of this type. 'We must assume,' argues Judge, 'that in some respect the politarchs were obliged to take cognizance of offenses against the "decrees of Caesar".'[51] But why – on what basis? Judge cites three pieces of evidence in the order of increasing specificity. First, there is an extant oath of personal loyalty by the inhabitants of Paphlagonia to the Caesarian house. This oath includes Roman and non-Romans alike and reads as follows:

I swear ... that I will support Caesar Augustus, his children and descendants, throughout my life, in word, deed and thought ... that in whatsoever concerns them I will spare neither body nor soul nor life nor children ... that whenever I see or hear of anything being said, planned or done against them I will report it ... and whomsoever they regard as enemies I will attack and pursue with arms and the sword by land and by sea ... [52]

Second, he cites a Cypriot oath of allegiance to Tiberius on his assumption of power. What is new here are the specific pledges to reverence (σεβάσεσθαι) and obedience (ὑπακούσεσθαι and πειθαρχέσειν). According to Judge, a 'formula of this kind might be sufficient to lead to the Thessalonians treating the oath as a "decree" of Caesar'.[53] Third, Judge points to an inscription from Samos which strongly suggests that local magistrates were responsible for administering the oath of loyalty as well as to receive complaints concerning violations of such an oath.[54]

Judge offers a probable explanation for the accuracy of the reference to the 'decrees of Caesar' in Acts 17. In all likelihood the politarchs in Thessalonica were responsible for administering the oath of loyalty and for dealing with violations of the oath. In

---

[50] Dio Chrysostom, *Nest.* 57.15.8; Judge, 'The Decrees of Caesar', p. 4.
[51] Judge, 'The Decrees of Caesar', p. 5.
[52] Judge, 'The Decrees of Caesar', p. 6.
[53] Judge, 'The Decrees of Caesar', p. 7.
[54] Judge, 'The Decrees of Caesar', p. 7.

view of this situation we need to ask whether there were elements in the proclamation of Paul and his co-workers in Thessalonica which might have been perceived as so politically inflammatory as to provoke the crisis described in Acts and whether the unusually strong civic cult in the city would have created an environment particularly hostile to early Christian proclamation and language.

It is difficult, if not impossible, to reconstruct the original Pauline message proclaimed in the city and all we can hope for are glimmers of it in the written correspondence. If 1 Thessalonians is at all representative of his original preaching then we certainly do find elements which could be understood or misunderstood in a distinctly political sense. In 2.12 God, according to the apostle, calls the Thessalonian Christians 'into his own kingdom'; in 5.3 there is a frontal attack on the *Pax et Securitas* program of the early Principate;[55] and in the verses just preceding this attack one finds three heavily loaded political terms: παρουσία, ἀπάντησις and κύριος. Milligan notes that παρουσία is related to 'the 'visit' of the king, or some other official'.[56] Dibelius also urges that when used as court language παροσίx refers to the arrival of Caesar, a king or an official.[57] Best has shown that ἀπάντησις refers to the citizens meeting a dignitary who is about to visit the city.[58] These two terms are used in this way by Josephus (*Ant.* 11.327ff.) and also similarly referred to by such Greek writers as Chrysostom. The term κύριος, especially when used in the same context as the two preceding terms, also has a definite political sense. As Deissmann has shown, the people in the eastern Mediterranean applied the term κύριος to refer to the Roman emperors from Augustus on, although the first verifiable inscription of the *Kyrios*-title in Greece dates to the time of Nero.[59] All of this, coupled with the

[55] W. H. C. Frend, *Martyrdom and Persecution in the Early Church* (Oxford: Blackwell, 1965), 96; see also p. 124, n. 69.

[56] G. Milligan, *St Paul's Epistles to the Thessalonians* (New York: Macmillan, n.d.), pp. 145–58.

[57] M. Dibelius, *An die Thessalonicher 1 II, An die Philipper* (HNT 11/3; Tübingen, 1937), pp. 14–15.

[58] E. Best, *The First and Second Epistles to the Thessalonians* (London: Adams and Charles Black, 1972). See p. 199 for bibliography.

[59] A. Deissmann, *Light from the Ancient East* (New York: Doran, 1922), pp. 351–8.

use of τὸ εὐαγγέλιον and its possible association with the eastern ruler cult,[60] suggests that Paul and his associates could easily be understood as violating the 'decrees of Caesar' in the most blatant manner.

We now turn to an examination of the civic cult of Thessalonica; important for a proper understanding of these activities is a brief sketch of the history of Thessalonica. The city was founded in 316 BCE by Cassander, a general in Alexander's army, and it was he who gave the city its name in honor of his wife, *Thessalonikeia*, who was the daughter of Philip II and the half-sister of Alexander. The new city included the ancient Therme and some thirty-five other towns. When Macedonia became a Roman province in 146 BCE, Thessalonica was made the capital and thus the center of Roman administration. The city supported the victorious Antony and Octavian prior to the famous battle of Philippi in 42 BCE, an event which ushered in a prosperous new era for Thessalonica. After Brutus' defeat, Thessalonica was able to celebrate its new status as a 'free' city with immunity from tribute and to establish games in honor of the victors. If Holland Hendrix's reconstruction of a Thessalonian inscription is correct,[61] then it 'is quite possible that the dedication was intended to honor Antony and Octavian who, as benefactors *par excellence*, assured the city's survival and freedom'.[62] The extensive coinage of Thessalonica underscores its prosperity which was certainly due to its status as a free city and its location as a main station on the famous Via Egnatia, which ran through the city on an east–west axis.

In his thesis, *Thessalonicans Honor Romans*, Hendrix shows not only that the Thessalonians' fortunes were determined heavily by Roman interests from the middle of the second century to the middle of the first century BCE, but also that in view of this

---

[60] P. Stuhlmacher, *Das paulinische Evangelium*, I (Göttingen: Vandenhoeck and Ruprecht, 1968), pp. 196–206.

[61] Hendrix, *Thessalonicans Honor Romans*, p. 41. The inscription reads as follows:
[The city? and the] negot[iant and]
[resident? R]omans [to M. Antony?]
[and C. Caes]ar [b]enefac[tors and saviors?]

[62] Hendrix, *Thessalonicans Honor Romans*, p. 42.

situation it was necessary for the Thessalonians to develop ways to honor their Roman benefactors so that they would be able 'to attract and sustain influential Romans' commitments and favors'.[63]

We have already explored the role of the gods, their importance as guardians of the city and the priesthood which stands at their service. As Roman benefaction gains in importance for the citizens of Thessalonica, increasingly the Roman benefactors are included as objects of honor alongside the gods. Hendrix dates this development at about 95 BCE and adds that while ' "the gods" of the city were due honors as the source of Thessalonica's continued well-being, important foreign agents of its immediate interests were acknowledged in concert with its divine sustainers ... Honors *for* the gods and Roman benefactors expressed a hierarchy of benefaction extending from the divine sphere into human affairs.'[64]

During the first century BCE the goddess Roma is joined to the Roman benefactors and 'it is clear that in establishing a priesthood for Roma and the Roman benefactors, Thessalonians acknowledged her divine status'.[65] While conventions concerning Roma may have been borrowed from elsewhere, her status and function in Thessalonica is quite different; she is not granted honors as an independent figure nor was she specifically related to an individual such as Augustus, but rather 'she was grafted onto a previously existing object of honor, the Roman benefactors ... As an object of devotion she was linked inextricably to those Romans who tangibly benefited the city.'[66] According to Hendrix's understanding of this development, once Roma is joined to the benefactors it now becomes easy for the priesthood of the gods to become associated with these Roman benefactors. Honors to the gods, Roma and the Roman benefactors become increasingly interrelated in the practice of the city.

---

[63] Hendrix, *Thessalonicans Honor Romans*, p. 253.
[64] Hendrix, *Thessalonicans Honor Romans*, p. 336.
[65] Hendrix, *Thessalonicans Honor Romans*, p. 287.
[66] Hendrix, *Thessalonicans Honor Romans*, p. 287.

But there is yet another important step in this trajectory: a temple of Caesar is built. This took place in the reign of Augustus and associated with this temple is a 'priest and agonothete of the Imperator'.[67] Most helpful as an aid in understanding this development is the numismatic evidence. From this it is clear that 'Thessalonica acclaimed Julius as god'.[68] These coins were minted in Thessalonica about 27 BCE and are the first coins which portray the heads of Romans.[69] In the case of Julius 'a Roman is designated explicitly as "god"'. Hendrix adds that although 'the title "son of god" [Θεοῦ υἱός] does not appear with Octavian/Augustus on any of the coins, the juxtaposition of the Divine Julius with his son may reflect Thessalonican awareness of the Imperator's status as *divi filius* and is indicative perhaps of local importance to it'.[70] Also significant in this overall process is that at this time the head of Augustus displaces the head of Zeus on the coins of the city.

This unequivocal numismatic designation of a Roman ruler as divine was, according to Hendrix, 'an extension of Thessalonica's earlier policies of monumental recognition for distinguished Romans whose benefactions were important to the city … because of his status as sole ruler and his supreme responsibility in assuring Thessalonica's well-being.'[71] Thus, 'Thessalonica added Augustus, his divine father and his successors to the honors granted "the gods and Roman benefactors" and "Roma and Roman benefactors".'[72] As a result of acknowledging 'the divine sanction of the new order'[73] a temple of Caesar is built and a priest and agonothete of the Imperator Augustus 'son of God' is appointed and now is given priority over the other priesthoods. In the evidence assembled by Hendrix one notes that in 'every extant instance in which the "priest and agonothete of the Imperator" is mentioned, he is listed first in what appears to be a

---

[67] Hendrix, *Thessalonicans Honor Romans*, p. 62.
[68] Hendrix, *Thessalonicans Honor Romans*, p. 108.
[69] Hendrix, *Thessalonicans Honor Romans*, p. 173.
[70] Hendrix, *Thessalonicans Honor Romans*, p. 170.
[71] Hendrix, *Thessalonicans Honor Romans*, pp. 299, 308.
[72] Hendrix, *Thessalonicans Honor Romans*, p. 308.
[73] Hendrix, *Thessalonicans Honor Romans*, p. 310.

strict observance of protocol. The Imperator's priest and agonothete assumes priority, the priest of "the gods" is cited next
followed by the priest of Roma and Roman benefactors.'[74] The
process of cult interaction and interrelationship proceeds, but it
is clear at this point in the history of Thessalonica which office
'demanded superior attention'.[75] Superior attention is called for
precisely because that 'particular strand of royal theology which
is most apparent in Thessalonica's honorific activity is the
attention paid to the legitimation of Augustus' rule and his
successors'.[76] Hendrix comments further that

> Augustus' dynastic prospects were publicly acclaimed on coin types
> honoring Gaius and Tiberius. Numismatic honors previously granted
> only selectively became a conventional feature of the city's coinage. The
> impact of developments in royal theologies and religious activities
> directed to rulers which had been cultivated in certain quarters of the
> Hellenistic Greek world and late Republican Rome are manifested clearly
> in the city's honors.[77]

Royal Theology and the Thessalonian Correspondence

Given this emphasis on royal theology in Thessalonica at the
time of Paul's visit and the accusation recorded in Acts that he and
his associates are 'all acting against the decrees of Caesar, saying
that there is another king, Jesus...' (17.7), let us proceed by
lifting out certain elements in 1 and 2 Thessalonians which we
believe are not unrelated to this overall political climate.

What situation(s) is Paul referring to with his several references to affliction and suffering in 1 Thessalonians? In 1.6 he
reminds the Thessalonians that they 'received the word in much
affliction [θλίψει πολλῇ]'; in 2.14 he refers to their suffering
(ἐπάθετε); in 3.3 he sends Timothy to them so 'that no one be
moved by these afflictions [θλίψεσιν].' This theme is well
summarized in 3.4: 'For when we were with you, we told you
beforehand that we were to suffer affliction [θλίβεσθαι]; just as it

---

[74] Hendrix, *Thessalonicans Honor Romans*, p. 312.

[75] Hendrix, *Thessalonicans Honor Romans*, p. 312.

[76] Hendrix, *Thessalonicans Honor Romans*, p. 311.

[77] Hendrix, *Thessalonicans Honor Romans*, p. 310.

has come to pass, and as you know.' What did Paul have in mind when he made this warning to the congregation during his visit and what exactly had come to pass?

Without yet engaging in the question of authorship, let us simply observe that 2 Thessalonians continues these themes of suffering (1.5), affliction (1.6) and intensifies them by the use of the term τοῖς διωγμοῖς (1.4) and the notion that God will 'repay with affliction those who afflict you' (1.6).

Also related to this are the Satan/tempter references. In 1 Thess. 2.18 Paul indicates that Satan repeatedly hindered him from visiting the Thessalonian congregation. Is this an indication that the political opposition to him remained so strong that it was impossible for Paul to re-enter the city? Is F. F. Bruce not on the right track when he suggests that 'Paul might well discern Satanic opposition behind the politarchs' decision'?[78] This also relates to the 'tempter' reference in 3.5: 'For this reason, when I could bear it no longer, I sent that I might know your faith, for fear that somehow the tempter [ὁ πειράζων] had tempted you and that our labor would be in vain.'[79] It is fully possible that the apostle is concerned that the political opposition and pressure on the young Christians might be so strong that they would be tempted to abandon their faith in Christ. That the climate of such a concern is a realistic possibility should be evident in light of our review of the civic cult in Thessalonica.

In the midst of this situation of affliction and suffering, produced in all likelihood by political opposition, 1 Thessalonians assures the congregation that God has chosen them (1.4)[80] and emphatically stresses the twin themes of hope and parousia. How does this emphasis fit into the overall perspective of the situation and what specifically caused Paul to place such emphasis on these twin themes of hope and parousia?

It is noteworthy that 1 Thessalonians opens in 1.3 and closes in 5.8 with the triadic formulation 'faith, love and hope'.

---

[78] F. F. Bruce, *The Acts of the Apostles* (Grand Rapids: Eerdmans, 1951), p. 327.

[79] Note also 1 Cor. 7.5: 'Satan tempts . . .'.

[80] The choice of this language may well be related to the persecution/affliction theme of the letter.

However, when Timothy reports back to Paul about the condition of the Thessalonian church he only brings the good news of their 'faith and love' (3.6). The element of hope is absent. This section of the letter ends with Paul praying that he might see them soon face to face so that he might 'supply what is lacking [τὰ ὑστερήματα] in their faith' (3.10). Given the strong emphasis on hope (ἐλπίς) in such strategic locations as 1.10, 2.19 and 3.13, locations which mark the closing of the first three chapters, and the fact that a similar situation exists with regard to the term παρουσία in 2.19, 3.13, 4.15 and 5.23, it is likely that what is lacking in the faith of the Thessalonians is the dimension of hope. This observation is underscored by what Dahl referred to as the 'superfluous rehearsals and reminders',[81] viz. the many 'you know' type references. When these are examined structurally the following pattern emerges:

1.5	καθὼς οἴδατε
2.1	Αὐτοὶ γὰρ οἴδατε
2.2, 5	καθὼς οἴδατε
2.9	Μνημονεύετε
2.10	ὑμεῖς μάρτυρες … ἐγενήθημεν
2.11	καθάπερ οἴδατε
3.3b–4	αὐτοὶ γὰρ οἴδατε … καὶ ἐγένετο καὶ οἴδατε
4.1–2	καθὼς παρελάβετε … οἴδατε
4.6	καὶ προείπαμεν ὑμῖν καὶ διεμαρτυράμεθα
4.10–11	καὶ γὰρ ποιεῖτε αὐτὸ … καθὼς ὑμῖν παρηγγείλαμεν
5.1	οὐ χρείαν ἔχετε ὑμῖν γράφεσθαι

These 'superfluous rehearsals and reminders' come to an abrupt halt in 4.13, the beginning of the section dealing with those persons who have died prior to the parousia. The verb ἀγνοέω, a word not found elsewhere in the Thessalonian correspondence, is used by Paul as a literary device to signal that new information is to follow. To indicate that the new information has come to an end, the apostle uses another rehearsal formula in 5.1: 'But as to the times and the seasons, brethren, you have no need to have anything written to you.' Thus, 4.13–18 is a section of critical importance for 1 Thessalonians; within the eschatological

---

[81] Nils Dahl in reflections made to the Society of Biblical Literature Paul Seminar in 1972 (unpublished), p. 2.

framework of Paul's initial proclamation, a new issue has arisen: What is the status of those who have died in Christ prior to the parousia? Negatively, Paul argues that the Thessalonian Christians should not be like the remainder of the gentile population who have no hope. Underscoring the accuracy of Paul's description of pagan hopelessness in the face of death are these observations by Ramsay MacMullen:

> In all the 'Oriental' cults in general, whether of Atargatis, Mithra, Isis or Cybele, the element of resurrection has received emphatic attention in studies old and new – attention emphatic but not always firmly controlled. It should really not be taken for granted, as it often is assumed, that people who believe a god might rise from death also believed in such a blessing for themselves as well. The conjecture needs support – and finds none.[82]

Paul's positive response to this issue is to refer to the faith they hold in common: 'we believe that Jesus died and rose again'. By the use of an apocalyptic 'word of the Lord' (4.15), the Apostle can draw the consequence that when the Lord comes 'the dead in Christ will rise first; then we who are alive ...' (4.16–17).

It is important to ask why this issue concerning the 'dead in Christ' (οἱ νεκροὶ ἐν Χριστῷ, 4.16) is so central to the letter, and, further, we must ask whether it is possible to identify those who have fallen asleep (τοὺς κοιμηθέντας, 4.14). F. F. Bruce makes a bold suggestion: 'perhaps those who "fell asleep" so soon (I Th. iv. 13) were victims of this persecution [the one referred to in Acts 17]'.[83] Bruce's suggestion is an unorthodox one in view of the fact that few scholars[84] discuss the matter of death by persecution this early in Christian history. Yet there are a number of items which could give positive support to Bruce's suggestion: 1) The use of κοιμάω in Acts 7.60 is remarkable: 'And as they were stoning Stephen, he prayed, "Lord Jesus, receive my spirit." And he knelt down and cried with a loud voice, "Lord, do not hold this sin against them." And when he had said this, he fell asleep [ἐκοιμήθη].' In this text the verb κοιμάω refers explicitly to one

---

[82] R. MacMullen, *Paganism in the Roman Empire* (New Haven: Yale University, 1981), p. 55.

[83] Bruce, *Acts*, pp. 327–8; unfortunately, Bruce does not mention this suggestion in his new commentary, *1 and 2 Thessalonians* (Word: 45; Waco, Texas: Word, 1982).

[84] Perhaps Frend, *Martyrdom and Persecution*, p. 83.

who has suffered death through persecution. 2) In 1 Thess.
2.14–16, which we have argued elsewhere as authentic,[85] Paul
makes a very clear parallel between the situation of the
Thessalonian church and that of the churches in Judea; they
'became imitators of the churches of God in Christ Jesus which
are in Judea' and they 'suffered the *same things*' (τὰ αὐτὰ ἐπάθετε)
from their countrymen and that clearly involves the dimension of
death (2.14–15). 3) The Thessalonian congregation became an
example to all the believers in Macedonia and in Achaia precisely
because they 'received the word in much affliction' (1 Thess.
1.6–8). Further they became 'imitators' of Paul, Silvanus and
Timothy (1 Thess. 1.6) in suffering, a theme which Paul articulates in 2.2: 'but though we had already suffered and had been
shamefully treated in Philippi, as you know, we had courage in
our God to declare to you the gospel of God in the face of great
opposition [ἐν πολλῷ ἀγῶνι].' Paul uses this same term, ἀγών,
only once again, in a very similar context, in Phil. 1.30. It is
precisely in this first chapter of Philippians that the apostle
expresses 'full courage' so that 'Christ will be honored in my
body, whether by life or by death' (Phil. 1.20) and it is in this same
letter that Paul once again expresses the possible nearness of
death: 'Even if I am to be poured as a libation upon the sacrificial
offering of your faith, I am glad and rejoice with you all' (Phil.
2.17). Most commentators are agreed that Paul is alluding to the
possibility of his own death as a martyr;[86] Lohmeyer goes even
further than this when he suggests that Paul and the congregation
are bound together in this threat of martyrdom. Referring to
Paul's anticipated trip to Philippi he remarks: 'Es ist eine Reise
zum Martyrium, genauer zu der dauernden persönlichen
Vereinigung von Apostel und Gemeinde im Martyrium.'[87]

---

[85] Donfried, 'Paul and Judaism', pp. 242–53. [Now also in this volume, pp. 195–208.

[86] J. Gnilka, *Der Philipperbrief* (HTKNT 10.3; Freiburg: Herder, 1968), pp. 154–5; J. B.
Lightfoot, *Saint Paul's Epistle to the Philippians* (London: Macmillan, 1891), pp. 118–19; E.
Lohmeyer, *Die Briefe an die Philipper, an die Kolosser und an Philemon* (MeyerK: Göttingen:
Vandenhoeck and Ruprecht, 1964), pp. 111–14.

[87] Lohmeyer, *Die Briefe*, p. 111. [ET: 'It is a journey toward martyrdom, more precisely,
a journey toward the permanent personal union of the Apostle and the congregation in
martyrdom.']

The question which, of course, arises in light of these suggestions is their persuasiveness: is it probable that the afflictions and
persecutions[88] in Thessalonica could lead to occasional deaths?[89]
When Paul in Rom. 8.35–36 speaks of tribulation, distress, persecution, famine, nakedness, peril and sword and then cites Ps.
44.23, 'For thy sake we are being killed all the day long; we are
regarded as sheep to be slaughtered', is he merely speaking
rhetorically? Otto Michel reminds us of an important point: 'Die
Aufzählung der Bedrängnisse wird bekräftigt durch das
Schriftwort Ps. 44.23. Das Rabbinat hat Ps. 44.23 gern auf den
Zeugentod (II Makk 7) gedeutet, und dies Getötetwerden galt im
Judentum als Erweis echter Gottesliebe.'[90] We are hard pressed
to see that Paul had any other intention in mind.

Bruce's conjecture concerning the identity of the dead in 1
Thess. 4.13–18 is, in our judgment, a reasonable hypothesis. If
our inclination is to take seriously the possibility of persecutions
in Thessalonica and elsewhere as leading to occasional death, do
we have any extra-biblical evidence which would lend further
credibility to this suggestion? The Paphlogonian oath of loyalty
to the Caesarian house in 3 BCE, which we cited earlier, compels
Romans and non-Romans alike to report cases of disloyalty and
to physically hunt down the offenders. The seriousness by which
this is meant to be taken – even to the point of death for those
who are disloyal – is self-evident. If this possible parallel has any
relevance for the political situation in Thessalonica at the time of
Paul, then certainly the apostle's 'political preaching' and his
direct attack on the *Pax et Securitas* (see 1 Thess. 5.3) emphasis of
the early principate was not likely to lead the citizens to give Paul
a warm or extended welcome.

Paul's review of his work in Thessalonica is found in 1 Thess.
2.1–12; this section is sandwiched between the themes of

---

[88] See also 2 Thess. 1.4.

[89] We certainly do not wish to imply any systematic persecutions.

[90] O. Michel, *Der Brief an die Römer* (MeyerK; Göttingen: Vandenhoeck and Ruprecht,
1963), p. 217. [ET: 'The enumeration of the afflictions is given support by reference to the
scriptural text in Ps. 44.23. The Rabbis readily interpreted Ps 44:23 as referring to
martyrdom and such a way of death was considered in Judaism as an indication of genuine
love for God.']

suffering and death. What is Paul intending to communicate? One important preliminary attempt to answer this question is the article by Abraham Malherbe.[91] Essentially he compares the Pauline language of these verses with that of the Cynic-Stoic philosophers and draws to our attention some significant parallels. Malherbe stops short, however, of suggesting the Pauline motivation which led to the composition of this 'apology'. In fact, at the close of his article, he invites us to move exactly in that direction. We would suggest the following as background to Paul's response: Paul had to leave Thessalonica hurriedly after a brief stay[92] due to the opposition originally mounted by the Jews of the city[93] but which had quickly spread to the non-Jewish population. As a result Paul travels to Athens but the Thessalonian Christians must remain and continue to experience the consequences of this attack. They experience persecution and, perhaps, in the case of a few, even to the point of death. It is not inconceivable that some, inside and outside the community, placed at least some blame on Paul for their difficult situation. Dio Chrysostom speaks negatively about certain philosophers who 'merely utter a phrase or two, and then, after railing at you rather than teaching you, they make a hurried exit, anxious lest before they have finished you may raise an out-cry and send them packing'.[94] Precisely because some may have viewed Paul in a somewhat similar way, it is necessary for him to speak of his deep affection and anguish for them during his absence.[95] Not to be confused with those wandering philosophers

---

[91] 'Gentle as a Nurse'; see n. 18 above.

[92] The reference to three weeks in Acts 17 deals with Paul's activity in the synagogue and not necessarily his total stay. Note Bruce, *Acts*, p. 324: 'We are not told what space of time elapsed between his leaving the synagogue and leaving the city.' See also G. Lüdemann, *Paulus, der Heidenapostel*, 2 vols (Göttingen: Vandenhoeck and Ruprecht, 1980), 1.203–4, for a brief discussion of his and other positions. [ET: *Paul, Apostle to the Gentiles: Studies in Chronology* (London: SCM Press, 1984)]. We are inclined to stress the brevity of Paul's visit to Thessalonica.

[93] There has always been a significant Jewish community in Thessalonica and now there is evidence for a Samaritan synagogue dating to the fourth century BCE. See B. Lifshitz and J. Schiby, 'Une Synagogue samaritaine à Thessalonique', *RB* 75 (1968) pp. 368–78.

[94] Dio Chrysostom, *Alex.* 32.11; see Malherbe, 'Gentle as a Nurse', p. 208.

[95] See our previous discussion above, pp. 24–5.

who did not become involved in the ἀγών of life, Paul reminds them that he and his co-workers preached the gospel of God to them 'in the face of great opposition [ἐν πολλῷ ἀγῶνι]' (1 Thess. 2.2), a reference placed very deliberately at the beginning of the apostle's 'apology'. Perhaps because of a further criticism that Paul deceived them by not telling them about the possibility of continued affliction, the apostle must defend himself against the charges of flattery and greed and must elsewhere in the letter repeatedly include himself as a participant in suffering and affliction – a suffering and affliction which he shared with them when present and now continues to share in Corinth. Certainly 1 Thess. 3.7, 'in all our distress and affliction', refers to Paul's situation at the time he is writing 1 Thessalonians. To demonstrate that his preaching was not a 'cloak for greed' (1 Thess. 2.5) the apostle recounts how hard Silvanus, Timothy and he worked[96] and how 'righteous and blameless' (1 Thess. 2.9–12) was their behavior toward the Christian community in Thessalonica.

Thus, we would argue that Paul's review of his relationship with the Thessalonian congregation in 1 Thess. 2 is in response to criticisms received from that Christian community which was upset not only by the severity of their afflictions, but also by Paul's rapid departure and apparent lack of concern. The letter is addressed to counter that misunderstanding of his relation to these Thessalonian Christians and to suggest that the Christian life is worth the affliction so that they may receive the salvation for which they have been destined (1 Thess. 5.9).

In terms of the substantive issue raised in 1 Thess. 4.13–18, Paul attempts to assure the community that those who have died will not be forgotten and those who are alive at the parousia will not have precedence. As we noted above, the apocalyptic language used serves to support this conclusion. We fully agree

---

[96] These comments taken together with 1 Thess. 4.10–12 'imply non-participation in public life. It is tempting to suggest that Paul's readers might have heard him taking a stand against the kind of political action that the philosophers were carrying on in Rome. They might understand that Paul was distancing himself from radical political activity' (E. Krentz, 'I Thessalonians: A Document of Roman Hellenism', 15, a paper presented to the 1 Thessalonians seminar of the Society of Biblical Literature, 1979).

with Koester that Paul's 'final daring play on the terms "death" (of Jesus), "being awake" and "being asleep" (of Christians) and "life" (with Jesus) seems to relativize also the problem of being alive or dead at the parousia'.[97] Koester, however, certainly goes beyond the text when he concludes that what 'started as apocalyptic instruction has thus become demythologized eschatology, describing faith, love and hope as the presence of eternity ... The timetable of eschatological expectations has been rendered meaningless.'[98] Given Paul's intention of wanting to relativize the problem of being dead or alive at the parousia, Marxsen is absolutely correct in his assertion that the theme of the parousia dominates 1 Thess. 4.13–5.11, and we would add, the entire letter.[99] The relationship between the problem of being dead or alive at the parousia and the centrality of the parousia to his thought is summarized by the apostle himself in 1 Thess. 5.9–10: 'For God has not destined us for wrath, but to obtain salvation through our Lord Jesus Christ, who died for us so that whether we wake or sleep we might live with him.'

The Problem of Second Thessalonians

Although it is impossible to rehearse thoroughly the very difficult and complex issue of 2 Thessalonians, a few tentative words need to be said. On the one hand, we are persuaded by Wolfgang Trilling's work that 2 Thessalonians is not from the hand of Paul;[100] on the other hand, we are not persuaded by Koester's analysis who also believes it to be non-Pauline but argues that it is considerably later than 1 Thessalonians and has no relationship with a concrete Thessalonian situation.[101]

---

[97] H. Koester, '1 Thessalonians – Experiment in Christian Writing', in *Continuity and Discontinuity in Church History*, (Festschrift George H. Williams; Leiden: Brill, 1979), p. 44.

[98] Koester, 'Experiment', p. 44; equally in error is Krentz's conclusion that 'the political tone triumphs over the apocalyptic' ('Document of Roman Hellenism', p. 14).

[99] W. Marxsen, *Der erste Brief an die Thessalonicher* (ZBK.NT 11.1; Zürich: Theologischer Verlag, 1979), pp. 63–7.

[100] W. Trilling, *Der zweite Brief an die Thessalonicher* (EKK XIV; Zürich: Benziger, 1980).

[101] H. Koester, *History and Literature of Early Christianity*, II, 2 vols (Philadelphia: Fortress Press, 1982), 2.242–6.

We understand 2 Thessalonians to be non-Pauline in the technical sense but that it is related to a concrete situation in Thessalonica. We would suggest that the specific situation is the continued and, perhaps, intensified persecution, an intensification that 2 Thessalonians refers to not only by use of the term τοῖς διωγμοῖς (1.4) and the harsh response to the afflicters (1.5–12), but also by the hostile description of the lawless one in 2 Thess 2.3–12. In terms of authorship, perhaps one of his two co-workers, who are listed as joint authors with Paul in both 1 and 2 Thessalonians, wrote the letter. It is not improbable to think that Timothy or Silvanus were in the city when the newest phase of the problem erupted. Since the first letter was co-authored by Paul, Silvanus and Timothy, neither Silvanus nor Timothy would have difficulty in co-authoring this second letter and modeling it after the first. But who is the more likely candidate – Silvanus (Silas) or Timothy? The answer is complicated by the fact that we do not have much information concerning either. Silvanus' Jerusalem background and his identification as a 'prophet' in Acts 15.32 might point to him as the author of 2 Thessalonians; but speaking against this is the absolute silence about Silas as an associate of Paul after their stay in Corinth (Acts 18.5). Pointing in the direction of Timothy are two facts: 1) we know from Acts that Timothy made at least two further trips to Macedonia (Acts 19.22; 20.4); and 2) the close association of Paul and Timothy in the authorship of at least four letters: 2 Corinthians, Philippians, 1 Thessalonians and Philemon.

Finally, a word about the κατέχον/κατέχων problem in 2 Thessalonians in the light of our study of cult interrelatedness in Thessalonica. In his 1967 study of the problem, C. H. Giblin drew some interesting links between the use of κατέχον/κατέχων in 2 Thessalonians and the cults of Serapis and Dionysus in Thessalonica and concludes that a 'generic allusion to pagan religious practice, especially to pseudo-prophetic seizure, would seem to account for Paul's choice of this particular term'.[102] This

---

[102] C. H. Giblin, *The Threat to Faith* (AnBib 31; Rome: Pontifical Biblical Institute, 1967), p. 201.

is a thesis that has been generally overlooked or rejected in the literature. Giblin's suggestion needs to be taken more seriously not only in the light of this study but also that of Ernst Koeberlein's work in which he shows that 'the mysteries instituted by Caligula and linked with Emperor worship partook of Isiacism, the colossal statue intended for in the Temple of Jerusalem being a blend of Neos Gaius and Zeus *Epiphane*'.[103] Based on Koeberlein's study Rex Witt is tempted to suggest that in the ἄνομος passage Paul is 'hitting out possibly at a Thessalonian cult in which Emperor worship was combined with the cult of Isis and Serapis'.[104]

Conclusion

The Greeks who were attracted to the Pauline mission grew up in a city filled with mystery cults and royal theology. Surely they would compare the gospel proclaimed by Paul with their pagan past; for this reason Paul skillfully selects his terminology for protreptic purposes. The language Paul uses, on the one hand, reveals continuities with their past practice, and on the other hand, reveals sharp discontinuities with their pagan past and intends to show them how the totality of their existence (note the unusual stress in 1 Thess. 5.23 on 'spirit and soul and body') has been transformed through the death of Christ into a new living relationship with him – whether awake or asleep (1 Thess. 5.10). Thus, for example, terms so common in the Egyptian cults of the day like εὐχαριστήριον and ἐκκλησιαστήριον are transformed by Paul so that they now stand in intimate relationship to Christ and his new community.[105]

It is our hope to have shown, even though in a cursory manner, that a knowledge of the interrelated cultic and historical background of Thessalonica, particularly the strong Roman presence and domination at the time of Paul, is an indispensable first step in the interpretation of the Thessalonian correspondence.

---

[103] Witt, 'The Egyptian Cults', p. 331. See further, E. Koeberlein, *Caligula und die aegyptischen Kulte* (Meisenheim am Glan: A. Hain, 1962).
[104] Witt, 'The Egyptian Cults', p. 331.
[105] Witt, 'The Egyptian Cults', p. 328; (ἐκκλησία: 1 Thess. 1.1; 2.14; 2 Thess. 1.4; εὐχαριστέω/εὐχαριστία: 1 Thess. 2.13; 3.9; 5.18).

3

꧁꧂

2 Thessalonians and the Church
of Thessalonica

It is with gratitude that I contribute this essay in honor of John Hurd. In over twenty years of friendship our common work on 1 and 2 Thessalonians has demonstrated both remarkable affinity[1] and substantial divergence.[2] Always, however, I have learned and been stimulated by John's creativity and originality and it has been a high privilege, over a long period of years and in a wide variety of Pauline seminars within the Society of Biblical Literature, to observe his careful analysis of texts and to engage his probing mind in dialogue. In what follows I will attempt to continue the conversation about a key concern to both of us and one for which no scholarly agreement has yet emerged.

In our article 'The Cults of Thessalonica and the Thessalonian Correspondence'[3] we argued that both the civic and religious cults of the city are a decisive factor in understanding the milieu in which the Thessalonian Christian congregation existed and that much of Paul's argument in 1 Thessalonians could be

---

[1]J. C. Hurd, 'Paul Ahead of His Time: 1 Thess. 2.13–16', in *Anti-Judaism in Early Christianity. I. Paul and the Gospels*, ed. Peter Richardson, Studies in Christianity and Judaism 2 (Waterloo, ON: Wilfrid Laurier University, 1986), pp. 21–36, and, 'Concerning the Structure of 1 Thessalonians' (unpublished; presented at the Paul Seminar, Society of Biblical Literature 1972 Annual Meeting, Los Angeles).

[2]J. C. Hurd, 'Concerning the Authenticity of 2 Thessalonians' (unpublished; presented at the Paul Seminar, Society of Biblical Literature 1983 Annual Meeting, Dallas).

[3]K. P. Donfried, 'The Cults of Thessalonica and the Thessalonian Correspondence', *NTS* 31 (1985), pp. 336–56; also pp. 21–48 in this volume.

interpreted with greater accuracy when these components were studied with care. In the comments that follow it will be urged that this same cultic background also serves as a critical factor for the comprehension of the intention of 2 Thessalonians. Since this has not been the usual interpretation of the setting of 2 Thessalonians it will be necessary at the outset to comment briefly on the setting of 2 Thessalonians in terms of its rhetorical intention, its authorship and its concrete background.

There is an emerging consensus that 2 Thessalonians belongs to the deliberative genre of rhetoric. This genre includes honor and advantage as the standard topics and in 2 Thessalonians these topics are used to advise the audience concerning their actions in the present and their outcome in the future. Recognizing that 2 Thessalonians is an example of deliberative rhetoric permits the interpreter to be sensitive to the argumentation of the letter. An examination of the various components of the rhetorical structure allows one to be perceptive to the neuralgic issues at stake in the dialogue this author is having with his audience. Thus, the *partitio* (2.1–2; statement of the proposition) immediately indicates that a major point of contention between the writer and his adversaries is related to the claim 'that the day of the Lord has already come' (2.2) and the *probatio* (2.3–15; proof) makes evident that the source of this false teaching is related to the Spirit (2.15). Another example of the importance of examining carefully the various rhetorical units can be seen in the exhortation in 2 Thess. 3.1–15. Hughes has demonstrated that even though 'exhortation is not a standard *pars orationis*, we are justified in identifying certain sections of certain letters in the Pauline corpus as exhortation sections, because of a variety of parallels to both "literary" and "nonliterary" letters, and because of the strong connection of deliberative rhetoric to exhortation'.[4] This last point is supported by the long section on exhortation (3.1–15), especially given the brevity of 2 Thessalonians, and the rather detailed mandate to work presented in four different ways (3.6–15). Even these

---

[4] F. W. Hughes, *Early Christian Rhetoric and 2 Thessalonians* (JSNTSup 30; Sheffield: JSOT Press, 1989), p. 64.

cursory glimpses at the rhetorical structure of 2 Thessalonians have provided us with some important indications concerning the goal that the author of this document is pursuing.

Contemporary scholarship is not of one mind concerning the authorship of 2 Thessalonians and the range of opinion is broad: some hold that the apostle is indeed the author; other scholars suggest that this is a pseudepigraphical letter written in the late first century to a situation quite different than the one addressed in 1 Thessalonians, even, many would insist, to a church other than Thessalonica itself. Factors most frequently mentioned in connection with the authenticity of 2 Thessalonians include: 1) the apparent literary dependence of 2 Thessalonians on 1 Thessalonians; 2) the tensions, if not contradictions, that are said to exist between 2 Thess. 2.3–12 and 1 Thess. 4.13–5.11; 3) the paucity of personal references and the formal, solemn tone of 2 Thessalonians; and 4) the references to forgery in 2 Thess. 2.2 and 3.17.[5]

For our present purposes it must suffice to examine briefly the first two items on this list, the first certainly being the most prominent topic in the scholarly debate.

Perhaps the single most important aspect of the discussion concerning the authenticity of 2 Thessalonians is the claim that *it reveals an unusual dependence on and imitation of 1 Thessalonians*, not only in terms of ideas but also terminology and phrases. The best-known advocate of this position is William Wrede who in his 1903 study compared 1 and 2 Thessalonians in parallel columns.[6] He determined that much of the first letter is repeated in the second, a fact not evidenced similarly in the remainder of the Pauline corpus. Even more striking is that many of these parallels occur in the same order. Such dependence, for example, can be seen in the relationship between 2 Thess. 1.4 and 1 Thess.

---

[5] See further G. Hollmann, 'Die Unechtheit des zweiten Thessalonicherbriefs', *ZNW* 5 (1904), 28–38 and J. Bailey, 'Who Wrote II Thessalonians?' *NTS* 25 (1979) pp. 131–45. See the discussion in R. Jewett, *The Thessalonian Correspondence: Pauline Rhetoric and Millenarian Piety* (Philadelphia: Fortress Press, 1986), pp. 3–18.

[6] W. Wrede, *Die Echtheit des zweiten Thessalonicherbriefs untersucht* (TU 9/2; Leipzig: Hinrichs, 1903).

1.6–8; 2 Thess. 2.13, 14 and 1 Thess. 2.12, 13; 2 Thess. 2.16 and 1 Thess. 3.11; 2 Thess. 3.1 and 1 Thess. 4.1; 2 Thess. 3.6, 7 and 1 Thess. 4.1–2; 2 Thess. 3.10–12 and 1 Thess. 4.10–12; 2 Thess. 3.16 and 1 Thess. 5.23. Unless one assumes coincidence or that Paul slavishly imitated his earlier letter, the only logical conclusion for Wrede is that of forgery. Wolfgang Trilling's two subsequent monographs, one a full-scale commentary on 2 Thessalonians, have served both to augment and to keep the insights and arguments of Wrede in the forefront of the recent discussion.[7] Based on a stylistic, form-critical and theological analysis of this second letter, Trilling concludes that although the vocabulary is in general Pauline, all other factors, particularly the style and rhetoric of this letter, suggest non-Pauline authorship.

To date there has been no comprehensively compelling refutation of Wrede's analysis. His investigation, reinforced and augmented by Trilling's studies, introduces a most persuasive series of arguments against the direct Pauline authorship of 2 Thessalonians. Yet in finding Wrede's literary study demonstrating the dependence of 2 Thessalonians on 1 Thessalonians forceful, we do not believe that this research either furnishes[8] or, by itself, provides the basis for any specific forgery hypothesis or discernible historical/social setting in which 2 Thessalonians was composed. Further, little compelling evidence has been provided in the literature to help understand how a letter purportedly addressed to Thessalonica by Paul would be pertinent and compelling to a non-Thessalonian church some thirty years after the apostle has died.

Despite this artificial similarity between the two letters, 2 Thessalonians exhibits a remarkably different eschatological emphasis and agenda. Thus it is argued that the eschatological assertions made in 2 Thess. 2.1–12 are incompatible with those

---

[7] W. Trilling, *Untersuchungen zum zweiten Thessalonicherbrief* (EThSt 27; Leipzig: St. Benno, 1972) and *Der zweite Brief an die Thessalonicher* (EKK XIV; Zürich, Einsiedeln and Köln, Neukirchen: Benziger and Neukirchener Verlag:, 1980). For a summary of Trilling's major observations, see C. A. Wanamaker, *Commentary on 1 & 2 Thessalonians* (NIGTC; Grand Rapids: Eerdmans, 1990), pp. 21–8.

[8] We thus reject Wrede's own attempt (*Die Echtheit*, esp. pp. 95–6) to place 2 Thessalonians as a forgery in the period 100–110 CE.

found in 1 Thess. 4.13–5:11. It is observed that the eschatology of the second letter is more thoroughly apocalyptic than the first and dependent on apocalyptic devices about time-calculations that are not only uncharacteristic of the first but, in fact, rejected there. Further, a dependence on the apocalyptic thought of Revelation is urged; so, for example, the idea of punishment and reward as coming from God (2 Thess. 1.5, 6) is found in Rev 6.10; 7.14; 11.18; 13.6; the phrase 'mighty angels' (1.7) is paralleled in Rev 19.14 as are the phrases 'flaming fire' (1.8) in Rev 19.12 and 'eternal destruction' (1.9) in Rev. 20.10.

Although we find the most cogent argument for non-Pauline authorship to be that of literary dependence, we are not persuaded that these critics have correctly or compellingly described the circumstances that prompted the writing of this letter, particularly those scholars who place it in the late first or early second century in a location other than Thessalonica. Compelling evidence simply has not been provided for these conjectures.

We are neither convinced that Paul wrote 2 Thessalonians nor that this letter is non-Pauline and written late in the first century and unrelated to a concrete situation in Thessalonica. While agreeing that 2 Thessalonians is non-Pauline in the technical sense we do suggest that it is related to a specific situation in Thessalonica. In all likelihood the circumstances that provided the primary motivation for the writing of 1 Thessalonians continued and escalated. 2 Thessalonians alludes to this intensification not only by use of the term τοῖς διωγμοῖς (persecutions; 1.4) and the harsh response to the afflictors (1.5–12), but also by the bellicose description of the lawless one in 2 Thess. 2.3–12. The question of authorship is more difficult. Timothy and Silvanus are listed as joint authors with Paul in both 1 and 2 Thessalonians; it is possible that one of these two Pauline co-workers wrote 2 Thessalonians, perhaps being present in the city as the problems which this letter addresses were emerging. In favour of Silvanus, on the one hand, is his identification as a 'prophet' in Acts 15.32; yet, on the other hand, following his time with Paul in Corinth (Acts 18.5) there is no further mention of

Silas. There are, however, several factors that speak in favor of Timothy's authorship: his key role as Paul's representative to the Thessalonian Christians (1 Thess. 2.1–10); two additional journeys to Macedonia (1 Cor. 4.17 [cf. 1 Cor. 16.10–11]; Acts 19.22 [cf. 20.4]);[9] and, the fact that he is associated with Paul and Timothy in the writing of 2 Corinthians, Philippians, 1 Thessalonians and Philemon.

Regardless which option one selects with regard to authorship, 2 Thess. 3.17 ('I, Paul, write this greeting with my own hand. This is the mark in every letter of mine; it is the way I write') presents difficulties for both positions. Those who select Pauline authorship have to resolve the problem that, if 1 and 2 Thessalonians are Paul's first letters, there is no evidence of a Pauline letter prior to 2 Thessalonians that contains a greeting in the hand of the apostle. Those who understand 2 Thessalonians as a pseudepigraphical letter must assume that the writer purposely inserted 2 Thess. 3.17 to mislead the readers into thinking that Paul was the actual author of the letter.

Before attempting to answer the question just raised, it is important to realize that 3.17 bears a close relationship to both 2 Thess. 2.2 ('not to be quickly shaken in mind or alarmed, either by spirit or by word or by letter, as though from us, to the effect that the day of the Lord is already here') and 2.15 ('So then, brothers and sisters, stand firm and hold fast to the traditions that you were taught by us, either by word of mouth or by our letter').[10] Several comments are in order.

First, there is an allusion to a problem related to an unspecified letter. Theses abound in attempting to explain this reference. In our view the letter that is being referred to in both cases is 1 Thessalonians. In 2.2 it appears that some persons misrepresented its meaning. In 2.15 the reference is again to 1

[9] In citing the references to 1 Corinthians, we assume that Timothy traveled from Ephesus to Corinth via Macedonia. This visit would have been earlier than the one mentioned in Acts 19.22 which is probably to be correlated with Phil. 2.22–24. Timothy could have authored 2 Thessalonians at either time, although we would opt for the earlier reference in 1 Cor. 4.17.

[10] Hughes, *Early Christian Rhetoric*, pp. 75–9.

Thessalonians, specifying in this case that it contains authentic traditions taught by Paul, Silvanus and Timothy which the Thessalonian Christians would do well to uphold and maintain.

Second, both in 2 Thess. 2.2 and 2.15 it is made clear that this unspecified letter, which in our view is 1 Thessalonians, was written by 'us', viz. Paul, Silvanus and Timothy. We have here, as we just observed, a case of joint authorship,[11] a situation that coheres nicely with the evidence in 1 Thess. 1.1 and elsewhere in that letter. Paul, Silvanus and Timothy are intimately involved not only in the joint authorship of 1 Thessalonians but also in a shared ministry that Paul describes as apostolic in 1 Thess. 2.7 where he refers to all three as 'apostles'. If one of them, probably Timothy, is writing in 2 Thessalonians on behalf of the apostolic group it would only be natural that Pauline tradition and authority receive an emphasis here that was not the case in the first letter.

Now if one of Paul's co-workers, probably Timothy, is the author of 2 Thessalonians, how would that affect our understanding of the Pauline autograph in 3.17? If one were to consider seriously a concept like that of the 'corporate personality' in ancient Israel or what Conzelmann and others have described as the 'Pauline school',[12] it may well be that this 'I' might be viewed more broadly. If, indeed, 2 Thessalonians is attempting to partially augment and correct a misunderstanding of 1 Thessalonians, and if Paul and Timothy were co-authors of that letter, could not Timothy refer to Paul in the way he does? Although Paul and his other two co-workers share in this same 'geistigen Eigentum' (intellectual property), it is Paul, who because of his high profile in Thessalonica, becomes the target

---

[11] This is not to deny that Paul is the primary author of 1 Thessalonians, even though the 'we' style is found throughout. The two exceptions to this 'we' style in 1 Thessalonians, viz. 2.18 and 3.5, serve to underscore both his deep concern for the Thessalonian Christians and to eradicate the notion that his absence is either the result of a low regard for them or the result of a neglect of the difficult situation that this church finds itself in. See further, K. P. Donfried, 'War Timotheus in Athen? Exegetische Überlegungen zu 1 Thess. 3,1–3', in *Die Freude an Gott – unsere Kraft* (Festschrift für Otto Bernhard Knoch; ed. J. J. Degenhardt; Stuttgart: Katholisches Bibelwerk, 1991), pp. 189–96; also found in this volume in English translation, 'Was Timothy in Athens', pp. 209–19.

[12] Hans Conzelmann, 'Paulus und die Weisheit', *NTS* 12 (1965–66), pp. 231–4.

of misunderstanding. If Paul is being attacked as a result of the gospel that he and Timothy jointly share, and further, since Timothy knows well what was intended in the original letter (1 Thessalonians), is it not possible that the final rhetorical clincher of 2 Thessalonians is to draw explicitly upon the Pauline apostolic authority, in which Timothy shares, as the final rebuttal to the misunderstandings rampant in Thessalonica? Certainly a letter from Timothy alone would not carry the same weight or be as effective in refuting distortions directed primarily at Paul.

Given our understanding that 2 Thessalonians is addressed to the same Christian community as 1 Thessalonians, and written not long after that first letter, the descriptions of the historical settings of Thessalonian Christianity described elsewhere need not be repeated and the reader is referred to them.[13] Thus our present task will be to understand the distinctive factors in Thessalonica that necessitated the composition of 2 Thessalonians. The letter reveals a continuance and intensification of the persecution attested to in 1 Thessalonians. Evidently the Thessalonian Christians' proclamation of the kingdom of God (2 Thess. 1.5) generates hostility among non-Christians (2 Thess. 1.8; 2.12). 2 Thess. 1.4 refers not only to ταῖς θλίψεσιν (afflictions), as in 1 Thessalonians, but also to τοῖς διωγμοῖς (persecutions). Whereas θλῖψις (affliction) needs to be specified according to its context, διωγμός always refers to persecution. But there is also a noteworthy reference to this later theme in 2 Thess. 2.15: 'So then, brethren, stand firm [στήκετε] and hold fast to the traditions that you were taught by us, either by word of mouth or by our letter.' This motif, 'stand firm', is part of a well-formed tradition of teaching in the context of persecution.[14]

Given this environment of protracted and escalated persecution, there are some in the congregation who are proclaiming that 'the day of the Lord is already here'. What was meant by this

---

[13] See Chapter 2 above.
[14] E. G. Selwyn, *The First Epistle of St Peter* (London: Macmillan, 1961), pp. 454–8.

slogan is not altogether clear.[15] It might refer either to a spiritu-alized, almost gnostic-like, understanding, viz., that there will not be any future, physical coming of the Lord, much like the problem described in 1 Cor. 15.12–28;[16] or it might suggest that the day of the Lord was at hand, that it would occur before long. Critical for the interpreter of 2 Thessalonians is to understand how this originally Jewish concept, the day of the Lord, would be interpreted in a congregation composed predominantly of Gentiles in a milieu permeated by Greco-Roman cults. For the author of this letter, contrary to some in the Thessalonian congregation, this event, this day of the Lord, will be real, dramatic, observable and future.

In all likelihood we are dealing with a misinterpretation of Paul's alleged 'realized eschatology' in 1 Thessalonians. The author of the second letter is not only concerned about this misreading but also with its consequences. For if the day of the Lord is already present, and not understood as a future event yet to be consummated, then, of course, the foundation of the Thessalonians' faith becomes very fragile. Our author responds to this dilemma by presenting an apocalyptic timetable that distances the present situation from the yet future day of the Lord. This shift in eschatological emphasis from the first letter does not mean, however, a contradiction between the two. Different situations call for distinct nuances and emphases.

There are two factors, both of which will be described more fully as we proceed, that suggest the day of the Lord is being misunderstood in a pseudo-spiritual, gnostic way: 1) the problem of the spirit in 2 Thess. 2.2 and 2.15; and 2) the identification of τὸ κατέχον/ὁ κατέχων in 2 Thess. 2.6 and 7 as a seizing or possessing power, some 'pseudocharismatic spirit or agent' that is

---

[15] The Greek verb translated as 'already here' is ἐνέστηκεν. Further references to its meaning can be found in Trilling, *Untersuchungen*, pp. 124–5; Trilling, *Der zweite Brief*, p. 78; H. Schenke and K. M. Fischer, *Einleitung in die Schriften des Neuen Testaments* (Berlin: Evangelische Verlagsanstalt, 1978), p. 192; Jewett, *Thessalonian Correspondence*, pp. 97–8).

[16] See further, K. P. Donfried, *The Dynamic Word* (San Francisco: Harper and Row, 1981), pp. 22–8.

'a false imitation of spiritual illumination and inspiration' and that has seized power.[17]

Not only must our author correct a false understanding of the day of the Lord, but he must also urge his readers to stand firm in their afflictions and not to be unsettled or troubled when some proclaim that the day of the Lord has already arrived. In order to accomplish this goal, 2 Thess. 1.5–13, which contains a major expansion of 1 Thessalonians, makes clear that the Lord's vengeance will come against those who are involved in this persecution against the Thessalonian Christians and that they will suffer 'the punishment of eternal destruction' when the Lord appears (2 Thess. 1.9). 2 Thess. 2.3–12, using strikingly apocalyptic categories and language and marking a major insertion into the framework of 1 Thessalonians, intends to combat the assertion made by some that 'the day of the Lord is already here' (v. 2). It is argued, on the contrary, that the day of the Lord is not yet here, or even close at hand, because certain future events about to be described must first take place. Glenn Holland has shown that we are dealing in this passage with a threefold apocalyptic schema in which a present phenomenon is portrayed and then personified at a future moment of crisis. What 'has been and continues to be active in the present, will in the future be unveiled as a personal force, part of the battle between the personalized forces of good and evil (cf. Dan. 10.18–11.1; Rev. 12.7–9).'[18]

This triple repetition of the impending crisis as already partially operative in the present is presented as follows in 2 Thessalonians 2:

Present	Future
ἡ ἀποστασία [the rebellion]	ὁ ἄνθρωπος τῆς ἀνομίας [the lawless one] (2.3–4)
τὸ κατέχον [the seizing power]	ὁ κατέχων [the seizer] (2.6–7)
τὸ μυστήριον τῆς ἀνομίας [the mystery of lawlessness]	ὁ ἄνομος [the lawless one] (2.7–8)

[17] C. H. Giblin, 'The Heartening Apocalyptic of Second Thessalonians', *TBT* 26 (1988), p. 353.

[18] G. S. Holland, *The Tradition that You Received from Us: 2 Thessalonians in the Pauline Tradition* (HUTh 24; Tübingen: J. C. B. Mohr, 1988), p. 112.

In each case it is apparent that what occurs in the future is a personification of those evil forces already operative in the present. Therefore the use of neuter and masculine participles of the verb κατέχω – is determined not by that to which these two participles refer but to the apocalyptic pattern itself.[19] In contemporary scholarship the most widespread translation for τὸ κατέχον/ὁ κατέχων is 'what is restraining/the one who restrains'. Giblin has urged an alternative translation: 'the seizing power/the seizer'.[20] This translation is defended on the following grounds:

1. κατέχειν is an intensive form of ἔχειν. Its usual meaning when followed by positive clauses and/or 'in contexts where death, curses, or demonic power are mentioned' is 'to hold on to, to seize, to grasp, to possess and to spellbind'.[21] Thus for Paul, Giblin points out, κατέχειν normally means 'to possess'. That is not to say that κατέχειν cannot mean 'to restrain' in the sense of 'to detain/hold on to', but when it does it is usually followed by a negative clause as in Luke 4.42.

2. Many exegetes understand κατέχον/ων as a benign restraining force such as the Spirit or the preaching of the gospel which keeps the lawless one at a distance. However, in the New Testament the gospel is described as unimpeded and 'not as itself impeding anything, much less, even indirectly, the Lord's coming'.[22] The relevant texts in the New Testament warn about the day of the Lord but never describe any force, benign or otherwise, as involved in devising a delay in its appearance.

In his 1967 study of 2 Thessalonians, Giblin drew some interesting links between the use of τὸ κατέχον/ὁ κατέχων in 2 Thessalonians and the cults of Serapis and Dionysus in Thessalonica and concludes that a 'generic allusion to pagan

---

[19] Holland, *Tradition*, p. 112.
[20] C. H. Giblin, *The Threat to Faith: An Exegetical and Theological Re-Examination of 2 Thessalonians 2* (AnBib 31; Rome: Pontifical Biblical Institute, 1967), p. 201. See now also Giblin's article, '2 Thessalonians 2 Re-Read as Pseudepigraphical: A Revised Reaffirmation of *The Threat to Faith*', in *The Thessalonian Correspondence*, ed. R. F. Collins (BETL 87; Leuven: University Press, 1990), pp. 459–69.
[21] Giblin, 'Pseudepigraphical', p. 465.
[22] Giblin, 'Pseudepigraphical', p. 466.

religious practice, especially to pseudo-prophetic seizure, would seem to account for Paul's choice of this particular term'.[23] This is a thesis that has been generally overlooked or rejected in the literature.[24] Yet Giblin's suggestion needs to be taken more seriously not only in light of our description of Thessalonica earlier in this volume but also in view of Ernst Koeberlin's work in which he shows that 'the mysteries instituted by Caligula and linked with Emperor worship partook of Isiacism, the colossal statue intended for the Temple of Jerusalem being a blend of Neos Gaius and Zeus Epiphanes'.[25] Based on Koeberlin's study Rex Witt is tempted to suggest that in the ἄνομος passage Paul is 'hitting out possibly at a Thessalonian cult in which Emperor worship was combined with the cult of Isis and Serapis'.[26]

This perspective is strengthened by a closer examination of the negative (2 Thess. 2.6a, 7b, 11a) and positive (2 Thess. 2.8, 13) references to the Spirit. Not unimportant is that 2 Thess. 2.13 concludes any further reference to the Spirit, either as a pseudo-spiritual activity or as Spirit-led sanctification. Further, in 1 Thess. 5.21, a letter our author(s) had clearly in mind, κατέχω is used precisely with regard to spiritual discernment and prophecy. Already in 1 Thess. 5, especially in verses 5–7 and 19–22, the apostle does not wish the gift of the Spirit to be confused with the excesses of the Dionysiac mysteries; for Paul the Spirit does not lead to 'Bacchic frenzies'. In short, then, this lawless one, this seizer, whose rebellion and seizing power is exercised in the present, will continue to mislead and confuse all people until the God of justice, through the manifestation of the Lord Jesus, will ultimately dethrone him. Therefore the eschatological

---

[23] Giblin, *Threat*, p. 201.

[24] It is heartening to note in Holland, *Tradition*, p. 114, that the work of τὸ μυστήριον finds its conclusion in the appearance of ὁ ἄνομος and is parallel to and contemporary with ἡ ἀποστασία and that he 'would suggest that the author is using the metaphor of a pagan mystery cult for the apocalyptic antagonism to Christ, a cult that is already "in operation" in the present'.

[25] E. Koeberlein, *Caligula und die ägyptischen Kulte* (BKP 3; Meisenheim am Glan: Verlag Anton Hain, 1962), pp. 21, 61 as cited in R. Witt, 'The Egyptian Cults in Ancient Macedonia', in *Ancient Macedonia II* (Thessaloniki: Institute for Balkan Studies, 1977), 1.331.

[26] Witt, 'The Egyptian Cults', 1.331.

day of the Lord has not yet arrived; much wickedness and lawlessness must yet be played out on the world's corrupt stage before God's ultimate show of victory.

Rhetorical criticism has made clear that the intentions of 1 and 2 Thessalonians are quite different. The rhetorical genre of the first letter is epideictic and has as its purpose to encourage and console, i.e. it is primarily a paracletic letter. The genre of the second letter is deliberative and has as its purpose exhortation, i.e. it is primarily a paraenetic letter.[27] These observations are confirmed by the use (or non-use) of three key verbs in the letters: παρακαλέω, παραγγέλλω and παραμυθέω.

Although the verb παρακαλέω has a wide range of meanings, in the two Thessalonian letters the translations 'to comfort, to encourage, to urge' are appropriate. The word is used eight times in the first letter (2.12; 3.2, 7; 4.1, 10, 18; 5.11, 14), but only twice in 2 Thessalonians (2.17; 3.12). The opposite pattern can be observed when we examine the usage of the verb παραγγέλλω which, in general, has the meaning 'to give orders, command or instruct'.[28] This word is used four times in the second letter (3.4, 6, 10, 12) but only once in the first (4.11) and this single reference in 1 Thess 4:11 has a quite different context from that of 2 Thessalonians. In the former, παραγγέλλω is twice preceded with the verb παρακαλέω (4.1, 10) which strengthens the view that this paraenesis 'was intended to reinforce them in their current forms of behavior rather than direct them to a different pattern of behavior';[29] in the latter, the primary section of ethical exhortation uses only the verb παραγγέλλω, which lends support to the perspective that 2 Thessalonians is attempting to change the future behavior of the Christians in Thessalonica. To further substantiate our thesis that paraenesis is found in the context of paraclesis in 1 Thessalonians and paraclesis in the context of

---

[27] This is not in any way to suggest a rigid demarcation between a 'paracletic' and a 'paraenetic' letter. Each may contain and combine both elements, although their overall emphasis and focus is different.

[28] W. Bauer, *A Greek-English Lexicon of the New Testament and Other Early Christian Literature*, ed. W. F. Arndt, F. W. Gingrich and F. W. Danker (Chicago: The University of Chicago, 1979), p. 613.

[29] Wanamaker, *1 and 2 Thessalonians*, p. 48.

paraenesis in 2 Thessalonians is the fact that the verb παραμυθέω, meaning 'to encourage, to cheer up, to console someone concerning someone' is found twice in 1 Thessalonians (2.12; 5.14) and not at all in the second letter.

2 Thessalonians, belonging to the genre of deliberative rhetoric, is urging the Thessalonian Christians both to believe and to conduct themselves in a different manner. The former intention is primarily located in the first proof, 2.1(3)–12, and the latter in the command to work, 3.6–15.

It is now to 2 Thess. 3.6–15 that we turn. In verse six both the source of Paul's authority is stated, 'in the name of our Lord Jesus Christ', as well as the command to work, expressed negatively, 'to keep away from every brother who is living in idleness (ἀτάκτως; used also in 3.11) and not according to the tradition [παράδοσις] that they received from us'. Central to our understanding of what is at stake in the argument is the meaning of ἀτάκτως (also ἀτακτέω in 3: 7) and παράδοσις.

With regard to ἀτακτέω, Louw and Nida write: 'Traditional translations have often interpreted ἀτακτέω in an etymological sense of "not being ordered" and hence with a meaning of "to behave in a disorderly manner," but this is quite contrary to the context.'[30] The adjective ἀτάκτως 'means primarily "out of order," "out of place," and ... is readily employed as a military term to denote a soldier who does not keep the ranks, or an army advancing in disarray'.[31] The verb ἀτακτέω has much the same meaning and 'is extended to every one who does not perform his proper duty'.[32] Is this original meaning really so contrary to the context as Louw and Nida would have us believe?

Since the interpretation of 2 Thess. 3.6–15 is heavily dependent on the translation of the Greek, it will be useful at this point to offer our own translation of verses 6–12:

---

[30] J. P. Louw and E. A. Nida, *Greek-English Lexicon of the New Testament based on Semantic Domains* (New York: United Bible Societies, 1988), I.768–9 [88.246–7].

[31] G. Milligan, *St Paul's Epistles to the Thessalonians* (New York: Macmillan, n.d.), p. 152.

[32] Milligan, *Thessalonians*, p. 153. [With regard to the use of this word group in 1 Thessalonians, see now K. P. Donfried, 'Paul and Qumran: The Possible Influence of סרך on 1 Thessalonians', in *The Dead Sea Scrolls Fifty Years After Their Discovery* (Jerusalem: The Magnes Press, 2000), pp. 1–9]; also pp. 221–31 in this volume.

Now we command you, brothers, in the name of our Lord Jesus Christ, to keep away from brothers who are not living a well-ordered life and are not in accord with the tradition that you received from us. For you yourselves know how you ought to imitate us; we did not depend on others for our support when we were with you and we did not eat anyone's bread without paying for it; but with toil and labor we worked night and day, so that we might not burden any of you. This was not because we do not have that right, but we waived our right in order to give you an example to imitate. For even when we were with you, we gave you this command: Anyone unwilling to work should not eat. For we hear that some of your number are leading ill-ordered lives, and, instead of attending to their own business, are busy with what does not concern them. Now such persons we command and exhort to attend quietly to their own work and to earn their own living.

This translation varies from several common translations in translating ἀτακτέω/ἀτάκτως as 'ill-ordered' or 'not well-ordered' rather than 'in idleness' and in translating περιεργάζομαι as 'not attending to their own business' rather than as 'busybody'.[33] This rendering of 2 Thess. 3.6–12 gives support to the thesis of Bengt Holmberg that the author of this letter is critical of a 'charismatic authority' being exercised by some in the congregation who are claiming that because of this self-claimed authority they are to be supported by others in the congregation.[34] This view of the situation also allows us to see the connection between the problem of the 'spirit' and the 'seizing power' that is already at work in the present. In this connection it is noteworthy that of only two references to οἴδατε[35] (you know) in this second letter, one of them appears in the first proof at 2.6a: 'And now you know by experience the seizing power'. Perhaps the use of the phrase 'you know' implies that this problem may have already been present in an embryonic fashion as Paul wrote the first letter (1 Thess. 1.9; 4.12–13, 14, 19–22).

This circumstance of an economic elitism by a few, based on the claim to charismatic authority, is refuted by 2 Thessalonians

---

[33] We have been greatly assisted in these renderings by the translation of Milligan, *Thessalonians*, p. 112.

[34] B. Holmberg, *Paul and Power* (Philadelphia: Fortress Press, 1980), p. 159. Not unimportant is the use of the word εὐτάκτος (good order) in 1 Clem. 42.2, a section dealing with church leadership.

[35] 2 Thess. 2.6; 3.7.

on the basis of tradition (παράδοσις), a term that is used in 2 Thess. 2.15 in the plural ('So then, brethren, stand firm and hold fast to the traditions that you were taught by us, either by word of mouth or by our letter'), and in 3.6 in the singular ('Now we command you, brothers, in the name of our Lord Jesus Christ, to keep away from brothers who are not living a well-ordered life and not in accord with the tradition that you received from us'). With Trilling we agree that the plural refers to a body of tradition and the singular to a specific item of that larger tradition.[36] The first reference is to the third argument of the second proof, viz. that by holding to the traditions already taught by Paul through word and letter they will make evident their orthodoxy. The second reference is found in the fifth section of 2 Thessalonians pertaining to exhortation. Again in this context the appeal is made to Pauline tradition: living an ill-ordered life does not accord with this tradition.

Although the term παράδοσις (tradition) does not appear in 1 Thessalonians, Caroline Vander Stichele[37] has examined the use of the verb παραλαμβάνω (to receive or accept) in 1 and 2 Thessalonians, discovering a significant connection between the two. The verb is used in 1 Thess. 2.13; 4.1 and in 2 Thess. 2.15 and 3.6. Further, Vander Stichele finds a 'striking similarity in place and formulation' between the use of the verb παραλαμβάνω in 1 Thess. 2.13 and 2 Thess. 2.15 and between 1 Thess. 4.1 and 2 Thess. 3.6.[38] With regard to the first linkage she points out that in addition to the formal agreements between the two, in both cases the author refers to himself as 'the source of tradition'.[39] Even though 2 Thess. 2.15 is a more explicit statement than 1 Thess. 2.13 and the fact that the latter one emphasizes more the reality that the Thessalonians accepted the word of God, nevertheless, both focus on a general rather than a particular tradition. In comparing 1 Thess. 4.1 and 2 Thess. 3.6 it is indicated that in

[36] Trilling, *Untersuchungen*, p. 116.
[37] C. Vander Stichele, 'The Concept of Tradition and 1 and 2 Thessalonians', in *The Thessalonian Correspondence*, pp. 499–504.
[38] Vander Stichele, 'Concept of Tradition', p. 501.
[39] Vander Stichele, 'Concept of Tradition', p. 502.

both cases we find παραλαμβάνω together with παρ᾽ ἡμῶν (from us) as well as the connection with the verb περιπατέω (to live, conduct oneself). Also, in these latter two verses a specific ethical issue receives attention.

The use of the term παράδοσις in 2 Thessalonians may have implications with regard to the issue of authorship. The absence of this term from 1 Thessalonians, it is argued, supports the non-Pauline authorship of 2 Thessalonians. Yet it could be argued that in view of the fact that παράδοσις is used elsewhere in the Pauline letters (1 Cor. 11.2 and Gal. 1.14), 2 Thessalonians is Pauline. More likely, however, is the conclusion that Vander Stichele reaches at the conclusion of her study: 'The structural agreement and the terminological affinity between 1 and 2 Thess. can hardly be accidental. It looks as if 2 Thess. used 1 Thess. as a model.'[40] The use of the term παράδοσις alone does not contribute significantly to solving the issue of authorship; rather, the critical issue is why the first letter serves as a model for the second.[41]

Not unrelated to this theme of παράδοσις in 2 Thessalonians is its relationship to sanctification. In 1 Thessalonians there is a strong emphasis on sanctification which is closely linked to the theme of the parousia. In 2 Thessalonians the terms ἁγιάζω (1 Thess. 5.23) and ἁγιωσύνη (1 Thess. 3.13) do not appear at all and the term ἁγιασμός (1 Thess. 4.3, 4, 7) is used only once in 2 Thess. 2.13. Obviously our author values the concept of sanctification, but because of the different pressures to which he is reacting, 'to be worthy' (1.5, 11) of God's kingdom and call is now presumed to be an adhering to the traditions that Paul and his associates have passed on to them. These include, on the one hand, adherence to Paul's teaching about the day of the Lord and the rejection of the idea inspired by some of the cults of Thessalonica that it is already here and, on the other hand, fidelity to Paul's instruction about leading an orderly life in a culture that prizes behavior quite the contrary.

It has become apparent, then, that the Thessalonian church is faced with a variety of dilemmas in the midst of an overall

---

[40] Vander Stichele, 'Concept of Tradition', p. 504.
[41] See our discussion on pp. 51–2 above.

situation of increased persecution. Even though one of Paul's co-
workers rather than the apostle himself is the author of the letter,
it makes perfectly good sense to read it as addressed to the
Thessalonian church sometime after the writing of 1
Thessalonians. The presence of the κατέχον/ων references, the
refutation of the belief that 'the day of the Lord is already here',
and the tendency toward a charismatic authority by a few in this
letter do suggest the possible influence of the pagan cults in
this crisis. The intention of the author of 2 Thessalonians
becomes evident as one observes the manner in which he
addresses and refutes these unsettling circumstances current in
the Thessalonian church.

Postscript

Both Still and Malherbe agree with our counsel that it is 'difficult
to imagine a setting where a letter specifically addressed to the
Thessalonians by Paul would be relevant and convincing to a
non-Thessalonian church some thirty or more years after the
Apostle's death'.[42] Quite correctly Malherbe insists that 'insuffi-
cient attention has been given to the difficulty of bringing such a
[pseudonymous] letter into circulation'.[43] The value of Still's
discussion is that he takes very seriously the continuity of the
Thessalonian context in discussing 1 and 2 Thessalonians,
although this remains more of an assertion than a factual demonstration. Malherbe shares a similar view as ours, viz. 'Paul was
writing to correct some of his readers' misunderstanding of 1
Thessalonians' but says little about the specific context that
would have called forth the misunderstanding or 2 Thessalonians
response to it. We have urged that in viewing side-by-side the
recommendations of Giblin and Holland one might be able to

---

[42] K. P. Donfried, '2 Thessalonians and the Cults of Thessalonica', in *Origins and Method: Towards a New Understanding of Judaism and Christianity. Essays in Honour of John C. Hurd* ed. Bradley H. McLean (Sheffield: Sheffield Academic Press, 1993), p. 132 (also in this volume, pp. 49–67); T. D. Still, *Conflict at Thessalonica: A Pauline Church and its Neighbours* (JSNTSup 183; Sheffield: Sheffield Academic Press, 1999), p. 58.

[43] A. J. Malherbe, *The Letter to the Thessalonians: A New Translation with Introduction and Commentary* (AB 32B; New York: Doubleday, 2000), p. 373.

find some insight into the situation in Thessalonica that produced 2 Thessalonians. Oddly, from our perspective, Still's study takes into account the work of Holland but not Giblin and Malherbe's commentary does just the opposite. Finally, Still and Malherbe have raised serious questions about the conclusions made about the purpose of the letter by those who hold to pseudonymity, but can only maintain this position by arguing for the Pauline authorship of 2 Thessalonians, a perspective we still have difficulty in sharing given Trilling's path-breaking studies on this issue.

4

1 Thessalonians, Acts and the Early Paul

Introduction

Until the late twentieth century 1 Thessalonians has been the stepchild of modern Pauline studies. Romans, Galatians and the Corinthian letters, in that order, have been the usual documents employed in the theological analysis and description of Pauline thought. Given this state of affairs, no doubt influenced by the Reformation's emphasis on justification by faith and its correlative devaluation of works of the law, many scholars have found it difficult to relate *this* construct of Pauline theology with either the portrait of Paul found in Acts or with that found in 1 Thessalonians. Vielhauer's influential argument that Luke presented a woefully distorted picture of Pauline theology in Acts is well-known.[1] Similarly, F. C. Baur, not being able to reconcile the Reformation's understanding of Pauline theology with that found in 1 Thessalonians, declared this letter as non-Pauline.[2] Although Baur's position, in contrast to Vielhauer's, has virtually no advocates today, the benign neglect of 1 Thessalonians in the overall study of Pauline theology today is simply a more subtle

---

[1] P. Vielhauer, 'On the "Paulism" of Acts' in *Studies in Luke-Acts*, ed. L. E. Keck and J. L. Martyn (Nashville: Abingdon, 1966), pp. 33–50.

[2] F. C. Baur, *Paul, the Apostle of Jesus Christ; His Life and Work, His Epistles and His Doctrine: A Contribution to a Critical History of Primitive Christianity*, 2 vols (London/ Edinburgh: Williams and Norgate, 1876).

way of affirming the Baur thesis. Since this generally acknowledged earliest letter of Paul cannot be made to fit the consensus
pattern of Pauline theology, it should not, so it is implicitly
argued, be taken too seriously. So, for example, there is not a
single reference to 1 Thessalonians in Vielhauer's essay. Although
the 1980s saw a revival in Thessalonian studies, they have often
been marked by an interest in the sociological/cultural setting of
the letter or in isolated passages or theological themes within it;
seldom does the letter itself, in its own right, receive attention as
a serious witness to the ethical and theological perspective of
Paul.[3] The reason for this state of affairs? – 1 Thessalonians is
apparently contradicted by the Pauline message found in
Galatians and Romans.

In light of much of the literature dealing with such issues as
Pauline chronology, the purpose of Acts and the re-evaluation of
Pauline theology, both in terms of its comprehensive whole and
in terms of its component parts, that is, its 'coherence'
and 'contingence',[4] I would suggest that we need to view Pauline
thought both more broadly and less restrictively as well as understanding that his theology developed over a far greater time span
than the traditional chronologies allow. The moment has indeed
arrived in Pauline studies to make a consistent distinction
between the early Paul and the late Paul; not to do so will
continue the marginalization of 1 Thessalonians, the distortion of
Pauline theology as a whole, as well as the relationship of Acts to
Paul.

The purpose of this paper is to suggest that 1 Thessalonians is
the key extant document for understanding the theology and
ethics of the early Paul and that it is this letter, rather than
Romans or Galatians, which more closely coheres with some of
the Lucan presentation of Paul in Acts. Further, it will be
suggested that the proper point of departure for the interpretation of 1 Thessalonians is not the thought patterns of the late

---

[3] A notable exception is R. F. Collins, *Studies on the First Letter to the Thessalonians* (BETL
66; Leuven: University Press–Peeters, 1984).
[4] J. C. Beker, *Paul the Apostle* (Philadelphia: Fortress Press, 1980).

Paul but rather those of the hellenistic church,[5] and particularly that of the Antiochene church, from which Paul received much of his theology and his training in missionary technique. Although perhaps overstated, there is much that is helpful in Siegfried Schulz's observation that in 1 Thessalonians 'die theologische Abhängigkeit von seiner hellenistischen Mutterkirche noch in gar keiner Weise gelockert war; vielmehr waren Theologie und Ethik des frühen Paulus sachidentisch mit der Verkündigung der hellenistischen Kirche'.[6] 1 Thessalonians reveals not only Paul's dependence on the theology of this hellenistic church which preceded him and of which he was a part, but also how a contingent, unforeseen situation in Thessalonica compelled Paul to move beyond that inherited theological context. As a result of this perspective it will be necessary to ask anew whether Acts is simply a gross distortion of Pauline theology as Vielhauer insists or whether, in fact, the Acts account is a *relatively* accurate reflection of the early Paul known to Luke and modified for this theological intent,[7] of the Paul often consistent with the theology and practice of the hellenistic church, and of the Paul *prior to* his major conflicts with Jewish Christianity as portrayed, for example, in Galatians.

Chronology

Since it has been precisely my rethinking of Pauline chronology[8] which has been a major factor in my willingness to posit an early and a late Paul, a few words need to be said about this topic. First, with regard to methodology, I acknowledge with most scholars

---

[5] See especially the discussion in S. Schulz, *Neutestamentliche Ethik* (Zürich: Theologischer Verlag, 1987), pp. 137–78.

[6] S. Schulz, 'Der frühe und der späte Paulus', *ThZ* 41 (1985), p. 236 [ET: 'the theological dependence on his hellenistic mother church had in no way been reduced; on the contrary, for the early Paul theology and ethics were identical with the proclamation of the hellenistic church'].

[7] See below for a further discussion of the purpose of Acts.

[8] See my article on 'New Testament Chronology' for *The Anchor Bible Dictionary*. ['Chronology, New Testament' in *The Anchor Bible Dictionary*, 6 vols, ed. D. N. Freedman; (New York: Doubleday, 1992), 1.1011–22.] See also, 'Chronology: The Apostolic and Pauline Period' in this volume pp. 99–117.

today that there are essentially only two sources for our knowledge of the Pauline period: the letters of the apostle himself and the events recorded by Luke in the Acts of the Apostles. Most New Testament scholars today give clear priority to the Pauline letters since Paul himself stands closest to the events he records. Further, it is increasingly recognized that Luke, in writing his second volume reshapes many traditions, just as he does in the Gospel, to cohere with his overall theological purpose. As a result, Acts becomes less useful as a source for exact chronological information since much of this information has been subjected to a larger theological program. While Acts can still be a valuable source of detailed and accurate information when separated from its programatic framework, as I have argued elsewhere,[9] it should never be given priority over the documents stemming from Paul and should only be used when it does not contradict assertions made by the apostle.

Although implementing this critical methodology is, according to its adherents, a requisite of rigorous historical research, its adoption does not make the task of establishing a chronology of the Pauline period easier. If anything, it reveals how tentative and highly speculative previous attempts have been and how tenuous all reconstructions must be. For when all is said and done, Paul gives us not one specific date! Inevitably, if one is to establish a possible chronology of this period, there will have to be some dependence on Acts. Recognizing this, one should be cautious to use Acts in a way which is both critical and plausible. Yet it must be acknowledged that from whatever perspective one views the data, *there can be no absolutely definitive chronology of this period*; all attempts must be tentative and subject to correction and revision!

For the purposes of this essay, I want to lift out for our consideration just a very few items from the larger chronological issues. In Gal. 1.21 the apostle asserts: 'Then [ἔπειτα] I went into the regions of Syria and Cilicia'. First, a brief word about the use

---

[9] K. P. Donfried, 'The Cults of Thessalonica and the Thessalonian Correspondence', *NTS* 31 (1985), pp. 336–56; see also pp. 21–48 in this volume.

of ἔπειτα. Many interpreters see it consistently referring back to the commissioning event; many others see it as consistently referring back to the immediately preceding event. The latter interpretation is strengthened by the parallel use in 1 Cor. 15.6–7. In Gal. 1.21, ἔπειτα is likely to refer to the immediately preceding event in verse 18: 'Then [ἔπειτα] after three years I did go up to Jerusalem'.

The critical question with regard to this verse in Galatians is not, hence, the referent of ἔπειτα but, rather, what is meant by the reference to the activity in Syria and Cilicia. Syria includes Christian centers in Damascus, the place of Paul's commissioning, and Antioch, an area where, by Paul's own description, he had worked (Gal. 2.11) and a city extensively referred to in Acts (11.19–30; 13.1, 14; 15.22–35; 18.22). In addition, Cilicia includes Tarsus, which, according to Acts 22.3, is Paul's native city. Is the intention of this reference in Gal. 1.15–2.1 to suggest that Paul spent some eleven (or fourteen) years only in Syria and Cilicia? Or, given the overall context of Paul's desire to distance himself from Jerusalem, does he merely wish to say that, 'then, after leaving from my fifteen day stay in Jerusalem, I did not stay around that area but I began moving as far away as Syria and Cilicia' without in any way wishing to suggest that he worked only in this area? How one interprets this reference to Syria and Cilicia will be crucial for the reconstruction of a chronology of the Pauline period. For those scholars who understand the reference to Syria and Cilicia as not limiting Paul's activity to these regions, the apostle was involved in missionary work as far away as Philippi, Thessalonica, Athens and Corinth very early in his career. They would urge that the reference in Phil. 4.15 to 'the beginning [ἀρχῇ] of the gospel' (RSV) literally refers to the beginning of Paul's independent missionary work in Philippi and that 1 Thess. 2.1–2 and 3.1–5 refer to Paul's continuing work during this period in Thessalonica, Athens and Corinth. This interpretation, to date not the majority one, allows for an 'uncrowding' of Paul's missionary work, for the maturing of his apostolic ministry and the development of his theology. Rather than an extended period of some eleven to fourteen years in Syria and Cilicia, this perspective allows for the beginnings of the European mission at a much earlier point in his apostolic career and does not reduce the remainder of his activity to such a severly limited timeframe. If one accepts this reading of the evidence, then it is probable that 1 Thessalonians stems from this early period, at least several years prior to the conference visit in Jerusalem.

Let us turn to certain chronological information provided by Luke, particularly the Gallio inscription and the edict of Claudius. In Acts 18.12 reference is made to Paul's visit to Corinth: 'But when Gallio was proconsul of Achaia, the Jews made a united attack on Paul and brought him before the tribunal.' Although the precise details, implications and context of the events described are disputed, there is little doubt that Paul made one of his visits to Corinth at the time that Gallio was proconsul of the province of Achaia. In light of the epigraphical evidence now in hand most scholars place Gallio's term of office in the years 51/52 CE, although 52/53 CE is also possible. While at first glance Acts 18.12 appears straightforward, caution must be exercised: Was Paul's visit to Corinth in the vicinity of 51/52 CE his first visit, or does Acts 18.12 actually refer to a subsequent one? Acts 18 may well conflate two or more Pauline visits to that city into one. Among the several factors pointing in this direction is the fact that in Acts 18.8 Crispus is the ruler of the synagogue and in 18.17 the reference is to Sosthenes as the ruler of the synagogue. It is fully possible that if Acts 18 is conflating at least two visits of Paul to Corinth, he may well have been in the city at a much earlier date.[10]

Another piece of information relating to secular history mentioned in Acts which may be useful in reconstructing Pauline chronology is the reference to the edict of Claudius in Acts 18.1–2. 'After this Paul left Athens and went to Corinth. There he found a Jew named Aquila, a native of Pontus, who had

---

[10] See G. Lüdemann, *Paul, Apostle to the Gentiles: Studies in Chronology* (London: SCM Press, 1984), pp. 157–63, and also his *Das frühe Christentum nach den Traditionen der Apostelgeschichte* (Göttingen: Vandenhoeck and Ruprecht, 1987), pp. 202–11.

recently come from Italy with his wife Priscilla, because Claudius had ordered all Jews to leave Rome. Paul went to see them'. It is likely that Suetonius in *Claud.* 25 is referring to this edict: '*Iudaios impulsore Chresto adsidue tumultuantes Roma expulit*'. Since Suetonius does not date this edict, one cannot be certain whether it is referring to one issued by Claudius in 41 CE or whether it is referring to disturbances later in his reign. Those who would argue against the early dating cite Dio Cassius' reference (60.6.6–7) that the large number of Jews effectively ruled out their expulsion and point to Orosius' reference (*Hist.* 7.6.15–16) that the edict occurred in Claudius' ninth year (i.e. 49 CE). Yet these references in themselves do not settle the issue. In the first place, there need not be any contradiction between Dio Cassius' assertions and Luke's characteristically exaggerated use of πᾶς (all) in Acts 18.2 and elsewhere. Further, there is the critical issue about the reliability of the information provided by Orosius, a fifth-century church historian.

If the Claudius edict is dated in 41 CE, then one would have strong evidence for the dating of Paul's first visit to the city at some point after the arrival of Aquila and Priscilla from Italy. If the more usual dating of this edict in the year 49 is to be accepted, this in and of itself would not speak against an earlier visit of Paul to Corinth, for it is difficult to know how thoroughgoing the conflation in Acts 18 is. For example, a case could be made that Acts 18.1 had its original continuation in verse 5 and that verses 2–4 are a retrojection made from a later period.

To place Paul's first arrival in Corinth as early as 41 is possible; yet some flexibility is in order since one does not know how long it took Aquila and Priscilla to travel to Corinth, nor if they went there directly. On this reckoning Paul's original visit to Corinth may have taken place sometime between the approximate period of 41–4. Additionally, it is most probable that he was also in Corinth during the years that Gallio was proconsul in 51/52. Some would place a visit by Paul to Corinth, usually his first, just before the Jerusalem Conference (e.g. Jewett)[11] and some just

---

[11] R. Jewett, *A Chronology of Paul's Life* (Philadelphia: Fortress Press, 1979), p. 99.

after (Lüdemann – an intermediate visit).[12] Thus, the Jerusalem Conference would be dated either c. 50/51 or 52. If Paul's first visit to Jerusalem was fourteen years before this conference visit, the date of that first visit would be c. 36–38, and his commissioning three years prior to the first visit would then be placed c. 33–35. Since in the view of this writer it is more likely that Paul was in Galatia, rather than Corinth, prior to the Jerusalem Conference, the first sequence of dates is preferred: c. 33, commissioning of Paul; c. 36, Paul's first visit to Jerusalem; c. 50, the Jerusalem Conference; c. 50–52, intermediate visit to Corinth. As a result we would date 1 Thessalonians about 43.

The Theology of 1 Thessalonians

General Comments

In his significant work, *Paul the Apostle*, J. Christiaan Beker has asserted that the 'triumph of God' is

> the coherent theme of Paul's gospel; that is, the hope in the dawning victory of God and in the imminent redemption of the created order, which he has inaugurated in Christ. Moreover, I claim that Paul's hermeneutic translates the apocalyptic theme of the gospel into the contingent particularities of the human situation. Paul's ability to correlate the consistent theme of the gospel and its contingent relevance constitutes his unique achievement in the history of Christian thought.[13]

Even more specifically, Paul 'locates the coherent center of the gospel in the apocalyptic interpretation of the Christ-event'.[14] The other side of this proposition is that 'the *character* of Paul's contingent hermeneutic is shaped by his apocalyptic core in that in nearly all cases the contingent interpretation of the gospel points – whether implicitly or explicitly – to the imminent cosmic triumph of God'.[15] We posit the correctness of this perspective for Paul in general, and especially for 1 Thessalonians.

---

[12] Lüdemann, *Paul, Apostle to the Gentiles*, p. 262.
[13] Beker, *Paul the Apostle*, p. ix.
[14] Beker, *Paul the Apostle*, p. 18.
[15] Beker, *Paul the Apostle*, p. 19.

This coherent theology of Paul, which overlaps to a degree with the early Christian missionary preaching of the hellenistic church, is developed, expanded, defended, articulated and elaborated as the apostle confronts new and unanticipated problems, challenges and risks in the missionary field. Thus, Paul's letters are expressions of his coherent theology, the gospel of the eschatological triumph of God in Jesus and its imminent conclusion, shaped by contingent situations.[16] The importance of 1 Thessalonians is precisely that it allows us to view the early missionary Paul before it is necessary for him to deal with many of the controversies which will develop subsequently in his apostolic career. The overarching message of 1 Thessalonians is that God has chosen, elected, the believers in Thessalonica and that they, because the gospel had been proclaimed to them in all power, have responded positively and joyfully, despite persecution, to this word of God.[17] As a result of this proclamation of God through Paul, the Thessalonian Christians have 1) 'turned to God from idols to serve a living and true God' (1.9) and 2) must 'wait for his Son from heaven whom he raised from the dead, Jesus, who rescues us from the wrath that is coming' (1.10). This response, this conversion to the living and true God has, then, two primary dimensions: ethical – 'to serve a living and true God' – and eschatological – 'to wait for his Son from heaven'. This twofold response is repeated, expanded and articulated at various points in the letter, most notably in chapter 4. The first half of that chapter is a further actualization of certain themes and beginning with 4.13 one finds a further, detailed elaboration of the eschatological dimension of God's prior election.

What is remarkable about 1 Thessalonians is the traditional character of the letter, namely, its close coherence with the theology of the hellenistic church. In many of its formulations

---

[16] On this entire subject see also the provocative article by Johannes Munck, '1 Thes 1, 9–10 and the Missionary Preaching of Paul. Exegesis and Hermeneutic Reflexions', *NTS* 9 (1963), pp. 86–110.

[17] On the theology of 1 Thessalonians see further Donfried, 'The Cults of Thessalonica', and 'The Theology of 1 Thessalonians as a Reflection of Its Purpose', in *To Touch the Text*, (Festschrift J. A. Fitzmyer; ed. M. P. Horgan and P. J. Kobelski (New York: Crossroad, 1989), pp. 243–60. [In this volume, pp. 21–48 and 119–38 respectively.]

and in its use of traditional materials it appears to be more pre-Pauline than 'Pauline'.[18] Over and over again Paul simply takes over traditions circulating in the hellenistic church and appropriated by that church from a variety of sources including hellenistic Judaism and, through it, popular hellenistic philosophy. These materials are so widespread in the letter that only a few passing references to this use of pre-Pauline materials must suffice: the triadic formula 'faith, hope and love'; the fragments of missionary preaching located in 1.9–10; the language of the popular philosophers and hellenistic cults in 2.1–12; the anti-Jewish topos of 2.13–16; the paraenetic elements in 4.1–12 and chapter 5; and certain phrases in 4.13–18, to just mention a few of these traditional elements. It is evident that 1 Thessalonians places Paul very precisely within the context of the hellenistic church's missionary movement, the very context in which he received much of his missionary training.

We must, of course, also ask what is uniquely Pauline in 1 Thessalonians? The Pauline contribution to those traditions which he inherited from Antioch and elsewhere are found precisely in those places where the apostle is shaping these earlier traditions in light of his apocalyptic gospel to meet a problem which has developed in the Thessalonian church, namely, some unexpected deaths, deaths which occurred before the parousia. How these deaths occurred, deaths which created such a crisis, is conjectural, but we have attempted to show elsewhere that they may have been the result of a 'lynch-mob', a small-scale, ad hoc type of persecution.[19] To deal with this issue Paul expands and applies the proclamation of the hellenistic church found in 1.9–10 in 4.13–18. What it means to wait for Jesus, not only in light of the fact they have turned to the true and living God from the idols but also because they have just recently experienced some

---

[18] See T. Holtz, 'Traditionen im 1. Thessalonicherbrief', in *Die Mitte des Neuen Testaments* (Festschrift E. Schweizer; ed. U. Luz and H. Weder; Göttingen: Vandenhoeck and Ruprecht, 1983); pp. 55–78, and R. H. Gundry, 'The Hellenization of Dominical Tradition and the Christianization of Jewish Tradition in the Eschatology of 1–2 Thessalonians', *NTS* 33 (1987), pp. 161–78.

[19] Donfried, 'The Theology of 1 Thessalonians', pp. 248–56; also pp. 119–38 in the volume.

unanticipated deaths, becomes the major goal of 4.13–18. In this pericope Paul applies his coherent gospel of the triumph of God to the contingent situation in Thessalonica. We see here Paul the theologian at work. That gospel which came in 'full conviction' (1.5) and in 'the Holy Spirit' (1.5) and is alive and 'at work' (2.13) in the believers must now be dynamically applied to and articulated in an unforeseen situation. We have here one of the first extant instances where Paul attempts to draw out the implications of his gospel for a situation hitherto not addressed. In so doing he develops a pattern which is then paralleled in an expanded way in his other letters as well. It is precisely at such points of specification and concretization that one sees vividly the relationship between coherence and contingency in Pauline thought.

1 Thess. 1.9–10 and 1 Thess. 4.13–18

Let us examine and illuminate this first major attempt of Paul the exegete by a more detailed comparison of 1 Thess. 1.9–10 and 1 Thess. 4.13–18.

1 Thess. 1.9–10[20]

ἐπεστρέψατε πρὸς τὸν Θεὸν ἀπὸ τῶν εἰδώλων
δουλεύειν Θεῷ ζῶντι καὶ ἀληθινῷ
καὶ ἀναμένειν τὸν υἱὸν αὐτοῦ ἐκ τῶν οὐρανῶν,
ὃν ἤγειρεν ἐκ νεκρῶν,
Ἰησοῦν τὸν ῥυόμενον ἡμᾶς ἐκ τῆς ὀργῆς τῆς ἐρχομένης.

The close relationship of these words to those found in the missionary proclamation of hellenistic Christianity prior to Paul is far reaching; ἐπιστρέφειν is found throughout Acts in such a

---

[20] For more detailed discussion of these verses, in addition to the commentaries, see C. Bussmann, *Themen der paulinischen Missionspredigt auf dem Hintergrund der spätjüdisch-hellenistischen Missionsliteratur* (Europäische Hochschulschriften. Reihe XXIII, Theologie; Bd. 3; Bern: Herbert Lang, 1971), pp. 39–56; P. Dalbert, *Die Theologie der hellenistisch-jüdischen Missionsliteratur unter Ausschluß von Philo und Josephus* (ThF 4; Hamburg, 1954); F. Hahn, *Christologische Hoheitstitel* (Göttingen: Vandenhoeck und Ruprecht, 1964); J. Munck, 'Missionary Preaching'; G. Schrenk, *Urchristliche Missionspredigt im 1. Jahrhundert, in Studien zu Paulus* (Zürich: Zwingli, 1954), pp. 131–40; U. Wilckens, *Die Missionsreden der Apostelgeschichte* (WMANT 5; Neukirchen-Vluyn: Neukirchener Verlag 1963), pp. 81–100.

context (Acts 3.19; 9.35; 11.21; 14.15; 15.19; 26.18, 20; 28.27). Paul, in addition to 1 Thessalonians, uses this verb only in 2 Cor. 3.16 and Gal. 4.9. Πρὸς τὸν Θεὸν is remarkably similar to the phrase ἐπιστρέφειν ἐπὶ Θεὸν ζῶντα of Acts 14.15. The term εἴδωλον is firmly embedded in Jewish hellenistic propaganda literature (e.g. Wis. 14.12, 24, 29) and the ethical lists influenced by it in the New Testament (1 Cor. 6.9; Gal. 5.20; Eph. 5.5; Col. 3.5).

The references to God as ζῶν and ἀληθινός are especially widespread in hellenistic Judaism (the former in *Sib. Or.* 3.763; *Jos. Asen.* 8.5; the latter in *Sib. Or.*, 3.621, 3.829; Wis. 12.27; *Let. Aris.* 140). The phrase Θεὸς ζῶν is used with frequency in the New Testament (Matt. 16.16, 26.63; Acts 14.15; Rom. 9.26; 2 Cor. 3.3, 6.16; 1 Tim. 3.15, 4.10; Heb. 3.12, 9.14, 10.31, 12.22; Rev. 4.9, 7.2, 10.6, 15.17); particularly noteworthy is the reference once again to Acts 14.15, a text which must command our attention below.

Ἀναμένειν is a *hapax legomenon* in the New Testament; however, it is found in the Septuagint (Jud. 7.12, 8.17; Job 2.9a, 7.2; Sir. 2.7, 5.7, 6.19; Isa. 59.11; Jer. 13.16; 2 Macc. 6.14). In Jud. 8.17; Sir. 2.7 and Isa. 59.11 the verb ἀναμένειν is found in an eschatological context similar to that of 1 Thess. 1.9–10.

Τὸν υἱὸν αὐτοῦ used to describe Jesus as the coming savior from heaven is not found in Paul despite the wide range of meaning which Paul can attribute to this phrase.[21] This, together with the absence of any reference to the death of Jesus and the fact that Paul uses σώζω rather than ῥύομαι in eschatological contexts dealing with the final return of Jesus, makes it once again probable that Paul is using here a pre-Pauline piece belonging to the hellenistic church, which itself took over this material from the missionary literature of Jewish hellenism and modified it (e.g. ὃν ἤγειρεν ἐκ νεκρῶν, Ἰησοῦν) in light of the Christ event and its own missionary needs.

Before moving on to 1 Thess. 4.13–18, reference must be made to two items. First, it should be added briefly that the

---

[21] Hahn, *Christologische Hoheitstitel*, pp. 319–33.

apocalyptic motif of ὀργή is already present in hellenistic Judaism, as for example, a quick perusal of *Let. Aris.* 254, *Sib. Or.* 3.309, 556, 632 and Wis. 16.6 and 18.20 reveal. Second, Wilckens has shown that not only do 1 Thess. 1.9–10 and Heb. 5.11–6.2 reveal a common schema, but that this is also shared by Acts 14.15–17 and 17.22–31 (but note also 26.20!).[22] It is interesting to observe that Luke never uses this material in the sermons presented in the first half of Acts. Perhaps we have here a witness to the fact that Luke, Barnabas and Paul shared in a common Antiochene tradition, a matter which we need to return to further on.

1 Thess. 4.13–18

The theme of 'waiting for his Son from heaven' (1.10) is one of the dominant emphases in 1 Thessalonians and this theme of the parousia is repeated at the end of every chapter.[23] As I have also shown, Paul uses what Dahl has referred to as 'superfluous rehearsals', namely, the repeated 'you know', throughout the letter.[24] However, at one critical point he does not use this formula and begins with a new introduction: οὐ θέλομεν δὲ ὑμᾶς ἀγνοεῖν (1 Thess. 4.13). Obviously the apostle and his associates wish to convey some new information. It is here in chapter 4 that Paul wishes to specify more exactly what he said in 1 Thess. 1.9–10 in view of the unexpected deaths in the Thessalonian congregation. It is possible that some drew an erroneous conclusion from his earlier statement, namely, that there would be no deaths before the parousia, a view which had been contradicted by the Thessalonian persecution. Paul's refutation of this perspective begins with a contrast similar to that found at the end of chapter 1 where a contrast is made between the message of idols, the consequences of which are here conveyed by references to those 'who have no hope', and that of the true living God.

---

[22] Wilckens, *Missionsreden*, pp. 86–91.
[23] See Donfried, 'The Cults of Thessalonica', p. 348; p. 40 in this volume.
[24] Donfried, 'The Cults of Thessalonica', p. 348; p. 40 in this volume.

The formula 'we believe that Jesus died and rose again' (πισ τεύομεν ὅτι Ἰησοῦς ἀπέθανεν καὶ ἀνέστη) is undoubtedly a pre-Pauline formula since Paul consistently uses the verb ἐγείρω instead of ἀνίστημι. This phrase repeats the content of 1.10, but does so more precisely; essentially, however, no new information is added. This pre-Pauline formula, 'Jesus died and rose', serves as the foundation of the new information which is to follow, namely, that the death and resurrection of Jesus is the basis for the belief that Christians will be united with Christ at his parousia.[25] The essential core of the new information is that 'God will bring with him those who have fallen asleep' (4.14) and this is confirmed with a word from the Lord (4.15). According to this word, when the Lord descends from heaven on the last day, 'the dead in Christ [οἱ νεκροὶ ἐν Χριστῷ] will rise first. Then we who are alive, who are left, will be caught up in the clouds together with them to meet the Lord in the air' (4.16–17).

Lüdemann is correct in defining Paul's hope in this letter as a parousia-hope and not a resurrection-hope. Further, he is also to be followed when he urges that the introduction of the resurrection of the prematurely deceased Christians does not decisively alter Paul's earlier view that the union of Christians with Christ will be at the parousia. This new information functions to preserve the eschatological hope of the early Paul and it does not introduce a new doctrine of resurrection-hope.[26] That only follows in 1 Corinthians.

There is an astonishing consistency between Paul's assertions in 1 Thess. 4.13–18 and in 1 Corinthians 15, and yet in 1 Corinthians Paul moves beyond his previous assertions. Now the problem is not death due to unexpected persecution but the problem of death itself. Thus in 1 Cor. 15.50 it is stated that 'flesh and blood cannot inherit the kingdom of God'. Because of Paul's imminent expectation of the parousia in 1 Thessalonians

---

[25] The phrase 'who died for us' in 1 Thess. 5.10 is a similar amplification of 1 Thess. 1.9–10.

[26] Gerd Lüdemann, 'The Hope of the Early Paul: From the Foundation-Preaching at Thessalonika to 1 Cor. 15.51–57', *PRSt* 7 (1980), pp. 196–7.

one finds neither any reflection on the problem of death itself nor any response to the challenges presented by hellenistic dualism.

This pattern of consistency with previous assertions as well as the expansion and the more precise articulation of such assertions in view of a new situation is a characteristic of Pauline thought which can be observed at many points in his letters. An example relevant to our discussion of 1 Thessalonians 4 and 1 Corinthians 15 is Paul's use of christology. In both letters it is christology that shapes the anthropological dimension. In 1 Thessalonians it is the connection between Jesus' resurrection and the fact that the believer is ἐν Χριστῷ which leads to Paul's assurance of the believer's union with Jesus at the parousia. To be ἐν Χριστῷ represents the fundamental act of inclusion into God's new eschatological event which will soon be completed at the parousia. In 1 Corinthians 15, where Paul has to come to terms with the problem of death itself as well as with the challenges posed by hellenistic dualism, christology once again offers the clue to the newly outlined anthropological assertions presented in that chapter. Paul's description of the heavenly man Jesus in 15.48 allows him to formulate a hitherto unexpressed perspective, namely, that, because the Christian will put on a new, spiritual body on the last day, death cannot deny Christian hope. Resurrection, understood in this way, now replaces the translation of Christians expressed in 1 Thessalonians 4. In 1 Cor. 15.52–53, the apostle asserts that 'at the last trumpet ... and we will be changed. For this perishable body must put on imperishability'. Here resurrection is not simply the method by which the dead believers are transferred as in 1 Thessalonians; rather, resurrection involves the transformation of all bodies, the survivors as well as the dead, on the last day.

Parousia and Christology

We have observed the absolute centrality of the parousia in the theology of 1 Thessalonians as well as Paul's concern to apply it specifically and consistently to the Thessalonian situation. The dominance of this concern helps us in understanding why Paul does not discuss in this, his earliest, letter such concepts as σῶμα, σάρξ or θάνατος, nor for that matter ζωή, ἁμαρτία, ἐλευθερία, νόμος, not to mention the absence of words having the root δικ-[27] or σταυρ-. What the apostle does discuss and with much frequency is παρουσία and the relationship of παρουσία to ἁγιωσύνη (ἁγιασμός, 4.3, 4, 7 and ἁγιάζειν, 5.23). For those who have been elected by God, ἁγιωσύνη is a critical factor for positive participation in the παρουσία, if it is to be σωτηρία rather than ὀργή (5.8–9). This is why he emphasizes the necessity for being ἄμεμπτος (3.13; 5.23). Thus, Paul uses the concept ἁγιωσύνη synonymously with the term δουλεύειν Θεῷ and then further applies this to the concrete situation in Thessalonica in 4.1–8 through his discussion of πορνεία (4.3) and πλεονεξία (4.6).[28] Earlier we noted that the response to God's election of these Christians was not only 'to wait' but also 'to serve a living and true God' (1.9). In other words, there is a very keen relationship between eschatology and ethics in 1 Thessalonians; in fact, one could argue that that very relationship between eschatology and ethics is the foundation of its entire theology.

The strong emphasis on the parousia also influences the christology of 1 Thessalonians. Such terms as ἐν Χριστῷ, ἐν κυρίῳ, and πνεῦμα are derived from a pre-Pauline baptismal tradition[29] in which the soteriological–ontological character of these terms is primary.[30] Yet for Paul these concepts are embedded in his

[27] Except δίκαιος in 2.10.

[28] Donfried, 'The Cults of Thessalonica', pp. 341–2; pp. 30–1 in this volume.

[29] See J. Becker, 'Die Erwählung der Völker durch das Evangelium', in *Studien zum Text und zur Ethik des Neuen Testaments* (Festschrift H. Greeven; ed. Wolfgang Schrage; Berlin: de Gruyter, 1986), p. 89. For Becker's further view that the ἐν Χριστῷ formula derives from Antioch, see his article 'Zum Schriftgebrauch der Bekenntnisschriften', in *Volkskirche – Kirche der Zukunft?*, ed. W. Lohff and L. Mohaupt (Hamburg: Lutherisches Verlagshaus, 1977), p. 100. See also R. F. Collins, 'Paul's Early Christology', in his *Studies*, pp. 253–84.

[30] U. Schnelle, *Gerechtigkeit und Christusgegenwart* (GTA 24; Göttingen: Vandenhoeck and Ruprecht, 1983), p. 112, describes the original intent of this 'lokal-seinhaftes', soteriological-ontological character of ἐν Χριστῷ: 'In diesem primär soteriologisch-ontologisch ausgerichteten 'in Christus'-Verständnis der Tauftradition ist nun der Ursprung der ἐν Χριστῷ-Vorstellung überhaupt zu vermuten: Durch die Taufe gelangt der Täufling in den Raum des pneumatischen Christus, konstituieren sich Christusgemeinschaft und neue Existenz und wird schließlich als Angeld auf die real in der Taufe begonnene Erlösung und Vollendung der Geist verliehen. Dieses Grundverständnis ist durch die Tauftraditionen als vorpaulinisch belegt, Paulus ist wohl der Tradent, nicht aber der Schöpfer der ἐν Χριστῷ-Vorstellung.'

apocalyptic structure and their meanings can only be derived from that perspective. We have already encountered the use of ἐν Χριστῷ in 1 Thess. 4.16. There it affirms that the communion with Christ inaugurated at baptism will not conclude with death but will continue right up to the final meeting with the Lord at the parousia. Here Paul takes the original soteriological-ontological sense of ἐν Χριστῷ and links it specifically to the eschatological hope which he is attempting to convey to the downcast Thessalonian Christians.

This apocalyptically transformed soteriological-ontological situation of being ἐν Χριστῷ becomes the basis for Paul's ecclesiology. Ἐκκλησία is constituted in Christ (1.1) in anticipation of the parousia. In this sense Paul's use of ἐν Χριστῷ in 2.14 (τῶν ἐκκλησιῶν τοῦ Θεοῦ τῶν οὐσῶν ἐν τῇ Ἰουδαίᾳ ἐν Χριστῷ Ἰησοῦ) can carry a broader ecclesiological meaning. In this latter reference the imitation of Christ in terms of suffering in persecution is accented and in 3.8 the motif of holding firm to the end (στήκετε ἐν κυρίῳ) is emphasized.[31] What allows one to be 'in Christ' and to remain 'in Christ', particularly during adverse conditions, is the working of God's Spirit. Πνεῦμα, in this sense of God's Spirit, occurs in 1 Thess. 1.5, 6; 4.8; 5.19. It is not only a sign of God's election and a source of one's soteriological and ontological placement 'in Christ', but also, and especially, a well-spring of joy in the midst of suffering. Since the Spirit is still being given to them in the present (note the use of the present participle διδόντα in 4.8), it serves as the carrier of the Christian congregation from its beginning through persecution to the parousia. Therefore Paul warns in 5.19 that the Spirit dare not be quenched.

In various ways, then, we have seen how Paul's parousia-hope allows the apostle both to actualize and transform the tradition in ways that are appropriate to the crisis in Thessalonica.

---

[31] Ἐν κυρίῳ is used in 5:12 in an instrumental sense within a larger context of ethical exhortation; the context of ἐν κυρίῳ Ἰησοῦ in 4:1 and ἐν Χριστῷ Ἰησοῦ in 5:18 are again ethical – the will of God is manifested in Jesus. [Now see also K. P. Donfried, 'The Assembly of the Thessalonians. Reflections on the Ecclesiology of the Earliest Christian Letter,' in *Ekklesiologie des Neuen Testaments* Festschrift Karl Kertelge; ed. R. Kampling and T. Söding; Freiburg, Basel, Wien: Herder, 1996, pp. 90–408; pp. 139–62 in this volume.]

Comparing the Theology of the Early Paul with that of the Late Paul

General Perspectives

Given the parameters of this essay, it will be impossible to enter into a more detailed comparison of the early and late Paul. Only selected examples will be probed further. It is, however, important to state the general principle, namely, that the proper starting point for the analysis of Pauline thought must be 1 Thessalonians particularly because it contains the key to the theology of the early Paul, and therefore, I would insist, also the key to understanding the theology of the late Paul. Therefore I fully agree with Siegfried Schulz when he declares that only 'eine Gesamtanalyse des 1 Thess kann die bisherigen Entwicklungshypothesen, die den frühen vom späten Paulus grundsätzlich unterscheiden, auf eine einigermassen sichere Grundlage stellen'.[32] In his *Neutestamentliche Ethik*[33] Schulz begins such an attempt and it is filled with keen insight. Since his major concern is with the ethics of Paul rather than his theology, it may be understandable why the concept of the law plays such a major role in the comparison of the late Paul with the early Paul. Yet, one must wonder whether a comprehensive analysis of the development of Pauline theology from its earliest to its latest phase ought not to be carried out by tracing the development of a term as central to Pauline thought as ἐν Χριστῷ.[34] Not only is this term used in *every* Pauline letter, but it has a pre-Pauline

---

[32] S. Schulz, 'Der frühe und der späte Paulus', *ThZ* 41 (1985), p. 234. [ET: 'only a complete analysis of 1 Thessalonians can provide a relatively certain basis by which one can attempt to distinguish, in a fundamental way, the early from the late Paul as proposed in various developmental hypotheses'.] See also U. Schnelle, 'Der erste Thessalonicherbrief und die Entstehung der paulinischen Anthropologie', *NTS* 32 (1986), pp. 207–24.

[33] S. Schulz, Neutestamentliche Ethik (Zürich: Theologischer Verlag, 1987), pp. 290–432.

[34] This might move us beyond the impasse that W. G. Kümmel, 'Das Problem der Entwicklung in der Theologie der Paulus', *NTS* 18 (1972), p. 457, referred to in his report of the 1971 SNTS Paul Seminar: 'Keine Einigung konnte erzielt werden in den Fragen, was bei der Annahme einer Entwicklung als bleibende Mitte der paulinischen Theologie anzusehen sei und wie das Verhältnis von Apokalyptik zu Anthropologie und Christologie im paulinischen Denken zu bestimmen sei.'

origin. This may well be the proper starting point for understanding the evolution of the Pauline theological trajectory.[35]

Although a whole range of additional topics need to be investigated,[36] we will limit ourselves to some very brief remarks concerning the theme of the law and the theme of justification in view of the fact that these seem to dominate the discussion about the validity of an early Pauline theology different from its later manifestation in Galatians and Romans. One other point needs to be made before proceeding to that discussion. If one posits an early and a more developed later Pauline theology, then it is requisite to ask what the major factors were which forced Paul to further amplify and develop his theology and ethics. Although such influences would have to be further defined through analysis of the individual letters, it is possible, at least tentatively, to suggest that it was the encounter with Christian, perhaps Jewish-Christian, gnosticizing tendencies, on the one hand, and with Judaizing Christian nomists on the other, that accounted for the maturation and evolution of Pauline thought.

The Problem of the Law in Pauline Theology

Why does 1 Thessalonians not contain the same intense discussions of the law as one finds in Galatians and Romans? In order to gain some perspective on this question, the following points need to be considered:

1) One should not posit a significant theological development of Paul's understanding of the law between Galatians and Romans. On the contrary, such a major development took place between 1 Thessalonians, written in the early 40s, and these later letters.[37]

---

[35] Schnelle, *Gerechtigkeit*, has made an interesting start in this direction.

[36] For example, a further development of our previous discussion of eschatology, flesh–spirit, sin, pre-existence christology and the whole range of related christological developments just alluded to, the theology of the cross, baptism and the church as the body of Christ, and the progress and maturation of the Christian in and according to the Spirit and ethics.

[37] Heikki Räisänen in his article 'Paul's Conversion and the Development of His View of the Law', *NTS* 33 (1987), pp. 405–6 and his *Paul and the Law* (WUNT 29; Tübingen, 1983); see also U. Wilckens, 'Zur Entwicklung des paulinischen Gesetzesverständnis', *NTS* 28 (1982), 154–90 and E. Larsson, 'Paul: Law and Salvation', in *NTS* 31 (1985), pp. 425–36.

2)   Paul was not introduced to 'justification' terminology at the time of his call,[38] but probably in connection with the Antiochian incident described in Gal. 2.11–17.[39] Räisänen puts the matter well: 'In view of the total absence of justification terminology in Gal. 2.11–17 one should *not* claim that Paul in this passage *grounds* his gospel of justification *sola gratia* and *sola fide* without works of the law in his call experience.'[40] Räisänen denies that Paul's sharp contrast between Judaism and Christianity in terms of achievement versus gift was present 'right at the beginning'. Rather, this is a result of the subsequent conflicts in which Paul became involved.[41]

3)   Räisänen posits that as a result of his call, Paul 'adopted in essence the view of the law of those Hellenistic Jewish Christians he had persecuted'.[42] This view of the law is a liberal one marked by ethical and spiritual reinterpretations of ritual stipulations. So in 1 Thess. 4.7 Paul can take up the distinction between 'uncleanness' (ἀκαθαρσία) and 'holiness' (ἐν ἁγιασμῷ), which was originally rooted in the ritual of the cult, and use it in a totally non-cultic way. Such an attitude, in and of itself, does not indicate hostility to the law, although it could clearly call forth anger from those, such as the persecutor Paul, who held to a more literal reading of the law. In this context Räisänen makes two assertions worth noting: i) 'In his writings this old relatively peaceful attitude toward the law shows through most clearly in 1 Thessalonians'.[43] ii) Further, in correctly noting the tensions in the Pauline view of the law, Räisänen asserts that these 'tensions are easier to understand if they can be seen as tensions between Paul's Antiochian heritage and new ideas he developed later. When Paul finds a new solution to a problem, he does not necessarily discard the old

---

[38] Räisänen, 'Paul's Conversion', p. 407.
[39] Note the intriguing suggestion made by Lüdemann, *Paul*, p. 58: 'The question remains to be asked whether there are indications in the content that Gal. 2.1ff. really does reflect a chronological rearrangement (out of interest for the issue at hand), that the event should be chronologically located before the Jerusalem Conference, and that this may have been *the* occasion for the conference.'
[40] Räisänen, 'Paul's Conversion', p. 407.
[41] Räisänen, 'Paul's Conversion', p. 412.
[42] Räisänen, 'Paul's Conversion', p. 413.
[43] Räisänen, 'Paul's Conversion', p. 415.

one.'[44] Räisänen makes an important point here, although the use of the term 'old' sets up more of a tension between the early and the late Paul than may be necessary. Does the late Paul contradict the early Paul? I would be more inclined to say that the late Paul, both in general and in relation to the issue of law presently under discussion, articulates more precisely what was already, at least implicitly, the theological structure of the early Paul. Already Paul's christology in 1 Thessalonians makes it clear that election is a gift of the Spirit and not a result of the law.

Justification Language in Paul

As is well-known, δικαιοσύνη and its cognates do not occur in 1 Thessalonians.[45] It is, of course, impossible to take up the whole problematic of justification in Paul in a brief paragraph. I have outlined my general perspective in 'Justification and Last Judgment in Paul'[46] and this has been further developed by K. R. Snodgrass in his essay 'Justification by Grace – to the Doers: An Analysis of the Place of Romans 2 in the Theology of Paul'.[47] I would argue that Paul's teaching on justification is nothing other than his teaching on election, sharpened by this theology of the cross, and applied to a series of polemical situations.[48] Seen in this way there is an amazing consistency between the emphasis on election and sanctification in 1 Thessalonians and justification and sanctification in Romans, between learning how to please God and to do his will in 1 Thess. 4.1–3 and the theme of obedience in Romans 6, between Paul's assertion in 1 Thess. 5.9 that 'God has destined us not for wrath but for obtaining

[44] Räisänen, 'Paul's Conversion', p. 414.

[45] See the exception mentioned in n. 27 above. Schnelle, *Gerechtigkeit*, p. 100, concludes: 'Aus diesem Sachverhalt ist die Konsequenz zu ziehen, daß es *die* paulinische Rechtfertigungslehre *gar nicht gibt.*'

[46] K. P. Donfried, 'Justification and Last Judgment in Paul', *ZNW* 67 (1976), pp. 90–110; now also pp. 253–78 in this volume. See also the new article on justification in this volume, pp. 279–92.

[47] K. R. Snodgrass, 'Justification by Grace – to the Doers: An Analysis of the Place of Romans 2 in the Theology of Paul', *NTS* 32 (1986), pp. 72–93.

[48] Such a development can already be seen in 1 Cor. 1.18–31. See the discussion in Becker, 'Erwählung', p. 100.

salvation through our Lord Jesus Christ' and that of Rom. 5.9, 'Much more surely then, now that we have been justified by his blood, will we be saved through him from the wrath of God.' When Paul remembers τοῦ ἔργου τῆς πίστεως (1 Thess. 1.3) of the Thessalonians, that definition of faith coheres remarkably well with the formula εἰς ὑπακοὴν πίστεως found in Rom. 1.5 and 16.26.

1 Thessalonians and the 'Paulinism' of Acts

There is much in Vielhauer's article that is perceptive and accurate; yet there is much that is in need of correction and modification. In his summary he concludes that 'the author of Acts is in his christology pre-Pauline, in his natural theology, concept of the law, and eschatology, post-Pauline. He presents no specifically Pauline idea.'[49] Is that correct? Vielhauer is to be followed in his observation that Luke has replaced the apocalyptic expectation and 'the christological eschatology of Paul by a redemptive historical pattern of promise and fulfillment',[50] although it should not be overlooked that there are places where the eschatological perspective of Paul in Acts shows remarkable similarity to that found in 1 Thessalonians,[51] particularly in the relationship between 1 Thess. 2.13–16 and Acts 28.17–31. Is it

[49] Vielhauer, 'Paulinism', p. 48.

[50] Vielhauer, 'Paulinism', p. 47.

[51] D. P. Moessner, 'Paul in Acts: Preacher of Eschatological Repentance to Israel', *NTS* 34 (1988), pp. 96–104. Moessner attempts to show certain Jesus–Paul parallels in Luke-Acts which reveal that 'Israel's disobedience to his voice brings about the *final* or *eschatological* judgment upon an unrepentant folk' (p. 97). He finds this parallel in a fourfold pattern: 'A. Israel's history is one long unremitting story of a stubborn, disobedient people; B. God has sent his messengers, the prophets, to plead repentance lest Israel bring upon itself the destruction of God's judgment. Jesus is the crowning prophet or messenger in the long line sent to Israel; C. Nevertheless, Israel *en masse* rejected all these prophets, even persecuting and killing them, and rejects Jesus' mission, as well; D. Therefore, God will bring upon Jesus' generation the "final judgment" for the whole history of the blood guilt of this disobedience' (p. 97). This fourfold pattern is remarkably similar to the contents of 1 Thess. 2.14–16. The same sharp rebuke of Israel found in 1 Thessalonians 2 is also found in Acts 13.40–46 (Pisidian Antioch), Acts 18.6 (Corinth) and Acts 28.25–28 (Rome). See also J. T. Sanders, 'The Salvation of the Jews in Luke-Acts', in *Luke-Acts. New Perspectives from the Society of Biblical Literature Seminar*, ed. Charles Talbert (New York: Crossroad, 1984), pp. 104–28.

accurate to fault Acts because it 'ascribes the motivation for the Jews' hostility toward Paul primarily to their jealous rivalry or to their disbelief in the messiahship of Jesus, but never to Paul's doctrine of freedom from the law (and thereby also from circumcision)?'[52] Is it not an overstatement to claim that 'Luke did know that Paul proclaimed justification by faith, but he did not know its central significance and absolute importance ...?'[53] Further, we must ask, 'central significance and absolute importance' to which Paul – the Paul of 1 Thessalonians or the Paul of Galatians? Further, Vielhauer concludes that 'the doctrine of the law which is in Acts, the "word of the cross" has no place because in Acts it would make no sense. The distinction between Luke and Paul was in christology.'[54] Again, we must ask, the distinction between Luke and which Paul – the early or the late Paul? – lies in christology? When Vielhauer surveys the contents of Paul's message in Acts he finds Luke describing it in such terms as 'kingdom' or 'kingdom of God' (19.8; 20.25; 28.23, 31); or simply as Jesus (19.13; 22.18); or, as 'Jesus, whom Paul asserted to be alive' (25.19); or, 'Jesus and the resurrection' (17.18).[55] This is then contrasted with the 'real Paul', namely, the late Paul, particularly the emphasis on the cross and justification, so as to demonstrate that Luke does not understand the genuine theology of the apostle. Thus, in contrast to the genuine Paul's theology of the cross, in Acts the 'exalted Messiah demonstrates his power in the mission of the church by directing the mission through the intervention of his Spirit (13.2, 1–17) and the miraculous effects of his "name." But his power as Messiah is not yet complete; his full messianic dignity will be established only at the parousia (3.19–21).'[56] When one looks at passages such as 1 Thess. 1.5 with its emphasis on the Spirit and miracles and the many references to the Lord's parousia and when one takes into account our previous discussion, then one has to ask whether Luke does not

---

[52] Vielhauer, 'Paulinism', p. 40.
[53] Vielhauer, 'Paulinism', p. 42.
[54] Vielhauer, 'Paulinism', p. 42.
[55] Vielhauer, 'Paulinism', p. 43.
[56] Vielhauer, 'Paulinism', p. 45.

in fact have a reasonable grasp of the early Paul's theology and whether Vielhauer's failure to distinguish between an early and a late Paul leads to results that are skewed. When Vielhauer asserts that 'Luke in composing his speeches made use of preformed material, as Dibelius has shown, the similarity with the speeches of Peter suggests that the christology of Acts 13 is also that of the earliest congregation, rather than that of Paul',[57] one has to ask whether he is not in error by drawing such a sharp distinction between the earliest congregation and Paul. Is there, in fact, not a far greater commonality between the earliest congregation, Luke and Paul, a commonality that would be greatly strengthened if it can be shown that Luke is a native of Antioch.[58]

Let us remind ourselves of some of the specific points that 1 Thessalonians and Acts share.

1) In 1 Thess. 1.6 Paul reminds the Thessalonian Christians that they had received the word in much affliction μετὰ χαρᾶς πνεύματος ἁγίου, words which are remarkably similar to Luke's account in Acts 13 of the persecution stirred up against Paul and Barnabas and how as a result the disciples were filled with χαρᾶς καὶ πνεύματος ἁγίου (13.52).

2) Paul's reference to the powerful deeds which accompanied his proclamation of the gospel in 1 Thess. 1.5 is also attested to in Acts 14.3, 10 and Acts 15.12 where Barnabas and Paul 'told of all the signs and wonders that God had done through them among the Gentiles'. This dimension of Paul's apostolic ministry is well summarized in Acts 19.11: Δυνάμεις τε οὐ τὰς τυχούσας ὁ Θεὸς ἐποίει διὰ τῶν χειρῶν Παύλου.

3) The same interchangeability of the terms 'gospel' and 'word' as found in 1 Thessalonians (1.5 and 2.13) is also found in the Pauline section of Acts (14.7, 21; 16.32; 17.11, 13).

4) The term 'apostle' appears only once in 1 Thessalonians (2.7) and then in the plural. That Paul is not intending to stress his apostolic authority by use of this term alone is obvious. In 1 Thessalonians 2, for example, it is Paul's apostolic activity and

[57] Vielhauer, 'Paulinism', p. 44.
[58] See nn. 67 and 68 below.

authority, and not necessarily the title 'apostle', which conveys his unique role within early Christianity. In fact, there is little in Paul's later concentration on the title 'apostle' that could not be derived from his understanding of this God-given responsibility as outlined in 1 Thess. 2.1–8. With regard to the Lucan presentation of Paul as apostle, Jervell makes a keen observation: 'Er verwendet den Titel nicht ... Die Taten des Apostels sind aber da, und Lukas will das seine Leser so konkludieren: Paulus ist der erste unter den Aposteln. Denn wie sonst sollen wir seine Wirksamkeit verstehen?'[59] In other words, sparse use of the title 'apostle' does not necessarily mean a minimalist understanding of Paul's apostolic call, whether the infrequent use of that title be noted in 1 Thessalonians or in Acts.

5) In 1 Thess. 3.2 Paul informs the congregation in Thessalonica that he is sending Timothy to them εις τὸ στηρίξαι ὑμᾶς καὶ παρακαλέσαι. Paul only uses the verb στηρίζω here in 1 Thessalonians (3.2, 13) and twice in Romans (1.11; 16.25). This same language is found in Acts 14.22 and 15.32. In fact, Acts 14.22 not only has much in common with the language of 1 Thessalonians (note also the use of the common term βασιλεία as in 1 Thess. 2.12) but it could well serve as a summary of the purpose of 1 Thessalonians as a *consolatio*:[60] Paul and Barnabas returned to Lystra and to Iconium and to Antioch and 'they strengthened [ἐπιστηρίζοντες] the souls of the disciples and encouraged [παρακαλοῦντες] them to continue in the faith, saying, "It is through many persecutions [θλίψεων] that we must enter the kingdom of God."' With its reference to faith, this verse is again remarkably reminiscent of 1 Thess. 3.2–3: 'to strengthen and encourage you for the sake of your faith, so that no one would be shaken by these persecutions [θλίψεσιν]'.

---

[59] J. Jervell, 'Paulus in der Apostelgeschichte und die Geschichte des Urchristentums', *NTS* 32 (1986) p. 384 [ET: 'He does not use the title ... However, the acts of an apostle are present and therefore Luke would like his readers to conclude: Paul is the first among the Apostles. Otherwise, how else are we to understand his efficacy?']; for a different perspective see W. O. Walker, 'Acts and the Pauline Corpus Reconsidered', *JSNT* 24 (1985), pp. 3–23.

[60] See further Donfried, 'The Theology of 1 Thessalonians', pp. 243–4 and 259–60; see also pp. 119–20 and pp. 37–8 in this volume.

6) It is remarkable that the theme of the suffering of Christ referred to in 1 Thess. 1.6 and 2.14 is referred to in Acts 17.3, exactly in that section of Acts dealing with Paul's activity in Thessalonica. It is of interest that in this same verse Luke also refers to the resurrection of Christ, using the identical verb that we noted earlier in 1 Thess. 4.14 (ἀνίστημι).

7) In 1 Thess. 5.12–13 Paul urges respect for 'those who labor among you, and have charge of you [προϊστάμενος] in the Lord and admonish you'. This fact is also attested to in Acts 14.23 and 20.28 even if Paul did not specifically refer to these leaders as πρεσβύτεροι or ἐπίσκοποι in 1 Thessalonians.

8) Given the understanding of 1 Thess. 2.14–16 which I have developed elsewhere,[61] I would want to assert that Luke not only has a clear perception of Paul's mission to the Gentiles (13.46–47; 22.21), but that he is also essentially accurate that Paul begins his mission to the Gentiles in the synagogue (Acts 13.14; 14.1; 17.1, 2; 19.8; see also 16.13).[62] I am convinced that the reference in Gal. 2.7–8 wherein Peter's and Paul's areas of responsibility are divided is essentially geographical and not religious. Thus Paul is concerned with proclaiming the gospel to Jews and Gentiles, even though his ultimate goal remains the Gentiles. The appropriateness of Paul beginning his mission in the synagogue is also enhanced when one reflects that the Gentiles most likely to be converted at first may well be those who were attracted to the synagogue and remained close to its periphery. Thus when Paul states in Acts 14.2 that 'the unbelieving Jews stirred up the Gentiles and poisoned their minds against the brothers', a situation also described in Acts 17.5 with reference to Thessalonica, he may well be accurate in his description.

Part of the perceived tension between Paul and Acts as described by Vielhauer is dependent on a thesis, perhaps most pointedly formulated by Käsemann: 'Der eigentliche Gegner des

---

[61] K. P. Donfried, 'Paul and Judaism', *Int* 38 (1984), pp. 242–53; also pp. 195–208 in this volume.

[62] Supporting the accuracy of Luke is Etienne Trocmé, 'The Jews as Seen by Paul and Luke', in *To See Ourselves as Others See Us*, ed. J. Neusner and E. S. Frerichs (Chico, CA: Scholars Press, 1985), p. 159.

Apostels ist der fromme Jude'.[63] Is this an accurate portrayal of the early Paul or of the late Paul – or of either? Is not Markus Barth correct in disputing such a portrayal for both?[64] When we set aside some of our preconceived ideas we will remember that in two places Paul refers to himself as a Ἑβραῖος, a Hebrew: first in Phil. 3.5, where the reference might only refer to his past when he asserts that he was born a Hebrew, a son of Hebrew parents; second, in 2 Cor. 11.22 where he certainly claims to be a Hebrew in the present. From the perspective of 1 Thessalonians what is unique about Paul's ministry is his assertion and proclamation that under the direction of Jesus Christ the Gentiles are to participate in God's promises to Israel and to share in their understanding and worship of the one true God. Such a message would suggest that Paul's intention is to be more a brother than an opponent of the Jew.

How, then, does one understand the attitude portrayed in 1 Thess. 2.13–16? As we have already noted, Paul the Jew was called to proclaim the triumph of God through Jesus Christ and its imminent eschatological conclusions to the Gentiles through the Jews in the diaspora. This latter point is important: Paul does not side-step Judaism to reach the Gentiles but first attempts to gain them as his allies. Precisely for this reason he generates so much opposition from many of his fellow Jews. Through the use of pre-Pauline materials, 1 Thess. 2.13–16 intends both to describe and evaluate the hostility of such Jews against Jesus, the churches in Judea, Paul and the church at Thessalonica.

Much of the material about Paul in Acts is a reflection of the early theology of Paul. Viewed from this perspective there is considerable common ground between Acts and 1 Thessalonians. As a result, a great deal of Vielhauer's work on the relation of Paul and Acts needs revision.[65] Often Luke is not distorting the

---

[63] E. Käsemann, 'Paulus und Israel', in *Exegetische Versuche und Besinnungen*, 2 vols (Göttingen: Vandenhoeck and Ruprecht, 1964), 2.195 ['Paul's actual opponent is the pious Jew'].

[64] M. Barth, 'Der gute Jude Paulus', in *Richte unsere Füße auf den Weg des Friedens* Festschrift H. Gollwitzer; ed. Andreas Baudis, *et al.*; München: Chr. Kaiser, 1979; pp. 107–37.

[65] Particularly important in this regards is the work of Jacob Jervell, including such essays as 'Paulus in der Apostelgeschichte und die Geschichte des Urchristentums', *NTS* 32 (1986), pp. 378–92 and the ones included in *The Unknown Paul* (Minneapolis: Augsburg, 1984).

theology of Paul in his writing of Acts; rather, he is concentrating on the early Paul, the Paul who has not yet engaged in the harsh polemics generated in the Galatian situation. As we know, Luke is interested in presenting harmony and unity in the early church, and the fact that the late Paul is engaged in such a harsh conflict with various groups of Judaizers does not fit the portrait that Luke is developing.

A word does need to be said about the personal relationship between Paul and Luke. Fitzmyer[66] swims against a strong tide in contemporary New Testament scholarship when he suggests that Luke may at times have been a companion of Paul, although not throughout his entire apostolic career. In fact, Luke would have been absent 'during the major part of his missionary activity, or during the period when Paul's most important letters were being written'.[67] Where Fitzmyer has to be taken seriously is in his support of the earlier positions of Strobel[68] and Glover[69] that Luke was a native of Antioch. This possible conjunction of Luke, Paul and the church at Antioch would assist in explaining a common background and allow us to understand how Luke had come to know Paul personally.

In further support of his position that Luke was at least a part-time associate of Paul, Fitzmyer tends to understand the 'we-sections' of Acts as diary material from Luke. I would like to agree with Fitzmyer because his is a plausible hypothesis which would allow a number of pieces to fall into place. And yet when I try to understand the relationship of Acts 16.10–17 to 20.5–15, both centered in Philippi, I cannot do so in a way that I find convincing. If one takes that material at its face value, Luke would have stayed in Philippi many years (why?) and would have had little or no contact with Paul. Perhaps that possibility needs to be explored more thoroughly than I have done. While not wishing to deny that Luke is using some firsthand source material in these

---

[66] J. A. Fitzmyer, *The Gospel According to Luke. I–IX* (AB 28; Garden City: Doubleday, 1982), pp. 47–51.

[67] Fitzmyer, *Luke*, p. 48.

[68] A. Strobel, 'Lukas der Antiochener', *ZNW* 49 (1958), pp. 131–4.

[69] R. Glover, 'Luke the Antiochene and Acts', *NTS* 11 (1964–65), pp. 97–106.

chapters, when all is said and done, I still find most convincing the hypothesis that the 'we-sections' are the result of the creative activity of Luke. Once one gets to Acts 16.10, his major Antiochene source of information, Barnabas, is gone. Much solid material which Luke has gathered is now framed with the eyewitness 'we'. When one views closely the relationship of 16.10–17 to 20.5–15 and then 21.1–18 to 27.1–28.16, I, for one, come to the conclusion that this is an editorial framing technique which allows Luke to report authoritatively the activities of Paul from Philippi to Rome once Barnabas has passed from the scene.

I am inclined to think, then, that Luke has a good sense of the total theology of Paul, including his late period.[70] For the purposes of his 'Christian consensus', as Kingsley Barrett phrases it so nicely,[71] Luke preferred to concentrate on and to shape the teaching and proclamation of the early Paul. Is that any less legitimate than the concentration of many on the late Paul? Is not the total Paul to be seen precisely in the combination of the early and the late Paul and in the development from the one stage to the other, as well as in attempting to understand the causes necessitating such further amplification and articulation of his early theology?

Conclusions

As a result of these reflections, often more programmatic than definitive, what conclusions might be reached?

1. Modern studies of Pauline chronology have suggested reasons for dating 1 Thessalonians in the early 40s of the first century. Although no chronology can claim to be conclusive, the theological development of Pauline thought would suggest more rather than less time and in general lends support to these revisions of what has been to date the more or less standard late dating of 1 Thessalonians.

[70] See further Walker, 'Acts', pp. 4–7.
[71] C. K. Barrett, 'Acts and Christian Consensus', in *Context* Festschrift P. Borgen; ed. P. W. Bockman and R. E. Kristiansen; Trondheim: Tapir, 1987, pp. 19–33.

2. 1 Thessalonians contains a fair amount of pre-Pauline material, material that has much in common with the hellenistic church and the Antiochene tradition. This tradition and its transformation, rather than the late Paul represented in Galatians or Romans, must be the starting point for understanding the evolution of Pauline theology. The major contribution of this letter to the study of Pauline thought is that it allows us to see how Paul's coherent theology of the gospel of the eschatological triumph of God in Jesus and its imminent conclusion shaped his inherited theological framework in light of the contingent situation he encountered in Thessalonica. This can be seen with particular clarity in the amplification of 1 Thess. 1.9–10 in 1 Thess. 4.13–18 and in the reshaping of the phrase ἐν Χριστῷ.

3. The phrase ἐν Χριστῷ may be an especially appropriate place to begin an examination of the development and maturation of Pauline theology since it appears in every Pauline letter.

4. Such Pauline themes as 'law' and 'justification' are contingent applications of the basic structure of Pauline thought found already in 1 Thessalonians. Thus, Paul's teaching about justification is nothing other than one specific application of his theology of election, sharpened by his theology of the cross, and necessitated by a series of polemical confrontations.

5. Although Luke places Paul within his larger theological program of unity and consensus, the portrait of the apostle he presents is more correct than Vielhauer leads us to believe. Luke does present some accurate accounts of the early Paul as well as some fleeting views of their common inheritance from the Antiochene tradition.

5

❦

Chronology: The Apostolic and Pauline Period

Introductory Comments

The apostolic and Pauline period in early Christian history is presently being reviewed with renewed scrutiny and much vigor. As a result, the chronological options are several, although it is possible to reduce the major options for this period to two: 1) the traditional approach, heavily dependent on the accuracy of the information and chronological framework found in the Acts of the Apostles, which understands Paul's primary apostolic work to have begun in 47–8 CE, and; 2) the approach pioneered by John Knox[1] and now argued in greater detail by others which is skeptical of the uncritical dependence on the chronological material provided by Acts, and suggests that Paul's apostolic work began as early as 37 or at the latest in 40.[2] It is thus clear that the decisive issue between these two major approaches is the evaluation of the chronological reliability of Acts.[3] But before these

---

[1] J. Knox, *Chapters in a Life of Paul*, ed. D. A. Hare, rev. ed. (Macon, GA.: Mercer University, 1987).

[2] G. Lüdemann, *Paul Apostle to the Gentiles: Studies in Chronology* (Philadelphia: Fortress Press, 1984).

[3] In addition to Knox, *Chapters* and Lüdemann, *Paul, Apostle to the Gentiles*, the following studies have helped inform our considerations: J. Finegan, *Handbook of Biblical Chronology; Principles of Time Reckoning in the Ancient World and Problems of Chronology in the Bible*, rev. ed. (Peabody, MA: Hendrickson Publishers, 1998); N. Hyldahl, *Die Paulinische Chronologie* (Leiden : E. J. Brill, 1986); E. A. Knauf, 'Zum Ethnarchen des Aretas 2 Kor 11,32', *ZNW* 74 (1983), pp. 145–7; K. Lake, 'The Chronology of Acts' in *The Beginnings of Christianity*, 5 vols, ed. F. J. Foakes Jackson and K. Lake (Grand Rapids: Baker, 1966), I.445–74; G. Ogg, *The Chronology of the Life of Paul* (London: Epworth, 1968); M. J. Suggs, 'Concerning the Date of Paul's Macedonian Ministry', *NovT* 4 (1960), pp. 60–8.

methodological considerations are discussed, it may be useful to provide a general overview of the traditional dating of the Pauline period, recognizing, of course, that individual scholars sharing this overall perspective may vary from this outline at some points.

Methodological Considerations

Given the remarks just made and the lack of consensus in evaluating the chronology of the apostolic and Pauline period, careful attention needs to be given to the issue of methodology in attempting to reconstruct the chronology of this period. To begin, it must be recognized that there are essentially only two sources for our knowledge of the Pauline period: the letters of the apostle himself and the events recorded by Luke in the Acts of the Apostles. Most New Testament scholars today give clear priority to the Pauline letters since Paul himself stands closest to the events he records. It is increasingly recognized that Luke in writing his second volume reshapes many traditions, just as he

Table 1: Traditional Dating

Event	Date (CE)
Conversion of Paul	33
First visit to Jerusalem	36
Famine visit	46
First missionary journey	47–8
Apostolic conference	49
Paul's arrival in Corinth	50
Paul leaves Corinth	autumn 51 or spring 52
Paul's arrival in Ephesus	autumn 53
Paul leaves Ephesus	summer 56
Paul's arrival in Corinth	late 56
Paul in Philippi	Passover 57
Paul's arrival in Jerusalem	Pentecost 57
Paul before Festus	summer 59
Paul's arrival in Rome	spring 60

does in the Gospel, to cohere with his overall theological purpose. Thus, for those scholars who maintain such a view of Luke's purpose, Acts becomes a less useful source for exact chronological information since much of this information has been subjected to a larger theological program. While Acts can still be a valuable source of detailed and accurate information when separated from its programmatic framework, it should never be given priority over the documents stemming from Paul and should only be used when it does not contradict assertions made by the apostle.

Although implementing this critical methodology is, according to its adherents, a requisite of rigorous historical research, its adoption does not make the task of establishing a chronology of the Pauline period easier. If anything, it reveals how tentative and speculative previous attempts have been and how tenuous all reconstructions must be. For when all is said and done, Paul gives us not one specific date. Inevitably, if one is to establish a possible chronology of this period, there will have to be some dependence on Acts. Recognizing this, one should be cautious to use Acts in a way which is both critical and plausible. Yet it must be acknowledged that no matter from what perspective one views the data, *there can be no absolutely definitive chronology of this period*; all attempts must be tentative and subject to correction and revision.

All scholars, no matter which chronological option they follow in their reconstruction of Paul's career, find it useful to distinguish carefully between the information found in the Pauline letters and that in the Acts of the Apostles. The first step will be to isolate certain information found in the Pauline correspondence which may have chronological implications.

The Pauline Correspondence

The information found in these letters might best be summarized in the following way: a) the revelation of the risen Jesus to Paul in Damascus (Gal. 1.12–16); b) the visit to Arabia and the return to Damascus (Gal. 1.17); c) 'then [ἔπειτα] after three years' the first visit to Jerusalem for fifteen days (Gal. 1.18) – the so-called 'acquaintance visit'; (d) then (ἔπειτα) activity in the regions of Syria and Cilicia (Gal. 1.21); e) then (ἔπειτα) after fourteen years a second visit to Jerusalem (Gal. 2.1) – the so-called 'conference' visit; f) activity in the churches of Galatia, Asia, Macedonia, and Achaia with special emphasis on the collection of the offering for Jerusalem (Gal. 2.10; 1 Cor. 16.1–4; 2 Cor. 8–9; Rom. 15.25–32) – the so-called 'offering' visit. Let us examine these individual pieces of information provided by the Pauline letters more closely:

a) The revelation of the risen Jesus to Paul in Damascus (Gal. 1.12–16).

This is often referred to as Paul's 'conversion', yet one should be most hesitant in using this term since it is not found anywhere in the text. In language reminiscent of prophetic imagery, the apostle declares that the God who had set him apart before he was born revealed 'his Son to me, so that I might proclaim him among the Gentiles'. Most accurately we have here a 'commissioning' event – the commissioning of Paul as one who is to preach Jesus Christ to the Gentiles.

In order to understand the context in which these remarks about commissioning, travel and chronology are made, one must remember that Paul is attempting to document the thesis that 'I did not receive it [the gospel] from man, nor was I taught it, but it came through a revelation of Jesus Christ' (Gal. 1.12). One aspect of the argument that this Pauline gospel is not dependent on any human authority is for the apostle to insist on his independence from Jerusalem. That is exactly the point which follows upon this 'commissioning' scene: 'I did not confer with flesh and blood, nor did I go to Jerusalem to those who were apostles before me' (Gal. 1.16–17). Not unimportant is to observe the word εὐθέως ('immediately, at once') in the text: 'I did not confer *immediately* with flesh and blood' (RSV). To understand very carefully this context is critical for an accurate perspective in interpreting the information which is to follow in the succeeding verses, viz. that Paul is primarily attempting to show his independence from Jerusalem and not to give detailed chronological information.

b) The visit to Arabia and the return to Damascus (Ga. 1.17)
To underscore the independence of his gospel and to insist that it came to him through a revelation of Jesus Christ, Paul asserts that following this revelation, he did not go immediately to Jerusalem but rather to Arabia and 'again I returned to Damascus' (Gal. 1.17). This Pauline description allows one to conclude that the location of the original commissioning was in Damascus, a fact which coheres with the embellished description of this event in the book of Acts (9.1–25; 22.1–21; 26.12–30). How long Paul was in Arabia or why he went there is unknown; how long he spent in Damascus is dependent on how one interprets the 'then' of Gal. 1.18. From the text before us it is reasonable to conclude that Paul spent his time in Damascus in the midst of a Christian community, a view that also accords with the information provided in Acts 9.19–22.

c) 'Then [ἔπειτα] after three years' the first visit to Jerusalem for fifteen days (Gal. 1.18) – the so-called 'acquaintance visit.' To what does the 'then' refer – to Paul's commissioning or to his return to Damascus? (Of course, if his stay in Arabia was a brief one, as it probably was, the commissioning event and his return to Damascus might be relatively close in time). However, since this is not the only occurrence of the adverb 'then' in the sequence of events to be described in Galatians, the interpretation of this word assumes great importance. Many interpreters see it consistently referring back to the commissioning event; many others see it as consistently referring back to the immediately preceding event. The latter interpretation is strengthened by the parallel use in 1 Cor. 15.6 and 7. Interpreted in this way, Paul remained with other Christians in Damascus for about three years (either two or three as a result of the ancient method of calculation) before making his first visit in Jerusalem since his call to preach Jesus Christ to the Gentiles. In keeping with his main thesis in this section, the apostle describes that he was only in Jerusalem with Cephas (Peter) for fifteen days and saw no one else except James the Lord's brother.

d) Then [ἔπειτα] activity in the regions of Syria and Cilicia (Gal. 1.21). In light of what has just been discussed, ἔπειτα ('then') is likely to refer to the immediately preceding event: 'I went to Jerusalem, then I went into the regions of Syria and Cilicia.' That the ἔπειτα refers back to the commissioning event is hardly possible.

The critical question with regard to this verse in Galatians is not, then, the referent of ἔπειτα but rather what is meant by the reference to the activity in Syria and Cilicia. Syria includes Christian centers in Damascus, the place of Paul's commissioning, and Antioch, an area where, by Paul's own description, he had worked (Gal. 2.11) and a city extensively referred to in Acts (11.19; 13.1, 14; 15.22; 18.22). In addition, Cilicia includes Tarsus, which according to Acts 22.3 is Paul's native city. Is the intention of this reference to suggest that Paul spent some eleven to fourteen years (see below) only in Syria and Cilicia? Or, given the overall context of Paul's desire to distance himself from Jerusalem, does he merely wish to say that 'then, after leaving from my fifteen-day stay in Jerusalem, I did not stay around that area but I began moving as far away as Syria and Cilicia' without in any way wishing to suggest that he worked only in this area? How one interprets this reference to Syria and Cilicia will be crucial for the reconstruction of a chronology of the Pauline period. For those scholars who understand the reference to Syria and Cilicia as not limiting Paul's activity to these regions, the apostle was involved in missionary work as far away as Philippi, Thessalonica, Athens and Corinth very early in his career. They would urge that the reference in Phil. 4.15 to 'the beginning [ἀρχῇ] of the gospel' (RSV) literally refers to the beginning of Paul's independent missionary work in Philippi and that 1 Thess. 3.1 refers to Paul's continuing work during this period in Thessalonica, Athens and Corinth. This interpretation, to date not the majority one, allows for an 'uncrowding' of Paul's missionary work, for the maturing of his apostolic ministry and the development of his theology. Rather than an extended period of some eleven to fourteen years in Syria and Cilicia, this perspective allows for the beginnings of the European mission at a much earlier point in his apostolic career and does not reduce the remainder of his activity to such a severely limited time-frame.

If one accepts this reading of the evidence then it is probable that 1 Thessalonians stems from this period prior to the conference visit in Jerusalem.

e) Then [ἔπειτα] after fourteen years a second visit to Jerusalem (Gal. 2.1) – the so-called 'conference' visit. In Gal. 2.1 Paul indicates that he made this second visit to Jerusalem 'by revelation' as opposed to being summoned by any human authorities. At the end of this meeting with James, Cephas and John, Paul relates how 'they gave to Barnabas and me the right hand of fellowship, agreeing that we should go to the Gentiles and they to the circumcised. They asked only one thing, that we remember the poor, which was actually what I was eager to do' (Gal. 2.9–10).

Paul uses ἔπειτα here for the third time. To what does it refer – back to his commissioning or back to the initiation of his activities in Syria and Cilicia? In view of the remarks made above, the more likely is the latter. Since his work in Syria and Cilicia began so very soon after his brief visit in Jerusalem, the fourteen-year period can accurately be said to describe the time between the first ('acquaintance') and the second ('conference') visit to Jerusalem.

f) Activity in the churches of Galatia, Asia, Macedonia and Achaia with special emphasis on the collection of the offering for Jerusalem (Gal. 2.10; 1 Cor. 16.1–4; 2 Cor. 8–9; Rom. 15.25–32). A general review of the Pauline letters suggests that his activities in this post-conference period were concentrated in Galatia, Asia, Macedonia and Achaia and that one important focus of the apostle's work was in collecting the offering for the poor in Jerusalem, which was a request made at the end of the Jerusalem meeting with James, Cephas, and John.

The major center for Paul's activities during this period was Ephesus (1 Cor. 16.8–9) and it is from here that Galatians, Philippians, Philemon and 1 Corinthians were written. From here he traveled to Macedonia with Timothy, making a first stop in Philippi (1 Cor. 16.5; 2 Cor. 2.13) where they met Titus (2 Cor. 7.5). If one sees 2 Corinthians as a composite document then it is possible that much, if not all of it, was written from Philippi. From Macedonia, which may have included a stop in Thessalonica, Paul heads on toward Corinth (2 Cor. 9.3–4; 12.4; 13.1). Finally, from Corinth, where the apostle writes Romans, he makes his final trip to Jerusalem.

g) *The final visit to Jerusalem (1 Cor. 16.3; Rom. 15.25–32) – the so-called 'offering' visit.* The last part of Paul's missionary activities that can be documented from his letters is this final trip to Jerusalem, although Acts continues on beyond Jerusalem until the apostle is placed in Rome. Paul's intention in making this last trip to Jerusalem is to 'make some contribution for the poor among the saints at Jerusalem' (Rom. 15.26). That Paul is anxious about this trip is evident from his request for the prayers of the Romans 'that I may be delivered from the unbelievers in Judea, and that my service for Jerusalem may be acceptable to the saints' (Rom. 15.31). There is no precise indication from the letters concerning the length of the period between the 'conference' visit and the 'offering' visit to Jerusalem.

The result of this rapid survey of chronological information provided us by the Pauline letters is that only two (other than the reference to fifteen days) references are given: three years between the return to Damascus and the first, acquaintance visit in Jerusalem, and fourteen years between the first and second visits to Jerusalem. This is where firsthand information from Paul ceases. From the letters there is no information whatsoever as to the year in which any of these visits or activities take place. The next task is to turn to Acts cautiously and critically to see whether reliable information can be found there which coheres with and does not contradict the primary evidence that has been derived from the Pauline letters.

The Acts of the Apostles

The relevant information in Acts having a possible bearing on Pauline chronology may be summarized as follows: a) the revelation of the Lord to Saul and his subsequent commissioning in

Damascus (Acts 9.1–25 – but notice the repetition of this event in 22.5 and 26.12); b) first visit to Jerusalem to meet with the apostles (9.26); c) preaching in Jerusalem followed by departure for Tarsus (Cilicia) and return to Antioch (9.28–30; 11.25–26); d) second visit to Jerusalem to bring relief in time of famine (11.29–30; 12.25); e) activity in Syria, Cyprus, and Galatia (Acts 13–14; the so-called 'first missionary journey'); f) third visit to Jerusalem for the apostolic council (15.1–29); g) activity in Galatia, Macedonia, Greece and Asia (15.36–18.21; the so-called 'second missionary journey'); h) fourth visit to Caesarea to greet the church, (Jerusalem?), Galatia and Phrygia (18.22); i) activity in Syria, Galatia, Asia, Macedonia and Greece (18.23–21.14; the so-called 'third missionary journey'); and j) fifth (final) visit to Jerusalem (21.11–16).

In order to compare this information with that found in the Pauline letters and to resolve the apparent contradiction concerning the number of visits to Jerusalem, it will be useful to examine this outline of Acts more closely:

a)   The revelation of the Lord to Saul and his subsequent commissioning in Damascus (9.1–25; 22.1–21; 26.12–30). Although Luke greatly embellishes the material found in Galatians 1, this event corresponds to Paul's description in Gal. 1.12–16 (see point a) on p. 102 above).

b)   First visit to Jerusalem to meet with the apostles (9.26). This information coheres well with the so-called 'acquaintance visit' recounted in Gal. 1.18 (see point c) on p. 103 above).

c)   Preaching in Jerusalem followed by departure for Tarsus (Cilicia) and return to Antioch (9.28–30; 11.25–26). This agrees only partially with Gal. 1.21 as discussed in point d) on pp. 103–5 above in terms of the departure, and then differs substantially from the letters in terms of a return to Antioch followed by point d) below, the second visit to Jerusalem.

d)   Second visit to Jerusalem to bring relief in time of famine (11.29–30; 12.25). There is no parallel for such a visit in the Pauline letters. This reference to a visit to Jerusalem is one of the two additional visits to Jerusalem which is described by Acts. When we discuss item j) below, we will observe that Luke gives no reason for this final visit to Jerusalem, a visit which in the letters is clearly described as the offering visit. One solution to the extra visits in Acts would be to suggest that the final offering visit is moved to this much earlier and likely incorrect position of Acts. Some would argue that although the tension between Jewish and Gentile Christians continued and perhaps intensified even into the last stages of Paul's apostolic ministry, Luke wished to suggest that these differences were essentially overcome at an early date.[4] This is the real motivation for Luke's rearrangement and modification of Paul's visits to Jerusalem.

e) *Activity in Syria, Cyprus, and Galatia (Acts 13–14; the so-called 'first missionary journey').* It is difficult to coordinate Acts' c), d), and g) with Paul's point d) above. Given our previous discussion that for Paul the reference to Syria and Cilicia was possibly only the starting point for activities that took him as far as Macedonia and Achaia, then it appears that Luke is fragmenting one longer visit into some smaller ones so that the Jerusalem visits can be rearranged according to his schema.

f) *Third visit to Jerusalem for the apostolic council (15.1–29).* The majority of New Testament scholars today would hold that this visit to Jerusalem corresponds with with e) on p. 105 above, the so-called 'conference' visit, although holding that Galatians describes a private meeting between Paul and the Jerusalem authorities, while Acts intends to describe a more public form of this meeting. If this correspondence is abandoned, then one is faced with a 'jungle of problems'[5] as well as a jungle of solutions. These include: 1) Gal. 2.1–10 does not describe the same Pauline visit to Jerusalem as Acts 15. Rather, the meeting referred to in Galatians is to be identified with the visit in Acts 11.27–30 (the famine visit) or with 18.22 or with a visit not mentioned in Acts.

---

[4] Knox, *Chapters*, pp. 71–3; Lüdemann, *Paul, Apostle to the Gentiles*, pp. 139–57.
[5] E. Haenchen, *The Acts of the Apostles; A Commentary*, trans. and ed. R. McL. Wilson (Philadelphia: Westminster Press, 1971), pp. 455–72.

2) Gal. 2.1–5 and 6–11 represent separate Pauline visits to Jerusalem, which are then identified with any of the three to five visits to Jerusalem by Paul described in Acts.

If one holds to the majority identification of Acts 15 with Galatians 2, then for Luke this is a third visit to Jerusalem while for Paul only a second. In view of the fact that in Acts 18.22 (h below) that visit to Jerusalem is totally unmotivated and fits into its context very awkwardly, it has been suggested that the original location for this visit was at 18.22 and that Luke retrojected it back to chapter 15 (f) for theological reasons: for the sake of the unity of the church this controversy had to be settled early, before he went to Asia Minor, Macedonia and Achaia. If this suggestion is correct, then after the elimination of d) and f), the activities described by Luke in c), e), and g) all fall into place as part of one 'missionary journey'.

g) *Activity in Galatia, Macedonia, Greece and Asia (15.36–18.21; the so-called 'second missionary journey').* As we have noted, it is possible that c), e), and g) are part of what took place during the fourteen-year activity described by Paul in Gal. 1.21.

h) *Fourth visit to Caesarea to greet the church, (Jerusalem ?), Galatia and Phrygia.* Aside from the fact that no reason whatsoever is given why Paul 'went up and greeted the church' (Acts 18.22) it is striking that in Acts 18.21 Paul is in Ephesus and then in verse 24, after having traveled to Caesarea, probably Jerusalem (although not referred to in the Greek text, many commentators argue that it is unlikely that the original, pre-Lukan itinerary did not mention a visit to Jerusalem if Paul had already traveled as far as Caesarea), Antioch and through the region of Galatia and Phrygia (all in three verses!), he is back in Ephesus. It is indeed possible that 18.22 was the original location for the conference visit which is now described in Acts 15.1–29 (f above).

i) *Activity in Syria, Galatia, Asia, Macedonia and Greece (18.23–21.14; the so-called 'third missionary journey').* This material coheres well with point f) in the Pauline section (pp. 105–6 above), although it is noteworthy that Luke eliminates what was so prominent for Paul in this period of his apostolic ministry – the collection. At this point one notes the consistency of Luke: not only does he eliminate the real reason for the final visit to Jerusalem in 21.11–26, viz. to present the collection in Jerusalem, but he also omits the collection as a primary objective during Paul's final activity in the areas described here in Acts 18.23–21.14.

j) Fifth (final) visit to Jerusalem (21.7–36). As we have already observed, this final visit is described in point g) in the Pauline section, although Luke omits the association with the offering and, as we suggested previously, retrojects this motivation to d) Acts 11.29–30; 12.25 – the 'famine' visit.

However one resolves the differences between the Acts account of Paul's activities and Paul's own account – and we have suggested only one general possibility here – all scholars will have to acknowledge that these apparent contradictions require explanation. Although a comparison of those events in the Pauline literature and Acts which have possible chronological implications have allowed an overview of their similarities and dissimilarities, one is still not in possession of concrete and precise chronological data. Therefore, it will be necessary to examine the book of Acts to see what other specific data it may provide and whether such evidence may be useful for determining the more exact limits of Pauline chronology, remembering the cautionary remarks already made concerning the transference of such information.

Chronological Information Provided by Luke

The Gallio Inscription and the Edict of Claudius

Reference is made in Acts 18.12 to Paul's visit to Corinth: 'But when Gallio was proconsul of Achaia, the Jews made a united attack upon Paul and brought him before the tribunal'. Although the precise details, implications and context of the events described are disputed, there is little doubt that Paul made one of his visits to Corinth at the time that Gallio was proconsul of the province of Achaia; most scholars place Gallio's term of office in the years 51–2 CE in light of the epigraphical evidence now in hand. While at first glance Acts 18.12 appears straightforward, caution must be exercised: Was Paul's visit to Corinth in the vicinity of 51–2 his first visit or does it refer to a subsequent one? Acts 18 may well conflate two or more Pauline visits to that city into one. Among the several factors pointing in this direction is the fact that in Acts 18.8 Crispus is the ruler of the synagogue. It is fully possible that if Acts 18 is conflating at least two visits of Paul to Corinth that he may well have been in the city at a much earlier date.

Another piece of information relating to secular history mentioned in Acts and which may be useful in reconstructing Pauline chronology is the reference to the edict of Claudius in Acts 18.1–2. There it is stated: 'After this Paul left Athens and went to Corinth. There he found a Jew named Aquila, a native of Pontus, who had recently come from Italy with his wife Priscilla, because Claudius had ordered all Jews to leave Rome. Paul went to see them'. It is likely that Suetonius (*Claud. 25*) is referring to this edict: '*Iudaios impulsore Chresto adsidue tumultuantes Roma expulit.*' Since Suetonius does not date this edict, one cannot be certain whether it is referring to one issued by Claudius in 41 or whether it is referring to disturbances later in his reign. Those who would argue against the early dating cite Dio Cassius' reference (60.6.6) that the large number of Jews effectively ruled out their expulsion and point to Orosius' reference (7.6.15) that the edict occurred in Claudius' 9th year (49). Yet these references in themselves do not settle the issue. In the first place, there need not be any contradiction between Dio Cassius' assertions and Luke's characteristically exaggerated use of πᾶς (the Lukan 'all') in Acts 18.2 and elsewhere. Further, there is the critical issue about the reliability of the information provided by Orosius, a fifth-century church historian.

If the Claudius edict is dated in 41 CE then one would have strong evidence for the dating of Paul's first visit to the city at some point after the arrival of Aquila and Priscilla from Italy. If the more usual dating of this edict in the year 49 is to be accepted, this in and of itself would not speak against an earlier visit of Paul to Corinth, for it is difficult to know how thoroughgoing is the conflation in Acts 18. For example, a case could be made that Acts 18.1 had its original continuation in verse 5 and that verses 2–4 are a retrojection made from a later period.

To place Paul's first arrival in Corinth as early as 41 is possible; yet some flexibility is in order since one does not know how long it took Aquila and Priscilla to travel to Corinth, nor if they went there directly. On this reckoning Paul's original visit to Corinth may have taken place sometime between the approximate period of 41–4. Additionally, it is most probable that he was also in Corinth during the years that Gallio was proconsul in 51–2. Some would place a visit by Paul to Corinth, usually his first, just before the Jerusalem Conference[6] and some just after.[7] Thus, the Jerusalem Conference would be dated either in c. 50–1 or 52. If his first visit to Jerusalem was fourteen years before this conference visit, the date of that first visit would be c. 36–8, and his commissioning three years prior to the first visit would then be placed c. 33–5. Since in the view of this writer it is more likely that Paul was in Galatia, rather than Corinth, prior to the Jerusalem Conference, the first sequence of dates is preferred: c. 33, commissioning of Paul; c. 36, Paul's first visit to Jerusalem; c. 50, the Jerusalem Conference, c. 50–2, intermediate visit to Corinth.

Aretas

In 2 Cor. 11.32–33 Paul states that at 'Damascus, the governor [ὁ ἐθνάρχης] under King Aretas guarded the city of Damascus in order to seize me, but I was let down in a basket through a window in the wall, and escaped from his hands.' The king referred to is Aretas (Arabic *ḥariṯa*) IV, who reigned at Petra over

---

[6] R. A. Jewett, *A Chronology of Paul's Life* (Philadelpha: Fortress Press, 1979).
[7] Lüdemann, *Paul, Apostle to the Gentiles*, p. 263 – an intermediate visit.

the Nabataean Arabs from 9 BCE to 40 CE. Although his kingdom extended to the vicinity of Damascus and although this city had been subject to his predecessors until the Romans took control of the city in 64 BCE, there is no definitive way of knowing when Damascus became subject to Aretas. One recent proposal suggests that such control over Damascus was only given to Aretas in 37 CE.[8] If this is the case, then the *terminus a quo* for the references in 2 Cor. 11.32–33 would be 37 CE and the *terminus ad quem* would be 40 CE, the year of Aretas' death. Yet, the text in no way suggests that Aretas controlled Damascus nor is this in any way necessary; 2 Cor. 11 asserts only that this leader was the representative (ὁ ἐθνάρχης – ethnarch) of King Aretas. In this case no *terminus a quo* can be reached. All that can be asserted is that this event took place before 40 CE.

The 'governor' (ὁ ἐθνάρχης) to whom Paul refers was, in all likelihood, the leader of the semi-autonomous Nabatean community in Damascus, a community which had been organized as an *ethnos* within the city, much as the Jews of Damascus would have been organized following the pattern of the Jews in Alexandria, viz. functioning as an *ethnos* within the city and under the leadership of an ethnarch.[9] In Gal. 1.17 it is asserted that immediately following his call to proclaim the gospel to the Gentiles, Paul 'went away into Arabia' (presumably to evangelize the Nabateans) and thereafter 'returned to Damascus'. Presumably the Nabatean community in Damascus and their leader took this opportunity to express their displeasure at the apostle's activity in the territory of the Nabatean Arabs.

A similar account is found in Acts 9.23–25. There is, however, one substantial difference: in Acts it is the Jews, while in 2 Corinthians it is the ethnarch of the Nabateans, who plots against Paul. Given the well-documented emphasis of Luke to portray the Jews as those hostile to the early Christian mission, the account of Paul is to be preferred.

---

[8] Jewett, *A Chronology*, pp. 30–3.
[9] See Strabo, *Geogr.* 17.798; Josephus, *Ant.* 14.117.

The Great Famine under Claudius

In Acts 11.28 Luke writes that one 'of them named Agabus stood up and predicted by the Spirit that there would be a severe famine over all the world; and this took place during the reign of Claudius'. This event is cited as the background of the first collection for the relief of the Jerusalem church. Although both Suetonius (*Claud.* 19) and Tacitus (*Ann.* 12.43) refer to widespread scarcity under Claudius, there was no famine over 'all the world' under Claudius; this phrase is undoubtedly an exaggeration. Either Acts is referring to a more local crisis, or it has intentionally retrojected an event which took place after 51 CE to this early point in the narrative.

The Death of Herod Agrippa I

The death of Herod Agrippa I, which occurred in 44 CE, is mentioned in Acts 12.23. The narrative continues in verse 25 with the reference that 'Barnabas and Saul returned from Jerusalem when they had fulfilled their mission' (RSV). This is certainly redactional and provides no firm chronological information.

Sergius Paulus

During the time that Paul and Barnabas were in Paphos on the island of Cyprus, they encountered a certain Bar-Jesus who 'was with the proconsul, Sergius Paulus' (Acts 13.7). Unfortunately the extant sources are ambiguous and do not provide a precise date for this proconsul's term of office. It has been shown that the famous inscription from Soli on the north coast of Cyprus,[10] which refers to a certain Proconsul Paulus, should probably be identified with Paullus Fabius Maximus, who was a consul in 11 BCE. Among the various inscriptions which may refer to a Sergius Paulus there is one from Pisidian Antioch with the name

---

[10] D. G. Hogarth, *Devia Cypria* (London: H. Frowde, 1889), p. 114.

L. Sergius Paullus; however, it is dated between 60–100 CE. Another inscription (*CIL* VI 31.545) placed in Rome between 41–47 CE also refers to a certain L. Sergius Paullus who was the curator of the Tiber; however, this reference does not specifically relate him to Cyprus. If he went to Cyprus after serving as one of the curators of the Tiber, perhaps in the late 30s, this time-frame would coincide with what we know elsewhere about Paul's travels.

The Trials under Felix and Festus

Acts 23.23–24.27 relate Paul's trial and imprisonment under M. Antonius Felix, procurator of Palestine. According to 24.27 the minimum period of time which elapsed was two years. The continuation of this situation is recounted in Acts 25.1–26.32. Here, Porcius Festus has succeeded Felix; in addition, Paul has an opportunity to present his case to King Herod Agrippa II. If the testimony of Josephus (*J. W.* 2.12.8; *Ant.* 20.7.1) is accepted, Felix arrived in Palestine during the summer of 55 CE when he was succeeded by Festus. This would place the trial of Paul in the year 55. But once again the evidence is contradictory[11] and it is possible that Festus succeeded Felix at a later date and a *terminus ad quem* of 60–1 has been argued.[12] This later dating is supported by Plooij's reading of Eusebius' *Chronicle* where the transfer of the procuratorship is placed in the tenth year of Agrippa II (59 CE).[13] If this later dating is accepted, it would cohere nicely with the view that Ananias, the high priest who censured Paul during his appearance before the Sanhedrin (Acts 23.1–5; 24.1), was probably replaced as high priest by Agrippa II in 59.[14]

---

[11] See Tacitus *Ann.* 12.54.

[12] Jewett, *A Chronology*, pp. 40–4.

[13] D. Plooij, *De Chronologie van het Leven van Paulus* (Leiden: 1918), p. 59. See also Ogg, *Chronology*, pp. 151–5.

[14] Josephus, *Ant.* 20.179.

Summary

Given the range of dates just discussed in Acts and the approach championed by J. Knox[15] and most recently especially by G. Lüdemann,[16] an alternative chronology to that given in Table 1 would be as follows, once again remembering that advocates of a similar approach may vary from one another in some details. Since this approach insists on the radical priority of the Pauline correspondence, it is important to follow the sequence of events found in the Pauline letters.

If one were to assume that the general sequence of the subsequent events outlined in Acts is accurate – two-year Caesarean imprisonment, hearing before Festus, and arrival in Rome – then

Table 2: Alternative Dating

Event	Date (CE)
The revelation of the risen Jesus to Paul in Damascus (Gal. 1.12–16)	33
The visit to Arabia and the return to Damascus (Gal. 1.17)	33
'Then [ἔπειτα] after three years' the first visit to Jerusalem for fifteen days (Gal. 1.18) – the so-called 'acquaintance visit'	36
Then [ἔπειτα] activity in the regions of Syria and Cilicia (and beyond) (Gal. 1.21)	36–50
Then [ἔπειτα] after fourteen years a second visit to Jerusalem (Gal. 2.1) – the so-called 'conference visit'	50
Activity in the churches of Galatia, Asia, Macedonia and Achaia with special emphasis on the collection of the offering for Jerusalem (Gal. 2.10; 1 Cor. 16.1–4; 2 Cor. 8–9; Rom. 15.25–32)	50–6
The final visit to Jerusalem (1 Cor. 16.3; Rom. 15.25–32) – the so-called 'offering visit'	56–7

---

[15] Knox, *Chapters*.
[16] Lüdemann, *Paul, Apostle to the Gentiles*.

the dates c. 57–9 for the first of these and a date of c. 60 for Paul's arrival in Rome would agree with the parameters of possible dates reviewed above.

While the traditional dating exhibited in Table 1 is still held by many, the chronology itemized in Table 2 is a viable alternative. It has these advantages: it incorporates the recent redaction-critical studies of Luke-Acts in its analysis; it eliminates the long and problematic 'silent period' early in Paul's career and intelligently explains the shape of Paul's apostolic activity in that period: it 'uncrowds' the entire career of the apostle and provides the context for a ministry that actively spanned a much longer period, thus allowing for the possibility of growth and development both in the apostolic ministry and theology of Paul. Such an approach would allow one to more readily speak of an 'early Paul' and a 'late Paul', and it would permit placing the concrete, contingent letters of Paul against a broader and wider spectrum of time and activity resulting in a more coherent understanding of the theology of this often complex and paradoxical apostle.

6

The Theology of 1 Thessalonians as a Reflection of Its Purpose

Introduction

During Paul's brief original visit to Thessalonica, which following the chronology of John Knox[1] we would place in the early 40s of the first century CE, he aroused such hostility (Acts 17.1–9; 1 Thess. 2.13–16) that he was forced to leave hurriedly. During both Paul's presence and his absence it was argued that he and his message were dangerous and fraudulent; such a critique would be equally valid from either a Jewish or a Roman perspective.[2] Following his hurried departure the persecution of his followers intensified.[3]

Paul writes this letter to the Thessalonian Christians in order to 1) console them and to encourage them to stand firm during continued persecution. Thus, we understand 1 Thessalonians not

---

[1] J. Knox, *Chapters in a Life of Paul*, ed. D. A. Hare; rev. ed. (Macon, GA: Mercer University, 1987), p. 86; see also G. Lüdemann, *Paul, Apostle to the Gentiles: Studies in Chronology* (Philadelphia: Fortress Press, 1984), pp. 195–200. Concerning further details with regard to chronology, see the following essays in this volume: 'The Cults of Thessalonica and the Thessalonian Correspondence', pp. 21–48, and, 'Chronology: The Apostolic and Pauline Period', pp. 99–117.

[2] We understand συμφυλετής in a local rather than in a racial sense. Thus, this reference by no means excludes those Jews who instigated the persecutions in Thessalonica. See further pp. 128–9 in this volume.

[3] For the further details of this argument see Donfried, 'The Cults of Thessalonica', pp. 347–52; also pp. 38–46 in this volume.

primarily as a 'paraenetic' letter[4] but as a 'paracletic' letter,[5] as a *consolatio*.[6] But in order to carry out effectively this purpose he must also 2) defend the message he proclaimed while present as originating from God and, therefore, as valid, and 3) defend himself against charges made concerning his motivation and behavior.

Persecution

External Witnesses

The theology of 1 Thessalonians is about a God who is present among his elect and suffering people and about a God who is leading them to their promised salvation. The theological themes found in the letter are a response to situations created by persecution and martyrdom as well as to the problem of living the Christian life in the midst of a pagan culture. Although the monograph by John S. Pobee[7] supports a position similar to the one we outlined in our 1984 SNTS lecture,[8] viz. that 1 Thessalonians is a church under attack, this has not been the usual interpretation of 1 Thessalonians to date.[9] Therefore it will be useful to review certain external data, that is, data other than

---

[4] Paul never uses the verb παραινέω, it is found only in Acts 27.9 and 22. For the position that 1 Thessalonians is a paraenetic letter see A. J. Malherbe, '1 Thessalonians as a Paraenetic Letter' (an unpublished seminar paper given at the 1972 meeting of the Society of Biblical Literature) and also his 'Exhortation in First Thessalonians', *NovT* 25 (1983), 238–56 [reprinted in A. Malherbe, *Paul and the Popular Philosophers* (Minneapolis: Fortress Press, 1989), pp. 49–66].

[5] Note the frequent occurrence of this word group: 1 Thess. 2.12, 13; 3.2; 4.1, 10; 5.11, 14. Interestingly enough there are only two occurrences in 2 Thess. (2.16 and 3.12).

[6] A further discussion of this genre will follow later in this essay.

[7] J. S. Pobee, *Persecution and Martyrdom in the Theology of Paul* (JSNT 6; Sheffield: JSOT Press, 1985), esp. p. 13.

[8] Donfried, 'The Cults of Thessalonica', esp. pp. 347–52; also p. 38–46 this volume.

[9] There are notable exceptions, of course. Willi Marxsen writes: 'Ich lasse es hier offen, wodurch es zur Verfolgung gekommen ist. Sicher aber ist, dass es eine Verfolgung gegeben hat. Die Frage, vor der nun die junge Gemeinde steht, lautet: Lohnt es sich denn überhaupt, Christ zu sein, wenn das in solche Bedrängnis führen kann? Wenn mann als Christ in der Gefahr steht, die bürgerliche Existenz – und mehr – zu verlieren, dann hört mann doch besser (wieder) auf die Goëten. Ich glaube … das wir es hier mit der Zentralfrage des ganzen Briefes zu tun haben' ('Auslegung von 1 Thess 4,13-18', *ZTK* 66 [1969], p. 24).

1 Thessalonians: 1) the evidence found in 2 Cor. 8.1–2; 2) the witness of Acts 17.1–9; and 3) the relationship of Jewish theologies of martyrdom to the theology of 1 Thessalonians.

2 Cor. 8.1–2

In these verses Paul commends the generosity of the churches in Macedonia despite their present condition: ἐν πολλῇ θλίψις. This reference is significant because it supports unequivocally the fact that there was a severe external threat present to the churches in Macedonia and that θλίψις is not simply a term indicating general eschatological woes as some would argue for 1 Thessalonians. Further, it seems improbable that Paul would be referring to the Macedonian churches and not have very clearly in mind the Thessalonian church,[10] which was a congregation located in the capital of the Roman province and which according to 1 Thessalonians itself (1.7) became an example to all the believers in Macedonia and beyond.

Acts 17.1–9

The account in Acts 17 of Paul's activities in Thessalonica informs us that the Jews together with some persons from the *agora* attacked the home of Paul's sponsor, Jason, with the hope of accusing Paul and his associates before the politarchs. Verses 6 and 7 continue that when 'they could not find them, they dragged Jason and some believers before the city authorities, shouting, "These people who have been turning the world upside down have come here also, and Jason has entertained them as guests. They are all acting contrary to the decrees of the emperor (τῶν δογμάτων Καίσαρος), saying that there is another king named Jesus." ' Elsewhere we have suggested that Luke is, in general, faithfully describing the reality of the Thessalonian situation.[11]

---

[10] So also V. Furnish, *II Corinthians* (AB 32A; Garden City: Doubleday, 1984), p. 400.

[11] K. P. Donfried, 'Paul and Judaism: 1 Thessalonians 2.13–16 as a Test Case', *Int* 38 (1984), p. 247; also pp. 200–2 in this volume. Donfried, 'The Cults of Thessalonica', pp. 342–6; also pp. 31–8 in this volume.

We have also attempted to explain what might be meant by the term δογμάτα Καίσαρος.[12] In all likelihood the politarchs in Thessalonica were responsible for administering an oath of loyalty and for dealing with violations of this oath. Given the hostility of the Jews toward Paul and the unusually strong civic cult active in the city, there would have been present in Thessalonica an environment particularly hostile to Paul's proclamation of the Christian gospel. Finally, the reference to the politarchs λαβόντες τὸ ἱκανόν may well refer to some decision whereby it was agreed that Paul must leave the city immediately and not return.

The relationship between the theology of martyrdom in Judaism and 1 Thessalonians

Paul's theology is apocalyptic theology modified by the Christ event.[13] Or to use the words of Beker, the coherent center of the gospel is located in the 'apocalyptic interpretation of the Christ event'. And thus 'the *character* of Paul's contingent hermeneutic is shaped by his apocalyptic core in that in nearly all cases the contingent interpretation of the gospel points – whether implicitly or explicitly – to the imminent cosmic triumph of God'.[14] It is precisely this perspective which dominates Paul's *consolatio* to the persecuted Thessalonian Christians.

If there is to be an imminent cosmic triumph of God, there must be a battle raging at present. In much apocalyptic literature the forces of Satan are at war against the forces of God as, for example, in Dan. 10.13–14. In fact, the presence of Satan is felt to be so real that it is often argued that Satan inhabits the persecutors.[15] This idea of a cosmic battle presently in progress appears to be reflected in 2.18 and 3.5. This latter verse indicates that the present is not only a time of persecution but may also be

---

[12] Donfried, 'The Cults of Thessalonica', pp. 342–6; also pp. 31–8 in this volume.

[13] Donfried, 'Paul and Judaism' pp. 242–53; also pp. 195–208 in this volume.

[14] J. C. Beker, *Paul the Apostle* (Philadelphia: Fortress Press, 1980), pp. 18–19.

[15] See, for example, 1 Kgs 22.26; *As. Mos.* 10.1; *Mart. Isa.* 1.8–9; 2.4–5, 8; 3.11; 4.2–3; 5.1; 7.9–10; 1QS 1.17–18; 3.23; Dan. 7.2–8; *1 En.* 89–90.

a time of apostasy, a feature which commonly occurs in the Jewish literature of persecution.

There are other related aspects of the Jewish theology of martyrdom found both in apocalyptic literature and beyond which have the possibility of illuminating a variety of themes found in 1 Thessalonians. Pobee has demonstrated that the martyr in biblical literature is characterized by three elements: 1) suffering which might or might not include death; 2) suffering as a witness to the martyr's zeal and devotion to God; and 3) a conviction about the omnipotence and transcendence of God.[16] These factors are summarized by the term *hallul ha-shem*, 'sanctification of the Holy Name'. Such was the obligation of every Jew who lived among the Gentiles. *Midrash Ps* 68.13, for example, compares Israel to a dove because they do not struggle when 'they are slaughtered for the sanctification of the Name'.

It is noteworthy that ἁγιασμός appears three times in 1 Thessalonians (4.3, 4, 7) and only three other times in the remainder of the Pauline corpus (Rom. 6.19, 22; 1 Cor. 1.30) and that ἁγιάζειν, used in 1 Thess. 5.23 is found only in four other places in Paul (Rom. 15.16; 1 Cor. 1.2; 6.11; 7.14). It is possible that the use of this idea in discussions about Jewish persecution provided one of the reasons why it was useful for Paul to stress the theme of 'sanctification' in 1 Thessalonians. Further, when Pobee observes that the 'martyr was the zealot, who by his suffering advertised his God',[17] one immediately recognizes remarkable resemblances to the thought world of 1 Thessalonians, especially to 1.7–8 and in a more limited sense to 4.10. If for Paul suffering was an advertisement for God then it followed especially that the situation of persecution was no excuse for moral laxity[18] or any behavior which would allow the non-Christian world to ridicule the work of God in Thessalonica.[19] Linked with this theme is the entire concept of

---

[16] Pobee, *Persecution*, p. 30.

[17] Pobee, *Persecution*, p. 30.

[18] This situation provides another reason why Paul uses the term. ἁγιασμός

[19] It is for this reason that Paul includes in this *consolatio* the exhortations found in 1 Thess. 4.1–12.

reward and punishment found in both the Jewish martyriological literature and in 1 Thessalonians (5.9: ὅτι οὐκ ἔθετο ἡμᾶς ὁ θεὸς εἰς ὀργὴν ἀλλὰ εἰς περιποίησιν σωτηρίας διὰ τοῦ κυρίου ἡμῶν Ἰησοῦ Χριστοῦ). From these selected examples it should be apparent that Paul is addressing a context quite similar to that addressed by this type of Jewish literature.[20]

Paul's Understanding of and Involvement with Persecution

The fact that Paul suffered and was persecuted for his apostolic work is beyond question. In addition to the important texts in 1 Thess. 2.1–4, 13–16, and 3.7, there is the evidence of 2 Cor. 4.7–12,[21] 2 Cor. 11.23–33, Gal. 6.17, and Phil. 1.20.[22] Pobee's conclusion is one to which most Pauline scholars would assent, viz. that Paul's 'persecution and sufferings were a *sine qua non* of Paul's apostolic ministry'.[23]

The issue for us is not, then, whether Paul was persecuted; the issue rather is how Paul understood those sufferings. Was his attitude that of the Stoics, who taught that one should accept afflictions cheerfully, with fortitude and with thanks?[24] Seneca, for example, writes. *nihil aeque magnam apud nos admirationem occupet quam homo fortiter miser.*[25] He even argues that to suffer affliction can serve as an example to others.[26]

We would suggest that the apparent similarities between Paul and the Stoics at this point are at best superficial. The Stoics

[20] A similar point is made in the first three chapters of Revelation: God will redeem those disciples and martyrs who do his will even though the entire world is disintegrating. Only after such obedience has been stressed in the Christian congregations of Asia Minor does the author proceed with his message of comfort and hope to those who are persecuted because of their discipleship. See further on this theme, K. P. Donfried, *The Dynamic Word* (San Francisco: Harper and Row, 1981), pp. 187–96.

[21] On this text as well as the overall theme of suffering in Paul, see the new work by Scott J. Hafemann, *Suffering and the Spirit* (Tübingen: Mohr, 1986).

[22] A further discussion of these and related texts (such as Rom. 8.17–18 and its use of πάσχειν) may be found in Pobee, *Persecution*, pp. 93–8.

[23] Pobee, *Persecution*, p. 106.

[24] Seneca, *Marc.* 24; *Polyb.* 2.1.5; *Ep.* 96.6; Cicero, *Tusc.* 3.32.77. See also the essay by R. Liechtenhan, 'Die Ueberwindung des Leides bei Paulus und in der zeitgenössischen Stoa', *ZTK* 3 (1922), pp. 368–99, esp. pp. 377ff.

[25] Seneca, *Helv.* 13.6. [ET: 'nothing rouses our admiration as much as a person who is brave in adversity'] See also his *Polyb.* 16.2; 1.4 and *Ep.* 21.33.

[26] *Polyb.* 5.4.

understand affliction as part of accepting fate;[27] for Paul, suffering is part of the cosmic struggle which is leading to God's triumphant victory. Whereas for the Stoics divinity is understood in terms of reason as the world principle,[28] for Paul God is the one who through Christ has inaugurated the imminent redemption of the created order. Thus, on the one hand, accepting persecution is a sign of obedience to the gospel; on the other hand, accepting it with joy is a gift of God given through the Holy Spirit.

Although Paul's attitude of accepting persecution with joy (1 Thess. 1.6) might be more appropriately compared with the Jewish martyrological literature where accepting sufferings with joy is an established motif,[29] there is a distinctive difference. For Paul, joy in any situation, especially in one involving persecution, is always an eschatological gift of the Spirit. It is rooted in faith and nurtured by the hope of God's imminent triumph. It is the result of a conscious relationship between the believer and Christ. No matter how difficult the immediate moment, the believer is always enabled to transcend this situation through prayer which allows the disciple to be strengthened through the eschatological gifts of the Spirit. Since these theological motifs permeate all of 1 Thessalonians, it is quite natural for Paul to write these words toward the end of his letter (5.16–19): Πάντοτε χαίρετε, ἀδιαλείπτως προσεύχεσθε, ἐν παντὶ εὐχαριστεῖτε, τοῦτο γὰρ θέλημα θεοῦ ἐν Χριστῷ Ἰησοῦ εἰς ὑμᾶς. τὸ πνεῦμα μὴ σβέννυτε. For Paul, then, suffering and affliction only make sense in the context of God's eschatological revelation in Jesus Christ.

Persecution and the Thessalonian Church

In addition to the similar context between 1 Thessalonians and that of the Jewish persecution literature, as well as the clear indications of persecution found in 2 Cor. 8.1–2 and Acts 17.1–9,

---

[27] Seneca, *Marc.* 21.4.
[28] Cicero, *Tusc.* 2.21.47.
[29] *4 Macc.* 10.20–21; 1.18–23; *3 Macc.* 4.1; Josephus, *Ant.* 2.299.

we must now examine both the explicit and implicit terminology in 1 Thessalonians which point to situations that affected the Christian church in Thessalonica.

Explicit Terminology

1.6: Καὶ ὑμεῖς μιμηταὶ ἡμῶν ἐγενήθητε καὶ τοῦ κυρίου, δεξάμενοι τὸν λόγον ἐν θλίψει πολλῇ μετὰ χαρᾶς πνεύματος ἁγίου.

If the Acts account of Paul's initial visit to Thessalonica is correct, as 1 Thess. 2.13–16 would indicate, then it is clear that Paul's message had as its consequence immediate hostility from the Jews. This was brought to the attention of the politarchs who at the outset already took limited action against the followers of Paul. Thus Paul reminds the Thessalonian Christians about two things: When they first became Christians they did so under the most adverse conditions, and that in doing so they already experienced the eschatological joy given by the Spirit. Their present situation of persecution should not surprise them since it is in direct continuity with the original context out of which their faith arose. In addition, Paul reminds them in 3.4 that he had forewarned them of precisely this type of future.

1.6 also reminds the hearers that as they suffer for the faith, they are not only imitators of Paul, Silvanus, and Timothy, but also of the Lord. Here Jesus serves as the prototype of the martyr, a theme that is then further developed in 2.13–16.[30] Yet we must ask even more precisely in what way the Thessalonian Christians were imitators of Paul and Jesus. The δεξάμενοι clause serves as an explanation of the imitation and Pobee is to be followed when he concludes that 'the content of the imitation is the fact of accepting affliction and persecution along with receiving the word of God. The point is the martyr spirit in which they accepted affliction with patience for the sake of God. Their

---

[30] Note Cerfaux's observation on this theme in 1.6: 'Can this be understood without reference to the human, or rather superhuman courage of Jesus in his passion? Have we not here the first model which is set up for our imitation – a model which is really human? ... By accepting death Christ has set us an example (see Rom. 15.3)' (L. Cerfaux, *Christ in the Theology of St Paul* [New York: Herder, 1959] pp. 182–3).

endurance of affliction has proven them to be zealous of the Lord.'[31] Contrary to other usages of the imitation motif in Greek or Jewish literature, *imitatio Christi* for Paul is not primarily a paraenetic emphasis but a literal one.[32]

2.13–16: Καὶ διὰ τοῦτο καὶ ἡμεῖς εὐχαριστοῦμεν τῷ θεῷ ἀδιαλείπτως, ὅτι παραλαβόντες λόγον ἀκοῆς παρ' ἡμῶν τοῦ θεοῦ ἐδέξασθε οὐ λόγον ἀνθρώπων ἀλλὰ καθώς ἐστιν ἀληθῶς λόγον θεοῦ, ὃς καὶ ἐνεργεῖται ἐν ὑμῖν τοῖς πιστεύουσιν. Ὑμεῖς γὰρ μιμηταὶ ἐγενήθητε, ἀδελφοί, τῶν ἐκκλησιῶν τοῦ θεοῦ τῶν οὐσῶν ἐν τῇ Ἰουδαίᾳ ἐν Χριστῷ Ἰησοῦ, ὅτι τὰ αὐτὰ ἐπάθετε καὶ ὑμεῖς ὑπὸ τῶν ἰδίων συμφυλετῶν καθὼς καὶ αὐτοὶ ὑπὸ τῶν Ἰουδαίων, τῶν καὶ τὸν κύριον ἀποκτεινάντων Ἰησοῦν καὶ τοὺς προφήτας καὶ ἡμᾶς ἐκδιωξάντων καὶ θεῷ μὴ ἀρεσκόντων καὶ πᾶσιν ἀνθρώποις ἐναντίων, κωλυόντων ἡμᾶς τοῖς ἔθνεσιν λαλῆσαι ἵνα σωθῶσιν, εἰς τὸ ἀναπληρῶσαι αὐτῶν τὰς ἁμαρτίας πάντοτε. ἔφθασεν δὲ ἐπ' αὐτοὺς ἡ ὀργὴ εἰς τέλος.

As we have shown in detail elsewhere,[33] these verses are not a later gloss but were included by Paul intentionally. That he is dependent on tradition and formulaic material is without question, but that alone cannot be used as an argument for a later addition to the original Pauline text. Thus we understand these verses as an important and integral part of this earliest extant Christian document.

As we have argued previously, it is necessary to pay careful attention to 1.6–9a in order to understand 2.13–16:

The themes of 'imitation' and 'affliction' from those earlier verses are taken up and expanded in 2.13ff., where the behavior of the Thessalonian converts is contrasted to that of the Jews. The Thessalonians accepted the

---

[31] Pobee's analysis of this verse in general is helpful. 'The internal construction of the sentence permits two interpretations of the δεξάμενοι clause: a) it explains μιμηταί, i.e. "in that you received the word with much affliction, with joy inspired by the Holy Spirit"; or b) it supplies the antecedent fact and ground of the imitation, i.e. "after that or inasmuch as you had received...." The obvious parallelism between the two parts of the verse will be destroyed unless the δεξάμενοι clause is taken as a participle of identical action. Also, the use of the two aorists, ἐγενήθητε and δεξάμενοι, in the two parts of the sentence suggests that the two are co-extensive action and the latter explicative of the former' (*Persecution*, pp. 69–70).

[32] Against Malherbe, 'Exhortation', pp. 246ff.; see also H.-H. Schade, *Apokalyptische Christologie bei Paulus* (GTA 18; Göttingen: Vandenhoeck and Ruprecht, 1981), pp. 118–26; see further M. Buber, 'Imitatio Dei', in *Israel and the World* (New York, 1963), pp. 66ff.; J. Schoeps, *Aus frühchristlicher Zeit: Religionsgeschichtliche Untersuchungen* (Tübingen, 1950), especially chapter 13; Xenophon, *Mem.* 1.63: οἱ διδάσκαλοι τοὺς μαθητὰς μιμητὰς ἑαυτῶν ἀποδεικνύουσιν; *Let. Aris.* 188, 210, 281; *4 Macc.* 9.23.

[33] Donfried, 'Paul and Judaism', pp. 242–53; also pp. 195–208 in this volume.

word of the apostles as the Word of God and it is therefore at work (ἐνεργεῖται) in them; the Jews in Judea (and the unbelieving Jews in Thessalonica) did not receive the apostolic proclamation as the Word of God but as the word of men. Thus, it is not at work in them, and as a result a negative description of these unbelievers is made in 2.15–16. As the Thessalonian Christians had welcomed Paul, so the Jews had hindered Paul and his associates from speaking to the Gentiles. The Thessalonian church became a model for the churches not only in becoming an imitator of Paul, Silvanus, and Timothy, but also in imitating the faithful endurance of the churches in Judea that were persecuted by the Jews. As the Thessalonians became an example for all the believers in Macedonia and in Achaia, so had the churches in Judea become a model for the Thessalonians. The believers in Judea and in Thessalonica had become examples of God's salvation which rescues 'from the wrath that is coming' (1.10) whereas the unbelieving Jews had become objects of God's wrath (2.16). This is summarized at the end of the letter: 'For God has destined us not for wrath but for obtaining salvation through our Lord Jesus Christ ...' (5.9). To summarize: by following the use of the thanksgiving theme in this letter, we note how the general thanksgiving of chapter 1 is further specified in chapter 2 with regard to suffering/affliction (see 3.4) and in chapters 3 and 4 with regard to the problem of hope (ἐλπίς); suffering and hope are two of Paul's main concerns in this letter to the Thessalonian congregation.[34]

If we understand τῶν ἰδίων συμφυλετῶν in a local rather than racial sense, viz. as not excluding the Jews who instigated the persecution,[35] then 'it makes perfectly good sense for Paul to draw a parallel between the situation of the Thessalonian church with that of the churches in Judea and to show that in both situations the Jews hindered the process of speaking to the Gentiles. Paul, having just recently experienced this rebuke at the hands of the Thessalonian Jews, and being aware of the ongoing afflictions of the Thessalonian church (3.3–4), turns to a preexisting tradition in his denunciation of the Jews in Judea and Thessalonica.'[36]

3.3: τὸ μηδένα σαίνεσθαι ἐν ταῖς θλίψεσιν ταύταις. αὐτοὶ γὰρ οἴδατε ὅτι εἰς τοῦτο κείμεθα.

---

[34] Donfried, 'Paul and Judaism', pp. 246–7; also p. 200 in this volume.
[35] Donfried, 'Paul and Judaism', p. 248; also pp. 200–1 in this volume.
[36] Donfried, 'Paul and Judaism', p. 248; also p. 202 in this volume. For a further discussion of these conclusions see now the further elaboration in Pobee, *Persecution*, pp. 35, 39–45, 70–1, 88–9.

Here we find another clear reference to the existential situation of the Thessalonians – continuing persecution. Paul, most anxious to know how they are coping under these circumstances, sent Timothy (3.1–2) εἰς τὸ στηρίξαι ὑμᾶς καὶ παρακαλέσαι ὑπὲρ τῆς πίστεως ὑμῶν so that no one would be 'beguiled away' from the faith. Chadwick[37] points to the original meaning of the *hapax legomenon* σαίνεσθαι as 'to wag the tail', 'fawn', or 'flatter'. Pobee suggests that its later metaphorical use as 'to deceive' or 'beguile' may be another of the several martyrological motifs found in 1 Thessalonians. Since beguiling is the work of Satan the use of this verb may be pointing directly to the present persecution as the work of Satan (2.18; 3.5).[38]

3.4: καὶ γὰρ ὅτε πρὸς ὑμᾶς ἦμεν, προελέγομεν ὑμῖν ὅτι μέλλομεν θλίβεσθαι, καθὼς καὶ ἐγένετο καὶ οἴδατε.

Paul reminds the Thessalonian Christians that, in addition to the persecution they experienced upon accepting the gospel, he and his co-workers warned them that suffering at the hands of their fellow citizens would continue. Therefore what they are now experiencing should not be unnecessarily unsettling since it does not come as an unannounced surprise.

Implicit Terminology

Now that it has been established that Paul is in fact writing to a church which had been and continues to be confronted by persecution, we can examine certain texts in 1 Thessalonians which confirm the same state of events, although more implicitly than the texts just reviewed.

1.4: εἰδότες, ἀδελφοὶ ἠγαπημένοι ὑπὸ θεοῦ, τὴν ἐκλογὴν ὑμῶν.

The phrase τὴν ἐκλογὴν ὑμῶν is of particular interest; ἐκλεκτός/ἐκλογὴ/ἐκλέγεσθαι language is not frequent in Paul[39] and always emphasizes God's initiative in choosing. The point in

---

[37] H. Chadwick, '1 Thess. 3.3, σαίνεσθαι', *JTS* 1 (1950), pp. 156–8.
[38] Pobee, *Persecution*, 136, n. 1.
[39] ἐκλεκτός: Rom. 8.33; 16.13; ἐκλογὴ: Rom. 9.11; 11.5, 7; ἐκλέγεσθαι: 1 Cor. 1.27–28.

1 Thess. 1.4 is again to mitigate any surprise in the continued persecution of the Christians. Surely God who has chosen them is aware of their present and future suffering; this is part of the cosmic battle which leads to the ultimate triumph of God. Paul's emphasis here is quite parallel to that in Rom. 8.33, τίς ἐγκαλέσει κατὰ ἐκλεκτῶν θεοῦ; θεὸς ὁ δικαιῶν, as well as to the verses that follow.[40] Thus, this widespread apocalyptic theme is used by Paul to assure the Thessalonians that the God who has selected them is the God who is the Lord of all history and who is in process of bringing it to conclusion. Persecution, then, is no cause to lose hope in God's forthcoming victory. The Holy Spirit is already present in their midst in the form of the eschatological gift of joy (1.6) and is at work in them through the gospel (2.13, ἐνεργεῖται ἐν ὑμῖν τοῖς πιστεύουσιν). We would thus agree with von Dobschütz's analysis.

> Die Erwählung ... ist für P. immer ein übergeschichtlicher, vorzeitiger Akt, der mit der πρόθεσις dem göttlichen Vorsatz Röm 9.11, 8.28, dem προορίζειν der göttlichen Vorbestimmung Röm 8.29f. zusammengehört als die Garantie der Heilsgewissheit; die Berufung κλῆσις ist davon zu unterscheiden als der geschichtliche Akt, durch den Gott seinen Heilsratschluss verwirklicht, indem er die Gnadenbotschaft wirksam an die Erwählten herantreten und das Evangelium bei ihnen Glauben wecken lässt – diese beiden Momente bringen v. 5 und v. 6 zum Ausdruck.'[41]

[40] For example, v. 35: 'Then what can separate us from the love of Christ? Can affliction (θλίψις) or hardship...?'; v. 39b: 'nothing in all creation ... can separate us from the love of God in Christ Jesus our Lord.'

[41] Ernst von Dobschütz, *Die Thessalonicher Briefe* (KEK X; Göttingen: Vandenhoeck and Ruprecht, [1909] repr. 1974), pp. 69–70. [ET: 'Election is for Paul always a transcendent, prehistoric action that, with the πρόθεσις of divine intention (Rom. 9.11, 8.28), belongs together with the προορίζειν of divine predestination (Rom. 8.29) as a guarantee of the certainty of salvation. The call (κλῆσις) is to be distinguished from this as the historic action through which God actualizes his decision for salvation insofar that he allows the message of grace to effectively approach the elect and that he permits the gospel to awaken faith among them; it is these two dimensions that v. 5 and v. 6 bring to expression.']. Similarly Holtz, 'Denn wie das Folgende zeigt, blickt ἐκλογὴ auf das Geschehen, durch das die Erwählung sich ereignete, Gestalt gewann, wirklich wurde' (T. Holtz, *Der Erste Briefe an die Thessalonicher* [EKK 13; Neukirchen-Vluyn: Neukirchener, 1986], p. 45), and Rigaux, 'L'élection et la vocation nous semblent deux facettes d'une même réalité: l'entrée concrète dans la réalisation du plan divin' (B. Rigaux, *Saint Paul. Les Épîtres aux Thessaloniciens* [EtB; Paris-Gembloux: Gabalda-Duculot, 1956], p. 372).

1.7: ὥστε γενέσθαι ὑμᾶς τύπον πᾶσιν τοῖς πιστεύουσιν ἐν τῇ Μακεδονίᾳ καὶ ἐν τῇ Ἀχαΐᾳ.

The Thessalonians have become an example (τύπος) precisely in having received the word in much affliction and presumably for having remained steadfast in the faith despite much suffering. Thus, they are *now* a model or pattern for the other congregations in Macedonia and Achaia to follow. This stands quite in contrast to the use of the words μιμητής and τύπος in 1 Cor. 4.16; 11.1; and Phil. 3.17 where those congregations *are being urged* to become imitators; in 1 Thess. 1.6–7 the Thessalonians *have already become* imitators of Jesus and Paul, not only because they believe, but precisely because they believe in a situation dictated by persecution. That is why they can serve as a model for other congregations. Once again it is apparent how persecution is a key factor in understanding the Thessalonian church and why Paul can hold them up as an example to be followed.[42]

2.18: διότι ἠθελήσαμεν ἐλθεῖν πρὸς ὑμᾶς, ἐγὼ μὲν Παῦλος καὶ ἅπαξ καὶ δίς, καὶ ἐνέκοψεν ἡμᾶς ὁ σατανᾶς.

In our discussion of σαίνεσθαι above we stated that since 'beguiling' is the work of Satan, the use of this verb in 3.3 may be pointing directly to the present persecution in Thessalonica as the work of Satan. If that is indeed the case then the term ὁ σατανᾶς in 2.18 may well refer to an agent of Satan, presumably an official of the Roman government, who is responsible for the persecution in Thessalonica, the expulsion of Paul and the prohibition of his further re-entry into the city.[43]

---

[42] This interpretation would thus disagree with Holtz when he states: 'Man wird aus einem solchen Satz keine Rückschlüsse nach beiden Richtungen ziehen dürfen, also auch auf die Situation der Glaubenden, denen die Thessalonicher zum "Vorbild" geworden sind' (*Thessalonicher*, p. 50). For an exegesis parallel to ours see W. Marxsen, *Der erste Brief des Paulus an die Thessalonicher* (ZBK.NT 11.1; Zürich: Theologischer Verlag, 1979), pp. 38–9.

[43] A similar understanding of this verse is articulated by Pobee, who states: 'That temporary ban on his missionary activities in Thessalonica Paul considered the work of Satan. Second, since the Jews had had a hand in the situation, fomenting the trouble which cut Paul's ministry short, their action was the work of Satan, on which God's wrath is later pronounced. Whatever the historical detail, the opposition to Paul's active ministry at Thessalonica that led to his enforced departure and continued absence from Thessalonica was interpreted as the work of Satan. This is the martyrological motif which interprets persecution and martyrdom as part of the cosmic battle between the forces of God and the forces of evil' (Pobee, *Persecution*, p. 99). Some of the other options in understanding this

3.5: διὰ τοῦτο κἀγὼ μηκέτι στέγων ἔπεμψα εἰς τὸ γνῶναι τὴν πίστιν ὑμῶν, μή πως ἐπείρασεν ὑμᾶς ὁ πειράζων καὶ εἰς κενὸν γένηται ὁ κόπος ἡμῶν.

1 Thess. 3.5, as we noted above, indicates that the present is not only a time of persecution but may also be a time of apostasy and, further, that this theme of apostasy is common in the Jewish literature of persecution. We have also pointed out that in this literature the presence of Satan is experienced with such reality that often it is argued that Satan inhabits the persecutors themselves. Thus, whether ὁ πειράζων refers to the local source of persecution or to Satan himself is not a critical question since in this literature a sharp distinction between Satan and his specific manifestations is often not made. That, even for Paul, Satan can be the specific source of temptation is evident from 1 Cor. 7.5 (ἵνα μὴ πειράζῃ ὑμᾶς ὁ σατανᾶς), although there the context is sexual and not one of apostasy. That 'the tempter' in 1 Thess. 3.5 is clearly related to their afflictions is apparent from the wider context, especially verses 3 and 4.[44]

4.13: περὶ τῶν κοιμωμένων . . .

Elsewhere we have suggested that the dead who are referred to in 1 Thess. 4.13–18 are those who may have died in some mob-action type of persecution in Thessalonica, and we strongly urge the reader to review that foundational argument.[45] Given our inclination to take seriously the possibility of persecution(s)[46] in Thessalonica and elsewhere as leading to occasional deaths, do we have any extrabiblical evidence which would lend further credibility to this suggestion? The Paphlogonian oath of loyalty to the Caesarian house in 3 BCE[47] compels Romans and

---

phrase are given by Rigaux, *Thessaloniciens*, p. 462. Holtz argues a position which is extreme: 'Da Paulus nicht sagt oder auch nur andeutet, welcher Mittel Satan sich für sein Werk bedient hat, ist jeder Versuch, sie zu bestimmen, hoffnungslose Raterei', p. 117.

[44] Marxsen (*Thessalonicher*, p. 55) is correct: 'Wären die Thessalonicher, um den Bedrängnissen zu entgehen, zu einem nicht von Christus geprägten Wandel ausgewichen, hätte sich darin gezeigt, dass sie dem Versucher erlegen sind. Dann wäre die Arbeit des Paulus in nichts zerfallen.'

[45] Donfried, 'The Cults of Thessalonica', pp. 349–50; also pp. 41–3 in this volume.

[46] 'Persecution' may be a somewhat misleading term and we should be pleased to find a more precise alternative. We have in mind neither systematic nor necessarily official persecution, but rather isolated and sporadic 'mob actions'.

[47] Donfried, pp. 342–4; also pp. 31–4 in this volume.

non-Romans alike to report cases of disloyalty and to physically hunt down the offenders. The seriousness by which this oath is meant to be taken – even to the point of death for those who are disloyal – is clear. If this possible parallel has any relevance for the political situation in Thessalonica at the time of Paul, then certainly the apostle's 'political preaching' and his direct attack on the *Pax et Securitas* emphasis of the early principate was likely to place him in a precarious situation.

In his publication subsequent to our 1984 SNTS lecture,[48] John Pobee has independently reached the same conclusion concerning the identity of κοιμώμενοι. Stressing with Nestle-Aland[26] the correctness of reading here the present rather than the perfect participle, Pobee concludes that the meaning of this present participle is that 'there is a reference to the continued and protracted persecution of Christians at Thessalonica which was taking the lives of some Christians'.[49]

Pobee also raises an important question concerning the interpretation of the following phrase in 4.14: καὶ ὁ θεὸς τοὺς κοιμηθέντας διὰ τοῦ Ἰησοῦ ἄξει σὺν αὐτῷ. The issue is whether διὰ τοῦ Ἰησου goes with κοιμηθέντας which precedes or with ἄξει which follows. If the διὰ τοῦ Ἰησου is to be taken with the second half then there is an element of redundancy in the σὺν αὐτω phrase. Pobee is to be followed in reading οἱ κοιμηθέντες διὰ τοῦ Ἰησου[50] and in understanding the διὰ as expressing attendant circumstance.[51] We fully follow Pobee's conclusion with regard to this phrase when he states that it 'refers to the Christians who died in their zeal for Jesus as was demonstrated by their patient endurance of persecution, before the parousia of Christ. The

---

[48] 'The Cults of Thessalonica', also pp. 21–48 in this volume.

[49] Pobee, *Persecution*, p. 113.

[50] Other scholars joining διὰ τοῦ Ἰησοῦ τοὺς κοιμηθέντας include Ephraim, Chrysostom, Calvin, Lightfoot, von Dobschütz, Dibelius and Frame; although their understanding of διὰ τοῦ Ἰησοῦ is certainly not identical.

[51] Pobee, *Persecution*, pp. 113–14. See also the detailed discussion of this issue in J. E. Frame, *Epistles of St Paul to the Thessalonians* (ICC; Edinburgh: T&T Clark, 1912), pp. 169–70, and especially his citation of Musculus: 'The faithful die through Christ, when on his account they are slain by the impious tyrants of the world.'

attendant circumstances of the death were the persecutions raging in the church of Thessalonica'.[52]

Paul's Defense of the Gospel

It is truly remarkable to note the significant emphasis Paul places on the theme of 'the word' and 'the gospel' in this brief letter, the combination of which is probably unparalleled in his other letters when calculated proportionate to their length. Λόγος, when referring specifically to the word of God, appears in 1.5, 6, 8; 2.13; and 4.15, 18. Εὐαγγέλιον appears in 1.5, 2.2, 4, 8, 9; and 3.2. When one observes the heavy concentration of occurrences in 1 Thess. 2.1–9 it may not be amiss to conclude that Paul's 'apology' is essentially an apology for the gospel.[53]

Nils Dahl has drawn attention to a phenomenon in 1 Thessalonians which he has referred to as 'superfluous rehearsals'.[54] What he has in mind here are the repetition of the οἴδατε (and related) phrases throughout the letter, examples of which can be found, for example, in 1.5; 2.1, 2, 5, 9, 10, 11; 3.3b–4; 4.1, 2, 6, 10, 11; and 5.1.[55] Why does Paul make such frequent reference to this phrase? At issue in Thessalonica is the validity of the gospel he preached. From our previous discussion we know that a frontal assault has been launched against its veracity. As a result, Paul must defend this gospel in two ways. First, he must defend it as a message originating from God. Second, and more particularly, he must bring to recollection the specific elements of his preaching and re-emphasize their validity lest they be regarded as irrelevant for the situation in Thessalonica. Thus, all the οἴδατε phrases in the letter are not simply to be regarded as 'superfluous rehearsals', but as key

[52] Pobee, *Persecution*, p. 114.

[53] See W. Marxsen, 'Auslegung von 1 Thess.' pp. 22–37, who quite rightly argues that these verses are an apology for the *gospel*. A similar point is made by A. Suhl, *Paulus und seine Briefe: Ein Beitrag zum paulinischen Chronologie* (Gütersloh: Mohn, 1975), p. 99.

[54] Nils Dahl in reflections presented to the Society of Biblical Literature Paul Seminar in 1972.

[55] For a more complete analysis of this phenomenon see Donfried, 'The Cults of Thessalonica', pp. 347–9; also pp. 39–41 in this volume.

elements in Paul's defense of the gospel he preached and presented to the Thessalonians during his initial visit. We would thus suggest that the overall defense of the gospel is intimately linked with the steady rehearsal of his gospel as valid.

There is another factor which needs to be considered in this context. It appears as if Paul's defense of his message as truly a word of God and the repetition and new application of his previous proclamation and teaching, pave the way for the new and decisive information and consolation which he is about to give in 4.13–18. What is presented here is ἐν λόγῳ κυρίου. This new information attempts to console the Thessalonian Christians at a most neuralgic point: some of them have died for the faith and now some are about to jettison a critical dimension of their faith, viz. hope. Paul's word of consolation would be worthless if he had not first attempted to demonstrate the validity of his prior preaching. Only then can the word of the Lord here presented as new information be considered as an effective response to the problem of death caused by persecution.

Paul's Defense of His Behavior

1 Thess. 2.1–12 has been interpreted in the most varied ways.[56] Given our understanding of 1 Thessalonians, we would argue that it is impossible for Paul to defend his message as a word of God unless he also defends the integrity of the messenger himself. Since not only Paul's gospel but also his person is under attack in Thessalonica, both must be defended.[57]

Critical is this question. Out of what context does Paul make his defense of gospel and messenger? Although Dio Chrysostom, for example, shares certain common phrases and language with Paul in distancing himself from the less than honorable popular wandering philosophers, that should not lead to the conclusion that the context of both is the same or

---

[56] See the literature cited by Collins, *Thessalonians*, pp. 183–91.

[57] Quite correctly Holtz (*Thessalonicher*, p. 94): 'Denn mit dem Boten steht und fällt die Botschaft.'

that Paul is not involved in a real 'Auseinandersetzung' with those who have falsely challenged his veracity and integrity.[58] One should not overlook the fact that the self-understanding of Paul and Dio are radically different. Paul is influenced by the conceptual world of Old Testament prophecy and the normative criteria of the true prophet which involves not only the content of teaching as deriving from God but also involves the moral behavior of the prophet as one accountable and acceptable to Yahweh.[59] The fact that in 2.6 Paul refers to himself and his two co-workers as 'apostles' does not nullify this point. We would argue that it is Paul's understanding of his prophetic role which informs his developing understanding of apostolate, an understanding which is still in its infancy in 1 Thessalonians.[60] Paul, operating out of a *prophetic context*, uses certain language also present in the popular rhetoric of the day to clarify to the Thessalonians the radical difference between himself and certain of the charlatan-type popular philosophers.[61]

---

[58] See here A. J. Malherbe, 'Gentle as a Nurse: The Stoic Background of 1 Thess. ii', *NovT* 12 (1970), pp. 203–17 [Reprinted in A. Malherbe, *Paul and the Popular Philosophers* (Minneapolis: Fortress Press, 1989), pp. 35–48]. As illuminating as Malherbe's work is, the following comments by Holtz are relevant: 'Indessen ist die Analogie deshalb nicht überzeugend, weil Dio tatsächlich popularphilosophischer Wanderprediger war ... und das natürlich auch wusste, während Paulus das nicht war und das ebenfalls wusste. Dio redet letzlich in eigener Autorität und musste sich daher zunächst aufbauen. Aufgrund genereller Erfahrung (die natürlich Malherbe anerkennt, 215f) konnte er das aktuell nur in Abgrenzung gegen andere Leute seiner Art tun. Paulus aber brauchte von der Sache und von der Autorität her, auf die er sich berief, eine generelle Verwechselung nicht zu fürchten. So muss eine Abgrenzung einen aktuallen Anlass haben' (Holtz, *Thessalonicher*, p. 93, n. 422).

[59] Literature on this theme includes: J. Murphy-O'Connor, *Paul on Preaching* (London and New York: Sheed and Ward, 1964), pp. 105–14; J. M. Meyers and J. D. Freed, 'Is Paul Among the Prophets', *Int* 20 (1966) pp. 40–53; D. Hill, *New Testament Prophecy* (London, 1975), pp. 111–12; J. Dunn, 'Prophetic "I" Sayings and the Jesus Tradition: the Importance of Testing Prophetic Utterances within Early Christianity', *NTS* 24 (1977–8), pp. 175–98; Collins, *Studies*, pp. 183–5.

[60] One needs to be careful not to read Paul's later understanding of his apostolate in this early period. Although in our judgment Ernest Best ('Paul's Apostolic Authority', *JSNT* 27 [1986] pp. 3–25) understates the importance of Paul's apostolic self-understanding, his criticism of the other extreme is urgently needed.

[61] At this point one should be somewhat more cautious than Collins when he states that Paul's 'language and his self-image ... are a product of his double roots' (Collins, *Thessalonians*, p. 191). Are both equally important?

A. M. Denis and Traugott Holtz[62] have attempted to show the influence of Deutero-Isaiah on Paul's thought. Holtz is more interested in the influence on Paul's theology as a whole. Thus, for Holtz, the background of Gal. 1.15, Paul's call to be an apostle to the Gentiles, is to be found in Isa. 49.1 and the interpretative background for Paul's understanding of suffering, as for example in 2 Cor. 4.8ff., is to be found in Isa. 50.5–7 as well as in Isa. 49.4 and 7.[63] Denis is more concerned with the influence of Deutero-Isaiah on 1 Thess. 2.1–6 and suggests that terms and phrases such as παράκλησις (e.g. 57.18; 66.11), ἀκαθαρσία (Isa. 52.1, 11), δόλος (Isa. 53.9) and ὅτι οὐ κενὴ γέγονεν (Isa. 59.4) are rooted in this prophetic book. In general these observations move in a right direction, especially the observations about the use and function of παράκλησις in Second Isaiah.[64]

Earlier we suggested that 1 Thessalonians has some elements in common with the genre *consolatio* (λόγος παραμυθητικός) in classical literature. Since Isaiah 40.1–55.13 is such a book of consolation,[65] it is little wonder that we would find striking similarities between it and 1 Thessalonians. Paul's intention in writing 1 Thessalonians is not much different from Second Isaiah's announced intention in 40.1. Παρακαλεῖτε παρακαλεῖτε τὸν λαόν μου, λέγει ὁ θεός.

Where we would differ from Malherbe[66] is not by denying that there are paraenetic elements in 1 Thessalonians but by denying that this is the overriding genre. Much closer to Paul's intention

[62] A. M. Denis, 'L'Apôtre Paul, prophète "messianique" des Gentils. Etude thématique de 1 Thes., II, 1–6', *ETL* 33 (1957), pp. 245–318; T. Holtz, 'Zum Selbstverständnis des Apostels Paulus', *TLZ* 91 (1966), pp. 322–30.

[63] 'So wird bei Deuterojesaja das Vorbild für das paulinische Leidesverständnis zu suchen sein', Holtz, 'Selbstverständnis', pp. 325 and 330.

[64] Earle Ellis suggests that παράκλησις has a particular connection with Christian prophecy even when that relationship is not explicitly indicated. See E. E. Ellis, 'The Role of the Christian Prophet in Acts', in *Apostolic History and the Gospel*, ed. W. W. Gasque and R. P. Martin (Exeter: Paternoster Press, 1970), pp. 55–67.

[65] For example, J. L. McKenzie, *Second Isaiah* (AB 20; Garden City: Doubleday, 1973), pp. 16–17: 'The opening words have given the Book of Second Isaiah the title of "Book of Consolation." Second Isaiah is much more than a book of consolation, but this is certainly a dominant theme.'

[66] Malherbe, 'Exhortation'.

is the genre *consolatio*,[67] a genre which, along with many other subcategories, includes paraenesis. 1 Thessalonians is a λόγος παραμυθητικός to a Christian church suffering the effects of persecution. Παραμυθεῖσθαι is used only in 1 Thess. 2.12 and 5.14 within the Pauline corpus. In fact the advice given in 5.14, παραμυθεῖσθε τοὺς ὀλιγοψύχους, is not far from the mark in describing the intention of the letter as an encouragement to the discouraged. They are discouraged precisely because 'hope' has become disengaged from their faith.[68] The preservation of Thessalonians in the canon is a testimony to its effectiveness in correcting by encouragement this situation of hopelessness among some in the church of Thessalonica.

---

[67] For a brief discussion of the genre and further literature, see the article 'Consolatio' in *The Oxford Classical Dictionary* (Oxford: Clarendon, 1970), p. 279. Also, Leichtenhan, 'Ueberwindung des Leides bei Paulus', 368-99, esp. 371ff. and now the discussion in the new publication by Stanley Stowers, *Letter Writing in Greco-Roman Antiquity* (Philadelphia: Westminster Press, 1986).

[68] See further Donfried, 'The Cults of Thessalonica', pp. 347–48; also pp. 39–40 in this volume. Also related to these remarks are the following comments made by W. Marxsen in connection with 1 Thess. 4.13–18, 'Auslegung', p. 32: 'Aber es geht hier nicht darum, ob die Heiden Vorstellungen von der Zukunft haben, sondern darum, ob ihre ἐλπίς in der πιστίς begründet ist. Die λοιποί haben deswegen keine Hoffnung, weil ihnen die πιστίς und damit der Grund für die ἐλπίς fehlt. So kann die λύπη angesichts von Todesfällen in der Tat charakterisiert werden als ein ὑστέρημα τῆς πίστεως.'

7

꙳꙳꙳

The Assembly of the
Thessalonians:
Reflections on the Ecclesiology of
the Earliest Christian Letter

τῇ ἐκκλησίᾳ Θεσσαλονικέων

Paul addresses his letter τῇ ἐκκλησίᾳ Θεσσαλονικέων ἐν θεῷ
πατρὶ καὶ κυρίῳ Ἰησοῦ Χριστῷ (1 Thess. 1.1) The language
used in this epistolary prescript raises several critical
questions. a) How should the term ἐκκλησία be translated and
interpreted? Is the term being used with already developed
Christian ecclesiological connotations or does it mean
'assembly' in the sense that any citizen of Thessalonica would
understand? b) Why does the author(s) use the *nomen
gentilicium*, 'of the Thessalonians', instead of the name of the
city? Why is this the only instance where Paul refers to the
church of the population rather than referring to the church
in the city as in 1 Cor. 1.2; 2 Cor. 1.1; Phil. 1.1; Rom. 1.7? c)
In the phrase ἐν θεῷ πατρὶ καὶ κυρίῳ Ἰησοῦ Χριστῷ, what
does the apostle intend with the unusual reference ἐν θεῷ
πατρι?

During the period in which Paul writes this letter the term
ἐκκλησία can refer to a regularly summoned political body or to
a more general public gathering as is apparently the case in Acts

19.32.[1] Conflict between Pauline proclamation and proper attention to Artemis create the need for this public gathering in the theater of Ephesus. An assembly of this type would not be unusual either in Ephesus nor in Thessalonica, where the civil and the religious are closely interwoven and where one can accurately speak of a 'royal theology'.[2] Our thesis is that ἐκκλησία in 1 Thess. 1.1 is being used in such a general, civic manner rather than in a way suggesting a developed Christian understanding of ecclesiology.[3] That Paul has an actual assembly in mind is also suggested by 1 Thess. 5.27 and, perhaps, it is alluded to in the use of ἀπάντησις in 1 Thess. 4.17.[4]

Why is 1 Thess. 1.1 the only instance where Paul uses the *nomen gentilicium*, τῇ ἐκκλησίᾳ Θεσσαλονικέων? The genitive Θεσσαλονικέων occurs regularly as a legend on the coinage of Thessalonica. What is especially noteworthy for our present purposes is that on a coin dated to the end of the end of the first century BCE, the obverse depicts the laureate head of Julius Caesar with the legend ΘΕΟΣ while the reverse pictures a bare head of Octavian with the legend ΘΕΣΣΑΛΟΝΙΚΕΩΝ.[5] For the first time in the city's coinage a Roman is explicitly referred to as 'god'. Hendrix adds that although 'the title "son of god" (θεοῦ υἱός) does not appear with Octavian/Augustus on any of the coins, the juxtaposition of the Divine Julius with his son may reflect Thessalonican awareness of the Imperator's status as *divi*

---

[1] See R. F. Stoops, Jr, 'The Social Context of Acts 19.23–41', *JBL* 108 (1989), pp. 73–91; see also the discussion in A. N. Sherwin-White, *Roman Society and Roman Law in the New Testament* (Oxford: Oxford University Press, 1963), p. 87, and, R. MacMullen, *Enemies of the Roman Order. Treason, Unrest, and Alienation in the Empire* (Cambridge, MA: Harvard University Press, 1966), pp. 170–2.

[2] K. P. Donfried and I. H. Marshall, *The Theology of the Shorter Pauline Letters* (Cambridge: Cambridge University Press, 1993), pp. 19–23; also, K. P. Donfried, 'The Cults of Thessalonica and the Thessalonian Correspondence', *NTS* 31 (1985), pp. 336–56, especially pp. 347–52; also pp. 21–48 in this volume.

[3] H. Merklein, 'Die Ekklesia Gottes: der Kirchenbegriff bei Paulus und in Jerusalem', in *Studien zu Jesus und Paulus* (WUNT 43; Tübingen: Mohr, 1987), p. 313. 'Für Paulus bedeutet dies. Er kann (und muß?) seinen hellenistischen Lesern den traditionellen Begriff der <<Ekklesia Gottes>> vom profanen griechischen Begriff der Ekklesia-Versammlung her erklären.'

[4] See the further discussion below.

[5] H. L. Hendrix, *Thessalonicans Honor Romans* (ThD diss., Harvard 1984), p. 170.

filius and is perhaps indicative of local importance attached to it.'[6] There are other coins illustrative of this same tendency. Among the most extensively attested Thessalonian issues from the Augustan period is the laureate head of Augustus with the legend ΚΑΙΣΑΡ ΣΕΒΑΣΤΟΣ on the obverse and a laurel-wreath surrounding the legend of the city, ΘΕΣΣΑΛΟΝΙΚΕΩΝ, on the reverse.[7] Another of these coins portrays a bare head of Gaius on the obverse with the legend ΓΑΙΟΣ ΣΕΒΑΣΤΟΣ ΥΙΟΣ, while the reverse contains the head of Augustus with the city legend ΘΕΣΣΑΛΟΝΙΚΕΩΝ.[8] The Tiberian issues are quite similar: on the obverse one observes Tiberius' head with the legend ΤΙΒΕΡΙΟΣ ΚΑΙΣΑΡ ΣΕΒΑΣΤΟΣ and on the reverse a head of Livia-Demeter with the city legend ΘΕΣΣΑΛΟΝΙΚΕΩΝ as well as ΣΕΒΑΣΤΗ.[9]

In a previous study we have already explored the role of the gods, their importance as guardians of the city and the priesthood which stands at their service.[10] As Roman benefaction gains in importance for the citizens of Thessalonica, increasingly the Roman benefactors are included as objects of honor alongside the gods. During the first century BCE the goddess Roma is joined to the Roman benefactors and 'it is clear that in establishing a priesthood for Roma and the Roman benefactors, Thessalonians acknowledged her divine status'.[11] While conventions concerning Roma may have been borrowed from elsewhere, her status and function in Thessalonica is quite different; she is not granted honors as an independent figure nor was she specifically related to an individual such as Augustus, but rather 'she was grafted onto a previously existing object of honor, the Roman benefactors ... As an object of devotion she was linked inextricably to those Romans who tangibly benefited the city.'[12] According to Hendrix's understanding of this development, once Roma is

---

[6] Hendrix, *Thessalonicans Honor Romans*, pp. 170–2.
[7] Hendrix, *Thessalonicans Honor Romans*, p. 180.
[8] Hendrix, *Thessalonicans Honor Romans*, p. 181.
[9] Hendrix, *Thessalonicans Honor Romans*, p. 185.
[10] Donfried, 'The Cults of Thessalonica', pp. 342–6; also pp. 31–8 in this volume.
[11] Hendrix, *Thessalonicans Honor Romans*, p. 287.
[12] Hendrix, *Thessalonicans Honor Romans*, p. 287.

joined to the benefactors it now becomes easy for the priesthood of the gods to become associated with these Roman benefactors. Honors to the gods, Roma and the Roman benefactors become increasingly interrelated in the practice of the city.

The unequivocal numismatic designation of a Roman ruler as divine is 'an extension of Thessalonica's earlier policies of monumental recognition for distinguished Romans whose benefactions were important to the city ... because of his status as sole ruler and his supreme responsibility in assuring Thessalonica's well-being'.[13] Thus, 'Thessalonica added Augustus, his divine father and his successors to the honors granted "the gods and Roman benefactors" and "Roma and Roman benefactors".'[14] As a result of acknowledging 'the divine sanction of the new order'[15] a temple of Caesar is built and a priest and agonothete of the Imperator Augustus 'son of God' is appointed and now is given priority over the other priesthoods. Further, in 'every extant instance in which the "priest and agono-thete of the Imperator" is mentioned, he is listed first in what appears to be a strict observance of protocol. The Imperator's priest and agonothete assumes priority, the priest of "the gods" is cited next followed by the priest of Roma and Roman benefactors.'[16] The process of cult interaction and interrela-tionship proceeds, but it is clear at this point in the history of Thessalonica which office demanded superior attention. Superior attention is called for precisely because that 'particular strand of royal theology which is most apparent in Thessalonica's honorific activity is the attention paid to the legitimation of Augustus' rule and his successors'.[17] Hendrix also observes that 'Augustus' dynastic prospects were publicly acclaimed on coin types honoring Gaius and Tiberius. Numismatic honors previously granted only selectively became a conventional feature of the city's coinage. The impact of developments in royal theologies

[13] Hendrix, *Thessalonicans Honor Romans*, pp. 299, 308.
[14] Hendrix, *Thessalonicans Honor Romans*, p. 308.
[15] Hendrix, *Thessalonicans Honor Romans*, p. 310.
[16] Hendrix, *Thessalonicans Honor Romans*, p. 312.
[17] Hendrix, *Thessalonicans Honor Romans*, p. 311.

and religious activities directed to rulers which had been culti-
vated in certain quarters of the Hellenistic Greek world and late
Republican Rome are manifested clearly in the city's honors.'[18]

Given this background, we would suggest that when Paul
addresses his letter τῇ ἐκκλησίᾳ Θεσσαλονικέων he is in fact
writing to an actual assembly gathered in Thessalonica. That
Paul has this in mind is also evident from the closing of the letter
where the phrase 'all the brethren', and the fact that he wants this
letter read aloud suggest a public assembly. Yet for the apostle, it
is not an assembly of Thessalonians gathered in the name of
Roma and the Romans leaders as ΘΕΟΣ or *divi filius*, but an
assembly gathered ἐν θεῷ πατρὶ καὶ κυρίῳ Ἰησοῦ Χριστῷ. The
apostle is clearly distinguishing and separating two types of
assemblies in Thessalonica, each comprising different groups
of people with substantially different allegiances and loyalties.[19]

The incorporative language of 1 Thess. 1.1, ἐν θεῷ πατρὶ καὶ
κυρίῳ Ἰησοῦ Χριστῷ, unique to the epistolary prescript of this
letter among the unquestioned authentic letters of the apostle, is
of critical importance for Paul because it helps him make clear in
what ways this ἐκκλησία is different from other 'assemblies'
in Thessalonica. Only here among his letters does he indicate
that the church is 'in God'. Although, as we will note below, the
phrase 'in Christ' is typical in expressing the incorporation of
the Christian into the fullness of Christ, the incorporative phrase
'in God' is not. Why does Paul use it here? Precisely because the
Thessalonians to whom this letter is addressed have 'turned to
God from idols, to serve a living and true God, and to wait for his
Son from heaven ...' (1.9–10). This is in striking contrast to the
coinage of ancient Thessalonica! Because these Thessalonians are
'in God'[20] and 'in the Lord Jesus Christ' they are not like the
pagans 'who do not know God' (4.5); they will live in holiness

---

[18] Hendrix, *Thessalonicans Honor Romans*, p. 310.

[19] A similar distinction between ἐκκλησία as 'assembly' and ἐκκλησία as 'church' can be
found in Acts, for example, in Acts 19.39 and 20.17.

[20] Obviously this interpretation of ἐν as incorporative presupposes and includes the
instrumental sense, viz. the incorporation into God and Christ is because of what God
accomplished in and through life, death and resurrection of Jesus Christ.

(4.7); they are θεοδίδακτοι (4.9); and they need not grieve as the pagans do because 'God will bring with him those who have fallen asleep' (5.13). As a result of their faith and incorporation in God the assembly of the Thessalonians is differentiated sharply from other assemblies in that city.

That Paul is intentionally engaging and challenging the political, civic and religious structures of pagan Thessalonica is suggested at several points in the letter and it is in dialogue with such an environment that he advances his ecclesiology. In 1 Thess. 1.10, one is to wait for Jesus as *divi filius*; in 2.12 God calls the Thessalonian Christians 'into his own kingdom'; in 5.3 there is an assault upon the *pax et securitas* program of the early principate; and in the verses just preceding this disapproval one finds explicit political terminology: παρουσία, ἀπάντησις and κύριος. Milligan notes that παρουσία is related to 'the "visit" of the king, or some other official'.[21] Dibelius also urges that when used as court language παρουσία refers to the arrival of Caesar, a king or an official.[22] Best has shown that ἀπάντησις refers to the citizens meeting a dignitary who is about to visit the city.[23] These two terms are used in this way by Josephus (*Ant.* 11.327ff.) and also similarly referred to by such Greek writers as Chrysostom.[24] The term κύριος, especially when used in the same context as the two preceding terms, also has a definite political sense. As Deissmann has noted, the people in the eastern Mediterranean applied the term κύριος to refer to the Roman emperors from Augustus on, although the first verifiable inscription of the

---

[21] G. Milligan, *St Paul's Epistles to the Thessalonians* (New York: Macmillan, n.d.), pp. 145–8.

[22] M. Dibelius, *An die Thessalonicher I II, An die Philipper* (HNT 11; third ed.; Tübingen: Mohr, 1937), pp. 14–15.

[23] E. Best, *The First and Second Epistles to the Thessalonians* (London: Adam & Charles Black, 1972), p. 199.

[24] J. Eadie, *Commentary on the Greek Text of the Epistles of Paul to the Thessalonians* (New York. Macmillan, 1877), p. 170 adds. 'Theophylact, after Chrysostom, likens the meeting to a king's entrance into a city – all its aristocracy coming out to meet him. The meeting is one of welcome and praise.' One might ask whether ἐκκλησία as assembly in 1.1 has any connection with the use of ἀπάντησις in 4.17. Is there perhaps the sense that at the parousia there will be an ἐκκλησία of the living and the dead that will be assembled to meet the Lord at his parousia?

Kyrios-title in Greece dates to the time of Nero.[25] All of this, coupled with the use of εὐαγγελίον and its possible association with the eastern ruler cult, suggest that Paul and his associates could easily be understood as violating the 'decrees of Caesar' in the most blatant manner, exactly as Acts 17 indicates. Beginning with the phrase τῇ ἐκκλησίᾳ Θεσσαλονικέων and continuing throughout the letter, Paul takes up political language prevalent in Thessalonica and thoroughly reinterprets it for an evolving Christian community.

The Formation of Paul's Ecclesiology

It is likely, then, that Paul uses the secular term ἐκκλησία as a starting point precisely so that he can develop its theological and christological character and thus show how this assembly differs from the other assemblies of the Thessalonians. As is apparent in his use of the phrase τῶν ἐκκλησιῶν τοῦ θεοῦ τῶν οὐσῶν ἐν τῇ Ἰουδαίᾳ ἐν Χριστῷ Ἰησοῦ in 1 Thess. 2.14, the apostle is in touch with a very early conception of the church. Assisted by pre-Pauline ecclesial traditions[26] and a perspective represented in the apocalyptic writings found in Qumran,[27] Paul will develop his eschatological understanding of the church, viz. the arena in which God's revelation in Jesus Christ has become present and active and in which the Holy Spirit is preparing those called in holiness in anticipation of the eschatological consummation. The assembly of the Thessalonians is no longer a democratic association of like-minded citizens, but it is the gathering of those who are 'in Christ Jesus', a phrase that is intimately linked with baptism in the Pauline correspondence.

God the Father has called together the assembly being addressed in 1 Thess. 1.1! As a result, the theme of election is foundational for understanding the unique character of this

---

[25] A. Deissmann, *Light from the Ancient East* (New York. Doran, 1922), pp. 351–8.

[26] A similar perspective is shared by J. Roloff, *Die Kirche im Neuen Testament* (GNT 10; Göttingen. Vandenhoeck and Ruprecht, 1993), pp. 102–7.

[27] See the discussion in the section 'Paul's Ecclesiology in the Context of First-Century Judaism' of this essay.

assembly of Thessalonians in Christ. It is the true and living God who is the one present among his elect and suffering people and who is leading them to their promised salvation. This thematic emphasis in 1 Thessalonians is intended to distinguish the Thessalonian Christians from their pagan environment, to respond to the situations of persecution, and perhaps martyrdom, as well as to challenge them to effectuate the Christian life as God's elect in the midst of a pagan culture.

The motif of election is a key theological component of this letter. The concept is expressly found or referred to in the following texts: εἰδότες, ἀδελφοὶ ἠγαπημένοι ὑπὸ [τοῦ] θεοῦ, τὴν ἐκλογὴν ὑμῶν in 1.4; εἰς τὸ περιπατεῖν ὑμᾶς ἀξίως τοῦ θεοῦ τοῦ καλοῦντος ὑμᾶς εἰς τὴν ἑαυτοῦ βασιλείαν καὶ δόξαν in 2.12; ἐκάλεσεν in 4.7; and, πιστὸς ὁ καλῶν ὑμᾶς in 5.24. In all cases, except the second, these expressions are linked to the verb καλέω. In the case of ἐκλογή it is related to the verb ἐκλέγομαι. In attempting to determine Paul's intent in using the concept of 'calling' or 'election', the most telling use of the motif is found in 1.4. For our purpose Bruce's more literal translation of ἐκλογή is to be preferred: 'knowing as we do (the genuineness of) your election, brothers so dear to God'.[28] But what does Paul mean when he speaks of their 'election' or 'selection'?

Of the seven occurrences of the noun ἐκλογή in the New Testament, Paul, in addition to this reference, uses it elsewhere four times (Rom. 9.11; 11.5, 7, 28) and it always has the meaning of divine choice. It is closely related to בחר in the Old Testament, a verb that consistently refers to divine choice or selection (1 Chr. 16.13; Pss. 89.3; 105.6, 43; 106.5, 23; Isa. 42.1; 43.20; 45.4; 65.9, 15, 22). In comparing this noun to the terms derived from καλέω in 1 Thessalonians, it can be said that ἐκλογή, meaning God's choice, election or selection, is the prior term, and that καλέω marks the act of realizing and actualizing this prior divine choice. Paul reminds the Thessalonian Christians that God has chosen them and that as a result of that selection they must now live out

---

[28] F. F. Bruce, *1 and 2 Thessalonians* (WBC 45; Waco, Texas: Word, 1982), p. 10.

the consequences of that choice and accept the privileges and responsibilities of the call into the kingdom of God.

The election of the Thessalonians is manifested in and through the apostolic preaching accompanied by the work of the Spirit and in the joyful acceptance of God's word by them. It is the gospel that announces God's election and calls the Thessalonians into being the ἐκκλησία of God. As a result of this action of God and their reception of it, they *are* the church; they do not enter into the church![29]

Given the rhetorical purpose of 1 Thessalonians, Paul serves as the κῆρυξ[30] to the Thessalonian assembly via this letter. The heart of his message is to make a public pronouncement to the assembly: Τοῦτο γὰρ ὑμῖν λέγομεν ἐν λόγῳ κυρίου, ὅτι ἡμεῖς οἱ ζῶντες οἱ περιλειπόμενοι εἰς τὴν παρουσίαν τοῦ κυρίου οὐ μὴ φθάσωμεν τοὺς κοιμηθέντας.[31] This is not the place to discuss the role of the κῆρυξ in the assembly or among the mystery cults and the Stoics, but some of the similarities with 1 Thessalonians are striking.[32] The herald opens the assembly with prayer, his report or announcement always represents that of a higher power, he must be trustworthy and also participates in oath-making. This background may shed light on the unusually strong language employed by Paul in 1 Thess. 5.27: Ἐνορκίζω ὑμᾶς τὸν κύριον ἀναγνωσθῆναι τὴν ἐπιστολὴν πᾶσιν τοῖς ἀδελφοῖς. The sense of it is something like 'I solemnly command you by the Lord' or, perhaps, even more to the point 'I bind you by an oath'.[33] Paul wishes to extract an oath from his hearers that this letter will be read to the assembly; they are to swear this by the Lord. Why? Because Paul, as the κῆρυξ of God, is announcing a word from the Lord to the Thessalonian assembly. The impact of this oath-making is strengthened by previous language in the letter to the effect that the 'Lord is an avenger' (4.6) and that those who

---

[29] J. Roloff, *Die Kirche*, p. 140, has expressed this point cogently. 'Der Apostel hat das Evangelium so zur Geltung zu bringen, daß dadurch *ekklesia* entsteht.'

[30] The concept, but not the term κῆρυξ, is used in 1 Thessalonians.

[31] A more complete discussion can be found in Donfried and Marshall, *Theology*, pp. 2–63.

[32] See the discussion by G. Friedrich, 'κῆρυξ', *TDNT* 3.689.

[33] J. B. Lightfoot, *Biblical Essays* (London: MacMillan, 1893), pp. 251–69.

disregard the instructions of the Lord 'disregard not man but God' (4.2, 8).

Paul, the herald, had previously entered the assembly of the Thessalonians with the gospel, the word of the Lord.[34] Through the apostolic parousia of this letter[35] he is planning to enter for a second time with an important announcement from the Lord concerning the Lord's parousia, viz. the proclamation that this gathered assembly of the Thessalonians, together with those who have died, will shortly meet (ἀπάντησις) the Lord (4.13–18). Because of this announcement, because of 'these words' (τοῖς λόγοις τούτοις), the Thessalonian Christians will be able to comfort each other (παρακαλεῖτε ἀλλήλους) in the midst of their difficult situation.

These observations may be able to account for another striking phenomenon in 1 Thessalonians. Given the brevity of this communication, it is at first surprising to realize that the term 'gospel' [εὐαγγέλιον] is used six times (1.5; 2.2, 4, 8, 9; 3.2) and its synonym, 'word' (λόγος) is used three times (1.6, 8; 2.13). This is a rather high percentage when compared with, for example, Romans.[36] In 1 Thessalonians Paul makes the following assertions about the gospel as word of God.

- that the gospel was proclaimed in Thessalonica, not only in word, but also in power and in the Holy Spirit and in full conviction (1.5), i.e. it is a performative word and it is actively at work (ἐνεργεῖται) in and among the believers (2.13); as a generating center it is foundational for the creation and continued existence of the church;
- that the Thessalonian Christians received the word in the midst of affliction (1.6). In so doing they became imitators of Paul and his associates, as well as the Lord. Further, by receiving the word in the midst of affliction they received it

[34] Note the interesting use of the εἴσοδος language in 1 Thess. 1.9 and 2.1.

[35] R. W. Funk, 'The Apostolic *Parousia*. Form and Significance', in *Christian History and Interpretation. Studies Presented to John Knox*, ed. William R. Farmer, *et. al.* (Cambridge: Cambridge University Press, 1967), pp. 249–68.

[36] Εὐαγγέλιον occurs nine times in Romans (1.1, 9, 16; 2.16; 10.16; 11.28; 15.16, 19; 16.25) and λόγος specifically as 'word of God', appears only once (9.6).

with joy inspired by the Holy Spirit (1.6); this is itself a sign of hope even if the Thessalonian Christians had not fully recognized it as such. Paul also acknowledges this existential situation when he asserts in 2.2 that he declared to them 'the gospel of God in the face of great opposition';

- that the word has proceeded out of Thessalonica to all the believers in Macedonia and in Achaia. In 1.8 Paul writes. 'For not only has the word of the Lord sounded forth from you in Macedonia and Achaia, but your faith in God has gone forth everywhere, so that we need not say anything.' As a result, whether intentionally or not, the Thessalonian church became a missionary base for the gospel. Despite the difficulty of their situation, the gospel, especially because it is the word of the suffering and risen Lord, has burst forth from Thessalonica in such a powerful way that they have become an example (τύπος, 1.7) to all the believers in Macedonia and Achaia. Perhaps Paul is wishing to suggest that they were not only a model in suffering but also, precisely because of their willingness to suffer, an example, an actualization, even if imperfectly, of that hope which is present in their midst now, although its consummation still lies in the future;
- that this gospel has been entrusted to Paul by God for the purpose of proclamation (2.4);
- that this gospel is something which is 'shared' by Paul with the Thessalonians and it is proclaimed without burden to them because Paul 'worked night and day' (2.8–9). In other words, he did not make demands of his new converts, even though he was an apostle;
- Timothy is God's servant in the gospel of Christ. It is Paul's hope as well as Timothy's that when the Christian community in Thessalonica is more thoroughly rooted in the gospel the result will be a firmer establishment, encouragement and stabilization of their faith in the midst of their current afflictions.

At the heart of the apostle's proclamation, then, is a God who is described as 'a living and true God', who raised his Son, Jesus, from the dead, with the resultant claim that this action will deliver the Thessalonian believers from the 'wrath' to come.[37] The intention of God goes beyond protecting the Christians from wrath; it includes salvation. Thus Paul can say in 5.9: 'For God has not destined us for wrath, but to obtain salvation through our Lord Jesus Christ.' The description of their present situation as one of waiting 'for his Son from heaven' underscores a pattern of 'already – not yet'. Already now, in the present, God acts decisively in the revelation, death and resurrection of his Son, but the imminent consummation, the approaching deliverance of 'the wrath to come' and the fulfillment of the promise of salvation is yet to occur.

The Thessalonians have heard and responded to the call of *this* God, as had Paul and his co-workers before them. Their response is in the form of having 'faith (πίστις) in him' (1.8), in turning to him rather than to the idols of Thessalonica (1.9) and in having courage in him (2.2). In light of this the term ἐκκλησία connotes a new meaning: the Thessalonian Christians are now a 'called out' community,[38] the church (ἐκκλησία), which is always a church '*in* God the Father and the Lord Jesus Christ' (1.1), and, as a result, they are now in fellowship with all the churches *of God*, including those in Macedonia, Achaia and Judea (2.14). Because of God's continual presence (3.9; 4.8, 17), Paul gives thanks, prays for and remembers the Thessalonian congregation without ceasing (1.2; 2.13; 3.9). As a result of these marvelous actions by God on behalf of the Thessalonians and because this living and true God is constantly present, the apostle can urge the Thessalonians to 'rejoice always, pray constantly, give thanks in all circumstances' (5.16–18).

---

[37] In 1 Thessalonians Paul uses the term 'God' [θεός] thirty-six times; in addition, God is described as 'Father' five times. The term 'Lord' [κύριος] is found some twenty-four times. In one-half of these cases it refers explicitly to Jesus (e.g. Lord Jesus Christ) and it is probable that Jesus is also the referent in the other twelve cases. Thus, there is no unambiguous reference to God as 'Lord'. When a distinction is intended, it is frequently one between 'God our Father' and the 'Lord Jesus Christ' (e.g. 1.1; 1.3; 3.11, 13).

[38] Etymologically ἐκκλησία derives from ἐκ and καλέω, meaning those who are called out. While we have no indication that Paul was aware of this etymological derivation, much in 1 Thessalonians explicitly supports such an understanding of the term.

Why does Paul take so much time to discuss the marvelous effect of his past εἴσοδος and proclamation of the gospel? Precisely to demonstrate to the disheartened Thessalonian Christians that the word of the Lord which the apostolic herald Paul is now announcing will be even more extraordinary in its effect than the original gospel. They will be with the Lord forever! God 'is faithful, and he will do it' (5.24). If the original Word established an ἐκκλησία in God and Christ, one from which the word was proclaimed so powerfully, then God's new word through Paul to the assembled Christians in Thessalonica will serve as a powerful encouragement in the midst of their loss of loved ones and in the presence of continuing persecution.

ἐν Χριστῷ

As we have already had opportunity to observe, the Thessalonian Christians are referred to as the elect because they are called forth by God through the Spirit-filled gospel; as a result, God gives 'his Holy Spirit to you [plural]' (4.8). This is why Paul can state that this elect, 'called out' community is '*in* God the Father and *in* the Lord Jesus Christ' (1.1). This new state of affairs is possible because 'Christ died for us' (5.9–10) and because of their faith (1.8; 2.13). Most often Paul refers to this new relationship *in* God and *in* Christ simply as ἐν Χριστῷ (2.14; 4.16;) or ἐν κυρίῳ (3.8; 5.12). Although it is not always easy to distinguish an instrumental from an incorporative meaning, we tend to view these references as belonging to the later category. In other words, this phrase means not only that the Christian community was brought into existence by God the Father and the Lord Jesus Christ through the preached word, but that there also exists a mystical and spiritual union with the Father and the Son made real through participation in the church as the eschatological 'called out' community which waits for the last day.[39] Fitzmyer has suggested the following different nuance between ἐν Χριστῷ and

---

[39] G. A. Deissmann, *Die neutestamentliche Formel 'in Christo Jesu'* (Marburg: N. G. Elwert, 1892).

ἐν κυρίῳ: 'Paul tells the Christian to become "in the Lord" what one really is "in Christ".'[40] As is clear from 1 Thess. 2.13 (ἐνεργεῖται ἐν ὑμῖν τοῖς πιστεύουσιν), the dynamic influence of Christ upon the Christian is fundamental.

The terms 'in Christ', 'in the Lord' and 'in the Holy Spirit' (1.5) are likely derived from a pre-Pauline baptismal tradition in which the emphasis on salvation is accentuated. For Paul these concepts are embedded in his manner of seeing and interpreting things apocalyptically and their meanings can only be derived from that perspective. When the apostle emphasizes in 1 Thess. 4.16 that the dead are 'in Christ' he affirms that the communion with Christ inaugurated at baptism will not conclude with death but will continue right up to the final meeting with the Lord at the parousia. Paul takes the original soteriological-ontological sense of 'in Christ' and links it specifically to the eschatological hope that he is attempting to make known to the downcast Thessalonian Christians. In 2.14 ('For you brethren became imitators of the churches of God in Christ Jesus which are in Judea') the ἐν Χριστῷ can also carry a broader meaning beyond simply being incorporated into Christ. Here the imitation of Christ in terms of suffering in persecution is accented and in 3.8 the motif of holding firm to the end (to 'stand fast in the Lord') is stressed.[41] What allows one to be 'in Christ' and to remain 'in Christ', particularly during adverse conditions, is the working of God's Spirit. Spirit, in the sense of God's Spirit, appears in 1 Thess. 1.5, 6; 4.8; 5.19. It is not only a sign of God's election and a source of one's soteriological and ontological placement 'in Christ', but also, and especially, a wellspring of joy in the midst of suffering. Since the Spirit continues to be given to them in the present (note the use of the present participle διδόντα in 4.8), it serves as the advocate and sustainer of the Christian congregation

---

[40] J. A. Fitzmyer, *Paul and His Theology. A Brief Sketch* (Englewood Cliffs, NJ: Prentice Hall, 1989), p. 90

[41] 'In the Lord' is used in 5.12 primarily in an instrumental sense within a larger context of ethical exhortation, but one should certainly not exclude the locative dimension; the context of 'in the Lord Jesus' in 4.1 and 'in Christ Jesus' in 5.18 are again ethical – the will of God is manifested in Jesus.

from its inception, in and through persecution, right up to the parousia. Therefore Paul warns in 5.19 that the Spirit dare not be quenched. In various ways, then, we can observe how Paul's parousia-hope allows the apostle both to actualize and transform the christological tradition he receives in ways that are appropriate to the circumstances in Thessalonica.

To be among the elect, to be ἐν Χριστῷ, is to be holy (ἐν ἁγιασμῷ; 1 Thess. 4.3, 4, 7). The context for living such a life 'in holiness' is provided for in the 'called out' community.[42] In it, those who are God-taught (4.9) receive God's sustaining and nurturing will and sanctification as they wait to inherit the kingdom (2.12). Although awaiting the future consummation, these believers are cognizant that this sanctified life must be lived out in the present; as members of the new, eschatological community of the end-time they must become exemplary in their love for one another. They are to build up one another as well as to engage in manual work because of the outsiders (4.9–12); they must not only strive to gain the respect of those outside the community, but there must be a healthy distance from them (1 Thess. 4.10–12). Those external to the 'called out' community are described, as we have noted, in a variety of ways: as idolaters (1.9–10); as those who oppose the gospel (2.14, 16); as those who are involved in πορνεία (4.3); as those who do not know God (4.5); and, as those who are without hope, and, as a result, grieve for those who have died (4.13).

For Paul, the God who elected and destined the believers for salvation also possesses a 'will' (θέλημα) which is to guide the Christians during this time of waiting. Not only is rejoicing, praying and giving thanks an expression of 'the will of God' (5.18), but also abstaining from 'unchastity' (4.3). To do the will of God is to please God (2.4; 4.1) and one dimension of that is 'to lead a life worthy of God, who calls you into his own kingdom and glory' (2.12). Pleasing God is doing the 'will of God, your sanctification [ἁγιασμός]' (4.3). For Paul, the Thessalonians already know what it means 'to lead a life worthy of God' because

---

[42] Note the similarity with Qumran: 1QM 10.10.

153

they have 'been taught by God [θεοδίδακτοι]' (4.9). Paul's ethical advice, given at several points in 1 Thessalonians, is thus a reminder of that which they already have been taught by God, the God who gives 'his Holy Spirit to you' (4.8). God's choice of the Thessalonian Christians, announced by Paul through the gospel and responded to in faith, is to be realized and actualized, despite all external adversities, through a lifestyle informed by love and established in hope. Repeatedly it becomes evident that Paul is in the process of transforming the non-Christian use of the term ἐκκλησία into a theologically descriptive reality for this congregation, viz. those who are 'called out' from among the citizens of Thessalonica (1.1) and are 'called into' the kingdom.

Paul urges the Christians in Thessalonica to love the brethren 'more and more' (4.9–10) and to 'encourage one another [παρακαλεῖτε ἀλλήλους] and to build one another up [οἰκοδομεῖτε εἰς τὸν ἕνα]' (5.11). 'Building-up' will become a key metaphor for Paul's understanding of the church in 1 Corinthians (8.1; 10.23, 14.3–5, 12, 17, 26 and elsewhere). To 'build-up' the church is for the believers to encourage one another to grow in sanctification, i.e. to produce spiritual maturity and stability, a theme that runs throughout the letter. The upbuilding and encouragement of the church is an ongoing and dynamic process. Strengthened by the gospel and uplifted by the coming of the Lord, the sanctified community is ever enabled to demonstrate the lordship of Christ throughout the world (ἐν παντὶ τόπῳ ἡ πίστις ὑμῶν ἡ πρὸς τὸν θεὸν ἐξελήλυθεν, 1.8) in word and deed.

The church of the Thessalonians is in relationship to the Father, to the Son and to the Holy Spirit (1.1–5), to other churches (1.8; 2.14) and to the apostle who first declared to them the gospel of God. Paul not only gives thanks for this community (1.2; 2.13; 3.9) but also prays for, consoles, exhorts, remembers and agonizes over them (1.2–13; 3.1). The intensity of the relationship between the founder and the believers is due to the fact that through their baptism they belong to one and the same eschatological family. Family structures, although transformed in Christ, are basic to the internal structure of the community and its relationship to the apostle. Because this is the case Paul can employ traditional kinship patterns in his association with the Thessalonian family; he is in solidarity with them as brother, father, nurse, orphan, or as beloved.

Although family structures lie at the heart of this new family in Christ, can anything further be said about the structures of leadership within this Thessalonian fellowship in Christ? Even though Paul does not accentuate the 'demands' (1.7) that Silvanus, Timothy and he might have made of the Thessalonians and even though Paul uses the phrase 'apostles of Christ' (1.7) in the plural, which certainly is not intended to emphasize his individual apostolic authority, there can be little doubt about his authoritative relationship. Paul has been 'approved by God' and 'entrusted with the gospel' (2.4); he can be gentle, consoling and encouraging, yet he can also admonish and adjure (ἐνορκίζω) 'by the Lord' (5.27).

As Paul has encouraged, exhorted and cared for the Thessalonian Christians, so they ought to act toward one another. But such a task requires leadership and guidance and it is to this subject that Paul turns in 5.12–13. 'But we beseech you, brethren, to respect those who labor among you and are over you [προϊσταμένους] in the Lord and admonish you, and to esteem them very highly in love because of their work.' From these verses it is apparent that there was leadership in this Thessalonian church, whatever form it may have taken, and that it is a leadership 'in the Lord'. It is a position not for self-aggrandizement or power, but one of service in the Lord who has suffered on behalf of all (5.10). This becomes the model for the kind of influence they are to exercise. These persons 'labor' on behalf of the others, they are 'over you' and they are 'those who ... admonish you'. Harnack argued these persons who 'toil, govern and admonish' are specifically 'office bearers of the congregation' who presumably had an 'appointment'.[43] Although this is an overstatement of the evidence, that the προϊστάμενοι are more than helpers is strongly suggested

---

[43] A. von Harnack, 'ΚΟΠΟΣ', *ZNW* 27 (1928), pp. 1–10. See further the positive evaluation of Harnack's position given by E. E. Ellis, *Prophecy and Hermeneutic* (Tübingen: Mohr, 1978), pp. 5–7.

by the inclusion of the function of 'warning' or 'exhorting' (νουθετέω) among their responsibilities. Horsely's examination of an inscription from Ephesus (c. 162–4 CE) that uses the term προΐστημι suggests 'the ease with which Graeco-Roman urban dwellers accepted the compatibility of the two notions of benevolent actions and structured authority'.[44] Also not irrelevant to this discussion is the reference to this same verb in 1 Tim. 3.4–5 where the role of the ἐπίσκοπος is being reviewed. 'He must manage his own household well, keeping his children submissive and respectful in every way, for if a man does not know how to manage [προστῆναι] his own household, how can he care for God's church?' Given the kinship and familial dimensions of Paul's relationship to the Thessalonian congregation, this role of leadership within that family should come as no surprise. Paul served as both benefactor and authoritative leader to this new family in Christ and it is essential that these functions continue in his absence. As these responsibilities are carried out by the leaders in their midst, the Thessalonian Christians are to esteem them 'very highly in love' (5.12). The same kind of affectionate relationship that existed between Paul and the Thessalonians should exist between the leaders and the people.

Paul's Ecclesiology in the Context of First-Century Judaism

As we have observed, Paul speaks τῶν ἐκκλησιῶν τοῦ θεοῦ τῶν οὐσῶν ἐν τῇ Ἰουδαίᾳ ἐν Χριστῷ Ἰησοῦ in 1 Thess. 2.14. Lying behind this plural reference to the 'churches of God' is the phrase ἐκκλησία τοῦ θεοῦ (1 Cor. 1.2; 10.32; 11.22; 15.9; 2 Cor. 1.1; Gal. 1.13) and this may well reflect the earliest Christian use and, in all likelihood, the self-designation of the early Jerusalem church itself.[45] This original term was then applied in the plural

---

[44] G. H. R. Horsely et al., New Documents Illustrating Early Christianity, 7 vols (North Ryde, NSW: Macquarie University, 1976–94), 4.74–82.

[45] L. Cerfaux, The Church in the Theology of St Paul (New York. Herder, 1959), pp. 95–117; P. Stuhlmacher, Gottes Gerechtigkeit bei Paulus (FRLANT 87; Göttingen, Vandenhoeck and Ruprecht, 1965), p. 211, n. 2: 'ἐκκλησία (τοῦ) θεοῦ scheint also doch eine alte Bezeichnung der Urkirche gewesen zu sein'.

to other churches as well (1 Thess. 2.14; 2 Thess. 1.4; 1 Cor. 11.16, 22). Stuhlmacher sees a parallelism between this usage of the singular and plural. 'das Verhältnis von essenischer Stammesgemeinde und Tochtergemeinden, die gemeinsam das eschatologische Bundesvolk darstellen'.[46] Several scholars[47] have urged that the formulation may be a translation of קהל אל, signifying the eschatological company of God, found in the Qumran texts 1QM 4.10 and 1QSa 2.4. In its wider context, 1QM 4.10 reads: 'When they set out for battle they shall write . . . on the sixth standard *Assembly of God* . . ., and they shall write the list of their names with all their order.'[48] Here one of the standards to be carried into the eschatological war will bear the title '*Assembly of God* . . .' In 1QSa 2.4 we find these words: 'And no man smitten with any human uncleanness shall enter the assembly of God; no man smitten with any of them shall be confirmed in his office in the congregation.'[49]

If the earliest Christian usage of ἐκκλησία τοῦ θεου derives from קהל אל as found in this apocalyptic environment, then the older position held by L. Rost[50] (and others)[51] is in need of revision. He urged that ἐκκλησία is derived from the Septuagint. However, קהל is translated in the Septuagint by both ἐκκλησία and συναγωγή; further, the Septuagint translates קהל יהוה with ἐκκλησία κυρίου or συναγωγὴ κυρίου, whereas the New Testament uses ἐκκλησία τοῦ θεοῦ. Certainly the Septuagint's ἐκκλησία τοῦ κυρίου would have been more appropriate to the double God and Christ references in the Pauline letters. Understanding קהל אל as a *technicus terminus* would help explain this unusual usage in earliest Palestinian Christianity. Although

[46] Stuhlmacher, *Gerechtigkeit*, p. 211, n. 2 [ET: 'the relationship between the Essene main community and their affiliates who together represent the eschatalogical people of the covenant'].

[47] K. Stendahl, 'Kirche, Im Urchristentum', *Die Religion in Geschichte und Gegenwart* (Tübingen: Mohr, 1959) *RGG* 3.1297–1304; Stuhlmacher, *Gerechtigkeit*, p. 211, n. 2; Fitzmyer, *Paul and His Theology*, pp. 95–6.

[48] G. Vermes, *The Dead Sea Scrolls in English* (New York: Penguin, 1995), p. 129.

[49] Vermes, *Dead Sea Scrolls*, p. 121.

[50] *TDNT*, 3.529, n. 90.

[51] See the superb critique of this position by J. Y. Campbell, 'The Origin and Meaning of the Christian Use of the Word ΕΚΚΛΗΣΙΑ', *JTS* 49 (1948): pp. 130–42.

קהל is infrequent in Qumran, when it is used it is in an exclusively eschatological sense. To refer to the community as a whole, or to the present manifestation of the community, it uses עדה (LXX = συναγωγή) and יחד.

In addition to the suggestion that the pre-Pauline use of ἐκκλησία τοῦ θεοῦ is similar to the phrase קהל אל found in the Dead Sea Scrolls, Paul's description of the church in 1 Thessalonians suggests acquaintance with concepts that are also evident in the Qumran community. Since 1 Thessalonians stands closest to the period of the pre-Christian Paul among the Pauline letters, the question arises quite naturally as to the kind of Judaism that may have influenced Paul.

In addition to the eschatological/apocalyptic contexts of each, there are other remarkable similarities between the Paul of 1 Thessalonians and the Qumran Community, including election and the calling of God, holiness/sanctification, the light/day–night/darkness contrasts, and the wrath/salvation dualism. For example, ἐκλογή, found only in 1 Thessalonians (1.4) among the Pauline letters,[52] shows an intimate connection with the Essenes who also regarded themselves as 'those chosen by (divine) benevolence' (1QS 8.6).[53] This is exactly what ἐκλογή is expressing in 1 Thessalonians, supplemented by the phrase ἀδελφοὶ ἠγαπη-μένοι ὑπὸ [τοῦ] θεοῦ. Previously I have written 'that Paul's teaching on justification is nothing other than his teaching on election, sharpened by his theology of the cross, and applied to a series of polemical situations';[54] in other words, justification is one way to articulate the controlling concept of election. Once this is recognized, then it becomes necessary to examine in detail the relationship between Paul and the Qumran Community not only in terms of their shared use of these concepts, but also with regard to such other inextricably interwoven concepts as sin, works of the law and salvation. It is likely that the influence of the Qumran community, rather than the Pharisaic–rabbinic tradition as

---

[52] It is also found in Acts 9.15; Rom. 9.11; 11.5, 7, 28; 2 Pet. 1.10.

[53] J. A. Fitzmyer, *Romans* (AB 33; New York: Doubleday), p. 605.

[54] Donfried, *Theology*, p. 66.

W. D. Davies and others have argued,[55] is determinative in shaping much of Paul's perspective of Judaism. This is true not only for categories such as election, but also for sin, which he uses in a way fundamentally uncharacteristic of the rabbinic tradition, as well as for Torah. Now in view of 4QMMT not only the phrase 'some of the deeds of the law' but also the relationship of this phrase to 'righteousness' can be seen anew and in a way not affirmative of the interpretations urged by Dunn and Gaston.[56]

How does one explain these commonalties between 1 Thessalonians and the community of Qumran?[57] Critical is the question raised by Fitzmyer. 'Where and how would he [Paul] have come into contact with this non-Pharisaic Palestinian Judaism, which some of the items in his theological teaching echo?'[58] Is the specific terminology and the broader conceptual similarities between the two mediated through earliest Christianity or was the pre-Christian Paul already influenced by the prophetic movement of the Qumran community? Since this community had a settlement in Jerusalem (by the Essene gate in the south of the city) as well as attracting followers throughout Palestine, contact between Paul and this movement is likely. Hengel suggests that the contact took place in Jerusalem when Paul studied at the Pharisaic בית מדרש.[59] In Josephus' *Vita* he shares a desire not only to study the teachings of the Pharisees and Sadducees, but also those of the Essenes. Would Paul, the inquisitive and highly intelligent 'graduate student' in Jerusalem, be any less motivated to be in dialogue with the teachings of the

[55] W. D. Davies, *Paul and Rabbinic Judaism: Some Rabbinic Elements in Pauline Theology* (Philadelphia: Fortress Press, 1965).

[56] See the discussion in K. P. Donfried, *The Romans Debate* (Peabody, MA: Hendrickson, 1991), pp. 299–326.

[57] To emphasize in this context the similarities is not intended to minimize the substantial differences between Paul and the Qumran community. The most glaring difference between the two is the coming together of Jews and Gentiles in Christ, so evident in 1 Thessalonians.

[58] J. A. Fitzmyer, 'Paul's Jewish Background and the Deeds of the Law', in *According to Paul: Studies in the Theology of the Apostle* (New York: Paulist Press, 1993), pp. 18–35, especially p. 35.

[59] M. Hengel, *The Pre-Christian Paul* (London: SCM Press; Philadelphia: Trinity Press International, 1991), p. 42. Further, he suggests that 1 Cor. 1.20 (σοφός [חכם], γραμματεύς [ספר], συζητητής [דרש]) gives insight into the milieu of this Pharisaic school.

Qumran community? To pursue this question forces to the forefront the issue of the pluralistic environment of Jerusalem prior to the 'progressive "unification"[60] of Palestinian Judaism under the guidance of the rabbinic scribes after 70 CE.

The exploration of Paul's dialogue with pluralistic pre-70 Judaism raises other questions. We know that Paul was a Pharisee and yet at key points he breaks with that tradition. Was there a predisposition to do so even prior to his call on the road to Damascus? Could he have received encouragement for such a move as a result of his contact with the prophetic movement of the Qumran community? Talmon's recent work is suggestive. He understands the Community of the Renewed Covenant as a 'third- or second-century crystallization of a major socio-religious movement which arose in the early post-exilic Judaism ... The development of the movement runs parallel to that of the competing rationalist stream which first surfaces in the book of Ezra, and especially in the book of Nehemiah, and will ultimately crystallize in Rabbinic or normative Judaism.'[61] And, he adds, the 'yahad's final dissent from the emerging brand of Pharisaic Judaism at the turn of the era constitutes the climax of the lengthy confrontation of these two streams'.[62] Does Paul's contact with the Community of the Renewed Covenant (יחד) facilitate his own dissent from the brand of Pharisaic Judaism that had shaped his own spirituality? Does this tension within Judaism predispose him toward the Jesus movement and its proposed solution to the very issues that had been and were still central to Paul's own religious reflection?

Concluding Observations

We began our observations on the ecclesiology of 1 Thessalonians by entering the pagan world of first-century

[60] Hengel, *The Pre-Christian Paul*, p. 44.

[61] S. Talmon, 'The Community of the Renewed Covenant. Between Judaism and Christianity', in *The Community of the Renewed Covenant: The Notre Dame Symposium on the Dead Sea Scrolls*, ed. E. Ulrich and J. VanderKam (Notre Dame, Indiana: University of Notre Dame Press, 1994), pp. 3–24.

[62] Talmon, 'The Community of the Renewed Covenant', p. 22.

Thessalonica and we concluded by observing some links with first-century Judaism. How does all of this fit together?

During the early 40s, the Thessalonian Christians had experienced suffering and death, probably as a result of an ad hoc persecution that resulted from the perceived threat posed by this community to the existing religious/civic cults of the city. By his emphasis on election the apostle assures these Christians that they have been chosen and loved by the God whose Son suffered, died, was raised and will come again in glory. It is this God who allows them to be his ἐκκλησία, and who continues to be present in their midst, encouraging, strengthening and calling them to fidelity. This declaration, with its emphasis on hope in the parousia of Jesus, will allow them to endure with assurance the daily tribulations that confront them. By announcing a specific prophetic word, Paul affirms that the proclamation of the death and resurrection of Jesus is a pledge that those who have died in Christ will not be forgotten at the parousia; they will, in fact, rise first, then those who are still alive. Together, then, this assembly of all the Thessalonians who are ἐν Χριστῷ will meet the Lord at his coming. The Lord's parousia gives meaning and encouragement to the suffering and hopeless Thessalonians. Moreover, this message of encouragement is given additional meaning by the emphasis placed on the new, called-out community in Christ, as well as to the ethical implications and expectations of such a distinct, corporate existence in the midst of a hostile and pagan world. The Spirit-filled gospel of faith, love and hope is the foundation of the church; in faith it calls the church into being, in love it permits the fellowship of believers to serve as a proleptic kingdom community and in hope it is assured of victory despite all the contrary signs that daily threaten to disable it. Certainly the goal and intention of this letter is to console and to encourage a desolate and discouraged people.

To emphasize the differences between their new existence in Christ from their former pagan idolatry, Paul skillfully takes up language and thought-patterns that these former pagans were familiar with and which still surround and encircle them. Primary among these is the phrase τῇ ἐκκλησίᾳ Θεσσαλονικέων. The remainder of the letter carefully transforms this language in light of God's revelation in Christ and explains to them how different their new existence '*in* God the Father and *in* the Lord Jesus Christ' is from their former existence. To help the Christians of Thessalonica grasp more fully their new life in Christ with all of its incorporative power, the apostle draws heavily upon pre-Pauline Christian tradition and a type of apocalyptic Judaism represented in the writings of the Qumran community.

8

❦

The Epistolary and Rhetorical Context of 1 Thess. 2.1–12

The Problem

One of the specific problems that this SNTS Seminar has set out to examine is how 1 Thess. 2.1–12 functions within the letter and in what ways epistolary and rhetorical criticism might assist us in addressing this question.

Since many scholars have argued that this text functions as an *apology* it will be useful to give a definition of this term so that we might attempt to avoid unnecessary ambiguity in our discussions: 'A work can be called an apology provided its content throughout aims at presenting a defense in answer to accusations against a certain person or group of persons or at overcoming or preventing opinions adverse to them.'[1]

A review of the literature suggests at least three major ways in which 1 Thess. 2.1–12 has been understood as an apology. 1) as an apology against specific opponents and concrete attacks. Some further specify it as an apology: a) against a Jewish attack;[2] b) against libertanists and gnostics who deny the resurrection;[3] 2) as

---

[1] J. A. Goldstein, *The Letters of Demosthenes* (New York: Columbia,1968), p. 98.

[2] R. A. Lipsius, 'Über Zweck und Veranlassung des ersten Thessalonicherbrief', *ThStKr* 27 (1854), pp. 905–34; J. E. Frame, *A Critical and Exegetical Commentary on the Epistles of St Paul to the Thessalonians* (ICC; New York: Scribners, 1912); W. Neil, *The Epistle of Paul to the Thessalonians* (Naperville: Allenson, 1957); B. Rigaux, *Saint Paul. Les Épîtres aux Thessaloniciens* (EtB; Paris-Gembloux: Gabalda-Duculot, 1956).

[3] W. Lütgert, 'Die Volkommenen im Philipperbrief und die Enthusiasten in

an apology determined by Paul's inner feelings;[4] 3) as an apology influenced by its hellenistic culture: a) determined by the milieu of wandering Cynic-Stoic philosophers, although there may not be a specific challenge that prompts the apology, or;[5] b) determined by the established rhetorical topos of the serious Cynic that wishes actually to dissociate his message from those of other wandering preachers.[6]

The last position (3b) has been especially argued by A. Malherbe in his now well known essay 'Gentle As a Nurse'. He lists a number of terms that are shared by Dio Chrysostom and Paul such as ἀγών, παρρησία, κενός, ἤπιος and βάρος. The real question is whether these terms share a similar field of meaning in the two different contexts. With regard to βάρος, for example, Malherbe comments that a 'special complaint is that the transients were sometimes brutally harsh rather than seeking to benefit their hearers'.[7] Further on we will suggest that Paul is using this phrase in a markedly different way. While Malherbe's essay provides much useful comparative material, it does not directly help us assess whether, based on these parallels, 1 Thess. 2.1–12 is an apology or not. For, on the one hand, he appears to suggest that Dio is contrasting his own philosophical ethos with

---

Thessalonich,' *BFChTh* 13 (1909), pp. 547–654; W. Hadorn, 'Die Abfassung der Thessalonicherbriefe auf der dritten Missionsreise und der Kanons des Marcion', *ZNW* 19 (1919–20), pp. 67–72; W. Hadorn, 'Die Abfassung der Thessalonicherbriefe auf der dritten Missionsreise des Paulus', *BFChTh* 24 (1919), pp. 157–284; B. Reicke, 'Thessalonicherbriefe', *RGG*³ 6.851–53; W. Schmithals, 'The Historical Situation of the Thessalonian Epistles', in *Paul and the Gnostics* (Nashville: Abingdon, 1972), pp. 128–318.

[4] E. von Dobschütz, *Die Thessalonicher-Briefe* (KEK X; Göttingen: Vandenhoeck and Ruprecht, [1909] repr. 1974).

[5] M. Dibelius, *Die Briefe des Apostels Paulus. II. Die Neun Kleinen Briefe* (HNT; Tübingen: Mohr, 1913); also speaking against a specific attack are von Dobschütz, *Die Thessalonicher-Briefe*, and A. Oepke, *Die Briefe an die Thessalonicher* (NTD 8; repr. of 1933 ed.; Göttingen: Vandenhoeck and Ruprecht, 1970).

[6] A. Malherbe, ' "Gentle as a Nurse": The Cynic Background to 1 Thess ii', in A. J. Malherbe, *Paul and the Popular Philosophers* (Fortress Press: Minneapolis, 1989), pp. 35–48 [originally in *NovT*12 (1970), pp. 203–17], followed by W. Marxsen, *Der erste Brief an die Thessalonicher* (ZB; Zürich: Theologischer Verlag, 1979); G. Friedrich, '1–2 Thessalonians', in J. Becker, H. Conzelmann and G. Friedrich, *Die Briefe an die Galater, Epheser, Philipper, Kolosser, Thessalonicher und Philemon* (NTD; Göttingen: Vandenhoeck and Ruprecht, 1981); H.-H. Schade, *Apokalyptische Christologie be Paulus* (GTA 18; Göttingen: Vandenhoeck and Ruprecht, 1981).

[7] Malherbe, 'Gentle as a Nurse', p. 45.

specific 'hucksters in mind'[8] and that 'there is no question of his having to defend himself against specific charges that he was a charlatan'.[9] But, then, on the other hand, he proceeds to say that in 'view of the different types of Cynics who were about, it had become desirable, when describing oneself as a philosopher, to do so in negative and antithetic terms. This is the context within which Paul describes his activity in Thessalonica. We cannot determine from his description that he is making a personal apology.'[10]

In the subsequent literature there have been several criticisms of Malherbe's proposal both by those who agree and those who disagree that 1 Thess. 2.1-12 is an apology. Wolfgang Stegemann, who stands in opposition to any form of the apology hypothesis, is extensive in his criticism of both Dibelius and Malherbe. Understanding Dibelius as drawing a vague relationship between Paul and the Cynics[11] and Malherbe a more specific one,[12] he criticizes both: 'Eine sprachliche Nähe zum kynischen Wortschatz muß also auch hier nicht zwangsläufig auf denselben Topos apologetischer Rhetorik verweisen.'[13] Traugott Holtz, who vigorously defends the apology position, is, however, in agreement: 'Indessen ist die Analogie deshalb nicht überzeugend, weil Dio tatsächlich popularphilosophischer Wanderprediger war und das natürlich auch wußte, während Paulus das nicht war und das ebenfalls wußte.'[14] Stegemann insists that one must inquire

---

[8] Malherbe, 'Gentle as a Nurse', p. 46.

[9] Malherbe, 'Gentle as a Nurse', p. 37.

[10] Malherbe, 'Gentle as a Nurse', p. 48.

[11] W. Stegemann, 'Anlaß und Hintergrund der Abfassung von 1Th 2,1-12', in *Theologische Brosamen für Lothar Steiger*, ed. Gerhard Freund and Ekkehard Stegemann (DBAT 5; Heidelberg, 1985), p. 398: 'Er rechnet also mit einer durch das "Milieu" bedingten Apologie, die durchaus keines aktuellen Anlasses bedurft habe.'

[12] Stegemann, 'Anlaß und Hintergrund', p. 399: 'Jedenfalls läßt sich für die von MALHERBE herangezogenen Beispiele nich ausschließen, daß sie auf reale, konkrete Vorwürfe reagieren.'

[13] Stegemann, 'Anlaß und Hintergrund', p. 399 [ET: 'A linguistic proximity to Cynic vocabulary must not necessarily point to the same topos of apologetical rhetoric'].

[14] T. Holtz, *Der erste Brief an die Thessalonicher* (EKK XIII; Zürich: Benzinger, 1986), p. 93, n. 422 [ET: 'Nevertheless the analogy is not persuasive since Dio was, in fact, a popular wandering philosopher and was indeed aware of this fact, whereas Paul was not and likewise was aware of this fact.']

about a 'spezifische Anlaß in den Verhältnissen der Gemeinde in Thessalonich diesen Text des 1. Thessalonicherbriefes motiviert haben könnte.'[15] Once again Holtz agrees with this, although he and Stegeman see the situation very differently: 'So muß seine Abgrenzung einen aktuellen Anlaß haben.'[16] Can one read 1 Thess. 2.1–12 in a mirror fashion so that the antithetical formulations are indications that Paul is countering charges made against him by opponents either within or outside of the church in Thessalonica? Lyons, seeing this text more broadly as an 'autobiography', indicates that any attempt to go beyond the current impasse must take into account that how 'an author approached his autobiography depended upon his relationship with his audience, the social setting of which and for which he wrote, and, most importantly, his intention (τέλος/*causa*) in writing'.[17] We now turn to the question whether epistolary criticism is able to assist in determining this *causa*?

The Epistolary Context

Particularly since Paul Schubert's study, *Form and Function of the Pauline Thanksgivings*,[18] the phrase 'form-critical analysis' has been used in a broad way. Charles Wanamaker reminds us that this phrase contains three originally distinct components:[19]

1. *Formal literary analysis* is primarily concerned with the study of 'formulaic features of ancient letters' such as the forms occurring at the opening and closing of an ancient letter, and

---

[15] Stegeman, 'Anlaß und Hintergrund', p. 401

[16] Holtz, *An die Thessalonicher* p. 93, n. 422. Similar is the criticism of J. Lambrecht, 'Thanksgivings in 1 Thessalonians 1–3', in *The Thessalonian Correspondence*, ed. R. F. Collins (BETL 87; Leuven: University Press, 1990), pp. 203–4; now also in *The Thessalonians Debate: Methodological Discord or Methodological Synthesis?*, ed. K. P. Donfried and J. Beutler (Grand Rapids/Cambridge: Eerdmans, 2000), pp. 135–62.

[17] G. Lyons, *Pauline Autobiography: Toward a New Understanding* (SBLDS 73; Atlanta: Scholars, 1985), p. 61.

[18] P. Schubert, *Form and Function of the Pauline Thanksgivings* (BZNW 20; Berlin: Töpelmann, 1939).

[19] C. A. Wanamaker, 'Epistolary vs. Rhetorical Analysis: Contradictory or Complementary?' in *The Thessalonians Debate: Methodological Discord or Methodological Synthesis?*, ed. K. P. Donfried and J. Beutler (Grand Rapids/Cambridge: Eerdmans, 2000), pp. 255–86.

other formulae involved either within the letter body or at its beginning and ending. Stowers refers to this as 'studies of structure and form'.[20]

2. *Thematic analysis* refers to the study of 'epistolary *topoi* or commonplace themes such as friendship and paraenesis, and the stock motifs which were used in relation to these themes'.[21]

3. *Form-critical analysis* attempts to isolate primary oral forms such as doxological units and paraenetic formulae which have been incorporated in the letters as written forms, but which received their shape in other, more oral contexts, such as the liturgy and the instruction of baptismal candidates. 'The fact that letters functioned in part as surrogates for oral communication encouraged the preservation of these traditions'.[22]

These various dimensions of the epistolary analysis of New Testament, Greco-Roman, Hebrew and Aramaic letters are invaluable for the understanding of these writings in many respects. John L. White, to cite one example, summarizes the components isolated by formal literary analysis:[23]

Opening
Address: Paul, an apostle of Jesus Christ, to the church of God at
____, sanctified (beloved, called, etc.) in Christ
Grace greeting: Grace to you and peace from God our Father and the Lord Jesus Christ.
Thanksgiving prayer: I thank God (always) for (all of) you, because of ..., and I pray that the Lord may make you increase (mature) in such activity so that you may be pure and blameless when Christ returns.

Body
Introductory formula: I want you to know, brethren, that... (I/we do not want you to be ignorant, brethren, that/of...). Or: I appeal to you, brethren, that ...
Transitional formulas: Often indicated by Paul's use of the vocative, 'brethren', and with request/disclosure phrases.
Concluding section/Paul's Apostolic Presence section

---

[20] Wanamaker, 'Epistolary vs. Rhetorical Analysis', pp. 256–7.

[21] Wanamaker, 'Epistolary vs. Rhetorical Analysis', p. 257.

[22] D. Aune, *The New Testament in Its Literary Environment* (LEC 8; Philadelphia: Westminster Press, 1987), p. 192.

[23] J. L. White, 'Ancient Greek Letters', in *Graeco-Roman Literature and the New Testament*, ed. D. E. Aune (SBLRBS 21; Atlanta: Scholars, 1988), p. 97.

1. Autobiographical (authoritative) reference to the letter and expression of confidence in the recipients' willingness to comply with Paul's instruction.
2. Identification/recommendation of Paul's messenger.
3. Announcement of Paul's anticipated (hoped for) visit.
4. Paraenetic section: Reminder of Paul's instruction, reference to Paul's/the congregation's former conduct, appeal to the example of Christ.
5. Prayer of Peace.

Closing

Closing greetings: from (to) third parties

The Holy Kiss greeting

Grace benediction: the grace of our (the) Lord Jesus Christ be with you (your spirit).

While valuing highly the many helpful letter components that have been identified, one must still inquire whether an epistolary analysis can help us discern, with substantial precision, the specific intentions, particularly the oral intentions, of the letter.[24] Such ambiguity, when it exists, can be attributed to the inability of this methodology to properly identify the parameters of the 'body' of the letter.

Such inexactitude with regard to the letter 'body' is highlighted in Paul Schubert's monograph, *Form and Function of the Pauline Thanksgivings*. The thanksgiving is a formal section in most of Paul's letters, normally concluding the letter opening and setting forth themes that will be taken up in the remainder of the letter. Simultaneously, Schubert concludes that 'the thanksgiving itself constitutes the main body of 1 Thessalonians. It contains all the primary information that Paul wished to convey'. In fact, he continues, 'the thanksgiving *is* the letter'.[25] Jan Lambrecht takes issue with what he considers to be Schubert's arbitrary classification of the pattern of the Pauline thanksgivings and the exclusion of 1 Thessalonians 4 and 5 from the 'body' of the letter. A similar concern is raised by David Aune in his suggestion that 1 Thessalonians 'is the only Pauline letter in which the

---

[24] K. Berger, 'Hellenistische Gattungen im Neuen Testament', *ANRW* II.25.2:1291, reminds us: 'Wie für die Briefe des Demosthenes, so gilt schließlich auch für die des Paulus: Sie sind Reden in Briefform.'

[25] Schubert, *Form and Function*, p. 26.

"concluding" hortatory section (4.1–5.22) constitutes the main part'.[26] Lambrecht issues a warning that needs to be heeded: 'The danger, however, lies in exaggeration, in increasingly inventive speciousness, in too much, often far-fetched and strained, genre hunting. One might wonder whether Paul consciously starts in 2.1 the body of his letter, deliberately composes in 2.17–3.13 an apostolic *parousia* or really intends in 2.1–12 and 2.17–3.8 a twofold epistolary recommendation.'[27]

As is evident from John Hurd's analysis of 1 Thessalonians, a too precise application of these identifiable components can lead to an overconfidence with regard to the structure of the letter. He suggests that this first letter of Paul 'has the *normal structure* [italics mine] of a Pauline letter: sender(s), recipient(s), greeting (1.1), thanksgiving (1.2–10), body (with renewed thanksgiving (2.1–16), apostolic visitation (2.17–3.13), paraenesis (4.1–5.22), blessing (5.23–24), and autograph coda (5.25–28)'.[28] The concept of a 'normal' letter with regard to the 'body' has not been demonstrated as can be seen by the vastly divergent views of what the parameters of the 'body' are in 1 Thessalonians.[29]

John White recognizes the limitations of epistolary analysis of the Pauline letters when he writes: 'Regarding the body portion of Paul's letters, common features are less evident than in the opening and closing. The recurrence of major motifs, and of an identifiable structure, seems to be limited to the closing section of the body.' When he continues that where 'the introductory part of the body is concerned, Paul introduces the message with

---

[26] Aune, *NT in Its Literary Environment*, p. 206.

[27] Lambrecht, 'Thanksgivings', in *Thessalonians Debate*, pp. 135–62. Note also I. H. Marshall, *1 and 2 Thessalonians* (NCBC; Grand Rapids: Eerdmans, 1983), p. 8: 'This characterisation of both sections of the letter [apostolic apology and apostolic *parousia*] is justified in terms of their content and the parallels detected with similar material in other letters. However, a closer analysis of the parallels suggests that it is over-precise and perhaps misleading to think of these as two specific "formal" parts of Pauline epistles which constitute structural elements in them. It would appear rather to be the case that here we have two themes which recur – for good contextual reasons – in various of Paul's letters in which he naturally expresses himself in similar ways.'

[28] J. C. Hurd, Jr, 'Thessalonians, First Letter to the,' *IDB* 4.900.

[29] See the chart in R. Jewett, *The Thessalonian Correspondence: Pauline Rhetoric and Millenarian Piety* (FFNT; Philadelphia: Fortress Press, 1986), p. 220.

conventional epistolary phrases: a disclosure formula in five cases (Romans, 2 Corinthians, Galatians, Philippians and 1 Thessalonians) and a request formula in the two remaining letters (1 Corinthians and Philemon)', two immediate questions come to mind: 1) whether to mark the beginning of the 'body' purely on the basis of conventional epistolary phrases is accurate; and, 2) whether the category 'body' is sufficiently vague and abstract to not only be unhelpful but perhaps misleading as well.

White moves in the right direction when he recognizes that the 'theological body is characterized by dialogical and argumentative features that are especially influenced by oral rhetorical traditions. The individual letters, or certain parts of them, reflect the influence of one or another type of argumentation.' Still, the limitations of this approach become evident when, without the benefit of a formal rhetorical analysis, White urges that 'hortatory reminder, and a paraenetic style, characterizes 1 Thessalonians'.[30]

Given the inability of epistolary criticism to provide a formal and structural analysis of the 'main body' of the letter, it can provide little assistance in solving the conundrum related to 2.1–12. Thus, we must ascertain whether a more sustained application of rhetorical criticism helps to illuminate the function of 1 Thess. 2.1–12 within the letter.

The Rhetorical Context

It is a major contention of this analysis that an awareness of the social situation in Thessalonica and a consideration of the structure of the letter itself will greatly assist the task of understanding the theology of 1 Thessalonians. The structure of a letter can be analyzed by employing the methodologies commonly referred to as epistolary and rhetorical criticism, analytical tools that can help determine Paul's intentions in writing this letter. The former explains how parts of letters are constructed; the latter, that is, Greco-Roman rhetorical criticism,

---

[30] White, 'Ancient Greek Letters', p. 99.

allows us to see more vividly why the letter is constructed the way it is as well as giving us further insight into the lived situation of the letter.[31] As we have resisted the imposition of existing epistolary categories on 1 Thessalonians, so we must be equally cautious to avoid a similar situation in the application of rhetorical criticism, especially when we are alert to the fact that this letter is a first attempt in Christian letter writing.

Theology, structure and social situation are closely interwoven in 1 Thessalonians and other Pauline letters. Thus rhetorical criticism can, by using its analytical tools, alert us not only to distinct emphases in a given letter but also to certain dimensions in the rhetorical situation, which gives suggestions about the larger social situation, that might otherwise have been overlooked. To recognize, for example, which of the three types (*genera*) of rhetoric, deliberative, judicial or epideictic, a document is tending towards already gives important clues both to its social situation as well as its intention. While being sensitive to the fact that there may be an overlap between these *genera*, it is useful to know that the proper time for deliberative rhetoric is the future, that the appropriate time for epideictic rhetoric is primarily the present, though often with reference to both the past and the future, and that the appropriate time for judicial rhetoric is the past. To be precise in identifying the different types of rhetoric, it is critical to note the standard topics that are common to each. For epideictic rhetoric these are primarily praise (for example, 1 Thess. 2.1–12) and blame (for example, 1 Thess. 2.14–16) and in deliberative rhetoric these standard topics are advantage and honor, namely, that which is expedient and/or harmful to the intended recipients. Thus the identification of these and other 'strategies of persuasion' will allow us to gain 'greater understanding of the author, the audience, and the author's purpose in communicating with the audience'.[32]

---

[31] For a further discussion see F. W. Hughes, *Early Christian Rhetoric and 2 Thessalonians* (JSNTSup 30; Sheffield: JSOT Press, 1989), pp. 19–50; and S. K. Stowers, *Letter Writing in Greco-Roman Antiquity* (Philadelphia: Westminster Press, 1986).

[32] F. W. Hughes, 'The Social Situations Implied by Rhetoric', in *Thessalonians Debate*, p. 243.

Understanding 1 Thessalonians as primarily an epideictic letter allows for some significant conclusions both about what Paul intended and what he did not intend to communicate. On the one hand, recognizing 1 Thessalonians as belonging to the epideictic genus of rhetoric allows us to see that the Thessalonian Christians have become the object of Paul's praise. Hughes summarizes the matter well:

> In fact, the strong use of epideictic rhetoric, as compared with deliberative and judicial rhetoric, reveals a great deal about the intention of the author in writing the letter. Epideictic rhetoric classically focused on the development of persuasive writing based on values held in common between the rhetor and the audience. Although Paul, like other persuasive writers, was quite capable of using features drawn from all the *genera* of persuasion, the fact that he did not do so in 1 Thessalonians would recommend the centrality of the epideictic topics of praise and blame to what he was trying to accomplish in the letter. Instead of praising the beauty of a mountain or river or of some honorific dead person, the apostle chose to modify this *genus* of rhetoric slightly, so that the recipients of the letter themselves were the object of Paul's praise. Paul's emphasis on praise reinforced the joyful relationship between the Thessalonians and their founder that had existed for some time – though the relationship was troubled by Paul's non-presence in Thessalonica during the congregation's recent difficulties, characterized by the deaths of some in the Thessalonian church. Paul's persuasive response to this bereaved congregation is to praise their faithfulness and love, to explain in an affective manner the reasons for his absence from the city (2.17–3.10), to confirm the teaching that he had given (the first two proofs: 4.1–8 and 4.9–12), and to add instruction that he had not conveyed previously (such as the material in 4.13–5.3). This additional direction is specifically not identified by the apostle as prior teaching but rather as revelation, as a 'word of the Lord' (4.15).
>
> Such a persuasive response, coupled with the skillfully crafted triad of virtues in 1.3, the listing of the *propositiones* in the *partitio* (3.11–13), including their careful and subtle recapitulation in the *peroratio* (5.4–11), all suggest that Paul either learned rhetoric in school or had developed an extraordinary gift for the subject in which he grasped the appropriateness of various rhetorical precepts for his letter without ever having formally learned them.[33]

On the other hand, since 1 Thess. 2.1–12 does not contain any explicit and sustained charges against Paul this letter cannot be categorized as belonging to the judicial genus of rhetoric. In

---

[33] Hughes, 'Social Situations', in *Thessalonians Debate*, pp. 252–3.

judicial rhetoric such charges would have to be taken up and defended in the *probatio* (proof) which is exactly what does not happen. While 1 Thess. 2.17–3.10 may possibly suggest some concerns about Paul's premature departure from Thessalonica, certainly one cannot, as a result of this understandable worry, conclude that Paul is arguing against opponents in this letter.

Although Greco-Roman rhetorical theory does not focus significantly on letters, the actual practice of rhetoric did include letters. Therefore one can speak of a 'rhetorical letter' and, perhaps, add that in terms of epistolary genre 1 Thessalonians approximates, but is not identical with, ancient letters of consolation. In terms of rhetorical genus there is a clear connection with epideictic rhetoric. Not unimportant for this particular linkage is the fact that among the two most important categories of the epideictic genus of rhetoric is the funeral speech (ἐπιτάφιος) and consolatory speech (παραμυθητικός). Paul's intention in writing 1 Thessalonians is, as we have urged,[34] to console a Christian community suffering the effects of persecution and death, to encourage the discouraged.

What follows is an abridgment and slight modification of the rhetorical structure of 1 Thessalonians proposed by F. W. Hughes:[35]

I. *Exordium* [Introduction] (1.1–10)
  A. Epistolary prescript (1.1)
  B. Thanksgiving prayer (1.2–10)
II. *Narratio* [Narrative[36]] (2.1–3.10)
  A. Introduction to *narratio* (address) (2.1)
  B. A description of Paul's first visit to the Thessalonians (2.1–16)
  C. Paul's desire for a second visit (2.17–3.10)
III. *Partitio* [Statement of Propositions[37]] (stated as an intercessory prayer; 3.11–13)

---

[34] See the discussion in K. P. Donfried, 'The Cults of Thessalonica and the Thessalonian Correspondence', *NTS* 31 (1985), pp. 336–56; also pp. 21–48 in this volume. And, further, in K. P. Donfried and I. H. Marshall, *The Theology of the Shorter Pauline Letters* (Cambridge: Cambridge University Press, 1993).

[35] F. W. Hughes, 'The Rhetoric of 1 Thessalonians', in *The Thessalonian Correspondence*, ed. R. F. Collins (BETL 87; Leuven: University Press–Peeters, 1990), pp. 94–116.

[36] Cicero in *Inv.* 1.27 defines the *narratio* in this way: 'The narrative is an exposition of events that have occurred or are supposed to have occurred.'

[37] In the *Rhet. Her.* 1.17 it is explained that this exposition or statement of proposition 'consists in setting forth briefly and completely, the points we intend to discuss'.

A. First petition: (transition from *narratio*): the topic of Paul's desired journey to the Thessalonians (3.11)
B. Second petition: the topics of the three-part *probatio* introduced (3.12–13)
  1. First topic: 'increase in love' (3.12–13)
  2. Second and third topics: 'being preserved at the Parousia' (3.13)
    a. Second topic: 'to establish your hearts blameless in holiness'
    b. Third topic: 'at the coming of our Lord Jesus Christ with all his saints'

IV. *Probatio* [Proof] (4.1–5.3)
  A. First proof: 'how it is necessary to walk and to please God' (4.1–8)
  B. Second proof: 'concerning brotherly love' (4.9–12)
  C. Third proof: 'concerning those who have fallen asleep' (4.13—5.3)
V. *Peroratio* [Epilogue] (5.4–11)
  A. Transition from previous section (5.4)
  B. Honorific description of Thessalonians (5.5)
  C. First consequence of description: wakefulness (5.6)
  D. Reasons for consequence: association of sleeping and drunkenness with night (5.7)
  E. Second consequence of argument: preparation for action (5.8–10)
  F. Third consequence of argument: console one another (5.11)
VI. Exhortation (5.12–22)
  A. Introduction of exhortation (5.12)
  B. First exhortation: concerning church order (5.12)
  C. Second exhortation: concerning church discipline (5.14–22)
VII. Final Prayers and Greetings (Epistolary Conclusion) (5.23–28)
  A. Intercessory prayer (5.23–24)
  B. A request for prayer (5.25)
  C. Final greetings (5.26–27)
  D. Final prayer (5.28)

1 Thessalonians 2.1–3.10 as Narratio

2.1   A. Introduction to *narratio* (address): 'For you know, brothers, our εἴσοδος to you' (see 1.9).

2.1–16 B. A description of Paul's first εἴσοδος to the Thessalonians

2.1   1. Negatively: 'not in vain'

2.2–16 2. Positively

2.2a   a. The prehistory of the visit: Paul's disaster in Philippi
    i) 'we had suffered'
    ii) 'we were shamefully treated'

	iii) The readers' relationship to the Philippi incident: 'you know'
2.2b	b. The visit to Thessalonica itself
	i) Statement of Paul's activity
	A) Summary: 'we had courage in our God to declare to you the gospel of God in the face of great opposition'
2.3–8	B) Concerning Paul's activity in Thessalonica
2.3	1) Stated negatively (concerning Paul's παράκλησις)
2.4	2) Stated positively (concerning Paul's apostolic office)
2.5	3) Stated negatively (concerning Paul's rhetorical methods)
2.6	4) Stated negatively (concerning Paul's motivations)
	5) Stated positively (concerning Paul's right as an apostle)
2.7	6) Stated positively (concerning Paul's activity as a pastor)
2.8	7) Summary of Paul's activity
	a) Statement: 'we were ready to share with you not only the gospel of God but also our own selves'
	b) Reason for activity: (relationship with readers) 'because you had become very dear to us'
2.9–12	C) Concerning Paul's behavior at Thessalonica (description of the ἦθος of Paul)
2.9	1) Paul as hardworking
	a) Calling of witnesses: 'For you remember, brethren'
	b) Statement of description: 'we worked night and day'
	c) Motive of Paul: 'that we might not burden any of you'
2.10	2) Paul as moral

		a) Calling of witnesses
		(A) 'you'
		(B) 'God also'
		b) Statement of description: 'how holily and righteously and blame-lessly'
2.11–12	3) Paul as fatherly	
2.11		a) Calling of witnesses: 'For you know how'
2.11–12		b) Statement of description: 'like a father with his children, we exhorted each one of you'
2.13–16	D) Concerning the Thessalonians' behavior	
2.13		1) In regard to reception of the gospel...
2.14–16		2) In regard to suffering...
2.17–3.10	C. Paul's desire for a second εἴσοδος	

An Overview of the Narratio

According to Quintilian the *narratio* 'consists in the persuasive exposition of that which either has been done, or is supposed to have been done'.[38] He and other rhetoricians urge that 'it should be lucid (*lucidam*), brief (*brevem*), and plausible (*verisimilem*)'.[39] Aristotle allows that the speaker may introduce himself and his adversary as being 'of a certain moral character'.[40] He also observes that the function of the *narratio* in epideictic rhetoric pertains 'most appropriately to the present, for it is the existing conditions of things that all those who praise or blame have in view. It is not uncommon, however, for epideictic speakers to avail themselves of other times, of the past by way of recalling it, or of the future by way of anticipating it.'[41]

The *narratio* builds upon the *exordium* and the latter functions both as a *captatio benevolentiae* and to introduce themes that will

[38] *Inst.* 4.2.31.
[39] *Inst.* 4.2.31–32.
[40] *Rhet.* 3.16.10.
[41] *Rhet.* 1.3.4.

be expanded further on in the discourse. Several themes mentioned in the *exordium* (Paul's behavior (1.5), the sufferings of Paul (1.6), the sufferings of the Thessalonians (1.6) and Paul's missionary intention (1.9) are elaborated further in the *narratio*. As the *narratio* is dependent on the *exordium*, so is the *probatio* dependent on the foundation laid by the *exordium*, *narratio* and *partitio*.

In studying the relationship between the *exordium* and the *narratio*, one observes that the integrity of Paul's past behavior is both a significant factor that led to the gospel's being accepted with full assurance (1.5; see 2.13) during his first visit and that that same integrity will also allow his current *paraclesis* to be accepted with the same full assurance. The power and effectiveness of the word is intimately linked with the credibility of the messenger; the truth of the divine logos is demonstrated by his ethos, that is, by Paul's embodiment of the gospel, and by his divine authorization (2.4, δεδοκι-μάσμεθα).[42] For these reasons, what is said in 1 Thessalonians, and especially, as we shall see, in the prophetic word announced by him in 4.15, is to be acknowledged as valid and authoritative.

It will be our contention that the first part of the *narratio* (2.1–16) of 1 Thessalonians is neither apologetic nor polemic, a fact that is confirmed by the absence of any charges or suspicions against Paul in the *probatio*. This first part of the narratio functions in the following three ways:

• It recounts the relationship of friendship established between Paul and the Thessalonians during the time of his founding visit (εἴσοδος, 1.9; 2.1), whereas the second part of the *narratio*, 2.17–3.13, concerns their relationship since Paul's departure (ἔξοδος) from Thessalonica and their separation (ἀπορ-φανισθέντες, 2.17).

[42] B. Henneken, *Verkündigung und Prophetie im 1. Thessalonicherbrief* (SBS 29; Stuttgart: Katholisches Bibelwerk, 1969), pp. 101 and 105, citing A. M. Denis, 'L'Apôtre Paul, prophete "messianique" des Gentils. Etude thématique de 1 Thess., II,1–6', *ETL* 33 (1957), pp. 245–318.

- The first part of the *narratio* serves to distinguish Paul's gospel and ethos from the error and delusion surrounding the Thessalonian Christians, specifically, from the idolatry of the heathen, namely, their false or non-existent understanding of God (4.5, τὰ ἔθνη τὰ μὴ εἰδότα τὸν θεόν). As a result these pagans have no hope and succumb to grief (4.13). It is this non-knowledge of God that leads to what Denis has called *l'erreur eschatologique*,[43] an error to which Paul must address his prophetic word in 4.15. One can understand much of 1 Thessalonians as a consistent clarification and application of what had taken place during Paul's first εἴσοδος when he reminds them that ἐπεστρέψατε πρὸς τὸν θεὸν ἀπὸ τῶν εἰδώλων δουλεύειν θεῷ ζῶντι καὶ ἀληθινῷ (1.9).

- The *narratio* also presents characteristics of Paul's ethos that the apostle will develop further in the *probatio*, especially in 4.1, 'Finally, brothers, we ask you and urge you in the Lord Jesus that, as you learned from us how you ought to live and to please God (as, in fact, you are doing), you should do so more and more.' Schoon-Jansen comments appropriately: '1 Thess. 2, 1–12 ist im Sinne unserer Definition keine Apologie, sondern die Beschreibung eine vorbildlichen Verhaltens, das die Gemeinde zur Nachahmung ermuntern soll.'[44]

Selected Exegetical Observations Within Part I of the Narratio *Concerning Paul's* εἴσοδος *(2.1–2)*

The *narratio* begins in 2.1: Αὐτοὶ γὰρ οἴδατε, ἀδελφοί, τὴν εἴσοδον ἡμῶν τὴν πρὸς ὑμᾶς ὅτι οὐ κενὴ γέγονεν. Three matters call for comment:

---

[43] Denis, 'L'Apôtre Paul, prophete "messianique" des Gentils', pp. 274–5.

[44] J. Schoon-Janßen, *Umstrittene 'Apologien' in den Paulusbriefen: Studien zur rhetorischen Situation des 1. Thessalonicherbriefes, des Galaterbriefes und des Philipperbriefes* (GTA 45; Göttingen: Vandenhoeck & Ruprecht, 1991), p. 64. In principle, K. Berger, 'Hellenistische Gattungen', p. 1287, evaluates this dimension of the text correctly, although the term 'Mahnrede' is an overstatement of Paul's intent and has the potential of misunderstanding 1 Thessalonians as primarily a paraenetic letter: 'Auch in 1 Thess 2,1–12 sind weder Anklage vor Gericht noch auch überhaupt ein bereits erfolgter persönlicher Angriff vorauszusetzen. Der Text ist – angesichts der Bedeutung des Motivs der Nachahmung des Lehrers in philosophischen Lehrbriefen – auch bereits voll verständlich als Mahnrede an "Schüler", die Paulus, ihr persönliches Vorbild, nachahmen sollen.'

1. As in other literature of antiquity, the possible offensiveness of autobiographical comments is reduced by using the 'we' or 'our', where 'I' or 'my' might have been expected. 'In this way', suggests Lyons, 'the corporateness and mutuality rather than the uniqueness of a claim appear to be emphasized.'[45]

2. The strong relationship between the meaning of εἴσοδος in 2.1 to the content of the εἴσοδος referred to 1.9, ἐπεστρέψατε πρὸς τὸν θεὸν ἀπὸ τῶν εἰδώλων δουλεύειν θεῷ ζῶντι καὶ ἀληθινῷ. Although he does not use this exact term again, the apostle in 3.10 is very much hoping for another εἴσοδος among the Thessalonians; however, since that is not immediately possible his letter must, in effect, be at least a temporary substitute until that new εἴσοδος may be possible. He very much hopes that the reception of this speech act will be as positive as the first reception of the word among them (for example, 1.9; 2.13).

3. What does Paul mean when he describes his εἴσοδος in 2.1 as οὐ κενή? How is one to translate οὐ κενή? As 'in vain' with the NRSV, as 'fruitless' with the REB, or as 'without effect' with the NAB or as 'pointless' with the NJB? The use of οὐ κενή here in 2.1 is different from its use in 3.5 where the concern is with 'the fruit of his labors'; here the concern is with 'the character' of his labors in Thessalonica.[46] A translation of οὐ κενή as 'has not been found empty' is to be recommended. The emphasis, then, is placed on the content of Paul's preaching and life rather than on its result. Rather than being 'empty', Paul's εἴσοδος had these characteristics:

- it was preceded by suffering;
- it was distinguished by boldness of utterance;

[45] G. Lyons, *Pauline Autobiography*, p. 69.

[46] J. Eadie, *Commentary on the Greek Text of the Epistles of Paul to the Thessalonians* (New York: Macmillan, 1877), p. 55.

- it was identified by absence of deceit, of uncleanness and of guile;
- it was identified by fidelity, by gentleness and disinterested self-denying love;
- it was marked by continuous and affectionate labor and toil.

That all of this had result, that it bore fruit, as suggested in 2.13, is not to be denied, but one must recognize that this is not the primary point being made in 2.1. 'Das Adjektive κενή bezeichnet also in diesem Kontext einen Mangel an Authentizität, die fehlende Übereinstimmung von Verkündigung und Existenz-weise des Verkündigers selbst.'[47] Precisely because this is not the case Paul negates the adjective κενή and emphasizes the <u>οὐ</u> κενή, that is, the *character* of his work in Thessalonica.

Paul wishes to stress the character and fullness of his entrance, as opposed to its vacuity, by reminding his readers about the prehistory of his visit, namely, the distress he experienced in Philippi: 'we had suffered', 'we were shamefully treated'. Following this he incorporates the reader's relationship to these events by adding 'you know'. Yet despite this state of affairs he reminds his audience in 2.2b that ἐπαρρησιασάμεθα ἐν τῷ θεῷ ἡμῶν λαλῆσαι πρὸς ὑμᾶς τὸ εὐαγγέλιον τοῦ θεοῦ ἐν πολλῷ ἀγῶνι. As we will suggest, this narrative is preparing for the words of encouragement that will be expanded in the *probatio*.

Not only does ἐπαρρησιασάμεθα play a significant role here, but also the insistent emphasis on ἐν τῷ θεῷ ἡμῶν. Despite having suffered cruelty and indignity in Philippi, Paul had the courage to preach the gospel in Thessalonica. Clearly his ability to proceed with assurance to this capital city of Macedonia despite these obstacles comes from God; it is part of the divine purpose of election (τὴν ἐκλογὴν ὑμῶν, 1.4) and that is why the apostle's message during his original εἴσοδος was received with πληρο-φορίᾳ πολλῇ. In this narrative section Paul is laying a foundation for his paraclesis, for a new form of εἴσοδος that is being

---

[47] Stegemann, 'Anlaß und Hintergrund', p. 403 [ET: 'In this context the adjective κενή represents a lack of integrity, a lack of consistency between the proclamation and the behavior of the proclaimer himself.']

communicated to this community. The intention of his encouragement is taking shape: just as hardships and persecutions had not deterred him so, too, should similar exigencies not deter the believers in Thessalonica from their fidelity to God.

Concerning Paul's Activity in Thessalonica (2.3–8)

In verse 3 Paul states negatively that his παράκλησις did originate ἐκ πλάνης οὐδὲ ἐξ ἀκαθαρσίας οὐδὲ ἐν δόλῳ. Three items require our consideration: παράκλησις, ἐκ πλάνης, and ἀκαθαρσίας.

1) παράκλησις In addition to the noun παράκλησις, the verb παρακαλέω is used eight times in this brief letter.[48] Thus, in 1 Thess. 5.9–11 Paul can write: 'For God has not destined us for wrath, but to obtain salvation through our Lord Jesus Christ, who died for us so that whether we wake or sleep we might live with him. Therefore encourage [παρακαλεῖτε] one another and build one another up, just as you are doing.' The concentration on this word group is not unusual given the fact that 1 Thessalonians has much in common with a λόγος παραμυθητικός, a word of consolation and encouragement to a Christian church suffering the effects of persecution.[49] Παραμυθέουαι is used only in 1 Thess. 2.12 and 5.14 within the Pauline corpus. In fact the advice given in 5.14, 'encourage [παραμυθεῖσθε] the fainthearted', is not far from the mark in describing the intention of the letter as one of encouragement to the discouraged. They are discouraged precisely because 'hope' has become disengaged from their faith as a result of unexpected deaths in their midst. The preservation of 1 Thessalonians in the canon is a testimony to its effectiveness in correcting, through encouragement, this atmosphere of hopelessness among some in the church of Thessalonica. Paul's intention in writing 1 Thessalonians resembles Second Isaiah's announced intention in 40.1: 'Comfort

---

[48] 2.12; 3.2, 7; 4.1, 10, 18; 5.11, 14.
[49] See Donfried, 'The Cults of Thessalonica'.

[παρακαλεῖτε], comfort [παρακαλεῖτε] my people, says your God.'
The use of παράκλησις coheres with the interpretation of 1 Thessalonians as a λόγος παραμυθητικός. When Paul refers to ἡ γὰρ παράκλησις ἡμῶν in 2.2 he means not only 'the words but also the disposition of the one who proclaimed them – his freedom won through persecution and his complete devotion to the readers and to the ministry (vv. 1–12), whose fruit is a purer faith, made stronger by suffering (vv. 13–14) and – retroactively – the comfort of the one who made the proclamation (3.7).' 1 Thess. 4.1 does not introduce 'an ethical appendix to the letter, but the contemporary renewal of the appeal with increase as its goal'. Containing an additional important insight is this further observation by Johannes Thomas: 'The paraclesis embeds the contemporary ... in the traditional on five separate occasions ... and consequently always aims at mutual comfort in the congregation.'[50] That is exactly why five of the occurrences of παρακαλέω are found in chapters four and five.

2) ἐκ πλάνης   The antithetical style that begins here 'should not be interpreted as Paul's defense of hypothetical accusations. Rather', Aune wisely reminds us, 'it is a technique that *amplifies* thought by contrasting ideas using negation, antonyms, and other devices.'[51] In fact, Paul employs the rhetorical device of antithesis throughout 1 Thessalonians as a way of expressing himself. Further, both antithetical parallelism and similar terminology as found here are used by hellenistic Judaism in its rejection of heathen idolatry, especially in texts such as the Wisdom of Soloman 11–15.

Paul's παράκλησις is not ἐκ πλάνης, not from error, but ἐκ τοῦ θεοῦ. The Thessalonians were converted to the true and living God (1.9); as a result they have been freed from the idolatry of the heathen and from the error of those who do not know God (4.5, μὴ ἐν πάθει ἐπιθυμίας καθάπερ καὶ τὰ ἔθνη τὰ μὴ εἰδότα τὸν

---

[50] J. Thomas, 'παρακαλέω' in *EDNT* 3.26.
[51] Aune, *NT in Its Literary Environment*, p. 206. Aune cites Aristotle, *Rhet.* 1409b–1410a; Pseudo-Aristotle [Anaximenes of Lampsacus], *Rhet. Alex.* 1435b; Hermogenes, *On Invention* 4.2.

θεόν). Similarly, Paul's gospel does not have its origin in such error or delusion. Here in this same verse (2.3), another sign of pagan error and delusion with regard to God is referred to as ἀκαθαρσία. It occurs again in 4.7 where it is explicitly connected to the conduct of 'τὰ ἔθνη who do not know God'. The correspondence to the language and thought world of the Wisdom of Soloman is remarkable, as is evident, for example, in 14.22: Εἶτ'α οὐκ ἤρκεσεν τὸ πλανᾶσθαι περὶ τὴν τοῦ θεοῦ γνῶσιν, ἀλλὰ καὶ ἐν μεγάλῳ ζῶντες ἀγνοίας πολέμῳ τὰ τοσαῦτα κακὰ εἰρήνην προσαγορεύουσιν.

In passing it should be added that the circumstances to which the apostle is addressing his paraclesis in 1 Thessalonians is far more similar to the situation described by the author of the Wisdom of Soloman than to that portrayed by the Cynic preachers. These brief comments suggest, then, that Paul's παράκλησις, both in terms of content and demeanor, is not related to paganism but originates with God. Thus, the entire first part of the *narratio* is an attempt by the apostle to distance himself and the Thessalonians from both pagan thought and practice.

In verse 4 Paul turns to make positive statements about his God-given task: ἀλλὰ καθὼς δεδοκιμάσμεθα ὑπὸ τοῦ θεοῦ πιστευθῆναι τὸ εὐαγγέλιον, οὕτως λαλοῦμεν, οὐχ ὡς ἀνθρώποις ἀρέσκοντες ἀλλὰ θεῷ τῷ δοκιμάζοντι τὰς καρδίας ἡμῶν. With regard to δεδοκιμάσμεθα the general intent is clear: Paul has been tested and approved by God prior to the initiation of his ministry and this accountability before the forum of God alone continues. That is why the word of God that he has proclaimed and continues to proclaim (literally 'to speak') is, in fact, truly the word of God, a fact that the Thessalonian Christians themselves acknowledge (2.13) and will hopefully also continue to acknowledge as a result of this speech-act known as 1 Thessalonians.

In Jer. 11.20 one finds a similar use of the verb δοκιμάζω: κύριε κρίνων δίκαια δοκιμάζων νεφροὺς καὶ καρδίας, ἴδοιμι τὴν παρὰ σοῦ ἐκδίκησιν ἐξ αὐτῶν, ὅτι πρὸς σὲ ἀπεκάλυψα τὸ δικαίωμά μου. God is here described as the one who 'tests/assays the kidneys and the heart'. Given the parallel in 12.3 (καὶ σύ, κύριε, γινώσκεις με, δεδοκίμακας τὴν καρδίαν μου ἐναντίον σου) it is probable that Jeremiah himself is being tested. The prophet is confident that as a result of God's definitive and conclusive 'test' he will be not be found wanting. Because Jeremiah has been examined and validated by God, God can pronounce to Jeremiah: 'I have made you a tester and refiner among my people so that you may know and test their ways' (6.27, δοκιμαστὴν δέδωκά σε ἐν λαοῖς δεδοκιμασμένοις, καὶ γνώσῃ με ἐν τῷ δοκιμάσαι με τὴν ὁδὸν αὐτῶν). This is precisely what Paul intends with the sending of his surrogate, Timothy, and the assessment given upon his co-worker's return from Thessalonica (3.6–10). As a result of the effective reception of Paul's paraclesis, now referred to as 1 Thessalonians, those 'in Christ' are expected to do their own 'testing' (5.20).

The relationship of this material in Jeremiah to this earliest Pauline letter is strengthened even further when one recalls the nature of the prophet's call in 1.5: Πρὸ τοῦ με πλάσαι σε ἐν κοιλίᾳ ἐπίσταμαί σε καὶ πρὸ τοῦ σε ἐξελθεῖν ἐκ μήτρας ἡγίακά σε, προφήτην εἰς ἔθνη τέθεικά σε. What we have here is a 'true internationalizing of the prophetic office'.[52] Recognizing a close relationship between the *narratio* of 1 Thessalonians and Jeremiah, Albert-Marie Denis proceeds to emphasize Paul 'comme un prophète messianique' and that the apostle stands at 'la charnière des deux plans: prophète messianique, il est apôtre des Gentils.'[53] Henneken's insightful monograph reaches a similar conclusion with regard to 2.1–4: 'Das Selbstverständnis des Apostel Paulus ist in ganz eigentümlicher Weise prophetisch geprägt.'[54] In addition, as we have seen and will continue to observe, many of the expressions found in 1 Thessalonians cohere quite precisely with Paul's definition of prophecy 1 Cor.

---

[52] W. L. Holladay, *Jeremiah*, 2 vols (Hermeneia; Philadelphia: Fortress Press, 1986), 1.34.

[53] Denis, 'L'Apôtre Paul, prophete "messianique" des Gentils', pp. 316–17 [ET: 'as a messianic prophet' and that the apostle stands at 'the juncture of two horizons: a messianic prophet who is apostle to the Gentiles'.]

[54] Henneken, *Verkündigung und Prophetie*, p. 98 [ET: 'The self understanding of the Apostle Paul is shaped prophetically in a very particular way.']

14.3: ὁ δὲ προφητεύων ἀνθρώποις λαλεῖ οἰκοδομὴν [see 1 Thess. 5.11] καὶ παράκλησιν [see 1 Thess. 2.3, 12; 3.2, 7; 4.1, 10, 18; 5.11, 14] καὶ παραμυθίαν [see 1 Thess. 2.12; 5.14].

1 Thess. 2.7 makes two positive assertions, the first concerning Paul's right as an apostle (δυνάμενοι ἐν βάρει εἶναι ὡς Χριστοῦ ἀπόστολοι) and the second concerning Paul's activity as a pastor (ἀλλὰ ἐγενήθημεν ἤπιοι ἐν μέσῳ ὑμῶν, ὡς ἐὰν τροφὸς θάλπῃ τὰ ἑαυτῆς τέκνα). Difficult exegetically is the phrase ἐν βάρει εἶναι. Does it refer to being burdensome with regard to the apostles' right to be supported financially or does it point to the honor that they might have expected to receive from the Thessalonians? The two meanings are not incongruous, although the first is to be given more weight. Drawing attention to what follows in this same verse, Stegemann writes: 'Diese *clementia*/ἤπιοι hat der Apostel Paulus walten lassen, indem er darauf verzichtete, seinen Unterhaltsanspruch als Apostel Christi einzufordern.'[55] Perhaps Paul is exploiting rhetorically the double sense of the phrase ἐν βάρει εἶναι, much like the Latin proverb: 'Honos propter onus.'[56]

With regard to the final part of 2.7, it must be emphasized that Paul is not talking about a 'mother'; rather, τροφός explicitly refers to a 'nurse'.[57] Understood in this way, this metaphor coheres precisely with the proposed understanding of ἐν βάρει. Stegemann has it exactly right: 'Doch Paulus sagt eben nicht, wie eine Mutter ihre Kinder hegt, sondern: wie eine Amme ihre eigenen Kinder hegt.... D.h. das Bild von der liebevollen Hingabe einer Amme an ihre eigenen Kinder muß auf dem Hintergrund ihre normalerweise für Entgelt

---

[55] Stegeman, 'Anlaß und Hintergrund', p. 408 (ET: 'Paul allowed this *clementia*/ἤπιοι to prevail insofar as he refrained from demanding his right to support as an apostle of Christ'). Similarly Wolfgang Schrage, *Der erste Brief an die Korinther* (1 Kor 1,1–6,11) (EKK VII/1; Zürich: Benzinger, 1991), pp. 346–7: 'Paulus hat gearbeitet, um niemandem zur Last zur Fallen (1 Thess 2,9 u.ö.), um so deutlich zu machen, daß er nicht das Ihre, sondern sie selbst sucht (2 Kor 12,14; vgl. auch 1 Kor 9,19).'

[56] G. Milligan, *St Paul's Epistles to the Thessalonians* (London: Macmillan, 1908), p. 21.

[57] See Donfried, 'The Cults of Thessalonica', p. 338; in this volume, pp. 24-5.

geschehenden Pflege eines fremden Kindes verstanden werden.'[58]

Concerning Paul's Behavior (2.9–12)

In 1 Thess. 2.9–12 correlations between the *narratio* and the *probatio* continue by means of a detailed description of Paul's ἦθος. Already in the summary of Paul's activity in 2.8 (οὕτως ὁμειρόμενοι ὑμῶν εὐδοκοῦμεν μεταδοῦναι ὑμῖν οὐ μόνον τὸ εὐαγγέλιον τοῦ θεοῦ ἀλλὰ καὶ τὰς ἑαυτῶν ψυχάς, διότι ἀγαπητοὶ ἡμῖν ἐγενήθητε) reference is made to the theme of love: he is willing not to burden them as an apostle of Christ because they are beloved. Here and elsewhere in the *narratio* intentional links are made with themes that will be taken up in the *probatio* (for example, love, in 4.9–12).[59]

Paul as hardworking in 2.9 (Μνημονεύετε γάρ, ἀδελφοί, τὸν κόπον ἡμῶν καὶ τὸν μόχθον· νυκτὸς καὶ ἡμέρας ἐργαζόμενοι πρὸς τὸ μὴ ἐπιβαρῆσαί τινα ὑμῶν ἐκηρύξαμεν εἰς ὑμᾶς τὸ εὐαγγέλιον τοῦ θεοῦ) picks up the theme of verse 6 (ἐν βάρει) and provides a model for what will be said in 4.11 (καὶ ἐργάζεσθαι ταῖς [ἰδίαις] χερσὶν ὑμῶν, καθὼς ὑμῖν παρηγγείλαμεν). Hock's sociological evaluation that for Paul work 'was also the source of much personal hardship and social humiliation' and, further, that he 'viewed his working at trade none too positively as toil, slavery, and humiliation',[60] coheres with Fee's theological insight that the apostle lists work as part of his apostolic hardships in 1 Cor. 4.6–13 in order to indicate to this church that ' "depriving" them of the privilege of helping him was... in keeping with his overall stance as a disciple of the crucified one'.[61] For Paul, Fee

---

[58] Stegemann, 'Anlaß und Hintergrund', p. 409 [ET: 'But Paul does not say as a mother protects her children; rather, as a wet nurse protects her children.... This means that the picture of the loving sacrifice of a wet nurse toward her own children must be understood against the background of normally receiving remuneration for the ongoing care of a child not her own.'].

[59] Schrage, *Der erste Brief an die Korinther*, p. 346: '1 Thess 4,9 stellt sie unter das Stichwort der Agape bzw. Philadelphia.'

[60] R. F. Hock, *The Social Context of Paul's Ministry: Tentmaking and Apostleship* (Fortress Press: Philadelphia, 1980), p. 67.

[61] G. D. Fee, *The First Epistle to the Corinthians* (NICNT; Grand Rapids: Eerdmans, 1987), p. 179.

continues, 'discipleship meant 'sharing in the sufferings of Christ,' not in its expiatory sense but in its *imitatio* sense (v. 16) – being in the world as Christ was in the world. Christ was really like this; those who would follow him must expect that they, too, will be like this.'[62]

The description of Paul as moral (2.10, ὁσίως καὶ δικαίως καὶ ἀμέμπτως), with the invocation of God and the Thessalonian Christians as witnesses, is undoubtedly intended to portray Paul as an example of the new life in Christ and to anticipate the *probatio*.

Verses 11–12 portray Paul as fatherly (ὡς ἕνα ἕκαστον ὑμῶν ὡς πατὴρ τέκνα ἑαυτοῦ). In the ancient world the father was responsible for the behavior of his children. Conversion requires socialization into a new lifestyle, and that is precisely what Paul is attempting to do both through his proclamation of the gospel, through the example of his own behavior and through this speech-act known as 1 Thessalonians. Through these means he is 'appealing, encouraging, and testifying' (παρακαλοῦντες ὑμας καὶ παραμυθούμενοι καὶ μαρτυρόμενοι) that they 'lead a life worthy of God, who calls you into his own kingdom and glory'. This strongly eschatological note is found throughout the letter and reaches its climax in 4.13–18. Eschatology and ethics are inextricably linked.[63]

Concerning the Thessalonians' behavior (2.13–16)

These verses are an integral part of the letter and with Wuellner we understand them as a digression within the *narratio*.[64] Such digressions often provide the basis for subsequent discussion, as, for example, in 4.13–18 where the suffering Thessalonians need once again to be comforted. In speaking so harshly about the

---

[62] Fee, *The First Epistle to the Corinthians*, p. 181.

[63] K. P. Donfried, 'The Kingdom of God in Paul', in *The Kingdom of God in 20th-Century Interpretation*, ed. W. Willis (Peabody, MA: Hendrickson, 1987), pp. 175–90, especially pp. 181–2; also pp. 233–52 in this volume.

[64] W. Wuellner, 'Greek Rhetoric and Pauline Argumentation', *Early Christian Literature and the Classical Intellectual Tradition*, (Festschrift Robert M. Grant, ed. W. R. Schoedel and R. L. Wilken (Théologie Historique 54; Paris: Beauchesne, 1979), pp. 177–88.

persecutors of the Jewish Christians, Paul 'makes a thinly veiled statement promising divine condemnation'.[65] Do we see here echoes of Jer. 11.20 where the testing and approval of the prophet leads to the condemnation of the opposition?

Paul, An 'Eschatologic Person'[66]

In our review of the problem of whether or not to understand 2.1–12 as an apology, we have already had opportunity to touch on the issue of Paul's self-identification, especially with regard to Malherbe's attempt to link these verses with the world of the Cynic wandering preachers. In light of our examination of the first part of the *narratio*, let us examine the text of this first extant Christian letter for additional clues that might help us understand something more about Paul's self-understanding and function.

The Spirit-Filled Word: 1 Thess. 1.6, 8; 2.13

In 1.8 Paul writes: 'For not only has the word of the Lord sounded forth from you in Macedonia and Achaia, but your faith in God has gone forth everywhere, so that we need not say anything.' The phrase 'the word of the Lord' is used synonymously with 'the gospel' (see 2.9), a term which Paul can also describe as 'the word of God' in 2.13. Since Paul had referred to the Thessalonians' imitation of Paul and the Lord in suffering just a few verses before (1.6), he uses again the term 'Lord' not only as a reference to the risen one to whom the church is responsible now and on the last day but also as a reminder that he whom they declare as Lord is also the one who was despised and suffered at the hands of human beings. Despite the difficulty of their situation, the gospel, especially because it is the word of the suffering and risen Lord, has burst forth from Thessalonica in such a powerful way that they have become an example (τύπος,

---

[65] C. A. Wanamaker, *Commentary on 1 and 2 Thessalonians* (NICNT; Grand Rapids: Eerdmans, 1990), p. 110.

[66] A. Fridrichsen, *The Apostle and His Message* (Uppsala: Almqvist-Wiksells, 1947), p. 3.

1.7) to all the believers in Macedonia and Achaia. Perhaps Paul is wishing to suggest that they were not only a model in suffering but also, precisely because of their willingness to suffer, an example, an embodiment, even if imperfectly, of that hope which is present in their midst now, although its consummation still lies in the future.

Given the brevity of 1 Thessalonians, it is at first surprising to realize that the term εὐαγγέλιον is used six times (1.5; 2.2, 4, 8, 9; 3.2) and its synonym, 'word' (λόγος), is used at least four times (1.6, 8; 2.13; 4.15),[67] a rather high percentage when compared with, for example, Romans.[68] This is largely due to Paul's emphatic attempt in the *narratio* to distinguish his gospel and ethos from that of the pagan context of Thessalonica. As a result he makes the following assertions about the gospel as word of God in 1 Thessalonians:

- the gospel was proclaimed in Thessalonica, not only in word, but also in power and in the Holy Spirit and in full conviction (1.5), that is, it is a performative word and it is actively at work (ἐνεργεῖται) in and among the believers (2.13); as a generating center it is foundational for the existence of the church;
- the Thessalonian Christians received the word in the midst of affliction (1.6). In so doing they became imitators of Paul and his associates, as well as the Lord. In addition, by receiving the word in the midst of affliction they received it with joy inspired by the Holy Spirit (1.6); this in itself is a sign of hope even if the Thessalonian Christians had not fully recognized it as such. Paul also acknowledges this existential situation when he asserts in 2.2 that he declared to them 'the gospel of God in the face of great opposition';
- the word has proceeded out from Thessalonica to all the believers in Macedonia and in Achaia. As a result, whether intentionally or not, the Thessalonian church became a missionary base for the gospel (1.8);

---

[67] See also 1 Thess. 1.5 and 4.18.

[68] εὐαγγέλιον occurs nine times in Romans (1.1, 9, 16; 2.16; 10.16; 11.28; 15.16, 19; 16.25) and λόγος, specifically as 'word of God', appears only once (9.6).

- this gospel has been entrusted to Paul in a special way by God (2.4);
- this gospel is something which is 'shared' by Paul with the Thessalonians and it is proclaimed without burden to them because Paul 'worked night and day' (2.8–9);
- Timothy is God's servant and Paul's co-worker in the gospel of Christ. It is Paul's hope that when the Christian community in Thessalonica is more thoroughly rooted in the gospel the result will be a firmer establishment, encouragement and stabilization of their faith in the midst of their present afflictions.

The Spirit-Filled Word: 1 Thess. 4.15

Paul's frequent description of his message as an effective, spirit-filled, divine *logos* together with his emphasis on the repetition and new application of his previous proclamation and teaching, paves the way for the unprecedented and decisive information and consolation which he is about to share with this church in 4.13–18. Thus, the *narratio* and the *probatio* are closely linked; the former prepares the way for the latter. At the heart of the pronouncement stands a 'word of the Lord' (ἐν λόγῳ κυρίου). This new information attempts to console the Thessalonian Christians at a most neuralgic point: some of them have died and now some are about to abandon a critical dimension of their faith, namely, hope. Paul's word of consolation would be ineffectual if he had not first attempted to demonstrate the efficacy of the word of God that he had preached previously. Only then can this word of the Lord, presented here as new information, that is, information not shared during his original visit in Thessalonica, be considered as a convincing intervention in response to the problem of death caused by persecution.

The first problem that needs to be resolved with regard to the phrase ἐν λόγῳ κυρίου in 4.15 is whether the contents of this 'word of the Lord' are limited to verse 15, verses 15–16, or verses 15–17. The second problem is the origin of this material. Options suggested include that it is a lost saying of Jesus, that Paul has freely adopted a saying of the historical Jesus, that the apostle has modified a word proclaimed by the risen Lord in the post-resurrectional period, or that we have here a prophetic announcement from the risen Lord through the prophet Paul.

Our proposal is that Paul is an ecstatic prophet, thoroughly shaped and influenced by the milieu of Jewish mystical-apocalypticism. Factors supporting this perspective of the apostle include a charismatic understanding of apostleship dependent on a vision of the risen Christ (Gal. 1.11–17); his attestation of mystical ascensions to the heavenly worlds (2 Cor. 12.1–10); and, his frequent use of Jewish mystical vocabulary, such as σύμμορφος (for example, Phil. 3.21) to describe the transformation experienced by the ones who are in Christ. Based on such an evaluation of Paul we would understand this 'word of the Lord' as one transmitted by the heavenly Lord to the prophet Paul. We are dealing, then, with a prophetic expression, not one stemming from the historical Jesus but from the risen Lord.

One should note in passing that the phrase ἐν λόγῳ κυρίου is situated in a similar context in the Septuagint. The 'man of God' speaks in 1 Kgs. 13.9, 'For thus I was commanded by the word of the Lord [ὅτι οὕτως ἐνετείλατό μοι ἐν λόγῳ κύριος λέγων]: You shall not eat food, or drink water, or return by the way that you came.' In our present context we must defer a more detailed treatment of this phrase to Henneken's instructive examination.[69]

According to the recent study by Helmut Merklein,[70] it is likely that the prophetic utterance is to be limited to verse 15b: 'We who are alive, who are left until the coming of the Lord, shall not precede those who have fallen asleep.' Verses 16–17 are further elaborations of the prophetic declaration using a variety of traditional, apocalyptic motifs. By means of an instructive comparison of 1 Thess. 4.13–18 with 1 Cor. 15.50–58, Merklein has discovered a number of parallels between these two chapters that give further support to limiting the prophetic word to verse 15b as well as allowing us to better comprehend it and its interpretation. With regard to 1 Thessalonians we note the following unfolding of the pattern: a) in 4.14a dimensions

[69] Henneken, *Verkündigung und Prophetie*, pp. 92–3.
[70] H. Merklein, 'Der Theologe als Prophet: zur Funktion prophetischen Redens im theologischen Diskurs', *NTS* 38 (1992), pp. 402–29.

of the gospel, already familiar to the recipients, are expressed; b) in 4.14b an introductory and transitional thesis is presented that must be confirmed and expanded by the yet to be announced prophetic word and its further elaboration; c) in 4.15b a hitherto unknown eschatological mystery is disclosed, although such prophetic revelation does not stand in contradiction to the gospel to which it is always subordinate; d) in 4.16–17 the interpretation of the prophetic word seeks to clarify matters not immediately evident from the gospel itself as a result of issues prompted by local, contingent situations and it is not, therefore, intended as a further dogmatic expansion of the gospel; e) in 4.18, the concluding part of this prophetic discourse, the theme of *consolatio* is unmistakable: 'Therefore comfort one another with these words [ἐν τοῖς λόγοις τούτοις].' The prophetic word of verse 15 is foundational for this paraclesis.

Our analysis of 1 Thess. 4.15–17, then, discloses that embedded in verse 15b is a prophetic word transmitted by the heavenly Lord to the prophet Paul, with verses 16–17 providing a further interpretation of this eschatological mystery. We have no evidence that this is a word from the historical Jesus and Merklein's study goes far to eliminate this as a serious option.

The Words of Prophets: 1 Thess. 5.19–21

'Der Apostel Paulus ist Prophet der mit Christus hereingebrochenen geisterfüllten (1 Thess. 4,8) Heils- und Endzeit, einer Zeit darum auch voller Bedrängnis, die er den Thessalonichern angesagt und vorausgesagt (vgl. 1 Thess. 3,4) hat. Das alles gibt seiner gesamten apostolischen Verkündigung eine prophetische Grundlegung und Färbung. Daneben ist Paulus auch Prophet im engeren Sinne der Weissagung, wie die Analyse von 1 Thess. 4.15–17 gezeigt hat.'[71] If one were to agree with Henneken's

---

[71] Henneken, *Verkündigung und Prophetie*, p. 103 [ET: 'The Apostle Paul is a prophet of the Spirit-filled (1 Thess. 4.8), salvific and eschatological period inaugurated by Christ. This is also a time filled with distress, a fact he has declared to the Thessalonians as well as having predicted it (see 1 Thess. 3.4). All of this gives his entire apostolic proclamation a prophetic basis and disposition. At the same time Paul is also a prophet in the more specific sense of prophecy as the analysis of 1 Thess. 4.15–17 has demonstrated.'].

profile of Paul, does 1 Thess. 5.19–21 (τὸ πνεῦμα μὴ σβέννυτε, προφητείας μὴ ἐξουθενεῖτε, πάντα δὲ δοκιμάζετε, τὸ καλὸν κατέχετε) have any relevance to our earlier discussion of the *narratio* of 1 Thessalonians?

Does προφητεία in this context refer to the gift of prophecy or to the words spoken by the person prophesying? The accusative plural of the noun suggests the latter. Perhaps the two different references in 5.19 and 5.20 suggest a differentiation between the gospel as the word of God handed on by the church but made alive by the Spirit and prophetic utterance as a Spirit-driven revelation of hidden mysteries that is primarily concerned with the encouragement of God's people. The first would be 'quenched' by refusing to listen to God's word and will and the latter would be 'despised' by treating it/them as irrelevant to the life of the congregation. The former is concerned with the announcement of the eschatological moment of salvation in the form of human weakness and frailty and thus as the embodiment of the suffering God, as incarnation in the present moment, whereas the latter is the dynamic announcement of God for the upbuilding, encouragement and consolation of the desolate. Such a differentiation would cohere well with our previous interpretation of the term paraclesis, namely, that it embraces the past and incorporates it into the present.

Therefore it is possible that 1 Thess. 5.19 and 20 are not referring to some general, abstract situation in the midst of the Thessalonian congregation, or to some aspect of conventional ethics, but are, rather, explicitly referring both to the gospel and the new word from the risen Lord that has been the central focus of this new speech-act itself. πάντα δὲ δοκιμάζετε would then refer to the testing of all dimensions of their life by the will of God as revealed by gospel and word of the Lord, in the same way that Paul was tested by God and found acceptable.[72] Thus, according to verse 22, they are not to follow the path of pagan culture (ἀπὸ παντὸς εἴδους πονηροῦ ἀπέχεσθε) but to follow the revealed will of God (τὸ καλὸν κατέχετε). Consequently, πάντα

---

[72] See above our previous discussion of Jeremiah.

relates to what follows and not to what precedes.[73] It is not a testing of the prophecies but, rather, all dimensions of life (πάντα) are to be tested by the gospel and by the prophetic word (προφητείας).

What, very briefly, is the relationship between Paul as prophet and Paul as apostle? The latter term appears only once in 1 Thessalonians (2.7) and in a plural form. It is obvious that this designation per se is not intended to be given major attention in this letter; consequently one needs to be careful not to import discussions about the epistolary *intitulatio* from Paul's later letters. To be an apostle is to proclaim the prophetic gospel to the Gentiles; but that can only be accomplished by the prophet who has been so authorized by God.

Conclusions

1) 1 Thess. 2.1–12 is not an apology of any sort, specific or general, and one ought not to read this text in a mirror fashion so that it could be argued that Paul is countering charges made against him. 2) Epistolary criticism does not assist us in a substantial way to interpret the intention of especially 1 Thess. 2.1–12 within the letter. 3) The identification of this text by rhetorical criticism as belonging to the *narratio* opens new possibilities for understanding its more precise function within the total act of communication. The *narratio* in 1 Thessalonians serves: a) to recount the relationship of friendship established between Paul and the Thessalonians; b) to distinguish Paul's gospel and ethos from the error and delusion of the idolatry of the heathen, and; c) to utilize the ethos of Paul as a model within the remainder of the paraclesis. This opens up the possibility of better understanding certain components of the first part of the *narratio* in relationship to the remainder of the letter. On the one hand we have noted how the *narratio* advances further what has been said in the *exordium*; and how, on the other hand, many of the themes developed in the *narratio* anticipate new actualization and elaboration in the *probatio*.

[73] Against Wanamaker, *Commentary on 1 and 2 Thessalonians*, p. 203.

9

❦

Paul and Judaism: 1 Thess. 2.13–16 as a Test Case

It has become increasingly evident that the creative ferment caused by such bold and provocative re-examinations of Pauline theology as those of Ernst Käsemann[1] has exercised considerable influence and has resulted in some significant new publications not only in Pauline studies in general,[2] but particularly with regard to the relationship of Paul and Judaism.[3] The large number of monographs in this area over the last few years is now a fact. Since a brief essay could not do even partial justice to these significant publications, we will concentrate on one, J. Christiaan Beker's *Paul the Apostle*.[4] Rather than presenting an abstract summary of his position,[5] it will be asked, after some brief

---

[1] Now summarized in E. Käsemann, *Commentary on Romans* (Grand Rapids: Eerdmans, 1980).

[2] P. Stuhlmacher, *Gerechtigkeit Gottes bei Paulus* (Göttingen: Vandenhoeck and Ruprecht, 1965) as well as his subsequent publications. See also the provocative structural introduction to the Pauline letters by D. Patte, *Paul's Faith and the Power of the Gospel* (Philadelphia: Fortress Press, 1983).

[3] See the two books by E. P. Sanders, *Paul and Palestinian Judaism* (Philadelphia: Fortress Press, 1977) and *Paul, the Law, and the Jewish People* (Philadelphia: Fortress Press, 1983). Also significant among such publications are Heikki Räisäänen, *Paul and the Law*, (WUNT 29; Tübingen: J. C. B. Mohr, 1983), W. D. Davies, *Jewish and Pauline Studies* (Philadelphia: Fortress Press, 1984), G. Lüdemann, *Paulus und das Judentum* (Munich: Chr. Kaiser, 1983) and P. Lapide and P. Stuhlmacher, *Paulus – Rabbi und Apostel* (Stuttgart/München: Calwer/ Kösel, 1981).

[4] J. C. Beker, *Paul the Apostle* (Philadelphia: Fortress Press, 1980).

[5] See Davies' critique of Beker in *Jewish and Pauline Studies*, p. 361, n. 16.

introductory comments, whether his understanding of Paul sheds new light on the controversial passage, 1 Thess. 2.13–16.

Beker acknowledges his dependence on Käsemann's thought:

> Käsemann's thesis – 'apocalyptic was the mother of all Christian theology' – opened up a new era of interpretation. As Klaus Koch says: 'Up to then apocalyptic had been for biblical scholarship something on the periphery of the Old and New Testaments – something bordering on heresy. Käsemann had suddenly declared that a tributary was the main stream, from which everything else at the end of the Old Testament and the beginning of the New was allegedly fed.'[6]

It is precisely this emphasis of Käsemann on the importance of apocalyptic for the understanding of Paul which Beker takes up in his attempt to portray a 'fresh understanding of Paul'.[7] Two key concepts are at the basis of such a fresh understanding: 'coherence' and 'contingency', namely, that there is a coherent center in Paul's theology which the apostle applies to the contingencies of different situations. This alone accounts for both the consistency and complexity of Pauline thought.

What is this coherent center in the theology of Paul?

> I posit the triumph of God as the coherent theme of Paul's gospel; that is, the hope in the dawning victory of God and in the imminent redemption of the created order, which he has inaugurated in Christ. Moreover, I claim that Paul's hermeneutic translates the apocalyptic theme of the gospel into the contingent particularities of the human situation. Paul's ability to correlate the consistent theme of the gospel and its contingent relevance constitutes his unique achievement in the history of Christian thought.[8]

Even more specifically, Paul 'locates the coherent center of the gospel in the apocalyptic interpretation of the Christ-event'.[9] The other side of this proposition is that 'the *character* of Paul's contingent hermeneutic is shaped by his apocalyptic core in that in nearly all cases the contingent interpretation of the gospel points – whether implicitly or explicitly – to the imminent cosmic triumph of God'.[10]

---

[6] Beker, *Paul the Apostle*, p. 143.
[7] Beker, *Paul the Apostle*, p. 143.
[8] Beker, *Paul the Apostle*, p. ix.
[9] Beker, *Paul the Apostle*, p. 18.
[10] Beker, *Paul the Apostle*, p. 19.

Beker's interpretation allows us to escape from the dead end search for a *centrum Paulinum*.[11] To ask whether 'righteousness' or 'justification' or 'reconciliation' or 'being in Christ', to cite simply some of the claims, is *the* basic Pauline category overlooks the fact that Paul's call – what Beker calls the 'primordial experience of the Christ-event'[12] – is brought into the language of Jewish apocalyptic, the language in which he lived and thought. Although the nature of the Christ-event alters the traditional apocalyptic language,[13] it is this *Christian* apocalyptic structure of thought which is the center of Pauline thought. As a result of this, it is necessary to distinguish between primary and secondary language. The primary language or its 'deep structure' is the 'Christ-event in its meaning for the apocalyptic consummation of history',[14] namely, the triumph of God, and the secondary language or 'surface structure' is the contingent interpretation by Paul of his Christian apocalyptic into specific situations. The triumph of God, the significance of the Christ-event for the apocalyptic consummation of history, is the primary language; and such specific symbols as 'justification' and 'reconciliation' belong to the secondary language. This distinction allows Beker not only to recognize the 'versatility of Paul's hermeneutic and the richness of his thought'[15] in applying his coherent gospel to the different local situations but also that this gospel allows for 'a wide diversity of interpretation without sacrificing its coherent center'.[16] These insights are then illustrated by a close examination of Galatians and Romans in which it is argued that the different attitudes of Paul toward the law in each, to take one illustration, is due to the fact that different contingent arguments are necessitated by the different contextual situations of each of these congregations. Yet these different contextual situations, which require different contingent

---

[11] Note the attempts of R. P. Martin, *Reconciliation* (Atlanta: John Knox, 1981) and J. Reumann, *Righteousness in the New Testament* (Philadelphia: Fortress Press, 1982).

[12] Beker, *Paul the Apostle*, p. 16.

[13] Davies (note 5 above) seems to miss this point in Beker's analysis.

[14] Beker, *Paul the Apostle*, p. 16.

[15] Beker, *Paul the Apostle*, p. 108.

[16] Beker, *Paul the Apostle*, p. 108.

arguments, do not invalidate the coherent core of Paul's gospel, which is 'motivated by the future consummation as God's goal with history and creation. All the ingredients to Paul's thought find their proper location only within this futurist flow.'[17]

In light of Beker's analysis, and contrary to the argument of Pierson,[18] Boers,[19] Koester[20] and others,[21] it can be demonstrated that neither all nor part of the text in 1 Thess. 2.13–16 is a later interpolation. All the arguments for interpolation cannot be reviewed here; there are, however, two primary ones which must be dealt with: 1) the structural argument, namely, that 2.13–16 does not fit into the flow of the letter, and 2) the anti-Jewish argument, namely, that Paul's assertions in this pericope are inconsistent with his assertions about the Jews in Romans. The first of these arguments has been refined by Daryl Schmidt;[22] he asserts that the embedding patterns of 2.13–16 reveal features not typical of the Pauline style elsewhere in 1 Thessalonians. There is no question about this; however, as we will attempt to show, this is due to Paul's use of traditional and formulaic material. The

---

[17] Beker, *Paul the Apostle*, p. 176.

[18] B. A. Pearson, '1 Thessalonians 2.13–16: A Deutero-Pauline Interpolation', *HTR* 64 (1971), pp. 79–94. For a rebuttal to this position see J. Coppens, 'Une diatribe antijuive dans I Thess. II, 13–16', *ETL* 51 (1975), pp. 90–5.

[19] H. Boers, 'The Form Critical Study of Paul's Letters. 1 Thessalonians as a Case Study', *NTS* 22 (1975/76), pp. 140–58.

[20] H. Koester, *History and Literature of Early Christianity*, 2 vols (Philadelphia: Fortress Press, 1982), 2.112–14.

[21] See the review of the literature in G. E. Okeke, '1 Thess. ii. 13–16: The Fate of the Unbelieving Jews', *NTS* 27 (1980), pp. 127–36.

[22] D. Schmidt, '1 Thess. 2.13–16: Linguistic Evidence for an Interpolation', *JBL* 102 (1983), pp. 269–79. On the basis of the evidence provided in his article I am not convinced that Schmidt's conclusion holds: 'Therefore, the interpolation hypothesis seems to be the best explanation...' (p. 276). Further, one needs to be very careful about not putting Paul into a hypothetical form-critical straight jacket, particularly if one is to take Koester's suggestion seriously about 1 Thessalonians being an experiment in Christian writing (H. Koester, '1 Thessalonians – Experiment in Christian Writing', in *Continuity and Discontinuity in Church History*, ed. F. F. Church and T. George [Leiden: E. J. Brill, 1979], pp. 33–44). Additionally, neither Schubert nor White argues that 1 Thess. 2.13–16 is an interpolation – not even on form-critical grounds! See P. Schubert, *Form and Function of the Pauline Thanksgivings* (BZNW 20; Berlin: Alfred Töpelmann, 1939), p. 17; J. L. White, 'The Form and Function of the Body of the Greek Letter: A Study of the Letter – Body in the Non-literary Papyri and in Paul the Apostle' (PhD Diss.; Vanderbilt, 1970), pp. 116–18. [Now available in published form with same title (2nd ed corrected; SBLDS 2; Missoula: Scholars Press, 1972).

more critical argument to which attention must be given is the second, the alleged anti-Judaism revealed in this text. Such a view is widespread. It is key to Pierson's position, 'I find it also virtually impossible to ascribe to Paul the *ad hominem* fragment of Gentile anti-Judaism in verse 15',[23] and it is even found in so conservative a scholar as Ernest Best: 'It must be allowed that 1 Th. 2.16c shows Paul holding an unacceptable anti-Semitic position.'[24] A similar concern is found throughout much of the literature.[25]

In order to understand verses 15–16, we must pay careful attention to verses 13–14. Paul uses the verb εὐχαριστέω twice for his own personal thanksgiving, in 2.3 and here in 2.13, and he uses the noun εὐχαριστία in 3.9 for a further word of thanksgiving. The first reference is very general and refers to their 'work of faith and labor of love and steadfastness of hope' as well as to the fact that the gospel proclaimed by Paul, Silvanus and Timothy 'came to you not only in word, but also in power and in the Holy Spirit and with full conviction'. This is followed by brief references to the integrity of Paul and his co-workers, that the Thessalonians became imitators of them because they received the word in much affliction (ἐν θλίψει) and that they 'became an example (τύπος) to all the believers in Macedonia and in Achaia'. Chapters 2 and 3, especially, are further specifications of this general thanksgiving. 1 Thess. 2.1–12 is an elaboration of the theme of apostolic integrity in the midst of affliction[26] and verses 13–16 are an intensification and expansion of the themes of 'imitation' and 'affliction' in relation to receiving the word. This further specification is signaled by the repetition of the theme of thanksgiving in 2.13 in a way similar to the function of the thanksgiving in 3.9 where it introduces the theme of supplying

[23] Pearson, 'Deutero-Pauline Interpolation', p. 85.

[24] E. Best, *The First and Second Epistles to the Thessalonians* (London: Adam and Charles Black, 1972), p. 122.

[25] This goes back at least as far as F. C. Baur, *Paul the Apostle of Jesus Christ: His Life and Work, His Epistles and His Doctrine*, 2 vols (London: Williams and Norgate, 1875–6) 2.84–97.

[26] Note the repetition of the εἴσοδος theme in 1.9 and 2.1.

'what is lacking' in their faith, the answer to which is given by Paul in the fourth chapter.

Therefore, to understand 2.13–16 we need to pay careful attention to 1.6–9a. The themes of 'imitation' and 'affliction' from those earlier verses are taken up and expanded in 2.13–16, where the behavior of the Thessalonian converts is contrasted to that of the Jews. The Thessalonians accepted the word of the apostles as the word of God and it is therefore at work (ἐνεργεῖται) in them; the Jews in Judea (and the unbelieving Jews in Thessalonica) did not receive the apostolic proclamation as the word of God but as the word of men. Thus, it is not at work in them and as a result a negative description of these unbelievers is made in 2.15–16. As the Thessalonian Christians had welcomed Paul, so the Jews hindered Paul and his associates from speaking to the Gentiles. The Thessalonian church became a model for the churches not only in becoming imitators of Paul, Silvanus and Timothy, but also in imitating the faithful endurance of the churches in Judea that were persecuted by the Jews. As the Thessalonians became an example for all the believers in Macedonia and in Achaia, so had the churches in Judea and in Thessalonica become a model for the Thessalonians. Both the believers in Judea and in Thessalonica became examples of God's salvation which rescues 'from the wrath to come' (1.10) whereas the unbelieving Jews had become objects of God's wrath (2.16). This is summarized at the end of the letter: 'For God has not destined us for wrath, but to obtain salvation through our Lord Jesus Christ' (5.9). To summarize: By following the use of the thanksgiving theme in this letter, we note how the general thanksgiving of chapter 1 is further specified in chapter 2 with regard to suffering/affliction (see 3.4) and in chapters 3 and 4 with regard to the problem of hope (ἐλπίς); suffering and hope are two of Paul's main concerns in this letter to the Thessalonian congregation.

It is now necessary to ask who the 'countrymen' (συμφυλέτης) are in 2.14. If we were to rely just on the surface information given in I Thessalonians a reasonable conjecture would be that 'Gentiles' are meant. If that were the only information at our disposal, it would indeed be in order to ask why Paul reacts so sharply to the Jews in the succeeding two verses. However, we do have additional data about Thessalonica in Acts 17.1–11a, where opposition to Paul and Silas by Jews is recorded.

To refer to Acts at this point raises the whole issue of the proper use of Acts in the interpretation of Paul. Hengel[27] and Jervell,[28] for example, are correct in calling into question the extreme scepticism which has dominated a large part of New Testament scholarship in recent years. This does not mean, however, an uncritical fundamentalism should be substituted. Rather, there must be the realism that Acts contains much valuable and accurate information about the Pauline mission even though the writers' theological tendencies are quite apparent. Thus, it would appear that the axiom of John Knox[29] still holds, namely, that the primary source of Pauline theology and mission strategy remains the authentic letters and that Acts may be used as a supplement where it does not contradict the primary source. Not only do I hold to this in principle, but increasingly I am persuaded of the historical accuracy of much of the material in Acts. For example, in Acts 17.8, Luke uses the phrase 'city authorities' (τοὺς πολιτάρχας). This unique term, used in Acts only with regard to Thessalonica, has been archeologically verified.[30] It is this kind of accurate detail that inclines one favorably toward the reliability of Acts at many points.

The information given in Acts 17 relevant to our exegesis of 1 Thess. 2.13–16 is this: Paul went into a synagogue of the Jews and made specific reference to the suffering (only here and in Acts 3.18) and resurrection of Christ;[31] some of the Jews were persuaded and joined Paul and Silas; additionally some devout Greeks (σεβομένων Ἑλλήνων) and 'not a few of the leading women' attached themselves to Paul and Silas; the Jews of

---

[27] M. Hengel, *Acts and the History of Earliest Christianity* (Philadelphia: Fortress Press, 1980).

[28] J. Jervell, 'Der unbekannte Paulus', in *Die Paulinische Literatur und Theologie. Skandinavische Beitraege*, ed. S. Pedersen (Aarhus-Goettingen, 1980), pp. 29–40.

[29] J. Knox, *Chapters in a Life of Paul* (Nashville: Abingdon, 1950), pp. 30–43.

[30] J. Finegan, *The Archeology of the New Testament* (Boulder: Westview, 1981), p. 108.

[31] Themes remarkably similar to the major emphases of 1 Thessalonians.

Thessalonica were jealous and 'taking some wicked fellows of the rabble, they gathered a crowd, set the city in an uproar' (RSV) and eventually 'the brethren' sent Paul and Silas to Beroea. The phrase 'some wicked fellows of the rabble' needs to be looked at more closely. In the Greek text we find the words προσλαβόμενοι τῶν ἀγοραίων ἄνδρας τινὰς πονηρούς. It is evident that a more literal and correct translation would be 'some wicked men from the agora' rather than 'wicked fellows of the rabble'. The Jews, in their anger, get some local Greeks from the marketplace to help them find Paul and his associates so that they can be exposed and brought before the authorities. Jews, together with Greeks, turn 'the city into an uproar' against the Paulinists. From the perspective of this account 'your own countrymen' (τῶν ἰδίων συμφυλετῶν) in 1 Thess. 2.14 is used 'in a local rather than racial sense... and need not therefore exclude all reference to those Jews by whom... the persecutions at Thessalonica were first instigated'.[32] Ἴδιος thus bears here a weakened force as it not infrequently does in hellenistic Greek. If Milligan is accurate in this, as I suggest he is, it makes perfectly good sense for Paul to draw a parallel between the situation of the Thessalonian church with that of the churches in Judea and to show that in both situations the Jews hindered the process of speaking to the Gentiles. Paul, having just recently experienced this rebuke at the hands of the Thessalonian Jews, and being aware of the ongoing afflictions of the Thessalonian church (3.3–4), turns to a pre-existing tradition in his denunciation of the Jews in Judea and Thessalonica.[33] As we now look more closely at 1 Thess. 2.15–16a we must keep in mind that it is precisely Paul, the former persecutor of Christians, who takes up a tradition which

[32] G. Milligan, *St Paul's Epistles to the Thessalonians* (New York: Macmillan, n.d.), p. 29.

[33] See the discussion by R. Schippers, 'The Pre-Synoptic Tradition in I Thessalonians II 13–16', *NovT* 8 (1966), pp. 223–34, especially pp. 231–34 and that of W. D. Davies, 'Paul and the People of Israel', in *Jewish and Pauline Studies*, pp. 123–52. Additionally, the study by O. H. Steck, *Israel und das gewaltsame Geschick der Propheten* (WMANT 23; Neukirchen-Vluyn: Neukirchener, 1967), is indispensable for a detailed study of this pre-Pauline and pre-Synoptic tradition.

at one time applied to him and which he now uses against his former colleagues.

We must now examine more closely the tradition upon which Paul is dependent in verses 15–16a. A careful examination of these verses shows they contain a tradition which is remarkably close to the Q text found in Luke 11.47–52. The Matthean parallel (Matt. 23.29–32) to Luke 11.47–48 adds the following: 'Thus you testify against yourselves that you are descendants of those who murdered the prophets. Fill up [πληρώσατε], then, the measure of your ancestors.' The similarity of this Matthean πληρώσατε to 1 Thess. 2.16a is obvious and it is fully possible that Paul may have been aware of this element of the tradition from his experience with the Antiochene church.[34] The reference to 'fulfill' in both 1 Thessalonians and Matthew is remarkably similar to Wis. 19.3–5 where the action criticized is like that of the Egyptians:

> For while they were still busy at mourning, and were lamenting at the graves of their dead, they reached another foolish decision, and pursued as fugitives those whom they had begged and compelled to depart. For the fate they deserved drew them on to this end, and made them forget what had happened, in order that they might fill up the punishment which their torments still lacked [ἵνα τὴν λείπουσαν ταῖς βασάνοις προσαναπληρώσωσιν κόλασιν], and that thy people might experience an incredible journey, but they themselves might meet a strange death.[35]

It would appear, then, that the opposition the Jews had given Paul throughout his apostolate, but particularly in Thessalonica, together with the past and present Jewish opposition to the Christian church in that city,[36] allowed Paul to use a form of this pre-synoptic tradition which had unusual appropriateness in his letter to the Thessalonians.

We are now in a position to take a closer look at the last words

---

[34] See I. H. Marshall, *The Gospel of Luke* (NIGTC; Grand Rapids: Eerdmans, 1978), p. 501.

[35] RSV. See F. W. Danker, *Jesus and the New Age* (St. Louis: Clayton, 1972), pp. 145–6.

[36] It is not unimportant to observe that after ἐκδιωξάντων, itself an aorist participle suggesting a definite event such as the events described in Acts 17, the following charges against the unbelieving Jews are made by use of the present participles expressing continuity.

in this text from 1 Thessalonians, 2.16b. The RSV translates the Greek as follows: 'But God's wrath has come upon them at last.' As we shall observe, the critical problem of this text resides in the final words, εἰς τέλος. The variations in the English translations attest to this. Instead of 'at last' the NEB uses the translation 'for good and all', in the sense of 'to the end'. Here a decisive event is clearly linked with some future consequences. These differences reveal the problem: Does εἰς τέλος have a backward or a future reference? Before we attempt to resolve this problem, let us look at the verse, piece by piece: ἔφθασεν δὲ ἐπ᾽ αὐτοὺς ἡ ὀργὴ εἰς τέλος.

Key to understanding this verse is the concept 'the wrath of God' which Paul uses elsewhere in 1 Thessalonians and in Romans. In 1 Thessalonians it is used in 1.10 where the future reference to this 'wrath' is beyond question; a present decision of faith has positive implications with regard to the coming wrath of God. 'Wrath' is used in a similar eschatological context in 5.9. The chapter opens with the reminder that the 'day of the Lord will come like a thief in the night' (v. 2) and just prior to verse 9 Paul refers to 'the hope of salvation' (v. 8) and then continues: 'For God has not destined us for wrath, but to obtain salvation through our Lord Jesus Christ'. The Greek word περιποίησις followed by an objective genitive has a definite future reference which the RSV correctly translates in the sense of 'destined us for'. What does it mean for our interpretation of 'wrath' in 2.16 that the other two uses of the term in 1 Thessalonians refer to a future event? How does this relate to Paul's point in 2.16 that 'God's wrath *has come*' and to the meaning of εἰς τέλος?

It is significant that the only other letter in which Paul uses the term 'wrath' is in Romans. It will be of particular interest to examine the usage of the term in that letter, for it is precisely the alleged tensions with regard to Paul's reference to the Jews/Israel in 1 Thessalonians and Romans that have led some to suggest that 1 Thess. 2.13–16 is a later interpolation. 'Wrath' is used ten times in Romans (1.18; 2.5, 8; 3.5; 4.15; 5.9; 9.22; 12.19; 13.4, 5). Let us examine the first appearance of this term in Rom. 1.18. It is critical to understand the context in which this text is found.

It follows verses 16–17 where Paul has defined the gospel and the fact that in it 'the righteousness of God is revealed through faith for faith'. Then follows verse 18: 'For the wrath of God is revealed from heaven against all ungodliness and wickedness of those who by their wickedness suppress the truth.' It is impossible to review the recent discussion of this verse,[37] and so we must state our understanding as tersely as possible, which, for the most part, is supportive of Cranfield's exegesis as well as Beker's overall perspective. The 'wrath of God' is an apocalyptic concept and the 'decisive perspective is the eschatological one';[38] reference to such texts as Zeph. 1.18 and Dan. 8.19 indicate how the last judgment can be referred to as the day of wrath. Although the world has stood under the judgment and wrath of God prior to the gospel, the 'eschatological present (of the gospel) implicitly illuminates the past'.[39] Cranfield asserts that the most natural way of taking verse 18 is to understand that God's wrath is also being revealed in the gospel so that 'basic to this revelation of the wrath of God in the preaching, is the prior revelation of the wrath of God in the gospel events'. In conclusion Cranfield adds that the full meaning of God's wrath is to be seen not 'in the disasters befalling sinful men in the course of history', but rather 'in its revelation in Gethsemane and on Golgatha'.[40] In verse 18 Paul makes clear that because of the gospel, namely, the death and resurrection of Jesus, all persons, Jews and Gentiles, stand explicitly under the wrath of God until such time that they accept His offer of new life in Christ as grace.

In Rom. 1.18–31 the Jew is at least implicitly included[41] in Paul's survey; in 9.22–24 there is explicit reference to the unbelieving Jews. Käsemann states the case well: In these verses the 'power of the final Judge (is) already manifested in the present, as in 1.18–3.20'.[42] In addition to the past reference, Paul

---

[37] See C. E. B. Cranfield, *A Critical and Exegetical Commentary on the Epistle to the Romans* (ICC; 2 vols; Edinburgh: T&T Clark, 1975), 1.106–10.

[38] Käsemann, *Romans*, p. 37.

[39] Käsemann, *Romans*, p. 35.

[40] Cranfield, *Romans*, pp. 109–10.

[41] Beker, *Paul the Apostle*, pp. 78–83.

[42] Käsemann, *Romans*, p. 270.

clearly recognizes both the present and future dimension of God's wrath, and the statements about the wrath of God in Romans move primarily between these two poles, some being closer to the one and others closer to the other. For example, 2.5, 8 and 5.9 clearly refer to the future exercise of God's wrath and 1.18 and 9.22 describe the present demonstration of that wrath. Rom. 5.9 is an important verse: 'Since, therefore, we are now justified by his blood, much more shall we be saved by him from the wrath of God.' In Christ, through justification, one neither experiences the wrath of God now nor in the future, a thought closely paralleled in 1 Cor. 11.32. Of the remaining 'wrath' verses in Romans, 12.19 is probably to a future reference, while 3.5 and 4.15 refer to the present exercise of God's wrath through the ruling authorities. To summarize: We have observed that the wrath of God in Romans refers to the death of Jesus, to the present and to the future. 'The death of Christ', suggests Beker, 'truly constitutes the eschatological judgment of the powers ... And God's apocalyptic judgment in the death of Christ will be confirmed in the last judgment...'.[43] Lying behind such an observation is the recognition that the cross marks the culmination of God's judgment and wrath; it is the apocalyptic turning point of history.

To return now to the meaning of 1 Thess. 2.16b: 'But God's wrath has come upon them εἰς τέλος.' Through the death of Christ, God's judgment and wrath has expressed itself. In 1 Thessalonians 2 this is applied particularly to the Jews, a perspective quite parallel to Rom. 1.18–3.20 and 9.22–24.[44] There is little question among contemporary exegetes that ἔφθασεν means 'has

---

[43] Beker, *Paul the Apostle*, p. 90. Note also C. E. B. Cranfield, 'A Study of 1 Thessalonians 2', *IBS* I (1979), pp. 215–26, especially p. 219. For one who regards such an interpretation as 'over-subtle' see I. H. Marshall, *1 and 2 Thessalonians* (NCB; Grand Rapids: Eerdmans, 1983), p. 81.

[44] This understanding of wrath as God's apocalyptic judgment in the death of Christ differs sharply from that of E. Bammel, 'Judenverfolgung und Naherwartung. Zur Eschatologie des Ersten Thessalonicherbriefs', *ZTK* 56 (1959), pp. 294–315. He argues that the wrath of God which has come upon the Jews is their expulsion from Rome by Claudius in 49 CE. See also O. Michel, 'Fragen zu I Thessalonicher 2,14–16: Anti-jüdische Polemik bei Paulus', in *Antijudaismus im Neuen Testament? Exegetische und systematische Beiträge*, ed. W. Eckert, *et. al.* (ACJD 1; München, 1967), pp. 50–9.

come, has arrived' and should not be understood as a prophetic aorist.[45] The real issue is whether εἰς τέλος refers to that same event in the past and is intensifying it, namely, the translation 'finally', or whether it is referring to the future, namely, 'until the end'.[46] We would argue for the latter meaning for three reasons: 1) the use of 'wrath' in 1 Thessalonians itself, with its present and future references; 2) the use of 'wrath' in Romans and its very similar present and future references; and 3) the use of εἰς τέλος in an apocalyptic context in the gospel tradition.

There is no need for us to review the evidence already provided for points one and two and so we shall turn immediately to the third point. The critical text is the one found in the Markan apocalypse, 13.12–13: 'Brother will betray brother to death, and a father his child, and children will rise against parents and have them put to death; and you will be hated by all because of my name. But the one who endures to the end [εἰς τέλος] will be saved.'[47] In light of this we would translate 1 Thess. 2–16b in this way: 'And now God's wrath has come upon them until the end.'

How does this understanding of 1 Thess. 2.16b in particular and 2.13–16 in general relate to the criticism of the inconsistency, if not contradiction, between this passage and what Paul has to say about Israel in Rom. 9–11?[48] We would suggest that the relationship between 1 Thessalonians and Romans is not one of inconsistency. In Romans, Paul does not negate what he said in his first letter but augments it; 1 Thessalonians does not contain the last word concerning Israel. Because of a specific problem in the Roman congregation, which we have described in detail elsewhere,[49] Paul needs to deal with the issue of the relation of Jew and Gentile in connection with the question of Israel's future.

---

[45] Okeke, 'The Fate of the Unbelieving Jews', p. 130.

[46] For the literature supporting the various exegetical possibilities see Marshall, *Thessalonians*, p. 81.

[47] See also the parallel in Matt. 24.13.

[48] See the excellent discussion in Davies, *Jewish and Pauline Studies*, pp. 123–52.

[49] K. P. Donfried, 'False Presuppositions in the Study of Romans', in *The Romans Debate*, ed. K. P. Donfried (Minneapolis: Augsburg, 1977), pp. 120–48; also now in *The Romans Debate: Revised and Expanded Edition* (Peabody, MA: Hendrickson, 2001), pp. 102–25. I am glad to note Beker's remarkably similar analysis.

Therefore, while not denying what he has said previously, he adds some new information in Rom. 11.25–32, namely, that at the end God's mercy will be extended to Israel in a mysterious way and all Israel will be saved. The negative statements about the Jews in 1 Thess. 2.13–16 are not denied in Romans; they are taken up in such statements as 10.21, 'But of Israel he says, "All day long I have held out my hands to a disobedient and contrary people"', or in 9.22–24 as we previously noted, or in 10.3 that Israel's striving after the law missed the mark. Having restated his case against the Jews, Paul then proceeds in Rom. 11 with the added information about God's great mercy toward Israel on the last day. 1 Thessalonians reports God's attitude of wrath toward the Jews from the death of Jesus until the last day; Romans adds that at the last day God's mercy will be revealed toward them in a mysterious and radically new way. In the words of Beker, 'Israel's eschatological destiny and privilege is therefore tied to God's original intention with her, that is, that Israel might perceive through Christ to know what it is to live by grace alone.'[50]

Beker's magesterial treatment of Paul has helped us to understand the apocalyptic context of the apostle with greater precision and therefore has assisted us in the re-evaluation of the function of 1 Thess. 2.13–16 both with regard to the coherent structure of Paul's theology in general and with regard to the contingent interpretation necessary to deal with the particular situation facing Paul in Thessalonica, a situation, as we noted, quite different from the contingent situation of Romans. Only when the contingent situation of each Pauline audience is comprehended can the coherent theology of Paul be understood; only when the coherent theology of Paul is understood can the contingent situation of each Pauline letter be comprehended. The interpreter is invited to enter precisely into that hermeneutical circle.[51]

---

[50] Beker, *Paul the Apostle*, p. 336.
[51] See my discussion of this same point in K. P. Donfried, *The Dynamic Word* (San Francisco: Harper and Row, 1981), especially pp. 197–9.

10

Was Timothy in Athens? Some Exegetical Reflections on 1 Thess. 3.1–3[1]

It is difficult for many commentators to reconcile the observations made in Acts 17.14–15 with those given in 1 Thess. 3.1–3. According to the text in Acts 17, Paul went to Athens from Beroea whereas Silas/Silvanus and Timothy were left in Beroea. The next and final reference to these particular Pauline co-workers in Acts 18.5 has them arriving in Corinth from Macedonia.

The tension between the two accounts in 1 Thessalonians and Acts suggested by some scholars can be summarized in this way: although Acts makes no reference to a visit by Timothy in Athens, such a visit is thought to be indicated by 1 Thess. 3.1–3.[2]

---

[1] This essay first appeared in *Die Freude an Gott – unsere Kraft* Festschrift Otto Knoch; ed. J. J. Degenhardt; Stuttgart: Katholisches Bibelwerk, 1991, pp. 189–96; as 'War Timotheus in Athen? Exegetische Überlegungen zu 1 Thess. 3,1–3', it appears here in English, in slightly revised form, for the first time.

[2] The view of T. Holtz [*Der erste Brief an die Thessalonicher* (2nd ed; EKK XIII; Zürich/Neukirchen-Vluyn: Benzinger/Neukirchener Verlag, 1986), p. 124] is typical: 'Denn wenn sich auch nicht zwingend aus dem Satz, daß Paulus beschloß, allein in Athen zurückzubleiben, ergibt, daß Timotheus von dort nach Thessalonich geschickt wurde, so ist das doch zweifellos sein einzig natürliches Verständnis.' [ET: 'Even though it cannot be compellingly concluded from the phrase referring to Paul's decision to remain alone in Athens that Timothy was sent from there to Thessalonica, yet that must be, without doubt, its natural meaning.'] See also the new commentary by S. Légasse, *Les Épîtres de Paul aux Thessaloniciens* (LD Commentaires 7; Paris: Cerf, 1999: 'Selon Paul (1 Th 3, 2.6), Timothée était d'abord avec lui à Athènes.' [ET: 'According to Paul (1 Thess. 3.2, 6) Timothy was initially with him in Athens.']

The NRSV translates it in this way: 'Therefore when we could bear it no longer, we decided to be left alone in Athens; and we sent Timothy, our brother and co-worker for God in proclaiming the gospel of Christ, to strengthen and encourage you for the sake of your faith, so that no one would be shaken by these persecutions. Indeed, you yourselves know that this is what we are destined for.' Several exegetical difficulties emerge in these verses. For the moment we limit ourselves to two:

1) To whom does the 'we' in 1 Thess. 3.1 refer? Does it include Paul, Timothy and/or Silas/Silvanus?[3] If so, then Acts does not acknowledge the simultaneous presence of these persons in Athens. G. Krodel offers one solution to this ambiguity:

> Naturally, one can harmonize the two accounts by postulating that Silas and Timothy met Paul in Athens (omitted in Acts) and that the apostle then sent Timothy to Thessalonica (omitted in Acts but stated in 1 Thessalonians) and Silas to Philippi, or some other place in Macedonia (omitted in Acts and in Paul's letters). Later, they both joined Paul in Corinth, as stated in 18.5. But there is a simpler explanation. Luke is wrong and Paul is right. Both companions traveled with Paul to Athens, from whence he sent Timothy to Thessalonica. He later rejoined Paul and Silas in Corinth. Nevertheless, we should recognize that Luke knew of a temporary separation of Timothy from Paul at this stage.[4]

Krodel's proposed solution, however, leaves unresolved several questions, especially with regard to the travel(s) of Silas/Silvanus. Had he remained in Macedonia? Or had Paul sent him here from Athens? Or did Silas/Silvanus remain with Paul in Athens and then travel with him to Corinth?

2) These ambiguities raise a further and primary question concerning the meaning of μόνοι in 1 Thess. 3.1. The plural form of μόνοι is linked to the plural of the verb ἐπέμψαμεν. But who is it, precisely, that remains in Athens 'alone', Paul and Silas/Silvanus or just Paul? Is this a genuine or simply a rhetorical plural? According to Marshall it is the former and he proposes that the 'best solution may be to assume that the thought is expressed loosely and that Paul means 'We (all three of us, or

---

[3] That these two names refer to one and the same person is disputed. See F. F. Bruce, *1 and 2 Thessalonians* (WBC 45; Waco, TX, Word Books, 1982), p. 6.

[4] G. Krodel, *Acts* (ACNT; Minneapolis: Augsburg, 1986), p. 322.

Timothy and myself) resolved that I should be left at Athens alone and that Timothy should be sent to you.'[5] However, this suggestion, with its use of the term 'loosely', carries with it considerable uncertainty and no compelling reason is given as to why the verb could not just as well be understood as a rhetorical plural.

The solutions proposed by both Krodel and Marshall are certainly within the realm of possibility and, one needs to acknowledge, perhaps, that there may be no other options in reconciling the differing information provided by 1 Thessalonians and Acts with regard to the journeys of these specific co-workers in relationship to those of Paul. Our position with regard to the overall credibility and accuracy of Acts has been published previously.[6] Although the theological framework of Acts is primarily the creation of Luke, the narrative within it contains a wealth of detailed, precise and accurate information. We reject two extremes found in Acts scholarship: either a radical rejection of the historical reliability of this volume or a literalist insistence on the accuracy of the entire volume. In fact, if one were to take the latter position, one would be compelled to find some harmonization between the two texts in question. However, by avoiding these two extremes one is in a position to at least raise the question whether the information presented in 1 Thess. 3.1–3 has been properly understood by many interpreters and whether, in fact, these two texts really contradict each other, as is often suggested.

Our thesis is straightforward: given the two sources at our disposal it can be argued that Timothy was never in Athens and that to understand 1 Thess. 3.1 otherwise creates more problems than it solves. In order to assess this proposal carefully, some fundamental questions must be asked: 1) whether the plural verbs

[5] I. H. Marshall, *1 and 2 Thessalonians* (NCBC; Grand Rapids, MI: Eerdmans, 1983), p. 90.

[6] K. P. Donfried, 'Paul and Judaism: 1 Thessalonians 2.13–16 as a Test Case', *Int* 38 (1984), p. 247; 'The Cults of Thessalonica and the Thessalonian Correspondence', *NTS* 31 (1985), pp. 336–56, and, '1 Thessalonians, Acts and Early Paul', in *The Thessalonian Correspondence*, ed. R. F. Collins (BETL 87; Leuven: University Press–Peeters, 1990), pp. 3–26. All three articles are now in this volume: pp. 195–208; 21–48; and, 69–98, respectively.

εὐδοκήσαμεν and ἐπέμψαμεν (together with the plural form of the adjective μόνοι) are not indeed to be understood as rhetorical plurals, i.e. that Paul is really only referring to himself; 2) the specific meaning of ἐπέμψαμεν; and, 3) the meaning of the explicit reference to Athens and the significance of ἐν Ἀθήναις for understanding the intention of Paul's argument.

The following observations are relevant in light of this proposal and the questions posed:

1) The plural form of the verbs ἐπέμψαμεν and εὐδοκήσαμεν, as well as the plural μόνοι, are best understood as rhetorical plurals referring only to Paul. Several factors point in this direction. As can be seen from the salutation, Paul is writing this letter in the presence of Silvanus and Timothy, most likely from Corinth. The assumption that 1 Thessalonians (or a part of this letter) was written from Athens based on the text of 3:1 is not immediately self-evident[7] and the older perspective that Paul wrote this letter from a city other than Athens is essentially correct.[8] Otherwise, would he not have written 'to be left alone *here*' rather than simply 'to be left alone *in Athens*'?

Paul, in all likelihood, writes this letter from Corinth in the presence of Silas/Silvanus and Timothy, shortly after their arrival in that city.[9] Looking back to the beginnings of the Thessalonian Christian community, the apostle writes in order to comfort, encourage and strengthen these Christians in the midst of ongoing persecution.[10] Only when the argumentation requires a specific reference to himself does he employ the first person singular rather than the rhetorical plural. Such is the case in both 1 Thess. 2.18 and 3.5. In both situations Paul emphasizes that his

---

[7] See, for example, R. Pesch, *Die Entdeckung des ältesten Paulus-Briefes* (Freiburg: Herder, 1984).

[8] F. J. Foakes Jackson and K. Lake, ed., *The Beginnings of Christianity*, 5 vols (Grand Rapids: Baker, 1966), 4.224; T. Zahn, *Introduction to the New Testament* (New York: Scribner's, 1917), pp. 207–24.

[9] Acts 18.5; 1 Thess. 3.6 (only Timothy is mentioned, although in 1 Thess. 1.1 Silvanus is also mentioned).

[10] See K. P. Donfried, 'The Theology of 1 Thessalonians', in *The Theology of the Shorter Pauline Letters*, ed. K. P. Donfried and I. H. Marshall (New Testament Theology; Cambridge: Cambridge University Press, 1993), pp. 243–60.

absence is neither due to diminished concern about this church nor because he has ignored the difficulties faced by this congregation. The entire letter allows Paul to reject emphatically such perceptions. 'As for us, brothers and sisters, when, for a short time [πρὸς καιρὸν ὥρας], we were made orphans by being separated from you – in person, not in heart – we longed with great eagerness to see you face to face. For we wanted to come to you – certainly I, Paul, wanted to again and again – but Satan blocked the way (2.17–18).' When Paul, writing this letter in collaboration with his two colleagues, wishes to refer to a past event that relates primarily to himself, he must then, of necessity, use the first person singular, which is exactly what he does here. This is the reason for the change from plural to singular in 1 Thess. 2.18 and 3.5, viz. we are dealing with a period in which Paul was alone, a situation that holds true for Athens and, probably, for his initial time in Corinth as well.

A superficial glance at 3.1 might give the impression that we are here not dealing with a rhetorical plural, a perspective that is widespread in the literature. But following upon a closer examination of these verses, and especially 3.5 ('For this reason, when I could bear it no longer, I sent to find out about your faith; I was afraid that somehow the tempter had tempted you and that our labor had been in vain'), such a perspective cannot be maintained. Once Paul has interrupted the first person plural in 2.18 with a specific reference to himself, he immediately takes up the redactional plural again. A second interruption occurs in 3.5, a verse that represents a partial paraphrase of 3.1–2 in the first person singular. The plural forms στέγοντες and ἐπέμψαμεν of 3.1–2 are replaced by a singular form in 3.5: στέγων and ἔπεμψα. This would confirm that plural μόνοι in 3.1 is conformed to the rhetorical plural of the verb. As his own testimony in 3.5 bears witness, it is specifically Paul who is anxious to know something about the status of the Christian church in Thessalonica.

2) Must the verb πέμπω necessarily suggest that the one who was sent to Thessalonica by Paul, Timothy, had to have been present with Paul in Athens at the time of the sending? We believe not and are one with von Dobschütz when he writes: 'es

kann sich auch durch den Auftrag an einen Entfernten vollziehen, nach Thess. zu gehen statt zu Paulus zurückzukehren: das trägt dem καταλειφθῆναι ἐν Ἀθ. μόνοι auch völlig Rechnung'.[11] In a similar manner Rigaux writes: 'Cela n'implique pas nécessairement que c'est d'Athènes que Paul renvoya Timothée à Thessalonique.'[12] In other words: Paul may have sent Timothy back to Thessalonica either while they were still together in Beroea or after Paul arrived in Athens. With regard to the latter, it is possible that those who accompanied Paul from Beroea to Athens (Acts 17.15) presented to Timothy, upon their return, Paul's request. Of these two options, we prefer the former since the latter suggests, dubiously, that Paul had received some new information in Athens. At any rate, the main intention of Paul's words in 1 Thess. 3.1–2 focuses on the fact that he will remain alone in Athens without the company and encouragement of his co-workers precisely because of his deep concern for the Thessalonian church. That this situation of being alone is caused by the departure of Timothy from Athens is simply not to be found in the text.

R. Pesch has argued that ἐπέμψαμεν should be understood as an epistolary aorist, that is, an aorist with a present meaning.[13] In this way he wishes to support his thesis that 1 Thessalonians in its canonical form is a redactional combination of two originally separate letters. The first was written in Athens and delivered to Thessalonica by Timothy and the second was written in Corinth. As a result Paul is not looking back to a past event but, rather, by using the aorist, he is expressing a present event, viz. the sending of Timothy to Thessalonica together with a letter. Pesch expands this observation by emphasizing that 1 Thess. 2.17–3.5 and 1 Thess. 3.6–10 represent two completely different situations in

---

[11] E. von Dobschütz, *Die Thessalonicher-Briefe* (KEK X; Göttingen: Vandenhoeck and Ruprecht, [1909] repr. 1974), p. 131. [ET: 'we could also be dealing with a commission to one who is distant to go to Thessalonica instead of returning to Paul: this interpretation gives due weight to καταλειφθῆναι ἐν Ἀθ. μόνοι.']

[12] B. Rigaux, *Saint Paul. Les Épîtres aux Thessaloniciens* (EtB; Paris-Gembloux: Gabalda-Duculot, 1956), p. 467. [ET: 'This does not necessarily imply that Paul sent Timothy to Thessalonica from Athens'].

[13] Pesch, *Die Entdeckung*, p. 61.

the apostolic work of Paul. The first represents an anxious time in Athens; the second reveals a confident period in Corinth resulting from the return of Timothy with his positive report about the situation in Thessalonica.

Using these arguments, together with the doublets and repetitions in 1 Thessalonians, Pesch reconstructs two originally separate letters:

Letter from Athens		Letter from Corinth	
	(Address)		(Address)
2.13–16	Thanksgiving	1.2–10	Thanksgiving and Retrospect
2.1–12	Retrospect		
2.17; 3.5	Sending of Timothy	3.6–10	Return of Timothy
		4.9–12	Concerning brotherly love
		4.13–18	Concerning 'those who have fallen asleep'
		5.1–11	Concerning 'times and seasons'
4.1–8	Exhortations	5.12–22	Exhortations
3.11–13	Conclusion (Concluding benediction)	5.23–27	Conclusion
		5.28	Concluding benediction

Pesch defends his understanding of ἐπέμψαμεν in 1 Thess. 3.2 as an epistolary aorist by referring to a series of other New Testament texts where the aorist functions in similar ways. This is a somewhat tenuous approach since it can only be the specific context that will determine how a given aorist is to be understood. Pesch seems unconcerned by the question as to why, in light of the broader context (2.17–3.5), it is only these two aorists in 3.1–2 (ἐπέμψαμεν and εὐδοκήσαμεν) that should be understood in this way. Further, he pays no particular attention to the Pauline paraphrase of these verses in 3.5 and he also does not explain how one can understand ἔπεμψα as an epistolary aorist. The text itself simply does not warrant the conclusion that these two verbs in 3.1–2 are, in fact, epistolary aorists.

If one accepts the likelihood that the broader context in which 3.1–2 is found allows for no other interpretation than that these verbs are *not* epistolary aorists, then one must conclude that

215

Pesch's search for other texts that would support his conclusion has not been successful. Nevertheless, let us review briefly some of the texts that Pesch draws upon to support his thesis that ἐπέμψαμεν in 1 Thess. 3.2 functions as an epistolary aorist: a) Phlm 12: without question this is an epistolary aorist and the entire letter is written from the perspective of an orally transmitted message. However, can this radically different situation and substantially distinct context really serve to justify Pesch's interpretation of 1 Thess. 3.2? b) Acts 15.22–23a and 25–27. For Pesch this report about persons sent from Jerusalem to Antioch with an accompanying letter is a compelling parallel for his understanding of 1 Thessalonians. This text is not, however, unproblematic. In the first place this 'letter' is not written by a particular individual to a specific congregation. The document simply wishes to convey a decision.[14] Second, it is not clear whether this 'letter' is a Lucan creation or whether it is derived from a source. In all likelihood Luke is describing a compromise agreement, one which probably arose in a variety of Christian churches that had a combined membership of former Jews and former Gentiles. This decision, either according to common understanding at the time or according to Luke's perception, derived from the apostolic period. In short, the completely dissimilar context as well as the unlike literary genre in which the infinitive πέμψαι occurs,[15] can hardly give weight to the argument that the use of ἐπέμψαμεν in 1 Thess. 3.2 is an epistolary aorist. c) 1 Cor. 4.17: Both to view this text as an epistolary aorist and to view it as a parallel to 1 Thess. 3.2 is highly questionable. In all likelihood, an event that has already taken place is being described. First, Timothy is not mentioned in 1 Cor. 1.1 and we have little reason to believe that he was present as Paul was composing this letter. Second, according to 1 Cor. 16.10 Timothy has already departed. Barrett reaches exactly the opposite conclusion from that of Pesch: 'It may be that *I have*

---

[14] ἔδοξε is a technical term for reaching an agreement about something at a meeting or assembly.

[15] Since the infinitive represents the focus, not the time of a given stem, it cannot be cited as a parallel for the epistolary aorist.

sent means, "I have sent word to Timothy, who has already set out for a different destination (Macedonia), that he should go on from there to visit you."[16] d) Phil. 2.19–24. Pesch's reference to this text also fails to convince. He asserts: 'This comparative text, with a renewed second word of commissioning, supports the fact that an actual sending is described in 1 Thess. 3.1–5.'[17] However, a problem with this view is that the ingressive infinitive πέμψαι clearly refers to the future.

As a result of these observations, we are not persuaded by Pesch's analysis of 1 Thess. 3.1–2. What Pesch considers the more or less corresponding nature of the parallels beyond 1 Thessalonians to which he has drawn attention cannot replace the more spontaneous and obvious context in which these verses are found. Read carefully, the original context reveals a quite logical and natural line of thought. The break between 1 Thess. 2.17–3.5 and 3.6–10 that Pesch proposes simply does not exist, especially if it is seen in light of Paul's intention to strengthen and encourage the church in Thessalonica.

3) If the argument of Paul in 1 Thess. 3.1–5 is to be correctly understood, then the position of ἐν Ἀθήναις in these verses needs to be taken quite seriously. The reference to Athens refers neither to the city in which 1 Thessalonians was written nor the city from which Timothy was sent. It is rather the city in which Paul 'decided *to be left alone*'.[18] This theme of being alone is critical for discerning the argument,[19] and von Dobschütz recognizes Paul's frame of mind well: for the apostle 'to remain alone in this unfamiliar environment, given his need for fellowship and

---

[16] C. K. Barrett, *A Commentary on the First Epistle to the Corinthians* (HNTC; New York: Harper and Row, 1968), p. 116. See also H. Conzelmann, *Der erste Brief an die Korinther* (Göttingen: Vandenhoeck and Ruprecht, 1969), p. 111, n. 19: 'ἔπεμψα ist nicht Aorist des Briefstils.' ['ἔπεμψα is not an epistolary aorist'].

[17] Pesch, *Die Entdeckung*, p. 62. ['Auch dieser Vergleichstext (auch mit der erneut doppelten Sendungsaussage) spricht dafür, daß in 1 Thess 3,15 eine aktuelle Sendung beschrieben ist.']

[18] P. Ellingworth and E. A. Nida, *A Translator's Handbook on Paul's Letters to the Thessalonians* (London: United Bible Societies, 1976), p. 52.

[19] *Rigaux, Les Épîtres aux Thessaloniciens*, p. 467: '-μόνοι, l'emphase est voulue, le mot étant rejeté à la fin de la phrase.' [ET: '-μόνοι, the emphasis is intentional since it is placed at the end of the phrase'].

dialogue, was indeed a great sacrifice; by weakening this theme one deadens the nerve center of the entire argument'.[20]

Our primary attention has been directed toward Timothy since Paul refers both to his sending and his return and we have found no compelling argument to suggest that he or Silas/Silvanus were with Paul in Athens. In all likelihood they remained in Macedonia following Paul's departure for Athens.[21] From there Timothy eventually travelled with Silas/Silvanus to Corinth in order to meet Paul. Their activities in Macedonia at this time are not specified in Acts or in 1 Thessalonians, with the exception of the latter's reference to Timothy's second visit in Thessalonica. Did either or both of them return to Philippi? That is possible, but never stated.[22]

By way of summary we can conclude: ἐπέμψαμεν in 1 Thess. 3.2 is a rhetorical plural and therefore requires the plural form μόνοι. Paul arrived in Athens without either Silas/Silvanus or Timothy and we have no information to suggest that these two co-workers were ever with Paul in that city. Paul was there alone and there is little reason to doubt the reliability of the information that is provided in Acts 17.14–15 ('Then the believers immediately sent Paul away to the coast, but Silas and Timothy remained behind. Those who conducted Paul brought him as far as Athens; and after receiving instructions to have Silas and Timothy join him as soon as possible, they left him') and 18.5 ('When Silas and Timothy arrived from Macedonia, Paul was occupied [in Corinth] with proclaiming the word, testifying to the Jews that the Messiah was Jesus'). In addition, we have questioned the viability of Pesch's contention that the verbs

---

[20] von Dobschütz, *Die Thessalonicher-Briefe*, pp. 130–1. ['allein bleiben in dieser fremden Umgebung, das war für ihn bei seinem Bedürfnis nach Gemeinschaft und Austausch sein schweres Opfer; es heißt den Nerv der ganzen Argumentation töten, wenn man dies Motive abschwächt.']

[21] Pesch, *Die Entdeckung*, p. 18: 'Jedenfalls blieb Silas in Beröa und arbeitete hier wohl an der Konsolidierung der Gemeinde' [ET: 'At any rate, Silas remained in Beroea and perhaps worked there in consolidating the congregation.']

[22] Pesch's suggestion (*Die Entdeckung*, p. 98) is totally speculative: 'Silas und Timotheus haben also, als sie nach Korinth kamen, eine finanzielle Unterstützung für Paulus aus Philippi mitgebracht.' [ET: 'Silas and Timothy brought financial support with them for Paul from Philippi to Corinth.']

ἐπέμψαμεν and εὐδοκήσαμεν are epistolary aorists and that, further, based on this hypothesis, one should understand the final form of 1 Thessalonians as composed of two originally separate letters. Neither aspect of this thesis finds even minimal support in the text of 1 Thessalonians.

11

Paul and Qumran: The Possible Influence of סרך on 1 Thessalonians

The Ambiguity of νουθετεῖτε τοὺς ἀτάκτους in 1 Thess. 5.14

Among the unresolved enigmas in 1 Thessalonians, Paul's first letter and thus the earliest extant Christian document, is the meaning of ἄτακτος in 1 Thess. 5.14. The phrase, νουθετεῖτε τοὺς ἀτάκτους, is rendered by the NRSV as: '[And we urge you, beloved,] to admonish the idlers'. The vast majority of commentaries understand the ἄτακτοι as 'idlers' or 'loafers'.[1] This translation is so ambiguous that one is hard-pressed to understand whom Paul is addressing and for what purpose. When Milligan urges that 'the special reference would seem to be to the idleness and neglect of duty which characterized certain members of the Thessalonian Church in view of the shortly-expected Parousia' he simply goes beyond the evidence of the text.[2] Is it

---

[1] For example, D. M. Martin, *1, 2 Thessalonians* (NAC 33; Broadman & Holman, 1995), p. 176: 'warn those who are idle'; C. A. Wanamaker, *The Epistle to the Thessalonians: A Commentary on the Greek Text* (NIGTC; Grand Rapids: Eerdmans, 1990), p. 197: 'idle or lazy'; F. F. Bruce, *1 and 2 Thessalonians* (WBC 45; Waco: Word, 1982), p. 122: 'loafers'; E. Best, *A Commentary on the First and Second Epistles to the Thessalonians* (BNTC; London: Adam and Charles Black, 1979), p. 222: 'admonish loafers'; J. E. Frame, *The Epistles of St Paul to the Thessalonians* (ICC; Edinburgh: T&T Clark, 1912), p. 197: 'idlers'.

[2] G. Milligan, *St Paul's Epistles to the Thessalonians* (London: Macmillan, 1908), p. 73. R. Jewett, *The Thessalonian Correspondence* (Philadelphia: Fortress Press, 1986), p. 104, moves in a similar direction and cites approvingly the position of Willi Marxsen [*Der erste Brief*, p. 71]: 'Judging from the details in 1 Thessalonians alone, Marxsen concludes that this group were "enthusiasts who because of the nearness of the parousia are no longer taking seriously the things of everyday life."'

possible to determine a meaning for ἄτακτος that coheres more closely with the rhetorical, ecclesiological and theological intention of 1 Thessalonians?[3]

The Testament of Levi and 4Qlevi^daram

A starting point for our investigation will be the Greek and Aramaic fragments of the *Testament of Levi*.[4] The relevant lines in the *Aramaic Testament of Levi f*rom the Cairo Geniza are located in a context of entering the Sanctuary and offering sacrifices:

> 30 After that, fine meal mixed with oil, after that pour out the wine and burn the frankincense over them; and let [all] your actions follow due order [Bod d: בסדך; Greek MS e: ἐν τάξει] and all your sacrifices be [acceptable] as a pleasing odor before the Most High God. 31 And [whatsoever] you do, do it in due order [Bod d: בסדך; Greek MS e: ἐν τάξει], [by measure] and weight, do not add anything that is not [fitting] and do not diminish from the amount.[5]

בסדך and ἐν τάξει are twice used equivalently in both fragments. In 1908 R. H. Charles suggested that these Aramaic and Greek fragments are versions of a common Hebrew text and that neither is the translation of the other.[6]

---

[3] See further K. P. Donfried in K. P. Donfried and I. H. Marshall, *The Theology of the Shorter Pauline Letters* (Cambridge: Cambridge University Press, 1993), especially pp. 1–7.

[4] The Aramaic fragments of the Testament of Levi from the Cairo Geniza are found in the Cambridge University Geniza Fragment T-S 16.94 and in the Bodleian Library Geniza Fragment, Ms Heb c 27 f 56. An infra-red photograph of the Cambridge fragments is published by J. C. Greenfield and M. E. Stone, 'Remarks on the Aramaic Testament of Levi from the Geniza', in M. E. Stone, *Selected Studies in Pseudepigrapha and Apocrypha* (SVTP: Leiden, E. J. Brill, 1991), pp. 228–46. Stone shares the judgment of Malachi Beit-Arié that these Aramaic Geniza texts 'were written before 1,000, that is at a period close to that of the palimpsest fragments of the Palestinian Talmud and of Genesis Rabba' (p. 230). The Greek and Bodleian Aramaic fragments are found in R. H. Charles, *The Greek Versions of the Testaments of the Twelve Patriarchs* (Oxford: Clarendon Press, 1908), p. 250. The Greek manuscript is from Mount Athos, Monastery of Koutloumous, Cod. 39 (cat. no. 3108), tenth century. For a detailed discussion of the issues see also H. W. Hollander and M. de Jonge, *The Testaments of the Twelve Patriarchs: A Commentary* (SVTP; Leiden: Brill, 1985), pp. 17–20.

[5] Text according to Bodleian d; translation by J. C. Greenfield and M. E. Stone in Hollander and de Jonge, *The Testaments*, p. 464.

[6] R. H. Charles, *The Testaments of the Twelve Patriarchs* (London: Adam and Charles Black, 1908), pp. lxx–lxxiii.

Following the publication of 1QLevi (1Q21) by J. T. Milik in 1955,[7] Greenfield and Stone concluded that 'the Geniza text was a medieval copy of a text similar to that which was found at Qumran, or was indeed based on a text which had come from the caves'.[8] In a subsequent paper Stone dated *The Aramaic Levi Document* to the third century BCE and suggested that it served as one of the sources of *The Book of Jubilees* and was influential in shaping the thought of the Qumran community in the second century.[9] Indeed, the term בסרך occurs in Frag 2, L 10, of 4QLevi[d]aram:[10] ו הו[א] עבדך בס[רך ו as reconstructed by Stone and Greenfield and which is translated: 'And [let your action follow due ord]er'.[11] סרך, a term without parallel in the Hebrew Bible,[12] may possibly have entered the vocabulary of the Qumran community as a result of the influence of *The Aramaic Levi Document*.

The Testament of Naphtali. and 4QTestament of Naphtali (4Q215)

The actual term, ἄτακτος, used in 1 Thess. 5.14, is found in the *Greek Testament of Naphtali*.[13] The text of *T. Naph*. 2.9 reads: οὕτως οὖν, τέκνα μου, ἐν τάξει ἐστὲ εἰς ἀγαθά, ἐν φόβῳ Θεοῦ, καὶ μηδὲν ἄκακτον ποιεῖτε ἐν καταφρονήσει, μηδὲ ἔξω καιροῦ αὐτοῦ.[14] Hollander and de Jonge translate 2.9–10 in this way: 'So

---

[7] DJD I 87–91.

[8] Greenfield and Stone, 'Remarks on the Aramaic Testament of Levi', p. 229.

[9] 'Enoch, Aramaic Levi and Sectarian Origins' in Stone, *Selected Studies*, pp. 247–58.

[10] The Qumran Cave 4 fragments consist of 4QLevi[a]aram, 4QLevi[b]aram, 4QLevi[c]aram and 4QLevi[d]aram.

[11] M. E. Stone and J. C. Greenfield, 'The Third and Fourth Manuscripts of *Aramaic Levi Document* From Qumran (4QLevi[c]aram and 4QLevi[d]aram)', *Le Muséon* 109 (1996), pp. 246–59.

[12] See further M. Weinfeld, *The Organizational Pattern and the Penal Code of the Qumran Sect* (NTOA; Göttingen: Vandenhoeck and Ruprecht, 1986). After reviewing the etymology of סרך, Weinfeld concludes: 'One has to admit however that although the etymology of סרך can be explained on the basis of cognate roots, the word סרך in its covenantal designation is not found in Hebrew besides Qumran' (p. 13).

[13] ἄτακτος is also found in HArt 9.23 (Artapanus) and ἀτακτέω in Prop (*Prophetarum vitae fabulosae*) 22.7; in the LXX only in 3 Macc. 1.19.

[14] M. de Jonge, *The Testaments of the Twelve Patriarchs: A Critical Edition of the Greek Text* (PVTG; Leiden: Brill, 1978), p. 116.

then, my children, be in order unto good, in the fear of God and do nothing disorderly in scorn or out of its due season. For if you tell the eye to hear, it cannot; so neither will you be able to do works of light while in darkness.'[15] In addition to this Greek recension, *T. Naph.* is found in two medieval Hebrew recensions.[16] This material was also incorporated by Rabbi Moses the Preacher of Narbonne (eleventh century) in his *Midrash bereshit rabbati*. In light of the four fragments that comprise 4QTestament of Naphtali (4Q215), Stone urges that 'R. Moses must have had a Hebrew or Aramaic source document and that, at a number of points, his citation is closer to 4QTestNaph than it is to TPN [= Greek recension of the Testament of the Twelve Patriarchs].'[17] Th. Korteweg and others would agree.[18]

The interpreter of 1 Thessalonians can learn much from a careful reading of *The Testament of Napthali*. In the verses under consideration, 2.9–10, one observes the ethical use of τάξις, i.e. the necessity to observe God's commandments (compare 1 Thess. 4.1–12) within the broader division between light and darkness (*T. Naph.* 2.7, 10; 1 Thess. 5.4–5). In *T. Naph.* 3 one of the illustrations for pursuing ethical behavior is that the sun, moon and stars 'do not change their order (ἀλλοιοῦσι τάξιν)' (3.2),[19] while the 'Gentiles changed their order (ἠλλοίωσαν τάξιν), having gone astray and having forsaken the Lord' (3.3).[20] The advice that the author of *T. Naph.* gives is straightforward: do not change the law of God by the disorderliness of your life and actions, because those who do so are like the Gentiles (see *T. Naph.* 4.1 and 1 Thess. 4.5). Contrariwise, the τάξις of the universe should lead one to the worship of the one true God (*T. Naph.* 3.3; 1 Thess. 1.9). Also, in *T. Naph.* 8.8–10 there is a very evident linkage between τάξις and ἐντολαί: 'Be, therefore, wise in God and prudent, understanding the order of his commandments (εἰδότες

---

[15] Hollander and de Jonge, *The Testaments*, p. 301.
[16] Hollander and de Jonge, *The Testaments*, pp. 25 and 296.
[17] M. E. Stone, 'The Hebrew Testament of Naphtali', *JJS* 47 (1996), p. 312.
[18] Hollander and de Jonge, *The Testaments*, pp. 296–7.
[19] See further M. E. Stone, 'The Parabolic Use of Natural Order in Judaism of the Second Temple Age', in Stone, *Selected Studies*, pp. 457–67.
[20] Hollander and de Jonge, *The Testaments*, p. 301.

τάξιν ἐντολῶν αὐτοῦ) and the laws of every activity, that the Lord will love you.'[21]

Thus, an examination of the Hebrew and Aramaic equivalents to the terms ἐν τάξει and ἄτακτος in the Napthali and, especially, in the Levi materials, suggests a nearness to the linguistic world of Qumran, especially if the proposed trajectory of development is persuasive. Yet the proximity of 1 Thessalonians to this particular segment of Second Temple Judaism is hardly surprising given both the similar use of theological concepts (e.g. election, holiness, apocalyptic eschatology)[22] and the utilization of identical terminology (e.g. קהל אל; בני אור).[23] Additional linkages between the two will be suggested as we proceed.

The Several Meanings of סרך in the Dead Sea Scrolls

For a term that has no antecedents in the Hebrew Bible, סרך appears with an amazing frequency in a variety of the DSS texts, but with a particular concentration in 1QS, 1QSa, 1QM, and CD. A survey of these texts allows one to conclude that this term is employed in three primary ways:

As a list of rules, i.e. ordered sayings in a small collection

A classic usage in this category is the very title of 1QS: [סרך היחד]. Also, 1QS 5.1: 'This is the rule [הסרך] for the men of the Community who freely volunteer to convert from all evil and to keep themselves steadfast in all he prescribes in compliance with his will. They should'.[24]

---

[21] Hollander and de Jonge, *The Testaments*, p. 318.

[22] See here D. Flusser, 'The Dead Sea Sect and Pre-Pauline Christianity', in D. Flusser, *Judaism and the Origins of Christianity* (Jerusalem: Magnes, 1988), pp. 23–74.

[23] See K. P. Donfried, 'The Assembly of the Thessalonians', in *Ekklesiologie des Neuen Testaments* (Festschrift Karl Kertelge; ed. R. Kampling and T. Söding; Freiburg: Herder, 1996), pp. 390–408. Now in this volume, pp. 139–62.

[24] F. G. Martínez, *The Dead Sea Scrolls Translated* (Leiden: Brill, 1994), p. 8; see also, for example, 1QS 6.8; 1QSa1.1; 1.6; 1.21.

As a group or classification of people organized according to a certain rule

This application of סרך is illustrated in 1QS 6.22: 'And if the lot results in him joining the Community, they shall enter him in the Rule [בסרך] according to his rank among his brothers for the law, for the judgment, for purity and for the placing of his possessions in common.'[25] The close coherence between the rule and community is evident in IQS 1.16–18: 'And all those who enter in the Rule of the Community [בסרך היחד] shall establish a covenant before God in order to a carry out all that he commands and in order not to stray from following him for any fear, dread or grief that might occur during the dominion of Belial.'[26] This intimate correlation between יחד, סרך and ברית is unique to the use of סרך/τάξις in Qumran. While there is an overlap between Qumran and the Greek literature of antiquity in the use of τάσσω/τάξις as rank or order, this covenantal/community dimension is absent in the latter.[27]

As a military formation

It is this application of סרך/τάξις that has the most frequent parallels in the Greek literature.[28] Typical of this usage is 1QM 5.3–4, 'When their army is complete, to fill a front line, the line will be formed of one thousand men, with seven forward formations per line, each formation in its own order [בסרך], each man being behind the other.'[29] As would be expected in 1QM, many of the specific rules (as above) refer to military matters.

---

[25] Martínez, *The Dead Sea Scrolls*, p. 10.

[26] Martínez, *The Dead Sea Scrolls*, p. 3.

[27] See the discussion in Weinfeld, *Organizational Pattern*; J. Licht, *Megilat HaSerakhim: The Rule Scroll: A Scroll from the Wilderness of Judea 1QS, 1Qsa, 1QSb: Text, Introduction and Commentary* (in modern Hebrew; Jerusalem: Bialik, 1965), especially p. 66 ; E. Qimron, *The Hebrew of the Dead Sea Scrolls* (Atlanta: Scholars Press, 1986) pp. 112, 116; and, Milligan, *St Paul's Epistles to the Thessalonians*, pp. 152–4. Further examples in this category might include 1QS 2.20; 2.21; 5.23.

[28] See further H. G. Liddell and R. Scott, *A Greek-English Lexicon* (Oxford: Clarendon, 1994), p. 1756.

[29] Martínez, *The Dead Sea Scrolls*, p. 98. See also 1QM15.5 and 1QSa1.23.

1 Thessalonians and the Possible Influence of סרך

Let us now probe 1 Thessalonians in greater detail. A careful examination of content and language suggests that 1 Thess. 5.12–15 refers back to 1 Thess. 4.1–12. This proposal coheres with our previously published rhetorical analysis of this earliest Pauline letter where we explained that 1 Thess. 5.12–15 was part of the concluding epistolary exhortation which is linked to the *probatio* in 4.1—5.3.[30]

Probatio [Proof]

A. First proof: 'how it is necessary to walk and to please God' (4.1–8)
B. Second proof: 'concerning brotherly love' (4.9–12)
C. Third proof: 'concerning those who have fallen asleep' (4.13—5.3)

The relevant texts are as follows:

Epistolary Exhortation

Ἐρωτῶμεν δὲ ὑμᾶς, ἀδελφοί, εἰδέναι τοὺς κοπιῶντας ἐν ὑμῖν καὶ προϊσταμένους ὑμῶν ἐν κυρίῳ καὶ νουθετοῦντας ὑμᾶς καὶ ἡγεῖσθαι αὐτοὺς ὑπερεκπερισσοῦ ἐν ἀγάπῃ διὰ τὸ ἔργον αὐτῶν. εἰρηνεύετε ἐν ἑαυτοῖς. παρακαλοῦμεν δὲ ὑμᾶς, ἀδελφοί, νουθετεῖτε τοὺς ἀτάκτους, παραμυθεῖσθε τοὺς ὀλιγοψύχους ἀντέχεσθε τῶν ἀσθενῶν, μακροθυμεῖτε πρὸς πάντας. ὁρᾶτε μή τις κακὸν ἀντὶ κακοῦ τινι ἀποδῷ, ἀλλὰ πάντοτε τὸ ἀγαθὸν διώκετε [καὶ] εἰς ἀλλήλους καὶ εἰς πάντας. (1 Thess. 5.12–15)

Probatio

Λοιπὸν οὖν, ἀδελφοί, ἐρωτῶμεν ὑμᾶς καὶ παρακαλοῦμεν ἐν κυρίῳ Ἰησοῦ, ἵνα καθὼς παρελάβετε παρ' ἡμῶν τὸ πῶς δεῖ ὑμᾶς περιπατεῖν καὶ ἀρέσκειν θεῷ, καθὼς καὶ περιπατεῖτε, ἵνα περισσεύητε μᾶλλον. οἴδατε γὰρ τίνας παραγγελίας ἐδώκαμεν ὑμῖν διὰ τοῦ κυρίου Ἰησοῦ. τοῦτο γάρ ἐστιν θέλημα τοῦ θεοῦ, ὁ ἁγιασμὸς ὑμῶν, ἀπέχεσθαι ὑμᾶς ἀπὸ τῆς πορνείας, εἰδέναι ἕκαστον ὑμῶν τὸ ἑαυτοῦ σκεῦος κτᾶσθαι ἐν ἁγιασμῷ καὶ τιμῇ, μὴ ἐν πάθει ἐπιθυμίας καθάπερ καὶ τὰ ἔθνη τὰ μὴ εἰδότα τὸν θεόν, τὸ μὴ ὑπερβαίνειν καὶ πλεονεκτεῖν ἐν τῷ πράγματι τὸν ἀδελφὸν αὐτοῦ, διότι ἔκδικος κύριος περὶ πάντων τούτων, καθὼς καὶ προείπαμεν ὑμῖν καὶ διεμαρτυράμεθα. οὐ γὰρ ἐκάλεσεν ἡμᾶς ὁ θεὸς ἐπὶ ἀκαθαρσίᾳ ἀλλ' ἐν ἁγιασμῷ. τοιγαροῦν ὁ ἀθετῶν οὐκ ἄνθρωπον ἀθετεῖ ἀλλὰ τὸν θεὸν τὸν [καὶ] διδόντα τὸ πνεῦμα αὐτοῦ τὸ ἅγιον εἰς ὑμᾶς.

Περὶ δὲ τῆς φιλαδελφίας οὐ χρείαν ἔχετε γράφειν ὑμῖν, αὐτοὶ γὰρ ὑμεῖς θεοδίδακτοί ἐστε εἰς τὸ ἀγαπᾶν ἀλλήλους, καὶ γὰρ ποιεῖτε αὐτὸ εἰς πάντας τοὺς ἀδελφοὺς [τοὺς] ἐν ὅλῃ τῃ Μακεδονίᾳ. Παρακαλοῦμεν δὲ

---

[30] Donfried, *The Shorter Pauline Letters*, pp. 1–9.

ὑμᾶς, ἀδελφοί, περισσεύειν μᾶλλον καὶ φιλοτιμεῖσθαι ἡσυχάζειν καὶ
πράσσειν τὰ ἴδια καὶ ἐργάζεσθαι ταῖς [ἰδίαις] χερσὶν ὑμῶν, καθὼς ὑμῖν
παρηγγείλαμεν, ἵνα περιπατῆτε εὐσχημόνως πρὸς τοὺς ἔξω καὶ μηδενὸς
χρείαν ἔχητε. (1 Thess. 4.1–12)

What we have in 4.1–12 is a small collection of rules, παραγγελίαι,
given by the Lord Jesus through Paul and his associates. The apostle
sternly warns that 'whoever disregards [ὁ ἀθετῶν] this, disregards
[ἀθετεῖ] not man but God, who gives his Holy Spirit to you' (4.8).
It is also evident in 1 Thessalonians that the ἐκκλησία (1.1) to which
Paul writes is organized around a certain principle, 'holiness' (ἐν
ἁγιασμῷ 4.7), and this is a fundamental consequence of what it
means to be ἐν Χριστῷ (4.16). These texts make it likely that the
ἄτακτοι are violating the first two understandings of סרך as
represented in the Qumran texts. As in *T. Naph.*, the ἄτακτοι of 1
Thessalonians are out-of-order with regard to the commandments
of God, standing on the side of darkness rather than light, and their
lack of ethical behavior indicates that they are more like the
Gentiles, who because of their idolatry, do not worship the one true
God. Texts such as 1 Thess. 1.9, 4.5, 4.13 and 5.5 show striking
similarities with this line of reasoning. We should also add that such
an interpretation of the ἄτακτοι has the support of no less an exegete
than John Chrysostom who considers these persons as acting in a
morally wrong way.[31] There is also a connection with the third use
of סרך in Qumran. The ἄτακτοι of 1 Thessalonians, because of their
being out-of-order with the commandments and the community of
God, are also out-of-order with another dimension of Pauline
advice, viz. adequate preparation for spiritual warfare: 'But, since we
belong to the day, let us be sober, and put on the breastplate of faith
and love, and for a helmet the hope of salvation' (1 Thess. 5.8).
1QM 6.14–15 reads: 'The horsemen of the rule [הסרך] shall be
between forty and fifty years old. They and their mounts [shall be
attired in breastplates], helmets and leggins and shall hold in their
hands circular shields and a spear of eight cu[bits].'[32] As the יחד of

---

[31] Chrysostom, *Hom 1 Thess.* v.14: He speaks of the ἄτακοι as πάντες οἱ παρὰ τὸ τῷ θεῷ
δοκοῦν πράττοντες ... πάντες οἱ ἁμαρτάνοντες (as cited in Milligan, *St Paul's Epistles to the
Thessalonians*, p. 153).
[32] Martínez, *The Dead Sea Scrolls*, p. 100 modified.

Qumran, so must the Thessalonian congregation be prepared for the struggle between light and darkness.

We must at least entertain the possibility that there is another dimension to this third use of the term סרך/τάξις that Paul may have in mind as he composes 1 Thessalonians, i.e. as order in the original military sense. In 1 Cor. 15.23 Paul shares his thoughts about the sequence of the resurrection: Ἕκαστος δὲ ἐν τῷ ἰδίῳ τάγματι ἀπαρχὴ Χριστός, ἔπειτα οἱ τοῦ Χριστοῦ ἐν τῇ παρουσίᾳ αὐτοῦ. That Paul has a similar meaning in mind when focusing on the ἄτακτοι in 1 Thessalonians might be suggested by the following phrases in 1 Thess. 4.13–18, where the reference is to those who have died unexpectedly, prior to the final consummation: 'For this we declare to you by the word of the Lord, that we who are alive, who are left until the coming of the Lord, will by no means precede [οὐ μὴ φθάσωμεν] those who have died' (v. 15); and again in verse 16: 'For the Lord himself, with a cry of command, with the archangel's call and with the sound of God's trumpet, will descend from heaven, and the dead in Christ will rise first [ἀναστήσονται πρῶτον].' Paul intends a distinct ordering of events with regard to meeting the Lord at his parousia: first those who have died and then only those who are still alive. Such an ordering, as described here in 1 Thess. 4.13–18, and similar to the use of τάγμα in 1 Cor. 15.23 as 'in the proper order', may be included in the reference to the ἄτακτοι in 1 Thess. 5.14. This is especially the case if one understands the meaning of νουθετέω in this context as primarily 'to instruct' rather than 'to warn, rebuke or chastise'.[33]

In 1 Thess. 4.18 Paul concludes the discussion of the prophetic word concerning those who have died with the words: Ὥστε παρακαλεῖτε ἀλλήλους ἐν τοῖς λόγοις τούτοις. Παρακαλέω in this context surely means 'to encourage, comfort or console'. If our tentative suggestion that the reference to the ἄτακτοι in 1 Thess.

---

[33] νουθετέω as 'to instruct' especially when followed with the accusative of person; *BAGD*, 544. For a similar use of νουθετέω in Paul see Rom. 15.14 and for a similar use of νουθεσία see 1 Cor. 10.11. In Eph. 6.4 and Philo, *Deus* 51–68, νουθεσία is used in conjunction with παιδεία. I thank Dr. D. Satran of Hebrew University for this Philo reference.

5.14 may refer back to 1 Thess. 4.13–18 then, if νουθετέω were to mean primarily 'to warn, rebuke or chastise', there would be a contradiction. How does one simultaneously console and chastise those who are grieving as the result of a confused eschatological time-table? More in accordance with the context is to interpret νουθετέω as 'to instruct'; if this is correct then the ἄτακτοι are being reminded of the instruction given in 4.13–18 and the proper sequence of meeting the Lord at the parousia. From such an implied use of τάγμα in 1 Thessalonians to the explicit use of τάγμα in 1 Cor. 15.23 is but a small step.

To summarize: the ἄτακτοι must be instructed in four areas by the leaders of the Thessalonian congregation: in the παραγγελίαι given by the Lord; in the way of holiness that is central to the life of the ἐκκλησία; in preparation for the spiritual warfare against the forces of darkness; and in understanding the proper order of events at the parousia. The first two areas of instruction cohere with the first and second proof, and the last two emphases cohere with the third proof.

The ἔργον of the Congregational Teacher/Leaders

These observations lead to another, one that transcends the limits of this paper, and must, therefore, remain very brief. Paul begins his epistolary exhortation in 5.12–13, i.e. the two verses preceding the reference to the ἄτακτοι, with these words: Ἐρωτῶμεν δὲ ὑμᾶς, ἀδελφοί, εἰδέναι τοὺς κοπιῶντας ἐν ὑμῖν καὶ προϊσταμένους ὑμῶν ἐν κυρίῳ καὶ νουθετοῦντας ὑμᾶς καὶ ἡγεῖσθαι αὐτοὺς ὑπερεκπερισσοῦ ἐν ἀγάπῃ διὰ τὸ ἔργον αὐτῶν. An appropriate translation would be: 'But we encourage you, brothers, to respect those who labor among you, and have charge of you in the Lord and instruct you; esteem them very highly in love because of their work.' We have argued elsewhere[34] that those referred to in these verses are the leaders of the Thessalonian church who are responsible for the well-being of the congregation. Given the suggestions made in this essay, what

---

[34] Donfried, *The Shorter Pauline Letters*, pp. 61–2.

is the meaning of the term ἔργον in the phrase 'esteem them very highly in love because of their work'?

1Q22 (1QWords of Moses), a text influenced by Deuteronomy, speaks about teachers whose particular work it is to expound the words of Torah. In col. II, lines 8–11, it is said: '[When] the covenant [has been estab]lished and the path [on which you must] walk [הדרך אשר תלכו] has been decreed, [choose for yourselves wise men who] will explain [חכים אשר יעשו לבאר] [to you and your so]ns all the words of this Law. [Be] very [careful,] for your lives, [to keep them, lest] the wrath [אף] [of your God] against you be enkindled and reach you ... And Moses [continued speaking] to the so[ns of Is]rael: Th[ese are the command]ments [מצוות] [which God] commands you to carry out.'[35]

In 1 Thess. 5.12–13, building on the Pauline assertions made in 1 Thess 4.1–3, reference is made to the selection of wise leaders (τοὺς προϊσταμένους ὑμῶν ἐν κυρίῳ) whose work it will be to instruct you (τοὺς νουθετοῦντας ὑμᾶς) in the commandments (παραγγελίας) which God commands (τοῦτο γάρ ἐστιν θέλημα τοῦ θεοῦ) them to carry out. As Paul encouraged the Thessalonians to walk (περιπατεῖν καὶ ἀρέσκειν θεῷ) on the path which God decreed, so must the leader/teachers, since those in Christ have not been destined for wrath (εἰς ὀργήν). The ἄτακτοι of 1 Thess. 5.14, within the context of this immediate discussion, are those persons who are out-of-order, disordered, both with regard to the rule of their community, viz. the commandments of God that lead to holiness, and with respect to the authority of the teachers in the Thessalonian congregation. Accordingly, we would translate 1 Thess. 5.14 as 'And we urge you, beloved, to instruct the disordered'. Having begun with the linguistic proximity of סרך/τάξις in Paul and Qumran, we are once again reminded of the conceptual proximity of the two as well.

---

[35] Martínez, *The Dead Sea Scrolls*, pp. 276–7 and DJD I, 93.

12

The Kingdom of God in Paul

To deal with the kingdom and kingdom of God references in the Pauline corpus is no simple task for it raises very profound and complicated issues with regard to the relationship of Paul to Jesus in general as well as Paul's use of the Jesus tradition in particular. While it is necessary to keep this larger issue in mind, method-ologically one should deal first with the specific Pauline passages in which this terminology is used and only once that has been done will it be appropriate to return to the larger questions just raised.

Paul uses kingdom/kingdom of God language in seven pas-sages: 1 Thess. 2.10–12; Gal. 5.21; 1 Cor. 4.20; 1 Cor. 6.9–10; 1 Cor. 15.24; 1 Cor. 15.50; and Rom. 14.17. Although I do not consider 2 Thessalonians as Pauline in the strict sense,[1] I will examine 2 Thess. 1.5 briefly in connection with 1 Thess. 2.10–12; some of the other deutero-Pauline passages will also be touched on briefly in the discussion of some of the above mentioned texts. I begin with 1 Cor. 15.24 for a variety of reasons, not least of which is the fact that recent treatments of kingdom passages in Paul omit mention of this most significant reference,[2] as well as the fact that its formal structure is unique among the kingdom

---

[1] See K. P. Donfried, 'The Cults of Thessalonica and the Thessalonian Correspondence', *NTS* 31 (1985), pp. 336–56; also pp. 21–48 in this volume.

[2] For example, G. Johnson, 'Kingdom of God Sayings in Paul's Letters', in *From Jesus to Paul* (Studies in Honour of Francis Wright Beare; ed. P. Richardson and J. C. Hurd; Waterloo: Wilfrid Laurier University, 1984), pp. 143–56 and G. Haufe, 'Reich Gottes bei Paulus und in der Jesustradition', *NTS* 31 (1985), pp. 467–72.

references in the Pauline letters. As I will show, 1 Cor. 15.24 defines the kingdom as both present and future. In light of this I would wish to test the thesis whether Rom. 14.17, 1 Cor. 4.20–21, and 1 Thess. 2.11–12 do not in fact have as their primary emphasis the presence of the kingdom, and whether 1 Cor. 15.50, 1 Cor. 6.9–10 and Gal. 5.21 do not have as their primary emphasis the kingdom as a still coming, future event. I also describe briefly their form and function in their respective contexts.

1 Cor. 15.24

Then comes the end, when he (Christ) delivers the kingdom to God the Father after destroying every rule and every authority and power.

This is a fascinating verse and yet one that has been virtually overlooked in previous discussions of the kingdom in Pauline thought. The kingdom is closely associated with Christ; it is something which he will deliver to God at the end when even Christ will be subjected to God so 'that God may be everything to every one' (15.28). If this is the case then clearly the concept of the kingdom for Paul is not an exclusively future one; in some sense the kingdom is present to those who are in Christ – it is a *present phenomenon* as well.

Conzelmann[3] shows Paul's indebtedness to the apocalyptic tradition in these verses of 1 Corinthians, particularly to the 'Apocalypse of the Ten Weeks' in *1 En.* 91–93 and *Sib. Or.* 4.47–91. Although influenced by this tradition Paul transforms it and transposes the messianic kingdom

into the present. For Christ is risen. His kingdom fills up the period between the resurrection and the consummation of the work of salvation after the parousia. It is not the kingdom of visible peace. This period is determined by the cross. Here the cosmological apocalyptic notions of the messianic kingdom disappear. It is Christologically speaking the time of the subjection of the powers, anthropologically speaking the time of the church, of the proclaiming of the death of Christ, of faith, of hope.[4]

---

[3] H. Conzelmann, *A Commentary on the First Epistle to the Corinthians* (Hermeneia; Philadelphia: Fortress Press, 1975), pp. 269–70.

[4] Conzelmann, *Corinthians*, p. 270.

Conzelmann is quite right when he asserts that 'the kingdom of the messiah does not lie in the future for Paul. And the present state of believers is determined by the presence of the Spirit as ἀπαρχὴ [first portion] of what is to come, by transformation into a new creation, and by faith, hope and love as advance gifts of the eschatological existence.'[5] This understanding of Paul's eschatology differs markedly from the interpretations of such scholars as Lietzmann[6] and Schweitzer,[7] who argue that in 1 Cor. 15.24 Paul means kingdom to refer to a 'messianische Zwischenreich' (messianic interim kingdom) which begins with the parousia and ends with the destruction of death. According to Lietzmann, Paul is referring precisely to this 'messianische Zwischenreich' when he uses the term συμβασιλεύειν Χριστῷ (to reign together with Christ) and when he refers to the dead in 1 Thess. 4.17 as reigning with Christ. That 1 Thess. 4.17 has this meaning is highly unlikely;[8] further, συμβασιλεύειν is used only in 1 Cor. 4.8. Not only must the precise context be understood, but also the connection with 1 Cor. 15.24. We will return to this point shortly.

The context of Paul's advice on the kingdom in 1 Cor. 15 is clear.[9] There are some in Corinth who have gotten their eschatological timetable mixed up. They believe that they have already received the fulness of God's eschatological gift in Christ in the present. The apostle wishes to show in 1 Cor. 15.20–34 that there is an important eschatological reservation which these Corinthians overlook. Thus Paul writes in verses 23–24: 'But

[5] Conzelmann, *Corinthians*, p. 270, n. 63. Also in agreement with this position is E. Käsemann (*Commentary on Romans* [Grand Rapids: Eerdmans, 1980], p. 377) when he states that the coming kingdom of God in 1 Cor. 15.24–25 'is the consummation of the already present lordship of Christ and has dawned with it … If Christ's reign is to be seen in the community, God's kingdom has already achieved anticipatory reality there. On earth this can take place only under assault.' Both Conzelmann's and Käsemann's emphasis on christology is important for only in this way can the kingdom of God be experienced in the present.

[6] H. Lietzmann, *An die Korinther I/II* (HNT 9; Tübingen: J. C. B. Mohr, 1959), p. 81.

[7] A. Schweitzer, *The Mysticism of the Apostle Paul* (New York: Holt, 1931), pp. 90–1.

[8] See Donfried, 'The Cults of Thessalonica', pp. 349–52.

[9] See the discussion in K. P. Donfried, *The Dynamic Word* (San Francisco: Harper and Row, 1981), pp. 22–8.

each in his own order: Christ the first fruits, then at his coming those who belong to Christ. Then comes the end, when he delivers the kingdom of God the Father after destroying every rule and every authority and power.' Although Christ has been raised, the resurrection of those in Christ is still *in the future*; although the kingdom is already present it will only reach its final goal in the future when 'every rule and every authority and power' is destroyed. Until then the kingdom is in conflict with the kingdoms of this world and the mark of the Christian is the cross and not kingship.

In all likelihood Paul's clarification of the eschatological timetable in 1 Cor. 15 is linked to certain assertions Paul makes in 1 Cor. 4.8–13. What we have here is the apostle's sarcastic paraphrase of the Corinthian misunderstanding of the Christian life. 'Already you are filled! Already you have become rich! Without us you have become kings [ἐβασιλεύσατε]! And would that you did reign, so that we might share the rule with you [καὶ ὄψελόν γε ἐβασιλεύσατε, ἵνα καὶ ἡμεῖς ὑμῖν συμβασιλεύσωμεν]'! Their understanding of the kingdom is that of eschatological fulfillment – already now they have been perfected and reign in the eschatological fullness of the kingdom. To all of this Paul issues a resounding 'no'! Paul's overall answer to this problem in 1 Corinthians is not dissimilar to the hymn[10] (perhaps Pauline?)[11] cited in the deutero-Pauline 2 Timothy: 'If we have died with him, we shall also live with him; if we endure, we shall also reign with him [συμβασιλεύσομεν]' (2.11–12). Not unimportant is the fact that this correction is given in a situation quite similar to the distortion being described in 1 Cor. 15: some 'have swerved from the truth by holding that the resurrection is past already' (2 Tim. 2.18).

To summarize: it is precisely to this wider problem of a misunderstood eschatological timetable that parts of 1 Corinthians are addressed and it is this situation that necessitates Paul's advice

---

[10] See M. Dibelius and H. Conzelmann, *The Pastoral Epistles* (Hermeneia; Philadelphia: Fortress Press, 1972), p. 109.

[11] For a general discussion of the problem see the discussion in C. K. Barrett, *The Pastoral Epistles* (The New Clarendon Bible; Oxford: Clarendon Press, 1963), pp. 7–12.

about the kingdom in chapter 15. It is present already, but not yet in its final, fulfilled eschatological sense; that is reserved for the end (τὸ τέλος, 'when he delivers the kingdom to God the Father,' 15.24). In the present the one in Christ lives under the sign of the cross not the sign of glory; the believer is called upon for the sake of the kingdom to endure.[12] It is precisely for this reason that Paul outlines the ignominy of his apostolic existence in 1 Cor. 4.10–12.

Rom. 14.17

For the kingdom of God is not food and drink but righteousness and peace and joy in the Holy Spirit.

The Roman church is facing tension.[13] The strong and the weak have different attitudes toward what is proper food etiquette for the Christian. 'One believes he may eat anything, while the weak man eats only vegetables' (Rom. 14.2); as a result a dispute arises. Paul reminds them that the gift of the kingdom, the gift of life in Christ, is righteousness, peace and joy. It is this which stands at the center of the kingdom; not food and drink. Given the controversy in the present life of the Roman church it is only natural that Paul would be stressing the *present* dimension and characteristics of the kingdom.

Haufe characterizes both this reference to the kingdom as well as that found in 1 Cor. 4.20 as an 'antithetischer Definitionssatz' (antithetical definition formula) in which a negative assertion preceeds the positive one.[14] Both employ an οὐ γὰρ ... ἀλλά construction. Rom. 14.17 replaces the ἐν of 1 Cor. 4.20 with a plain ἐστίν statement. Käsemann has suggested that we are dealing with a polemical declaration in Rom. 14.17.[15] Haufe[16]

---

[12] Note here our previous reference to 2 Tim. 2.12: 'if we endure, we shall also reign with him'.

[13] See K. P. Donfried, *The Romans Debate: Revised and Expanded Edition* (Peabody, MA: Hendrickson, 2001), pp. 102–25.

[14] Haufe, 'Reich Gottes', p. 469. Haufe proceeds to indicate that this is not an antithetical definition formula in the strict sense since it is not giving a comprehensive definition of the kingdom, but one that is relevant and limited to the specific situation the apostle is addressing.

[15] Käsemann, *Romans*, p. 377.

[16] Haufe, 'Reich Gottes', p. 469.

challenges this and prefers to see the 'pädagogisch-didaktische Interesse' (pedagogical-instructive interest) central on the basis that Paul is dependent on a 'popularphilosophischen Schulbetriebes' (the activity of the popular philosophical school). If this is, in fact, the case, there is no reason why he could not modify that form to meet his needs.

We see no reason to accept here Johnson's[17] interpretation of δικαιοσύνη (righteousness) in a general sense and not in its technical Pauline usage. Given the overall polemical nature of Romans 14, we are inclined to Käsemann's interpretation.[18] He suggests that Paul is criticizing both the positions of asceticism and freedom that are opposing each other in Rome on this issue of food. Rather than set up a new set of Christian virtues, Paul reminds the Roman Christians that they have been placed 'in the realm of eschatological grace. Righteousness is not right action but divine power. Peace is openness toward everyone. Joy is standing under an open heaven. Not feelings but realities are here described as the marks of the inaugurated lordship of God and Christian fellowship.'[19] Käsemann also correctly reminds us that verse 18 ('he who thus serves Christ is acceptable to God and approved by men') is closely connected with the preceding verse. ' "Serving Christ" sums up what has been said. It is the essence of the kingdom of God manifest in fellowship.'[20]

1 Cor. 4.20

For the kingdom of God does not consist in talk (ἐν λόγῳ) but in power (ἐν δυνάμει).

We have already had opportunity to comment on this verse in connection with our discussion of Rom. 14.17. It can be described as an 'antithetischer Definitionsatz', although such an understanding does not mean that it is intending to give an

---

[17] Johnson, 'Kingdom of God Sayings', p. 152.

[18] Käsemann, *Romans*, p. 377.

[19] Käsemann, *Romans*, p. 377. Note also the excellent discussion in C. E. B. Cranfield, *The Epistle to the Romans*, 2 vols (ICC; Edinburgh: T&T Clark, 1979), 2.717–19.

[20] Käsemann, *Romans*, p. 377.

exhaustive definition of the kingdom of God; rather, as we shall see, it is concentrating on one dimension of that new reality in light of certain misunderstandings present in the Corinthian congregation.

A major problem in the Corinthian church is its members' arrogant boasting. Previously it was noticed how they claim already to be filled and to be reigning with Christ, viz. that already now they are living fully in an eschatological existence which, for Paul, in its finality is reserved for the future. The apostle indicates that during his forthcoming visit he 'will find out not the talk of these arrogant people but their power' (1 Cor. 4.19). Immediately thereafter follow the words that we are interested in: 'For the kingdom of God does not consist in talk but in power.'

Although δύναμις (power) is used by Paul in a variety of ways, here he appears to be referring to the powerful deeds which accompanied his apostolic preaching. This is certainly the case in 2 Cor. 12.12: 'The signs of a true apostle were performed among you in all patience, with signs and wonders and mighty works [δυνάμεσιν].' Our understanding is well stated by Victor Furnish: 'Failing any indication to the contrary, Paul must be using the phrase *signs and wonders and deeds and power* in the way his readers would naturally take it – namely, with reference to some kind of miraculous occurrences, perhaps healings, which took place (despite the silence of Acts 18) when he was preaching the gospel to them.'[21] This same intention appears also to be present in, for example, 1 Cor. 2.4: 'my speech [ὁ λόγος μου] and my message were not in plausible words of wisdom, but in demonstration of the Spirit and of power [δυνάμεως]'; in Rom. 15.19: 'For I will not venture to speak of anything except what Christ has wrought through me to win obedience from the Gentiles, by word and deed, by the power of signs [ἐν δυνάμει σημείων] and wonders, by the power of the Holy Spirit ... so that I have fully preached the gospel of Christ'; and in 1 Thess. 1.5: 'for our gospel came to you not only in word [ἐν λόγῳ], but also in power [ἐν δυνάμει]

---

[21] V. Furnish, *II Corinthians* (AB 32A; Garden City: Doubleday, 1985), p. 556.

and in the Holy Spirit and with full conviction'. In his attempt to deal with those in Corinth who placed an excessive premium on sophisticated rhetoric and polished preaching, Paul makes clear that these are not the primary marks of the kingdom – it is not demonstrated by talk, in the sense just discussed, but by power. As the power of God is revealed in his kingdom by the gospel accompanied by signs demonstrating the authority of this new reality, so the Corinthians must give witness to the transformative power of the gospel not in their boasting but in the actuality of a new redeemed community living by and under the power of ἀγάπη (love) as an eschatological gift.[22]

If we have interpreted Paul's intention correctly, then there are a number of Synoptic echoes of this theme. However one interprets Mark 9.1, it is noteworthy that the 'kingdom of God has come ἐν δυνάμει (in power)'. Paul's emphasis would be quite similar to the Matthean summary of Jesus' activity in 9.35: 'And Jesus went about all the cities and villages, teaching in their synagogues and preaching the gospel of the kingdom, and healing every disease and every infirmity.' A similar emphasis is found in the Q passage Matt. 12.28//Lk. 11.20: 'But if it is by the Spirit of God that I cast out demons, then the kingdom of God has come upon you.'

According to 1 Cor. 4.20 the kingdom of God is present and provides the context for the life of the Corinthian church. In asserting this we need to remember what was said above: the presence of the kingdom of God through the Christ event in an anticipatory way does not reduce the eschatological nature of this kingdom.

1 Thess. 2.11–12

We exhorted each one of you and encouraged you and charged you to lead a life worthy of God, who calls you into his own kingdom[23] and glory.

[22] See especially 1 Cor. 12 and 13.
[23] Paul does not use the more customary phrase, 'kingdom of God', because he has just referred to God and obviously wishes to avoid redundancy.

These verses follow Paul's defense of his motives and behavior during his initial visit to Thessalonica. Verse 10 summarizes much of Paul's appeal in verses 1–8, viz. that the Thessalonians should know 'how holy and righteous and blameless was our behavior to you believers' precisely because Paul and his co-workers were not interested in pleasing men but God, the very God who entrusted his gospel to them. Since Paul's behavior results from that gospel which he preached to them, he reminds them of his proclamation when he was present among them. Two further points need to be emphasized in connection with this reminder. First, καλεῖν (to call) is in the present. This stresses the present and continuing nature of the event in which they now participate and which will be consummated in the future. Second, just for clarity, we need to remind ourselves once again that Paul *orally communicated* this message about the kingdom during his presence in Thessalonica. In short, we have evidence that this term was rooted in his oral preaching.[24]

The point of Paul's original exhortation was this: since God has called and continues to call the Thessalonian Christians, they are expected to live a life that is being transformed continually by the gospel. In 5.5 Paul reminds them that already now 'you are all sons of light and sons of the day'; thus the result is: 'since we belong to the day, let us be sober, and put on the breastplate of faith and love, and for a helmet the hope of salvation' (5.8). By repeating the triadic formula 'faith, love and hope' in 5.8,[25] Paul indicates clearly his understanding of the Christian life as eschatological – as already, not yet. Already now, partially and proleptically, through Christ and his gospel, God's rule and glory[26] have broken into this transient world and are at work in them.[27] Thus the Thessalonian Christians have 'turned to God

---

[24] Since 1 Thess. 2.12 is found in the general context of the great thanksgiving and in the specific context of Paul's 'apology' we cannot accept Haufe's ('Reich Gottes', 468) characterization of this verse as a 'Drohwort' (threatening word). It simply does not function this way in 1 Thess. 2.

[25] Note 1 Thess. 1.3.

[26] Note, for example, the use of δόξα (glory) in 2 Cor. 3.18; it is something which is already present in the Christian community.

[27] Note 1 Thess. 2.13.

from idols, to serve a living and true God, and to wait for his Son from heaven' (1.9–10).[28] The newness of their life in Christ has already begun and will be completed on the last day. As a result, 'God has ... destined us ... to obtain salvation through our Lord Jesus Christ' (5.9).

The use in 1 Thess. 2.12 of the adverb ἀξίως (worthy), more infrequent in the Pauline corpus, may well suggest that Paul is dependent on an early Christian baptismal tradition, a suggestion strengthened when one notes the similar use of this adverb in Phil. 1.27, Eph. 4.1, and Col. 1.10.[29] Haufe[30] suggests that this same baptismal context lies behind the kingdom references in 1 Cor. 4.20–21 and 1 Thess. 2.11–12, except that in these two cases Paul develops them in a new way under the influence of the forms of popular philosophical schools.

As previously indicated, I shall comment briefly on 2 Thess. 1.5, even though I do not hold it to be from the hand of Paul: 'This is evidence of the righteous judgment of God, that you may be made worthy of the kingdom of God, for which you are suffering.' The author of this document has just praised the congregation for its faith and love and offers support in all their 'persecutions and in the afflictions' which they are enduring. Their steadfastness during these difficulties is a sign that they will be made worthy of the kingdom of God. Given both the change in language nuance between 1 Thess. 2.12 and 2 Thess. 1.5[31] and the strongly apocalyptic language of 2 Thess. 1.5–12, it is apparent that an eschatological shift has taken place in the under-standing of the kingdom for the author of 2 Thessalonians. It is now strictly a future phenomenon and Wolfgang Trilling is to be

[28] Note the overall similarity with the deutero-Pauline Col. 1.13: 'He has delivered us from the dominion of darkness and transferred us to the kingdom of his beloved Son.' We will discuss the baptismal context of these verses below.

[29] So R. Schnackenburg, *Der Brief an die Epheser* (EKK; Neukirchen-Vluyn: Neukirchener, 1982), p. 164. See also n. 59 below.

[30] Haufe, 'Reich Gottes', p. 469.

[31] The difference between εἰς τὸ περιπατεῖν ὑμᾶς ἀξίως τοῦ θεοῦ τοῦ καλοῦντος ὑμᾶς εἰς τὴν ἑαυτοῦ βασιλείαν καὶ δόξαν and εἰς τὸ καταξιωθῆναι ὑμᾶς τῆς βασιλείας τοῦ θεοῦ, ὑπὲρ ἧς καὶ πάσχετε is quite substantial: 'to lead a life worthy of God, who called you into his own kingdom and glory' and 'That you may be made worthy of the kingdom of God for which you are suffering'.

followed when he states: 'Die strenge Zukünftigkeit steht ausser Frage.'[32] We now turn to those Pauline passages which view the kingdom as primarily a future event.

1 Cor. 15.50

I tell you this, brethren: flesh and blood cannot inherit the kingdom of God, nor does the perishable inherit the imperishable.

In his attempt to show that the resurrection is future and bodily, as opposed to something already fully experienced spiritually, Paul attempts to demonstrate that a future bodily transformation must precede entrance into the kingdom of God.[33] In verses 42–46 the apostle argued that what 'is sown is perishable, what is raised is imperishable ... It is sown a physical body, it is raised a spiritual body ... But it is not the spiritual which is first but the physical, and then the spiritual.' It is precisely to underscore this point that he adds in verse 50 that 'flesh and blood', viz. the physical, cannot inherit the future kingdom. Only when this physical body is transformed on the last day, can one enter the kingdom. Thus, what characterizes human existence in the present is the physical body; what characterizes life in the future consummated kingdom is a transformed, spiritual body.

The phrase βασιλείαν θεοῦ κληρονομῆσαι (to inherit the kingdom of God) here in 1 Cor. 15.50 is virtually identical with the phrase found in 1 Cor. 6.9–10 and Gal. 5.21: βασιλείαν θεοῦ οὐ κληρονομήσουσιν. In all likelihood this expression is pre-Pauline[34] and derives from a baptismal-paraenetic context of the early church. In 1 Cor. 6.9–10 and Gal. 5.21 it is connected with a list of negative conditions by which one is certain to be excluded from the kingdom.[35] In connection with these last two references, Haufe's use of the category 'Drohwort' (threatening word) is

---

[32] 'There is no doubt about the radical futurity [of the kingdom].' W. Trilling, *Der Zweite Brief an die Thessalonicher* (EKK; Neukirchen-Vluyn: Neukirchener, 1980), p. 50.

[33] Donfried, *Dynamic Word*, pp. 22–8.

[34] Note that only in these three kingdom references the article is omitted before βασιλεία, a phenomenon not found in the other kingdom references in Paul.

[35] Note the modified form of this phrase in the deutero-Pauline Eph. 5.5.

more accurate. However, although the 'Sprachmilieu' (language environment)[36] of 1 Cor. 15.50 is originally the same, its intention is quite different and therefore 1 Cor. 15.50 cannot function as a 'Drohwort'.[37] Given the misunderstanding of the eschatological timetable in Corinth, the apostle takes up this traditional phrase as a teaching device and applies it to the mis-understandings at hand.[38] Against such a new threat Paul has to modify this common tradition which may originally stem from baptismal paraenesis.[39]

1 Cor. 6.9–10

Do you not know that the unrighteous will not inherit the kingdom of God (θεοῦ βασιλείαν οὐ κληρονομήσουσιν)? Do not be deceived; neither the immoral, nor idolaters, nor adulterers, nor sexual perverts, nor thieves, nor the greedy, nor drunkards, nor revilers, nor robbers will inherit the kingdom of God (βασιλείαν θεοῦ κληρονομήσουσιν).

As already intimated in our discussion of 1 Cor. 15.50, these verses, together with verse 11, are probably cited by Paul from an earlier tradition which is rooted in baptism and is then coupled with a post-baptismal list of vices which define, negatively, the requirements of the kingdom.[40] Hahn insists that the 'kingdom of God' language as used here is derived from this earlier tradition, since only the references to the kingdom in the present (1 Cor. 4.20; Rom. 14.17) have a claim to authentic Pauline usage.[41] By use of this tradition, which reveals certain tensions with the

---

[36] Haufe, 'Reich Gottes', p. 469.

[37] Which Haufe, 'Reich Gottes', pp. 468–9, acknowledges.

[38] There is a similarity between 1 Cor. 15.50 and John 3.3–5 (and Matt. 18.3) and it is fully possible that members of the Corinthian congregation were misunderstanding a Johannine-like tradition in the sense of eschatological fulfillment in the present.

[39] See our discussion below and also the discussion in C. H. Dodd, *Historical Tradition in the Fourth Gospel* (Cambridge: University Press, 1963), pp. 358–9, and R. E. Brown, *The Gospel According to John (I–XII)* (AB 29; Garden City: Doubleday, 1966), pp. 143–4.

[40] For a complete analysis of this tradition see F. Hahn, 'Taufe und Rechtfertigung', in *Rechtfertigung* (Festschrift für Ernst Käsemann; ed. J. Friedrich, W. Pöhlmann, P. Stuhlmacher; Tübingen: J. C. B. Mohr, 1976), pp. 104–9; and U. Schnelle, *Gerechtigkeit und Christusgegenwart* (Göttingen: Vandenhoeck and Ruprecht, 1983), pp. 37–44.

[41] A statement such as this requires caution, since Paul in many cases will take up traditions and use them to express his theological or ethical purpose. Hahn, 'Taufe und Rechtfertigung', p. 105, n. 41.

apostle's theology,[42] Paul is making it clear that certain types of behavior will void the future inheritance of the kingdom even for those who have been baptized and justified. These actions are not magical and guarantee nothing in and of themselves. Although the original apocalyptic nature of the phrase kingdom of God is evident,[43] in this text it is placed in a paraenetic context.[44] As Conzelmann[45] correctly recognizes, this raises the whole question of the relationship of indicative and imperative in Pauline thought. Precisely because justification for Paul is not simply a point in past time but is a continuing event,[46] he makes it clear that the one who is in Christ must now lead a life congruent with the gift that has been given in baptism and which continues to be given in the Spirit through the congregation. His intention in citing this tradition becomes especially evident in verse 18: 'Shun immorality'. Those who participate in prostitution[47] will be excluded from the future kingdom.[48]

This pre-Pauline tradition is consistent with the words attributed to Jesus in Mark 1.15: 'The time is fulfilled, and the kingdom of God is at hand; repent, and believe in the gospel.' There also appears to be a close proximity with the M tradition, especially as formulated in Matt. 25.34: 'Then the King will say to those at his right hand, "Come, O blessed of my Father, inherit [κληρονομήσατε] the kingdom prepared for you from the foundation of the world."' Not only do we have the same verb as in 1 Cor. 6.10, but also the fact that such inheritance is dependent on a certain type of ethical behavior. But before we discuss these parallels more extensively it will be well to review the kingdom reference in Gal. 5.21 first and then return to this issue.

[42] See Hahn, 'Taufe und Rechtfertigung', p. 104.

[43] See Conzelmann, *1 Corinthians*, p. 106.

[44] Schnelle, *Gerechtigkeit*, p. 38.

[45] Conzelmann, *1 Corinthians*, p. 107.

[46] See Hahn, 'Taufe und Rechtfertigung' pp. 117–24; Donfried, *Dynamic Word*, pp. 50–64.

[47] Probably temple prostitution, although for a different perspective see the discussion in J. Murphy-O'Connor, 'The Corinth that Saint Paul Saw', *BA* 47 (1984), pp. 147–59.

[48] Here, contrary to Schnelle (see n. 41), we see the section beginning with 1 Cor. 6.9 as looking forward toward the issue of prostitution rather than backward to the issue of Christians involved with lawsuits against one another.

Gal. 5.21

I warn you, as I warned you before, that those who do such things shall not inherit the kingdom of God [βασιλείαν θεοῦ οὐ κληρονομήσουσιν].

The first part of this verse, which serves as a 'quotation formula' for the remainder, suggests that Paul's advice about the kingdom is not a novelty but was included in his previous communications with this congregation, a fact also paralleled in 1 Thess. 2.12.[49] Both in its present form and in its previous oral form, this kingdom reference as well as the wider context appear to come from a tradition including early Christian baptismal instruction.[50] The tension with Pauline theology can be seen at several points, perhaps most pointedly in the use of κληρονομεῖν (inherit) which is in tension with the use of that term elsewhere in Galatians.[51]

Given the strong possibility that some Galatian Christians misunderstood Paul's use of the term 'freedom',[52] Paul uses this traditional material in a paraenetic context to warn the Galatian Christians that certain types of activity, viz. 'works of the flesh', are not only inappropriate for those who are now in Christ but that those who do them shall not inherit the kingdom of God. Indisputably the apocalyptic dimension of the kingdom is being stressed in this verse. As we noted previously there are parallels to this use of kingdom language in M and to this we shall now turn.

The 'inherit the kingdom of God' formula found in 1 Cor. 6.9–10 and Gal. 5.21[53] finds its most striking parallel in Matt. 25.34, a passage which is unique to the M tradition.[54] Although Matt. 25.34 is a positive reference to those who will enter the kingdom, its opposite is found, although in a substantially modified form, in 25.41. Obviously if one is to be thrown into the eternal fire one will not inherit the kingdom. Also related to this tradition are those synoptic references about not entering the

---

[49] For a further discussion of this see H. D. Betz, *Galatians* (Hermeneia; Philadelphia: Fortress Press, 1979), p. 284.

[50] Betz, *Galatians*, p. 284.

[51] Gal. 3.18, 29; 4.1, 7, 30.

[52] Note Gal. 5.13.

[53] In modified form also in 1 Cor. 15.50.

[54] Note similar but not exact uses of 'to inherit' in Matt. 5.5 and 19.29.

kingdom of God (Mark 10.15 and parallels; Matt. 5.20; 7.21; 18.3).[55] Haufe[56] rightly shows the practical interchangeability of εἰσέρχομαι (to enter) and κληρονομεῖν (to inherit) in the Septuagint.[57] This, too, points to a common early Christian tradition. The fact that this language about 'inheriting the kingdom' is found neither in its negative nor positive form in Q once again suggests that we are dealing with an early Christian baptismal-paraenetic tradition in which this material was first used for catechetical instruction. Thus it was the needs of the earliest Christian communities which necessitated the transformation of Jesus' proclamation of the kingdom to meet the requirements of its baptismal and post-baptismal instruction and other paraenetic necessities. That is not to say that the original message of Jesus was lost sight of; rather it was taken up, expanded, and applied in new situations.

Conclusion

What tentative conclusions may be reached? Let us attempt to divide our summary into three parts: Paul's use of kingdom language; Luke's description of Paul's proclamation in Acts; the relationship of Paul's use of kingdom language to that of Jesus and the Synoptic tradition.

1) With regard to Paul's use of kingdom language it can be concluded that Paul understands that the kingdom of God is consummated in the future but that it has already achieved anticipatory reality in the present through the resurrection and reign of Christ. The 'already–not yet' nature of the kingdom is especially evident in 1 Cor. 15.50. Further, we found that Rom. 14.17, 1 Cor. 4.20–21, and 1 Thess. 2.12 stressed the presence of the kingdom and that 1 Cor. 15.50, 1 Cor. 6.9 and Gal. 5.21 emphasized its futurity. With regard to those texts stressing the presence of the kingdom we noted that they stem from a

---

[55] Note in this connection our previous discussion of John 3.5.
[56] Haufe, 'Reich Gottes', p. 470.
[57] Deut. 4.1; 6.18; 16.20.

baptismal context, although Rom. 14.7 and 1 Cor. 4.20–21, with their οὐ γὰρ … ἀλλά structure characteristic of an 'antithetischer Definitionsatz' (antithetical definition formula) reveal a further development through the influence of the popular philosophical schools. Those texts stressing the apocalyptic nature of the kingdom, 1 Cor. 15.50, 1 Cor. 6.9 and Gal. 5.21 also stem from a baptismal context, although they are all marked by a specific tradition using the verb κληρονομεῖν (to inherit). At this point we noticed some noteworthy relationships with M and other parts of the synoptic tradition, but not with Q.

Since all these texts, with the possible exception of 1 Cor. 15.50, derive from a baptismal context,[58] how can one describe their differences, especially the οὐ γὰρ … ἀλλά construction, on the one hand, and the κληρονομεῖν construction, together with the absence of the article before βασιλεία, on the other? Perhaps one might suggest that Rom. 14.17, 1 Cor. 4.20–21 and 1 Thess. 2.12 are modified for their present contexts from a more kerygmatic tradition and that 1 Cor. 15.50, 1 Cor. 6.9, and Gal. 5.21 derive from a tradition that was originally intended to offer specific, perhaps post-baptismal, ethical instruction.

2) As we turn our attention to Acts, we notice that in Acts 14.22, 19.8, 20.25 and 28.23, 31, Luke describes Paul as preaching the kingdom of God. While in the first text there is a clearly future reference to the kingdom ('through many tribulations we must enter the kingdom of God'), the other three verses, while not excluding a future reference, are not oriented to a particular time and might well be emphasizing the present nature of the kingdom.[59] While not wishing to deny Luke's theological intention in shaping his view of

---

[58] 'Baptismal context' is a somewhat vague term although it is widely used in the literature. Such a context can involve both indicative and imperative elements. Perhaps one should refer to the former as 'baptismal' (viz. kerygmatic) and to the latter as 'post-baptismal' (viz. paraenetic). One should not overlook the fact that the former can easily be transformed to fit the needs of the latter; precisely because this happens it becomes more important to attempt to isolate the original *Sitz im Leben* of each.

[59] So, for example, F. F. Bruce, *The Acts of the Apostles* (Grand Rapids: Eerdmans, 1960), p. 480.

Paul, we would disagree with Jürgen Roloff,[60] for example, when he understands the kingdom references in Acts as merely Luke's way of summarizing the teaching of Jesus. The fact remains that Paul used this term both in his oral preaching and paraenesis as well as in his written letters. One must be a bit more cautious before assigning every instance of such terminology to the hand of Luke, as Roloff apparently does.

One other passage in Acts needs to be reviewed briefly in light of our discussion of Paul and his use of kingdom language: Acts 17.6–7. The scene is Thessalonica and the accusers of Paul and his followers argue before the city authorities that these 'men who have turned the world upside down have come here also, and Jason has received them; and they are all acting against the decrees of Caesar, saying that there is another king, Jesus'. Paul's categorical statement in 1 Thess. 2.12 that he did speak to the Thessalonians about the kingdom during his presence in the city should help us to understand the relative accuracy of the Acts 17 account, not only with regard to Paul's use of king/kingdom language but also with regard to the fact that this language may well have served as the catalyst for the animosity he and his co-workers aroused in Thessalonica.[61]

3) Finally we come to the question whether our study can offer some assistance in helping us understand the relation of Paul's proclamation about the kingdom of God to that of Jesus and the synoptic tradition. There are obvious points of contact between them, the most evident being that both Paul and Jesus used the phrase 'kingdom of God'. Beyond this there are some more substantive relationships as well. We divided the Pauline references to the kingdom of God into present and future. This accords well with the Synoptic tradition. The apocalyptic notion of the kingdom is found both in the triple tradition (Mark 14.25 par.) and in Q (Matt.

---

[60] J. Roloff, *Die Apostelgeschichte* (NTD; Göttingen: Vandenhoeck and Ruprecht, 1981), p. 283.

[61] For a more complete discussion of this position see Donfried, 'The Cults of Thessalonica', pp. 342–52. In this volume, pp. 31–46.

6.10//Luke 11.2) as well as in various single traditions. The present nature of the kingdom is especially evident in the Q tradition (Matt. 12.28//Luke 11.20). Additionally the references to ἐν δυνάμει (in power) in 1 Cor. 4.20 may well be influenced by the triple tradition (Mark 9.1 par) and this is not unrelated to the theme expressed in Matt 9.35 concerning the teaching and healing ministry of Jesus. We also observed a specific relationship to the M tradition and its use of κληρονομεῖν (e.g. Matt. 25.34 and 5.19). This verb appears to be used almost synonymously with εἰσέρχομαι (to enter) not only in the M tradition (5.20) but also in the triple tradition (Mark 10.14 par; Mark 10.15 par; Mark 10.23–25 par) and in the Markan tradition as well (9.47).

For the most part these observations are in agreement with the conclusions reached by F. Neirynck.[62] We would agree fully when he states that there 'is no trace ... in the Pauline letters of a conscious use of a saying of Jesus. Possible allusion to such sayings (on the basis of similarity of form and content with gospel sayings) also show significant differences, and a direct use of a gospel saying in the form it has been preserved in the synoptic gospels is hardly provable'.[63] One can also concur with Neirynck when he states that 'Paul's knowledge of the Q tradition or pre-Q collection ... cannot be demonstrated'[64] since the paucity and anonymity of such possible allusions make it most doubtful whether Paul was specifically referring to them as sayings of Jesus.

Reference must also be made to Nikolaus Walter's insightful study.[65] In general he agrees with Neirynck's conclusions: Paul quotes no sayings of Jesus but he is familiar with the Jesus tradition. Walter shows that in the extant Pauline letters the Jesus tradition is used primarily in paraenetic contexts,[66] but also

---

[62] F. Neirynck 'Paul and the Sayings of Jesus', in *L'Apôtre Paul: personnalité, style et conception du ministère* (BETL 73; Leuven, University Press–Peeters, 1986), pp. 265–321.

[63] Neirynck, 'Paul and the Sayings of Jesus', p. 320.

[64] Neirynck, 'Paul and the Sayings of Jesus', p. 320.

[65] N. Walter, 'Paulus und die urchristliche Tradition', *NTS* 31 (1985), pp. 498–522.

in sections in which Paul defends his apostolic ministry.[67] Walter cites 1 Cor. 4.11–13 and 9.14; we would add 1 Thess. 2.11–12. Further, when Paul cites the Jesus tradition it is usually without reflection and it is used with enormous freedom, viz. he can refer to it and yet not be bound by it (e.g. 1 Cor. 9.1–18).

The Jesus–Paul debate is an enormously complex one and cannot be reviewed here.[68] However, our study does show that Paul is dependent on the teaching of Jesus as reflected in the synoptic tradition, particularly with regard to the concept kingdom of God. Thus we would agree with S. G. Wilson that references to Jesus' teachings are rare;[69] however, we would add the kingdom of God references to his short list of such teachings. Further, we would suggest that Paul's use of the phrase 'kingdom of God' supports those scholars who would wish to show that a fundamental unity and continuity between Jesus and Paul can be detected in the several central themes which are common to both.[70] Some may object to our citing the kingdom of God references in this context because of their brevity and their fragmentary nature. To this we would respond, by way of summary, with the helpful conclusion reached by Nikolaus Walter: 'Aber jene Auffassung von der sachlichen Überein-stimmung des paulinischen Evangeliums mit der Botschaft Jesu kann auch bestehen, wenn der – natürlich nicht entbehrliche – Traditionszusammenhang sich sehr viel indirekter oder (um es

---

[66] The following statement of Walter ('Paulus und die urchristliche Tradition', p. 515) seems to interpret the paraenetic context quite broadly: 'Der von Paulus aktiv "gepflegte" Ausschnitt aus dem Bestand von Jesustradition, den er möglicherweise gekannt hat, hat es meist in der einen oder anderen Weise mit der Grundlegung und den Grunderkenntnissen seiner Verkündigung und Theologie (aber nicht mit den zentralen christologisch-soteriol-ogischen Aussagen . . .) oder aber mit seiner apostolischen Existenz zu tun.' ['That regularly preserved selection from the survival of the Jesus tradition by Paul, which he possibly knew, has in one way or another something to do with the fundamental and basic understandings of his proclamation and theology (but not with his central christological-soteriological assertions) or have something to do with his life as an apostle.']

[67] Walter, 'Paulus und die urchristiche Tradition', pp. 508–13.

[68] See the useful review by S. G. Wilson 'From Jesus to Paul: The Contours and Consequences of a Debate', in *From Jesus to Paul* (Festschrift F. W. Beare; ed. P. Richardson and J. C. Hurd; Waterloo: Wilfrid Laurier University, 1984), pp. 1–21.

[69] Wilson, 'From Jesus to Paul', p. 7.

[70] For example, eschatology. See Wilson, 'From Jesus to Paul', p. 10, and the literature cited there.

mit Bildern aus dem Bereich der Optik zu sagen) mit Strahlenbündelungen, -brechungen, -spiegelungen, auch mit partiellem Strahlenausfall und andererseits mit Anreicherungen von fremder Herkunft vollzogen hat.'[71]

---

[71] Walter, 'Paulus und die urchristliche Tradition', p. 518. A translation of this sentence, worked out in conjunction with Prof. Walter, might read as follows: 'But such an understanding of the substantial agreements of the Pauline gospel with the message of Jesus can also exist when the continuity of traditions has taken place quite indirectly, through (to use images from the realm of optics) the emission and common focusing, refraction, and reflection of rays. This continuity of tradition can take place even though there may be a partial "fading-out" of certain traditions and the embellishment of others through materials of foreign origin, such as certain non-Jesus, for example, Jewish-Hellenistic, traditions.'

13

❦

Justification and Last Judgment in Paul

(For Günther Bornkamm on his 70th Birthday)

Introduction

The relationship between justification and last judgment in Paul has been both a source of division between Roman Catholicism and Protestantism[1] and a source of confusion within much of contemporary Protestant thought.[2] A re-examination of this difficult and troublesome theme in light of the advances in contemporary biblical studies may help not only to achieve greater clarity with regard to this theme but also to assist in removing some of the falsely erected barriers which still cause

---

[1] For a brief review of the dialogue between Roman Catholicism and Protestantism on this subject, see H. Küng, 'Katholische Besinnung auf Luthers Rechtfertigungslehre heute', in *Theologie im Wandel* (TThR I; München: Erich Wewel Verlag, 1967), pp. 449–68; also, J. Wicks, ed., *Catholic Scholars Dialogue with Luther* (Chicago: Loyola Press, 1970).

[2] 'The discussion of justification at the Fourth Assembly of the Lutheran World Federation at Helsinki in 1963 captured the attention of the churches and the public particularly on account of the fact that it came to no tangible conclusion. It became clear to all who are theologically concerned not only how important is a new consideration of the doctrine of the sinner's justification by faith alone, but also how difficult such an undertaking is ... On many points the study groups were indeed able to reach a concluding consensus, but on other points either opinions diverged or one only arrived at the formulation of questions, not answers. This report cannot, therefore, attempt to show a well-rounded picture' ('Justification Today', *LW*, Supplement to No. 1, 1965, p. 14). The 'Affirmation of Faith' study, produced in 1973/74 by the Lutheran Church in America, reflects considerable ambiguity with regard to the concept of justification, both in the responses solicited from the laity and in the theological section.

division within Christianity. In short, the re-exploration of this nerve-center of division could have important theological and ecumenical implications.

Such an effort, however, raises the question of approach, viz. the style of scholarship employed in dealing with this problem area. The amount that has been written in this century on the twin themes of justification and judgment is vast;[3] but what is

[3] What follows is some of the most important literature on the subject: M. Barth, *Justification* (Grand Rapids: Eerdmans, 1971), especially pp. 74–82; G. Bornkamm, 'Der Lohngedanke im Neuen Testament', in *Studien zu Antike und Urchristentum* (BEvT; München: Chr. Kaiser Verlag, 1959), pp. 69–92; H. Braun, *Gerichtsgedanke und Rechtfertigungslehre bei Paulus* (UNT 19: Leipzig: J. C. Hinrichs'sche Buchhandlung, 1930); R. Bultmann, 'ΔΙΚΑΙΟΣΥΝΗ ΘΕΟΥ', *JBL* 83 (1964), pp. 12–16; H. Conzelmann, 'Die Rechtfertigungslehre des Paulus: Theologie oder Anthropologie?' *EvTh 28* (1968), pp. 389–404; R. C. Devor, *The Concept of Judgment in the Epistles of Paul* (PhD diss., Drew University, 1959); G. Didier, *Désinteressement du Chrétien. La rétribution dans la morale de Saint Paul* (Théologie 32; Paris: Aubier, 1955); F. V. Filson, *St Paul's Conception of Recompense* (UNT 21; Leipzig: J. C. Hinrichs'sche Buchhandlung, 1931); C. Haufe, *Die sittliche Rechtfertigungslehre des Paulus* (Halle: Max Niemeyer, 1957); J. Jeremias, 'Paul and James', *ExpTim 66* (1954–5), pp. 368–71; W. Joest, *Gesetz und Freiheit* (Göttingen: Vandenhoeck and Ruprecht, 1956), especially pp. 138ff. and 165ff.; E. Jüngel, *Paulus und Jesus* (HUTh 2; Tübingen: J. C. B. Mohr, 1962), especially pp. 66ff.; E. Käsemann, 'Gottesgerechtigkeit bei Paulus', *ZThK 58* (1961), pp. 367–78 [ET: '"The Righteousness of God" in Paul', in *New Testament Questions of Today* (Philadelphia: Fortress Press, 1969), pp. 168–82]; E. Käsemann, 'Sentences of Holy Law in the New Testament', in *New Testament Questions of Today* (Philadelphia: Fortress Press, 1969), pp. 66–81; E. Käsemann, *An die Römer* (HNT 8a; Tübingen: J. C. B. Mohr, 1973), especially pp. 48–56; K. Kertelge, *'Rechtfertigung' bei Paulus* (NTAbh 3; Münster: Verlag Aschendorf, 1966); G. Klein, 'Gottes Gerechtigkeit als Thema der neuesten Paulus-Forschung', *VF 12* (1967), pp. 1–11; E. Kühl, *Rechtfertigung auf Grund Glaubens und Gericht nach den Werken bei Paulus* (Königsberg: Wilh. Koch, 1904); S. Lyonnet, 'Gratuité de la justification et gratuité du salut', in *Studiorum Paulinorum Congressus Internationalis Catholicus 1961*, 2 vols (AnBib 17–18; Rome: Pontifical Biblical Institute, 1963), 1.95–100; S. Lyonnet, 'Justification, jugement, rédemption, principalement dans l'épitre aux Romains', *RechBib 5* (1960), pp. 166–84; U. Luck, 'Der Jakobusbrief und die Theologie des Paulus', *TGI 61* (1971), pp. 161–79; L. Mattern, *Das Verständnis des Gerichtes bei Paulus* (ATANT 47; Zürich: Zwingli, 1966); C. F. D. Moule, 'The Judgment Theme in the Sacraments', in *The Background of the New Testament and Its Eschatology*, ed. W. D. Davies and D. Daube (Cambridge: University Press, 1964), pp. 464–81; C. Müller, *Gottes Gerechtigkeit und Gottes Volk* (FRLANT 86; Göttingen: Vandenhoeck and Ruprecht, 1964); E. Plutta-Messerschmidt, *Gerechtigkeit Gottes bei Paulus* (Tübingen: J. C. B. Mohr, 1973); Calvin J. Roetzel, *Judgement in the Community* (Leiden: Brill, 1972); K. H. Schelkle, 'Lohn und Strafe nach dem Neuen Testament', *BibLeb 10* (1969), pp. 89–95; H. Schuster, 'Rechtfertigung und Gericht bei Paulus', in *Stat Crux Dum Volvitur Orbis* (Festschrift H. Lilje; ed. G. Hoffmann and K. H. Rengstorf (Berlin: Lutherisches Verlagshaus, 1959), pp. 57–67; H. M. Shires, *The Eschatology of Paul in the Light of Modern Scholarship* (Philadelphia: Westminster Press, 1966), especially pp. 103–24; K. Stendahl, 'Justification and the Last Judgment', *LW 8* (1961), pp. 1–7; K. Stendahl, 'The Apostle Paul and the Introspective Conscience of the West', *HTR 29* (1963), pp. 199–215; P. Stuhlmacher, *Gottes Gerechtigkeit*

rather disconcerting, however, is that much of this literature is rambling, repetitive and contradictory. How can such a style of 'solo' scholarship, where everyone does his 'own thing', to use a current American expression, really help the churches and the ecumenical movement? If New Testament scholarship is to have a credible impact upon the theology of the churches, I remain convinced that the direction of the future must lie in something approximating a team approach. Such an approach has the advantage of not only bringing together a variety of scholars with different areas of expertise, but also allowing these scholars to discuss and to learn from one another, so that the final product will transcend the individual result which any one of them would have or could have produced alone. Aside from the possible theological and ecumenical contributions which may have been made in *Peter in the New Testament*[4] (a jointly produced volume by an eleven-person, joint American Roman Catholic and Protestant team over a two-year period), it might be valuable for us to ask whether it contains a style of academic collaboration which has potential for the future. It is particularly important to raise this issue in light of the fact that the most recent monograph in this area, J. A. Ziesler's *The Meaning of Righteousness in Paul*, summarizes the disappointing present state of affairs very succinctly: 'There is little sign of an emerging consensus'.[5] Given the lack of consensus on a theme of such vital importance, the purpose of this paper is to deal with the relationship of justification to last judgment in light of the contemporary discussion so as to provide, hopefully, a stimulus for further team-oriented research.

---

bei Paulus (FRLANT 87; Göttingen: Vandenhoeck and Ruprecht, 1965), especially pp. 228–336; R. V. G. Tasker, *The Biblical Doctrine of the Wrath of God* (London: Tyndale Press, 1957); G. P. Wetter, *Der Vergeltungsgedanke bei Paulus* (Göttingen: Vandenhoeck and Ruprecht, 1912); J. A. Ziesler, *The Meaning of Righteousness in Paul* (SNTSMS 20; Cambridge: Universtiy Press, 1972).

[4] *Peter in the New Testament*, (ed. R. E. Brown, K. P. Donfried and J. Reumann (Minneapolis and New York: Augsburg Publishing House and Paulist Press, 1973).

[5] Ziesler, *The Meaning of Righteousness*, p. 14. This is also demonstrated in the studies by Klein and Plutta-Messerschmidt (see n. 3).

Justification

The starting point for any understanding of the function of the last judgment in the theology of Paul must be his understanding of justification. Only when one has come to terms with justification can one understand the proper importance of last judgment and its relationship to justification. Because this basic fact has been overlooked in many of the studies on last judgment in Paul, one finds many divergent approaches and results.

It is precisely because justification must be the starting point for any discussion of last judgment in Paul that we find ourselves today in a situation most conducive to a reevaluation of these two themes in Pauline theology. Not only has justification been a subject intensely discussed over the last decade, but some genuine advances have been made in the understanding of this theme. If one grants that there have been some genuine new advances with regard to understanding justification, then the time may be ripe to relate these new insights to the concept of last judgment.

It is Käsemann who must be credited with igniting the critical discussions on justification with his 1961 article on ' "The Righteousness of God" in Paul'.[6] Käsemann argues vigorously and forcefully that justification, together with the corollary term, 'righteousness of God', is much more than simply God's gift to man. When understood in this limited way, as is the case with Bultmann,[7] not only does the gift character become isolated, resulting in an unbalanced individualism, but also the eschatological tensions in Pauline theology, particularly between beginning and end, are either reduced to insignificance or entirely ignored. For Käsemann, justification and the term 'righteousness of God' certainly include the gift character, but they are viewed as part of a much broader historical and eschatological context: 'δικαιοσύνη θεοῦ is seen as God's sovereignty over the world revealing itself eschatologically in Jesus'.[8] God's gift to man in Jesus Christ is a manifestation of the God who has been

---

[6] See n. 3.
[7] See n. 3.
[8] Käsemann, 'Righteousness of God', p. 180.

faithful to his people and who reveals himself in sovereignty and power (Macht). When this larger context of the sovereign God revealing himself is ignored, 'the inevitable result is that the Pauline anthropology is sucked under the pull of an individualistic outlook'.[9] The value of Käsemann's approach to justification is that it avoids this danger of absolutizing the meaning of the term as 'gift' in individualistic categories. Rather, justification is regarded as 'Gabe und Aufgabe'. It contains a present and a future dimension – it is 'a matter of promise and expectation'.[10]

The gift involved in justification is not automatic; it remains a gift only as long as there is daily allegiance and obedience to Christ. For this reason Paul can speak of present and future judgment as an integral part of his theology. The righteousness of God which is revealed in Christ recaptures man for the sovereignty of God; this sovereign God acts not only in mercy but also in judgment to those who reject Him, to those who no longer remain obedient, and who consequently fail to actualize His promise.

Käsemann's provocative essay has touched off a healthy and significant debate.[11] Perhaps more important are the numerous dissertations and monographs which are significantly indebted to the challenges of Käsemann. We will make brief reference to the work of Stuhlmacher[12] and Ziesler;[13] more extensive reference will be made to the work of Kertelge,[14] who, together with Käsemann, has provided a basis for a new understanding of the relationship between justification and last judgment in Paul.

Stuhlmacher, substantially influenced by the perspective of his teacher, Käsemann, with regard to justification, deepens and broadens his insights, particularly with regard to the apocalyptic background of the phrase 'righteousness of God'. Somewhat one-sided over against Käsemann's original essay is, however, the

[9] Käsemann, 'Righteousness of God', p. 176.
[10] Käsemann, 'Righteousness of God', p. 170.
[11] See especially the work of Klein and Plutta-Messerschmidt referred to in n. 3.
[12] See n. 3, and also the monograph of Müller cited there.
[13] See n. 3.
[14] See n. 3.

enormous stress on the faithfulness of the creator God to his creation, to the point that the salvific aspect of justification is far too greatly minimized. In Käsemann's essay, the 'Macht' and 'Gabe' character of God's righteousness is held in better balance.[15]

Important for our present purposes are the comments Stuhlmacher makes with regard to the last judgment. His awareness that the last judgment needs to be discussed in relationship with justification, a fact frequently ignored, and his often perceptive critique of other treatments of last judgment in Paul is heartening.[16] However, although Stuhlmacher's general comments[17] concerning justification and last judgment move in a direction similar to that of Käsemann, they do not really represent an advance beyond him. While Stuhlmacher makes some helpful reflections, he has a tendency toward imprecision, perhaps caused by the fact that he presents no extensive analysis of the most important judgment texts[18] and fails to even refer to many potentially significant ones.[19]

We must turn to the problematic areas in Stuhlmacher's analysis. First, it must be asked whether it is accurate to speak of '[das] Problem der doppelten Rechtfertigung'.[20] Paul himself does not use this terminology and we will have to explore below whether it is not more accurate to make a distinction between justification and salvation, than between a first and a second justification. Second, Stuhlmacher asserts: 'Die Lösung liegt für Paulus darin, daß er das Gericht nach den Werken für den Christen als Gericht über die diesem noch anhaftende σάρξ versteht, daß ihm aber die Taufgabe des Geistes Pfand und Siegel für die auch das Gericht überdauernde Treue des Schöpfers zu

---

[15] Kertelge, *Rechtfertigung bei Paulus*, p. 307, develops this criticism of Stuhlmacher.

[16] For a critique of Braun and Filson, see Stuhlmacher, *Gottes Gerechtigkeit*, p. 51; of Schlatter, p. 53; of Bultmann, pp. 57 and 229; of E. Schweizer, p. 67; of Jüngel, pp. 68 and 230; of Kuss, p. 229; of J. Jeremias, p. 229; of Joest, p. 230.

[17] Stuhlmacher, *Gottes Gerechtigkeit*, pp. 228–36.

[18] For example, 1 Cor. 3.10–15 or 1 Cor. 5.3–5.

[19] For example, Rom. 14.10 or 2 Cor. 5.10.

[20] Stuhlmacher, *Gottes Gerechtigkeit*, p. 229 ['the problem of double justification']; see also Jeremias, 'Paul and James', n. 3.

dem Getauften bleibt'![21] What does this really mean? Why are there no textual references? Shortly after this, Stuhlmacher continues: 'Wer die Liebe läßt . . . gewährt dem Christus keinen Raum in sich und über ihn gewinnt daher die ἁμαρτία auch dann Gewalt, wenn er in der Taufe mit Gottes Geist beschenkt war. Doch auch in diesem Falle ist sich Paulus noch gewiß, daß Gott seine designierte Neuschöpfung am Tage des Gerichtes retten wird: I. Kor. 5.5 (vgl. 3.15).'[22] To accept Stuhlmacher at this point, without any exegesis of 1 Cor. 5.5 whatsoever,[23] would be to conclude that there is an irresolvable conflict in Paul's theology.

What is helpful in Stuhlmacher's analysis is the stress on obedience as the connecting link between justification and last judgment. Thus he approvingly cites Fuchs' assertion that 'die Rechtfertigung erfolge nicht durch die Werke, aber *im* Werk des Gehorsams'.[24] But no sooner is this said, than an exegesis of Phil. 3.12–16 and 2.12–13 follows which can only be judged to be awkward; in reality he disagrees with both Fuchs and Käsemann and basically underrates the ultimate importance of obedience as one part of the solution to the justification/judgment problem. It is ultimately useless to speak of 'eine zur Endrechtfertigung führende und nach des Menschen freistellender Tat rufende Bewährungsethik . . .'[25] in which obedience is ultimately insignificant and final salvation is an assured possession guaranteed by the creator's faithfulness to the baptized Christian. In short, Stuhlmacher's critique of others is helpful, but he himself does

---

[21] Stuhlmacher, *Gottes Gerechtigkeit*, pp. 230–1 [ET: 'The solution for Paul lies in the fact that he understands the judgment according to works for the Christian as the judgment with regard to the still persisting σάρξ but that the baptismal gift of the Spirit's pledge and seal remains as a sign of the Creator's enduring fidelity to the baptized even at the judgment'].

[22] Stuhlmacher, *Gottes Gerechtigkeit*, p. 231 [ET: 'Whoever departs from love does not allow Christ any place within him and then ἁμαρτία wins power over him even if he was graced with God's Spirit at baptism. But even in this case Paul is still certain that God will save his designated new creation on the day of judgment: 1 Cor. 5.5 (compare 3.15).']

[23] For Stuhlmacher, *Gottes Gerechtigkeit*, p. 231, to cite Rom. 9.6a in support of his analysis is beside the point.

[24] Stuhlmacher, *Gottes Gerechtigkeit*, p. 231 [ET: 'justification does not result because of works but *in* the work of obedience.']

[25] Stuhlmacher, *Gottes Gerechtigkeit*, p. 235 [ET: 'an ethic of accountability that calls the human being as a result of the decision that frees him and that leads to final justification …']

not present a consistent or persuasive solution to the problem. The element of obedience already found in Käsemann, and waiting to be developed more profoundly, finally becomes a paradoxical and confused item in Stuhlmacher's analysis. One wonders whether Stuhlmacher's creativity is perhaps hindered at this point because of an overriding theological concern which he himself expresses in this way: 'Es geht hier ja in der Tat um Recht oder Unrecht der Reformation.'[26] However, that should not be the issue in a New Testament analysis: the issue is to correctly understand Paul, not the Reformation.

It would be beyond the limits of this paper to review extensively Ziesler's dissertation, *The Meaning of Righteousness in Paul*.[27] We can only refer to it where it deals with the relationship of justification to last judgment. While Ziesler's monograph contains many valuable insights concerning the linguistic and contextual background of the terms δικαιόω and δικαιοσύνη, it is disappointingly weak with regard to our concern. That is not to say that we are trying to judge Ziesler exclusively in terms of our categories, although we maintain that one cannot adequately discuss the meaning of righteousness in Paul without viewing it in relationship to last judgment.

What is perplexing in Ziesler's discussion is, on the one hand, his avowed high regard for Käsemann's position,[28] together with his concern for overcoming the traditional Roman Catholic–Protestant split in understanding the concept of righteousness in Paul, and, on the other hand, his seemingly paradoxical statement 'that justification essentially belongs to the Judgment, the Christian has heard the verdict on him already, a verdict which he continually needs to hear until the Judgment'.[29] What is disconcerting is that there are several naive discussions concerning justification and judgment without reference to the basic texts. Ziesler concludes that he has arrived 'at an exegesis which

---

[26] Stuhlmacher, *Gottes Gerechtigkeit*, pp. 230–1, n. 3 [ET: 'This indeed raises the question of whether the Reformation was right or wrong.']

[27] See n. 3.

[28] Ziesler, *The Meaning of Righteousness*, pp. 13–14.

[29] Ziesler, *The Meaning of Righteousness*, p. 209.

satisfies the concerns of both traditional Catholicism and traditional Protestantism. Nothing is lost: justification is entirely by grace through faith, it is declaratory, yet on the other hand, Paul's ethical seriousness is fully allowed for'.[30] This conclusion, although seemingly desirable, is problematic because the full implications of and motivation for 'Paul's ethical seriousness' are not explored.

These reservations should not cause us to overlook some of Ziesler's positive insights, even if they are not carried through as concisely and consistently as one would like. For example, in relation to Phil. 3.9, he comments: 'We may say, therefore, that righteousness exists in the believer only as he is in Christ – he never possesses it, but rather participates in it by faith, in so far as he is "in Christ". Having righteousness by faith, and having it in Christ, are identical; should he cease being in Christ his righteousness would cease, for it exists only in and through this relationship'.[31] What is unclear is how this correct observation relates to the previously quoted statement dealing with the assurance of the Christian at the last judgment. Part of Ziesler's ambiguity may be attributed to the absence from his discussion of the Pauline concept of obedience.[32] We would assert that it is the obedient Christian, the one who remains in Christ, who will be saved on the last day. Nevertheless, Ziesler's stress on the participation of the believer in Christ is very valuable. In his conclusions concerning the meaning of δικαιοσύνη θεοῦ in 2 Cor. 5.21 (which he believes is parallel to Phil. 3.9 and 1 Cor. 1.30) one can observe not only the helpful influence of Käsemann and Stuhlmacher, but also Ziesler's own contribution:

> We suggest rather that it [δικαιοσύνη θεοῦ] means that we are taken up into and share the covenant loyalty which hitherto has been God's alone. This is not possession: believers neither become righteous, nor have the righteousness of God, both of which would imply possession, at least of a quality. Instead, they 'become the righteousness of God in him,' an

[30] Ziesler, *The Meaning of Righteousness*, p. 212.

[31] Ziesler, *The Meaning of Righteousness*, p. 149; see Lyonnet, 'Gratuité', p. 109, for a similar perspective on this point.

[32] This motif is well-developed not only by Kertelge (see p. 257 above) but also by Käsemann, *An die Römer* (HNT 8a; Tübingen: J. C. B. Mohr, 1973), pp. 48–56.

expression which avoids the other and unsatisfactory formulations, and emphasizes *participation in*, not possession of, God's righteousness.[33]

We turn now to a book written before Ziesler's, also indebted to Käsemann, and one which is of central significance: Karl Kertelge, *Rechtfertigung bei Paulus*.[34] Here is a study which develops the pregnant suggestions of Käsemann's earlier article[35] and which presents us with some highly fruitful insights towards understanding the relationship of justification to last judgment.

One of Kertelge's fundamental themes[36] is based upon Käsemann's observation that when Paul speaks of the 'gift of righteousness' in Rom. 5.17, he is referring to a gift which is both present and future, already received and still expected. For both Kertelge and Käsemann, God's righteousness is a gift in the present, but a gift which at the same time recognizes God's sovereign power and the fact that the redeemed person is placed under that power in obedient service. This grace and power of God as 'promise' presupposes an eschatological framework of 'already' – 'not yet'. For the justified person salvation is not yet completed in the present; it has still to be consummated and fulfilled on the last day. Only as the Christian waits and hopes, is he or she saved (Rom. 8.23–25; Gal. 5.5). Kertelge suggests that both Bultmann and Conzelmann have not properly understood this dimension of Pauline thought.[37] Bultmann overstresses the present nature of δικαιοσύνη and Conzelmann dismisses the 'not yet' dimension of salvation as a polemic primarily directed against Corinthian enthusiasts.[38] As a correction of this typical

---

[33] Ziesler, *The Meaning of Righteousness*, p. 160. What is disappointing here is that Ziesler's rich insights are not carried through more consistently, especially with regard to the relationship between justification and last judgment.

[34] See n. 3.

[35] Käsemann, 'God's Righteousness in Paul', see n. 3.

[36] Kertelge, *Rechtfertigung bei Paulus*, p. 133.

[37] Kertelge, *Rechtfertigung bei Paulus*, p. 152.

[38] Stuhlmacher argues in a similar fashion concerning the background of Phil. 3.12–16 (*Gottes Gerechtigkeit*, pp. 235–6). Both Ziesler (*The Meaning of Righteousness*, pp. 148–51) and Kertelge (*Rechtfertigung bei Paulus*, pp. 234–36) present a better balanced exegesis of Phil. 1 and 3. To acknowledge that Paul is arguing with those who are distorting the Christian gospel does not lead to the conclusion that Paul himself distorted his own theology in the process of presenting a counter-argument.

misunderstanding of Paul, Kertelge summarizes his understanding: 'Beides ist also in gleicher Weise zu betonen, die
Gegenwärtigkeit des Heiles als eschatologische Bestimmung des
Gerechtgesprochenen, Glaubenden und die Erwartung der
eschatologischen Vollendung des gegenwärtigen Heilsstandes.'[39]

What is the critical component or link between the already
realized dimension of salvation experienced in justification and
that which is yet to be actualized? Kertelge, again acknowledging
his dependence upon Käsemann, demonstrates in both a creative
and detailed way that the critical component is 'obedience'.[40]
'Der Glaube bedeutet bei Paulus immer Gehorsam gegen den
Heilswillen Gottes und enthält insofern ein aktives Element, als
der Mensch den Anspruch Gottes entspricht.'[41] This interpretation is demonstrated by a careful exegesis of Romans 6,
particularly verses 12–23. Sanctification (6.19 – εἰς ἁγιασμόν),
the development and maturation of the Christian life in Christ is
an integral part of justification and can only be accomplished in
obedience to the will of Christ (παριστάνετε ἑαυτοὺς δούλους εἰς
ὑπακοήν, Rom. 6.16). Sanctification serves both to elucidate and
to preserve what has taken place in justification. Only when this
is carried out in obedience will God fulfill what he has begun.

Limitations of space have prohibited us from the thorough and
complete analysis which Kertelge's work deserves. Yet, we cannot
move on until at least one other aspect of his study has been
explored: its specific contribution to an understanding of last
judgment. While we will attempt to show that Kertelge and
Käsemann have provided the basic structural foundation for our
own understanding of the relationship between justification and
last judgment, Kertelge himself fails to specifically connect his

[39] Kertelge, *Rechtfertigung bei Paulus*, p. 155 [ET: 'Both need to be equally emphasized:
the contemporaneity of salvation as an eschatological determination of the one who has
been justified, the believer, and the expectation of the eschatological fulfillment of this
present state of salvation.']

[40] Kertelge, *Rechtfertigung bei Paulus*, pp. 159–225, 250, 266, 275, 281, 285. See also
Mattern, *Gericht bei Paulus*, pp. 172–3; Käsemann, *Römer*, p. 55, and; Shires, *Eschatology*,
p. 117.

[41] Kertelge, *Rechtfertigung bei Paulus*, p. 225 [ET: 'For Paul faith always mean obedience
to the salvific will of God and therefore it contains an active element as a person complies
with the claim of God.']

own creative insights to the theme of last judgment. He correctly suggests that even though the theme of last judgment is not an integral component of the doctrine of justification per se, one should not think that the last judgment 'für Paulus theologisch völlig bedeutungslos wäre und nur als Relikt aus der vorchristlichen Zeit beibehalten würde'.[42] Yet he fails to demonstrate explicitly why the concept of a last judgment still has meaning for Paul and why this motif occurs so frequently in the Pauline letters. We will hope to show below that if one accepts the general contents of Kertelge's position, then one negative role which the last judgment will play is the withholding of the final gift of salvation from those baptized Christians who have been disobedient. It is indeed regrettable that Kertelge did not bring his otherwise keen observations to bear more fully on this problem of last judgment in the Pauline letters.

Thus far we have attempted to show that justification must be the starting point for an understanding of Paul's last judgment terminology. We then reviewed selected new studies on justification which appear to have set the stage for a reevaluation of the relationship of last judgment to justification in Paul. Before we proceed to discuss Paul's specific remarks about last judgment, it will be helpful to review briefly his attitude toward the entire scope of the Christian life, from beginning to end.[43]

For Paul, justification is the beginning of the Christian life. As persons receive the revelation of the sovereign creator in Jesus Christ by faith, their broken relationship with God becomes whole and is restored. God now offers new Christians, through the gift of his Spirit, the possibility of leading a new life which is both obedient to him and responsive to the needs of their fellow humans. The Spirit permits us to live ἐν ἁγιασμῷ, traditionally referred to as sanctification. As we continue to participate obediently in the process of sanctification granted by God, this process will lead to the final fulfillment of that which began in

---

[42] Kertelge, *Rechtfertigung bei Paulus*, p. 257 [ET: 'was for Paul totally without meaning theologically and was only retained as an artifact from the pre-Christian period'.]

[43] At several points we are indebted to Käsemann. See the review of his position on pp. 256–7 above, and his further exposition in *Römer*, pp. 48–56.

justification, namely, the gift of salvation to be consummated at the last day.[44]

The fact that sanctification is the process of living out the Christian life between justification and the last day is made clear at several points; specifically Rom. 6.19 and 22: 'For just as you once yielded your members to impurity and to greater and greater iniquity, so now yield your members to righteousness for sanctification [τῇ δικαιοσύνῃ εἰς ἁγιασμόν] ... But now that you have been set free from sin and have become slaves of God, the return you get is sanctification [εἰς ἁγιασμόν] and its end, eternal life.' Sanctification, based upon justification, leads to the final gift of salvation, eternal life.[45] That the life of the Christian is in fact a process which has a beginning and an end-point is also made abundantly clear in 1 Corinthians and Philippians. In language very similar to the synoptic logion 'many are called but few are chosen' (Matt. 22.14), Paul warns the Corinthians that there is nothing automatic about the Christian life. He reminds them that not every athlete receives a prize (1 Cor. 9.24–27) and that, in fact, God was not pleased with the behavior of Israel (1 Cor. 10.1–13).[46] It is only the Christian who both competes (τρέχω) in the race and who is pleasing to God (10.5) who will receive the prize (βραβεῖον). This is exactly Paul's point in Phil. 2.12 where he urges the Philippians to work out their 'own salvation with fear and trembling'. The seriousness with which Paul affirms that salvation is not yet a fully possessed gift is affirmed in Phil. 3.12–16: 'Not that I have already obtained this [the resurrection from the dead] or am already perfect; but I press on to make it my own ... I press on toward the goal for the prize of the upward call of God in Christ Jesus.' In short, the Christian life is a process which begins in justification, is actualized in sanctification and is consummated with salvation. Critical for the final reception of

---

[44] See further the discussion in G. T. Montague, *Growth in Christ* (Fribourg: Regina Mundi, 1961).

[45] A similar point is made in 1 Thess. 5.23–24.

[46] C. F. D. Moule aptly comments that 'the baptized Christian is no safer in playing fast and loose with his privileges than were the Israelites who had been "baptized" in the land and the sea' ('The Judgment Theme in the Sacraments', in *The Background of the New Testament and Its Eschatology*, ed. W. D. Davies and D. Daube [Cambridge, 1956], p. 472).

salvation is our continued obedience and continued reception of God's freely offered gift of the Spirit who is at work in the believer as a part of the body of Christ.[47]

This brief discussion should assist our understanding of a Pauline text which is of fundamental importance: Rom. 5.9–10: 'Since, therefore, we are now justified [δικαιωθέντες νῦν] by his blood, much more shall we be saved [σωθησόμεθα] by him from the wrath of God. For if while we were enemies we were reconciled [κατηλλάγημεν] to God by the death of his Son, much more, now that we are reconciled shall we be saved [σωθησόμεθα] by his life.'[48] What is crystal clear from this text is that Paul, speaking to a Christian congregation, refers to justification as a past event in which they have already participated, and salvation as a future event in which they have yet to participate fully. In this particular text Paul expresses a strong confidence that the one who is justified shall also be saved on the day of wrath. But what is of interest is that despite Paul's strong confidence, he does not simply conflate salvation with justification. They remain two distinct points along the trajectory of the Christian life. Nor should one think that Rom. 5.9–12 is a unique text. The regular pattern in the Pauline letters is that δικαιόω refers to the beginning of the life in Christ, and that σώζω (and σωτηρία) refers to an event yet to be consummated. A few examples must suffice. In his discussion of baptism in Romans 6, Paul writes in verse 7: 'For he who has died is freed [δεδικαίωται–perfect] from sin.' Not only is the event of death with Christ and justification a past event, but Paul also is very careful to point out in this context that resurrection is a future possibility, not a present reality.[49] We died with Christ so that 'we too might walk [περιπατήσωμεν–subjunctive] in newness of life' (v. 4). Also important as a summary expression of Paul's intent in using

---

[47] Stendahl, 'Justification and the Last Judgment', 7, comments: 'Consequently, to be a member of the church is by definition to be justified, and he who remains in the church will be saved. If someone backslides, he will not be saved.'

[48] For a further discussion of this verse, see especially Lyonnet, 'Gratuité', pp. 101–2.

[49] See the further discussion in K. P. Donfried, *The Setting of Second Clement in Early Christianity* (Leiden: E. J. Brill, 1974), pp. 142–4.

δικαιόω is the formula, perhaps pre-Pauline,[50] in 1 Cor. 6.11: 'But you were washed, you were sanctified, you were justified [ἐδικαι-ώθητε] in the name of the Lord Jesus Christ and in the Spirit of our God.' More important than observing the obvious, viz. that justification refers to a past event for the Christian, is the less frequently noted fact that for Paul σῴζω and σωτηρία have an explicit future reference.

Two texts in particular support Paul's use of the future passive of σῴζω in Rom. 5.9–10 to indicate the futurity of the consummated gift of salvation: 1 Thess. 5.8, where he refers to the 'hope of salvation' (ἐλπίδα σωτηρίας) which is immediately followed by the thought that God has destined us (ἔθετο) to obtain (εἰς περιποίησιν) salvation, and Rom. 13.11, where the Romans are reminded that 'salvation [σωτηρίας] is nearer to us now than when we first believed'. This clearly indicates that salvation is a future event towards which the Christian moves; it is not yet a present possession. It is unimaginable for Paul[51] that a Christian could properly confess, 'I have been saved.' At most the Christian can assert that he or she is in the process of being saved – 1 Cor. 1.18 (σῳζομένοις). The Christian can give thanks not because he or she is already saved, but 'because God chose you ... to be saved [εἰς σωτηρίαν], through sanctification [ἐν ἁγιασμῷ] by the Spirit' (2 Thess. 2.13).

The Pauline pattern which we have observed might be summarized in this way:

justification – a past event, which has present implications through sanctification;

sanctification – a present event, dependent upon a past event, justification, which has future implications, viz. salvation;

salvation – a future event, already anticipated and partially experienced in justification and sanctification and clearly dependent upon them.

---

[50] See H. Conzelmann, *Der Erste Brief an die Korinther* (Göttingen: Vandenhoeck and Ruprecht, 1969), pp. 129–30. One should remember, however, that pre-Pauline does not mean anti-Pauline.

[51] But not for the Pauline school – for example, Eph. 2.5–8.

Even in those occasional texts where Paul uses σώζω in a present tense, there is no ground for a confusion which would suggest that salvation is now fully possessed or that the process leading to it is automatic. This can be seen in 1 Cor. 15.1–2: 'Now I would remind you, brethren, in what terms I preached to you the gospel, which you received, in which you stand, by which you are saved [σώζεσθε], *if you hold fast* [εἰ κατέχετε] – unless you believed in vain.' Yes, the gospel is the means of salvation – but only if one holds fast to its power, only if one is obedient to its claim (Rom. 6.16–17). When one does not hold fast, when one is not obedient, then that person has believed in vain (1 Cor. 15.2). In other words, the gospel is both 'Gabe' and 'Aufgabe'.

In light of these observations, we shall propose the following preliminary thesis concerning the relationship of justification to last judgment, a thesis which of necessity will have to be amplified and clarified as we proceed: Paul affirms that the person who has received the gospel of God's gracious mercy by faith and who has been justified through it, will receive the final gift of salvation at the last judgment. This is purely an act of God's grace which the believer will receive if he or she remains obedient to the gift of God and his Spirit. For the people who have been justified, but who then make a mockery of God's gift by their gross abuse and disobedience, such will not receive the gift of salvation at the last judgment and they will suffer the wrath of God (Rom. 5.9–10). Thus the final criterion at the last judgment is, for Paul, not how many good works someone has performed – this is irrelevant since it is the Spirit which enables people to do those deeds of love – but whether someone has held fast and remained obedient to their new life in Christ.[52] It is the criterion of the obedience of faith (Rom. 1.5 and 16.25) which will enable us to understand many of the Pauline last judgment texts to which we now turn.[53]

---

[52] Stendahl, 'Justification and the Last Judgment', p. 5, puts the matter well: 'The danger is not to get a little worse, and the hope is not to get a little better (ethically, or in terms of faith). It is sharpened in the simplified black and white of all eschatological situations: the dangers of apostasy.'

[53] See P. S. Minear, *The Obedience of Faith* (SBT 19; London: SCM Press, 1971).

Last Judgment

The Pauline texts dealing with last judgment can essentially be divided into four categories:

- texts describing the universal judgment of all people, including non-Christians;
- texts describing the judgment of Christians who have remained obedient;
- texts describing the judgment of the apostolic work (ἔργον) of Christian missionaries;
- texts describing the judgment of Christians who have not been obedient to the hope of the gospel.

Within the limitations of this paper, our primary focus will be on the third and fourth categories, with only brief remarks directed to the first and second.

The fact that Paul expects a universal judgment for all persons could clearly be assumed from his doctrine of the righteousness of God and justification, particularly since those themes are derived from the Old Testament and apocalyptic Judaism. However, Paul does not leave us guessing in this matter of a universal last judgment: he explicitly describes such a judgment for us. Two texts, one from a deutero-Pauline[54] and one from a Pauline letter must suffice. According to 2 Thess. 1.8–9, when God appears at the last day he will inflict 'vengeance upon those who do not know God and upon those who do not obey the gospel of our Lord Jesus. They shall suffer the punishment of eternal destruction and exclusion from the presence of the Lord and from the glory of his might.' This identical point is reiterated in Rom. 2.5–6: 'But by your hard and impenitent heart you are storing up wrath for yourself on the day of wrath when God's righteous judgment will be revealed. For he will render to every man according to his work.' This category of Pauline judgment

---

[54] See our discussion of 2 Thess. on pp. 49–67 in this volume.

texts can be summarized very briefly in the apostle's own language: 'all ... will be judged' (Rom. 2.12).

As we will hope to show, Paul expects a last judgment for Christians which can have different results: salvation for the Christians who have been obedient in faith and wrath for those who have been disobedient to their calling in Christ.[55] We turn now to the former of the two categories.

It is the intention of the gospel which the apostle proclaims to lead people εἰς σωτηρίαν (for example, Rom. 1.16). While salvation begins already now in the present (2 Cor. 6.2), its final manifestation is still to be found in the future (Rom. 13.11; 1 Thess. 5.8–9).[56] Justification can never be equated with salvation: justification is the beginning of the Christian life, salvation its consummation and fulfillment. How does one move from one to the other? Paul answers very concisely in 2 Thess. 2.13: 'God chose you from the beginning to be saved, through sanctification [ἐν ἁγιασμῷ] by the Spirit and belief in the truth.' Salvation is the natural and expected end result for the justified person through sanctification! Only through εἰς ἁγιασμόν will one be pure and blameless on the day of Christ. To be pure and blameless on the day of Christ is an overriding concern of Paul for all his congregations (Phil. 1.10–11; 1 Cor. 1.8).

A concise summary of Paul's theology can be found in the deutero-Pauline Colossians. In describing who will be found irreproachable on the last day, it presents the all-important Pauline conditions: 'provided [εἴ γε] that you continue [ἐπιμένετε] in the faith, stable and steadfast, not shifting [μετακινούμενοι] from the hope of the gospel' (1.23). It is the Christian who remains steadfast and firm,[57] in short, obedient to the hope of the gospel, who will receive the final gift of salvation. It is in this fact (viz. that consummated salvation is still a future event) that the apostle's entire paraenesis is anchored. Because the

---

[55] This is parallel to the dual meaning of ἡμέρα – as the day of salvation (ἡμέρα σωτηρίας – 2 Cor. 6.2) and as the day of wrath (Rom. 2.5); see also Roetzel, *Judgement*, p. 83.

[56] See our previous discussion above, p. 267.

[57] Phil. 1.27–30, 4.1; Rom. 14.4; 1 Cor. 7.37, 15.50–58, 16.13; Gal. 5.1; 1 Thess. 3.8; 2 Thess. 2.5.

Christian must stand firm in sanctification, Paul warns his churches to be: ἀνέγκλητοι (1 Cor. 1.8; Col. 1.22); ἄμεμπτοι (1 Thess. 3.13, 5.23; Phil. 2.15); εἰλικρινεῖς and ἀπρόσκοποι (Phil. 1.10). In short, Christians must work out their salvation in fear and trembling.

Even though Paul stresses that justification is purely an act of God's mercy and that sanctification is entirely the gift of God's spirit, he is quick to warn his audience that these involve their active participation and obedience to God's continued goodness. Otherwise they will be like the people of Israel with whom God was not pleased; 'for they were overthrown in the wilderness. Now these things are warnings for us, not to desire evil as they did' (1 Cor. 10.5–6). And so, because Paul wants to present his bride pure and blameless on the last day (2 Cor. 11.2), he reminds his congregation of this last day in no uncertain terms. No one should transgress 'because the Lord is an avenger [ἔκδικος] in all these things' (1 Thess. 4.6). We must be careful not to despise our brother or sister because we must all appear 'before the judgment seat of God [βήματι τοῦ θεοῦ]' (Rom. 14.10) where 'each one may receive good or evil, according to what he has done in the body' (2 Cor. 5.10). To simply dismiss these texts as relics from Paul's Jewish past is to fundamentally misunderstand the scope and richness of Pauline theology.[58]

There are at least two texts which by the very nature of their context must be placed in a separate category: 1 Cor. 3.1–15 and 1 Cor. 4.1–5. 1 Cor. 3.15 ('If any man's work is burned up, he will suffer loss, though he himself will be saved, but only as through fire') can only be correctly interpreted if one understands the entire pericope in which it is found. Because Lieselotte Mattern does not take the context in which this verse is placed with sufficient seriousness, one is forced to sharply disagree with her conclusion, partially based on 1 Cor. 3.15: 'Hat Paulus ohne jede Einschränkung und ohne jede Bedingung den Christen Freiheit vom Vernichtungsgericht zugesagt ... und haben 1. Kor. 3,15;

---

[58] Representative of such a position would be Bultmann. See the discussion in Stuhlmacher, *Gottes Gerechtigkeit*, p. 229.

5,5; 11,21 gezeigt, daß diese Freiheit weder durch die Untauglichkeit des Werkes noch durch eventuelle 'Sünde' des Christen verspielt werden kann, dann scheint daraus eine Heilsgewißheit zu sprechen, die einer Sicherheit des Heils sehr nahe kommt.'[59] The question, however, is whether or not Paul is speaking about the sins of individual Christians in 1 Cor. 3.15. Is this a case where what Stendahl refers to as 'the introspective conscience of the West' has overlooked both the missionary context of 1 Cor. 3, as well as its apocalyptically conditioned language?

We would contend that 1 Cor. 3.5–15 has nothing to do with the sins of individual Christians nor with their consequent salvation in spite of their sins. In fact, we would even go so far as to argue that the verb σῴζω in verse 15 has nothing to do with christology and is used here in an entirely secular sense of 'to rescue, to deliver from danger or harm'.

The issue in 1 Cor. 3 is party strife, viz. whether in the minds of the Corinthians Paul or Apollos is superior. Paul, in this entire section, addresses himself to the absurdity of such a competitive attitude. It is clear that some members of the Corinthian congregation are disputing the effectiveness of Paul's ministry and apostleship, as becomes evident in Paul's response in 1 Cor. 4.3–5:

> But with me it is a very small thing that I should be judged by you or by any human court. I do not even judge myself. I am not aware of anything against myself, but I am not thereby acquitted. It is the Lord who judges me. Therefore do not pronounce judgment before the time, before the Lord comes, who will bring to light the things now hidden in darkness and will disclose the purpose of the heart. Then every man will receive his commendation from God.

He not only warns the Corinthians, filled with pride, against judging his stewardship prematurely, but also points out that on

---

[59] Mattern, *Gericht bei Paulus*, pp. 110–11 [ET: 'If Paul promised the Christian's exemption from a damning judgment, without any restrictions or any conditions, … and if 1 Cor. 3.15, 5.5, 11.21 have shown that this exemption cannot be lost whether through the unsuitability of works or through potential sin, then a confidence of salvation seems expressed that comes very close to a certitude of salvation.']

the last day[60] God will reveal all that now seems to be hidden in darkness – in this case, the trustworthiness (πιστός) of Paul's relationship to the Corinthians (1 Cor. 4.2). The apostle reminds this congregation that it is finally the Lord who will judge (4.4) the effectiveness of his laborer's work and it is finally the Lord who will either burn up the ineffective labor or reward the competent work, an action which Paul may view as similar to the one given to the good and faithful steward in Matt. 25, viz. the 'well done' macarism.

1 Cor. 3.10–15 is also a warning to those charged with the responsibility of caring for the Corinthian church to take care how they build on the foundation, since on the last day the quality of building materials will be revealed through fire. The good will survive and the remainder will be destroyed. That laborer who has built a house with cheap materials, i.e. ministered to the Corinthians via short cuts, with worldly wisdom rather than the cross of Christ, that man will be pulled out of his rubble heap just in the nick of time. Barrett remarks that the 'workman caught in the flames of his own badly constructed house runs the risk of being engulfed in them. In fact, he will escape, but it will be as one who dashed through flames . . ., safe, but with a smell of fire upon him.'[61] The entire thrust of our argument has been that neither 1 Cor. 3.15 nor 4.5 has anything to do with the good works of individual Christians or with their personal salvation; both deal with a concrete situation in the life of the Corinthian congregation concerning the validity and effectiveness of apostolic ministry. Paul, on the one hand, uses a well-known apocalyptic illustration (Isa. 26.11, 31.9, 66.24; Dan. 7.9–14) to warn the Corinthians about premature judgment; on the other hand, he employs the argument that all apostolic work, good or bad, is known to God and will be judged by him on the last day.[62]

---

[60] This point is made both in 1 Cor. 3.13 and 4.15.

[61] C. K. Barrett, *A Commentary on the First Epistle to the Corinthians* (HNTC; New York: Harper and Row, 1968), p. 89.

[62] See also the discussion in Devor, *Concept of Judgment*, pp. 433ff. While his sharp distinction between reward and salvation is untenable, he provides a series of perceptive insights.

Thus far we have reviewed last judgment texts in Paul which deal with universal judgment, the gift of salvation for obedient Christians at the last judgment and God's scrutiny of apostolic work on the last day. We now turn to those texts which postulate a negative outcome for disobedient Christians on the last day. In proposing such a fourth category of Pauline judgment texts we stand in direct opposition to such scholars as Kühl[63] who holds that once the believer has been justified, salvation will result in an irrevocable manner.

There are several texts which indicate that Paul not only warns Christians about a possible rejection by God if they abandon the hope of the gospel, but which also flatly state that God can and will reject disobedient Christians. Such warning is explicitly found in 1 Cor. 10 and 1 Cor. 11.27–32, and implied in Gal. 6.7, the text dealing with sowing and reaping. Less clear are 2 Thess. 1.8–9, where it is stated that vengeance will be inflicted 'upon those who do not know God and upon those who do not obey the gospel of our Lord Jesus', and 1 Cor. 6.9, where the rhetorical question is raised, 'Do you not know that the unrighteous will not inherit the kingdom of God?' It is unlikely that the 2 Thessalonians passage refers to Christians; the text in 1 Corinthians is more difficult to interpret. Ambiguity also surrounds the understanding of Gal. 5.21b, 'I warn you, as I warned you before, that those who do such things shall not inherit the kingdom of God.' We are, however, inclined to see both the 1 Corinthian[64] and the Galatian texts as referring to Christians, since both are found in paraenetic contexts addressed to Christians.

---

[63] E. Kühl, *Rechtfertigung auf Grund Glaubens und Gericht nach den Werken bei Paulus* (Königsberg, 1904), pp. 11, 15, 20. See also Devor, *Concept of Judgment*, p. 370.

[64] Roetzel, *Judgment in the Community*, p. 129, holds with Käsemann that Paul is seeking to restore the important dimension of 'eschatological reservation' in 1 Cor. 6.9–11. Paul is stressing two factors: '1) He challenges the eschatological certainty of the Corinthians. You do wrong, Paul says, and "you know, don't you, that wrongdoers will not inherit the Kingdom of God" ... Paul thus underscores the point that apart from continued vigilance in Christ there is no guarantee of salvation. 2) He speaks of the Kingdom of God as a future inheritance not a present possession.'

These preliminary references bring us to the single most important passage in this category of judgment texts: 1 Cor. 5.1–8. It is one of the most troublesome Pauline judgment texts and the one most frequently used as a support for the argument that the baptized Christian is guaranteed salvation, especially verse 5: 'you are to deliver this man to Satan for the destruction of the flesh, that his spirit may be saved in the day of the Lord Jesus'. The exegetical difficulty which this text presents can be seen, for example, in Conzelmann's inability to reach a firm conclusion. He concludes his discussion with two unanswered questions: 'the saving of the πνεῦμα. This is an enigmatic statement. Does the baptized man possess a *character indelebilis*? Or is the intention precisely that the Spirit should be taken from him?'[65]

Those who interpret this verse as supporting guaranteed salvation are all dependent on what has become the widely accepted translation of the Greek text, typified by the American Revised Standard Version: 'you are to deliver this man to Satan for the destruction of the flesh, that his spirit may be saved in the day of the Lord Jesus'. But where in the Greek text does one find any αὐτοῦ which would permit us to translate 'his spirit' rather than 'the spirit'? It does not exist. Is there any other contextual warrant for translating πνεῦμα as the condemned person's spirit, other than the exegetical bias of 'the introspective conscience of the West'? Much to be preferred is the more literal translation of the King James Version: 'To deliver such a one into Satan for the destruction of the flesh, that the spirit may be saved in the day of the Lord Jesus.'[66]

While this translation may be the more literal, does it assist us in understanding Paul's intention? It does, for by taking seriously the fact that Paul refers to 'the spirit' rather than 'his spirit', one is forced to rethink the whole matter. Our thesis is, quite simply, that Paul is not at all referring to the offender's spirit, but God's

---

[65] Conzelmann, *Korinther*, p. 118. The English text is taken from the English translation of Conzelmann's commentary: *1 Corinthians: A Commentary of the First Epistle to the Corinthians* (Hermeneia; Philadelphia: Fortress Press, 1975), p. 98.

[66] This verse is correctly translated by both Roetzel, *Judgement in the Community*, p. 123, and R. Jewett, *Paul's Anthropological Terms* (Leiden: E. J. Brill, 1971), p. 124.

Spirit present in the Corinthian congregation.[67] He is telling the Corinthians to cast out the work of the flesh and to return it to its proper source, Satan, so that God's Spirit may continue to be present and thus preserve the congregation for the last day (cf. 1 Cor. 1.7–8). This understanding stands parallel to the succeeding verses which speak of the old and the new lump, and coheres very well with 1 Cor. 3.16–17: 'Do you not know that you are God's temple and that God's Spirit dwells in you? If any one destroys God's temple, God will destroy him. For God's temple is holy, and that temple you are.'[68] In fact, this understanding agrees with much of the exhortation present in 1 Corinthians, viz. that the presence of God's spirit in the Corinthian church by no means leads to guaranteed assurances about their status before God (e.g. see 1 Cor. 10.5–6, 12). Thus, the focus of Paul's concern in 1 Cor. 5 is not primarily that of one person's sin, but the arrogance of a congregation which would tolerate this and fail to realize that the presence of such 'fleshly' actions jeopardizes the entire church's standing before God. His mandate is clear: rid yourselves of all corruption so that God's spirit may be saved, i.e. may continue to dwell in your midst (1 Cor. 3.16).[69] Commenting on the function

---

[67] Roetzel's study, *Judgement in the Community*, is helpful by its very title in moving emphasis away from the purely individual aspects of judgment in Pauline thought to that of the entire congregation: 'Paul's emphasis falls on the corporate aspects of judgment. This finding is apparent in the prominent role the church plays in Paul's judgment allusions. In both the present and the future, the church stands at the center of Paul's thought about the Day of the Lord ... If the church attempts to take the fruits of salvation without assuming the responsibilities that go with them the judgment portends loss and possible ruin ... While Paul ... is not unmindful of the individual believer, the individual member of the church is first and foremost a social being' (p. 178). These perceptive insights are not, unfortunately, applied with consistency to 1 Cor. 5.5–15, where the salvation of the individual is the primary concern for Roetzel (pp. 123–4).

[68] See further discussion of these verses in Barrett, *1 Corinthians*, pp. 90–2, and Conzelmann, *Korintherbrief*, pp. 96–7.

[69] That the use of the term 'spirit' in these verses differs from his ordinary usage is acknowledged by Bornkamm and von Campenhausen in H. von Campenhausen, *Ecclesiastical Authority and Spiritual Power* (Stanford: University Press, 1960), pp. 134–5, n. 50. Bornkamm is supported by the fact that in 1 Corinthians, Paul, when using the terms σάρξ and πνεῦμα with reference to a person, does not use them in a dualistic but in a wholistic sense – see especially 1 Cor. 7.34; also 2 Cor. 7.1 and 1 Thess. 5.23. Note also Barrett's uneasiness in understanding the term 'spirit' in 1 Corinthians 5 (*1 Corinthians*, p. 126); further discussions in R. Bultmann, *Theology of the New Testament*, I (New York: Scribner's, 1951), pp. 203–10; and, Jewett, *Paul's Anthropological Terms*, pp. 119–25.

of the Spirit in this verse, Conzelmann remarks: 'But for Paul the Spirit is not a habitual possession, but a gift, and moreover a gift to the community.'[70]

This interpretation of the Spirit's function within the life of the Corinthian congregation found in 1 Cor. 5.5, is similar to other statements made by Paul. In 1 Corinthians itself, in addition to 3.16–17, one should note the relevant discussion about the Spirit and the flesh in 2.10–3.4, which serves as the substructure of the practical implications and actions taken in chapter 5. Also, Paul's comment in Gal. 5.5 is helpful for an understanding of 1 Cor. 5.5: 'For through the Spirit, by faith, we wait for the hope of righteousness.' Since it is only through the Spirit that one hopes for the final gift on the last day, it is critical for the congregation, by faith, to permit God's Spirit to dwell in its midst. It is for this reason that Paul must outline so carefully the radical difference between the desire of the flesh and of the Spirit in Gal. 5.16–26, and must categorically state in 5.21b: 'I warn you, as I warned you before, that those who do such things shall not inherit the kingdom of God'. Paul is quite explicit that the gift of the Spirit at baptism (1 Cor. 12.12–13) does not grant an indelible mark which automatically leads to salvation. Rather, the one who has been baptized must continue to receive and share in the gift of God's Spirit (Phil. 2.1) and, as a result, be obedient to His will. Even the deutero-Pauline Ephesians (4.30) recognizes that it is possible to 'grieve the Holy Spirit'. Apparently both the Corinthians and the Galatians were in danger of confusing the gift of the Spirit with the full payment, rather than recognizing it to be only the first installment (ἀρραβών) of that which is yet to come if the Christian continues to participate in the Spirit.[71] Finally, Paul's words in 1 Thess. 4.6–8, that the Lord is an avenger (ἔκδικος) to everyone who

---

[70] Conzelmann, *Korintherbrief*, p. 97, n. 92. English translation is taken from *1 Corinthians*, p. 78, n. 92.

[71] See also N. Q. Hamilton, *The Holy Spirit and Eschatology in Paul* (SJTOP 6; Edinburgh: Oliver and Boyd, 1957), p. 32; C. K. Barrett, *A Commentary on the Second Epistle to the Corinthians* (New York: Harper and Row, 1973), pp. 78–81, and J. S. Vos, *Traditionsgeschichtliche Untersuchungen zur Paulinischen Pneumatologie* (Assen: van Gorcum, 1973).

disregards (ὁ ἀθετῶν) the Holy Spirit given by God, further supports our interpretation of 1 Cor. 5.5.

While Paul's primary concern in this pericope is the Christian community, his comments concerning the sinner do have important implications for the overall theme concerning the relationship between justification and last judgment. Paul's point with regard to this offender appears to be clear and consistent: anyone who is baptized, justified and a member of the church but who is not obedient to the gift and possibility of his new existence, will not be tolerated.[72] Those who are disobedient live in the realm of Satan, in the realm of the flesh, and thus corrupt the body of Christ. Both in his formula of exclusion in 1 Cor. 5.5[73] and in his citation of Deut. 17.7 in 1 Cor. 5.13, 'Drive out the wicked person from among you', Paul is very consistent: the church member who is flagrantly disobedient no longer belongs to the realm of those who are being saved, but to the realm of those who are perishing (1 Cor. 1.18). The apostle urges his congregation to acknowledge the obvious for the sake of the Spirit.

Relevant to this discussion are Käsemann's remarks with regard to 1 Cor. 11.26–34: 'The self-manifestation of Christ calls men to obedience and this means that, at the same time it calls them to account before the final Judge who is already today acting within his community as he will act towards the world on the Last Day – he bestows salvation by setting men within his lordship and, if they spurn this lordship, they then experience this act of rejection as a self-incurred sentence of death.'[74]

---

[72] Against Mattern, *Gericht bei Paulus*, p. 106.
[73] See the discussion and citation of other literature in Barrett, *1 Corinthians*, p. 126.
[74] E. Käsemann, *Essays on New Testament Theses* (London: SCM Press, 1964), p. 126.

14

❦

Justification and Last Judgment in Paul – Twenty-Five Years Later

Responses and Advances

My original article, 'Justification and Last Judgment in Paul',[1] opened with these words: 'The relationship between justification and last judgment in Paul has been both a source of division between Roman Catholicism and Protestantism and a source of confusion within much of contemporary Protestant thought. A re-examination of this difficult and troublesome theme in light of the advances in contemporary biblical studies may help not only to achieve greater clarity with regard to this theme but also to assist in removing some of the falsely erected barriers which still cause division within Christianity. In short, the re-exploration of this nerve-center of division could have important theological and ecumenical implications.' This essay was originally delivered as a lecture at the Roman Catholic sponsored *Colloquium Biblicum Lovaniense* at the University of Louvain (KU Leuven) in 1974; the ecumenical context and intention of my reflections as a Lutheran theologian were explicit both then and now.

The responses to my interpretation of Paul's understanding of justification and last judgment were immediate, varied and sustained. Immediately following this lecture in Louvain, my close friend, the late Raymond E. Brown, and I were walking

---

[1] For original publication see n. 2 below. In this volume, pp. 253–78.

toward the exit of the College of Pope Adrian VI when we met the late Monsignor Josef Coppens, the president of the *Colloquium Biblicum Lovaniense* for that year. Professor Coppens graciously thanked me for the lecture and added words to the effect that 'you are more Catholic than the Catholics!'[2] As we stepped away, Professor Brown looked at me and said, 'Karl, you have just received the imprimatur!' In a similar vein, the Roman Catholic scholar, Benedict T. Viviano, OP, wrote to me that 'I was especially moved by your article(s) on judgment in Paul. If you are right, as I believe you are, I see little further reasons for a Reformation split. Whenever I teach Romans I emphasize the importance of your work.'[3] And during the Easter Triduum of 1998, one year before the Lutheran–Roman Catholic Joint Declaration on Justification was signed,[4] the late Cardinal John O'Connor cited this essay from the pulpit of St Patrick's Cathedral in New York City, urging the new confirmands and the gathered congregation to take seriously the words describing Paul's perspective with regard to the sanctified life.[5]

A significant Lutheran voice, dependent on the previous criticism of Ernst Synofzik,[6] demurred. John H. P. Reumann, citing my description of the relationship of justification, sanctification and salvation, which he describes as a 'three-stage pattern'[7] in a way I never did, concluded that it 'is demonstrably wrong (cf. Synofzik, pp. 152–4), as is shown not only by the compromises Donfried has introduced in his description but above all by the

---

[2] Professor Coppens was the President of the *Colloquium Biblicum Lovaniense* in 1974 and my original lecture, 'Justification and Last Judgment in Paul', was included in the volume he edited, in *La Notion biblique de Dieu*, ed. J. Coppens (Gembloux: J. Duculot, 1976), pp. 293–313 (with French summary attached). He very graciously permitted the essay to be simultaneously published in *ZNW* 67 (1976), pp. 90–110, and an abbreviated version in *Int* 30 (1976), pp. 140–52. Much of this material is also to be found in my book, *The Dynamic Word: New Testament Insights for Contemporary Christians* (San Francisco: Harper and Row, 1981), pp. 50–64.

[3] Letter dated 18 October 1996.

[4] 31 October 1999.

[5] 11 April 1998.

[6] E. Synofzik, *Die Gerichts- und Vergeltungsaussagen bei Paulus: Eine traditionsgeschichtliche Untersuchung* (GTA 8; Gottingen: Vandenhoeck and Ruprecht,1977), pp. 152–4.

[7] J. Reumann, *Righteousness in the New Testament* (Philadelphia/New York: Fortress/Paulist Press, 1982), p. 82.

Pauline texts themselves.'[8] At this point Reumann is uncritically dependent on Synofzik, even to the point of using his exact language in English translation. James Dunn has correctly observed that Synofzik misses the point and that 'to force Paul's dialectic between grace and judgment into an antithesis … throws his theology into confusion'.[9] Joseph Fitzmyer, inadvertently confusing Reumann's (i.e. Synofzik's) language for mine, suggests rather that in 'Pauline thinking they [justification, sanctification and salvation] represent rather three effects of the Christ-event, each of which has a past, present, and future aspect. More has to be said about the way Paul speaks of "salvation" in Romans as a whole; here Reumann has obscured the issue somewhat.'[10] Fitzmyer's use of the phrase 'three effects of the Christ-event' is helpful and coheres fully with what I was intending to express.

The clearest articulation of the major interpretative goals of my essay have been both succinctly and accurately stated in paragraph 15 of the Lutheran–Roman Catholic Joint Declaration on the Doctrine of Justification:

> In faith we together hold the conviction that justification is the work of the triune God. The Father sent his Son into the world to save sinners. The foundation and presupposition of justification is the incarnation, death and resurrection of Christ. Justification thus means that Christ himself is our righteousness, in which we share through the Holy Spirit in accord with the will of the Father. Together we confess: By grace alone, in faith in Christ's saving work and not because of any merit on our part, we are accepted by God and receive the Holy Spirit, who renews our hearts while equipping and calling us to good works.[11]

This statement, especially its last sentence, captures well the dialectic in Paul's theology: justification as an act of grace that calls for and energizes the transformation of the believer in faith (see 1 Thess. 2.14 and 2 Cor. 3.18).[12] It is precisely this

---

[8] Reumann, *Righteousness in the New Testament*, p. 82.

[9] J. D. G. Dunn, *Romans 1–8* (Dallas: Word, 1988), p. 85.

[10] In Reumann, *Righteousness in the New Testament*, 213.

[11] *Joint Declaration on the Doctrine of Justification/the Lutheran World Federation and the Roman Catholic Church* (Grand Rapids: Eerdmans, 2000), paragraph 15.

[12] See further my comments in 'Augsburg, 1999: By Grace Alone – Some Reflections by a Participant', *Pro Eccl* IX (2000): pp. 5–7.

indicative/imperative intention that Paul has in mind when he uses the phrase 'the obedience of faith' (Rom. 1.5 and 16.26).

Justification and the Dead Sea Scrolls

John Reumann's critique proceeds further to state that in my analysis 'Rom. 2.6–11 is not discussed' and, further, that my interpretation is 'open to a synergistic emphasis on the third use of the law'.[13] Given the dialectical relationship between justification and last judgment in Paul for which I had argued, these verses in Romans both support and augment that understanding of Paul. Paul writes these words in Romans 2:

> But by your hard and impenitent heart you are storing up wrath for yourself on the day of wrath, when God's righteous judgment will be revealed. For he will repay according to each one's deeds: to those who by patiently doing good seek for glory and honor and immortality, he will give eternal life; while for those who are self-seeking and who obey not the truth but wickedness, there will be wrath and fury. There will be anguish and distress for everyone who does evil, the Jew first and also the Greek, but glory and honor and peace for everyone who does good, the Jew first and also the Greek. For God shows no partiality.

With Käsemann[14] and others one must recognize that the judgment Paul refers to in verses 3 and 5 needs to be understood in light of his teaching on justification by grace through faith. When the apostle argues in verse 6 that 'he will repay according to each one's deeds [τὰ ἔργα αὐτοῦ]', the specific reference to the 'good deeds' (ἔργου ἀγαθοῦ) that follow are correctly understood as the result and fruit of faith. This is the case not only here and in verse 10 (τῷ ἐργαζομένῳ τὸ ἀγαθόν), but also in 2 Cor. 9.8 ('And God is able to provide you with every blessing in abundance, so that by always having enough of everything, you may share abundantly in every good work [πᾶν ἔργον ἀγαθόν]'), and Phil. 1.6 ('I am confident of this, that the one who began a good work among you will bring it to completion by the day of Jesus Christ [ἔργον ἀγαθὸν]').

---

[13] Reumann, *Righteousness in the New Testament*, p. 82, n. 84
[14] E. Käsemann, *Commentary on Romans* (Grand Rapids: Eerdmans, 1980), p. 58.

With regard to Rom. 2.1–11, Fitzmyer comments that the 'Jews are no exception to the teaching of Paul's gospel that no one comes to salvation without God's grace; no one comes to justification on the basis of deeds only.'[15] In verse 6, 'For he will repay according to each one's deeds', by his direct reference to Ps. 62.12 (LXX 61.13) and Prov. 24.12, Paul is challenging an established principle of Judaism. One might appropriately ask whether there were precedents within Judaism that encouraged Paul and allowed him to hold concurrently his assertions about justification by faith and judgment according to deeds. Elsewhere we have suggested that Paul seems to be influenced by elements of thought that are found in the scrolls found at Qumran.[16] Might that be the case here as well? In verse 5 ('But by your hard and impenitent heart you are storing up wrath for yourself on the day of wrath, when God's righteous judgment will be revealed'), the term that Paul uses for 'God's righteous judgment', δικαιοκρισίας τοῦ θεοῦ, a term quite different from his earlier use of δικαιοσύνη γὰρ θεοῦ, has the sense of God's distributive justice. It has been suggested that the phrase is equivalent to צדק משפטי ('just judgments') in 1QH 1.23, 30.[17] Further, Fitzmyer suggests that the Pauline clause that follows in verse 6, 'For he will repay according to each one's deeds', is remarkably close to כיא את אל משפט כול חי והואה ישלם לאיש גמולו ('for with God resides

---

[15] J. Fitzmyer. *Romans: A New Translation with Introduction and Commentary* (AB33; New York: Doubleday, pp. 297–8. Fitzmyer, in a longer comment, affirms the major perspective of my original article on 'Justification and Last Judgment'. Fitzmyer maintains that 'it is precisely the motif of God's judgment that must be retained for the sake of the message of justification by grace through faith. God has the right to judge the world and to recompense humanity according to its deeds. This Pauline message of judgment is what the Christian needs to hear first (see 3.6), and in the light of that message the message of justification by grace through faith takes on new meaning. It is only in the light of divine judgment according to human deeds that the justification of the sinner by grace through faith is rightly seen. Hence there is no real inconsistency in Paul's teaching about justification by faith and judgment according to deeds. Judgment according to deeds may be a relic of Paul's Jewish background, but it has become an important and integral element in his teaching' (p. 307).

[16] K. P. Donfried, 'Paul and Qumran: The Possible Influence of סרך on 1 Thessalonians', in *The Dead Sea Scrolls Fifty Years After Their Discovery* (Jerusalem: The Magnes Press, 2000), pp. 148–56; pp. 221–31 in this volume.

[17] J. A. Fitzmyer, 'Paul and the Dead Sea Scrolls', in *The Dead Sea Scrolls After Fifty Years*, vol. 2, ed. P. W. Flint and J. C. Vanderkam (Leiden: Brill, 1999), pp. 599–621, here p. 615.

the judgment of all the living, and He shall pay each man his recompense') in 1QS 10.18.[18]

If there is such proximity to the conceptual world of the Qumran community, the *yahad*, one to which Paul could react both positively and negatively, we need to explain the relationship between Paul's self-assertion that he was 'circumcised on the eighth day, a member of the people of Israel, of the tribe of Benjamin, a Hebrew born of Hebrews; as to the law, a Pharisee; as to zeal, a persecutor of the church; as to righteousness under the law, blameless' (Phil. 3.5) and any possible influence from Qumran. Shemaryahu Talmon, who prefers to call the group reflected in the scrolls by their own self-description, viz. as the Community of the Renewed Covenant or, simply the *yahad*,[19] understands this Community of the Renewed Covenant as a 'third- or second-century crystallization of a major socio-religious movement which arose in the early post-exilic Judaism.... The development of the movement runs parallel to that of the competing rationalist stream which first surfaces in the book of Ezra, and especially in the book of Nehemiah, and will ultimately crystallize in Rabbinic or normative Judaism.' And, he adds, that the '*yahad*'s final dissent from the emerging brand of Pharisaic Judaism at the turn of the era constitutes the climax of the lengthy confrontation of these two streams'.[20] As a result one must ask whether Paul's contact with the Community of the Renewed Covenant facilitated his dissent from the brand of Pharisaic Judaism that had shaped his own spirituality? Does this tension within Judaism predispose him toward the Jesus movement and its proposed solution to the very issues that had been and were still central to his own religious struggle?

In this context as well, it appears that the Qumran scrolls may be a tributary to Paul's theological reflection. One need only listen to the following texts:

[18] *The Dead Sea Scrolls: A New Translation*, ed. M. O. Wise, M. G. Abegg, Jr and E. M. Cook (San Francisco: Harper, 1996).

[19] See CD 6.19, 8.29.

[20] S. Talmon, 'The Community of the Renewed Covenant', in *The Community of the Renewed Covenant: The Notre Dame Symposium on the Dead Sea Scrolls* (Christianity and Judaism in Antiquity Series, 10; ed. E. Ulrich and J. VanderKam; Notre Dame, Indiana: University of Notre Dame, 1994), pp. 3–24, here p. 22.

My iniquities, rebellions, and sins,
    together with the wickedness of my heart,
belong to the assembly of perverse flesh
    and to those who walk in darkness.
For mankind has no way,
    And man is unable to establish his steps
since judgment is with God
    and perfection of way is out of His hand.
All things come to pass by His knowledge;
He establishes all things by His design
    and without Him nothing is done.

As for me,
    if I stumble, the mercies of God
    shall be my eternal salvation.
If I stagger because of the sin of flesh,
    my judgment shall be
    by the righteousness of God which endures for ever.
When my distress is unleashed
    He will deliver my soul from the Pit
    and will direct my steps to the way.
He will draw me near by His grace,
    and by His mercy will He bring my judgment.
He will judge me in the righteousness of His truth
    and in the greatness of His goodness
    He will pardon all my sins.
Through His righteousness he will cleanse me
    of the uncleanness of man
    and of the sins of the children of men,
that I may confess to God His righteousness,
    and His majesty to the Most High.
    (1QS 11.9–15)[21]

I lean on Thy grace
    and on the multitude of Thy mercies,
for Thou wilt pardon iniquity,
    and through Thy righteousness
    [Thou wilt pardon man] of his sin.
Not for his sake wilt Thou do it,
    [but for the sake of Thy glory].
For Thou hast created the just and the wicked.
    (1QH 11.36–40)[22]

---

[21] G. Vermes, *The Complete Dead Sea Scrolls in English* (New York: Penguin, 1997) with modification.

[22] Vermes, *Complete Dead Sea Scrolls.*

The theme of human sinfulness and wickedness, the assertion that 'judgment shall be by the righteousness of God' and the emphasis on the mercy of a gracious God in whom human right-eousness is rooted are remarkably analogous to Paul's teaching about justification by grace. A closer examination of this termin-ology is revealing. The term δικαιοσύνη θεοῦ, 'the righteousness of God', is used by Paul in Rom. 1.17, 3.5, 21, 22; 10.3; and 2 Cor. 5.21, often in close connection with his comments on justi-fication. It is not insignificant that the exact phrase 'the righteousness of God' is not found in the Old Testament but that it is only found in 1QM 4.6 as צדק אל and in 1QS 10.25; 11.12 as צדקת אל. This prior usage of the concept by the *yahad* would indicate that it was not created by Paul. Also, at the beginning of the passage cited above, 1QS 11.9, there is a striking parallel to Paul's use of σαρκὸς ἁμαρτίας ('sinful flesh'; Rom. 8.3) and צול בשר ('perverse flesh').[23] In addition, there are further examples of Paul's negative meanings for σὰρξ ἁμαρτίας, as in Rom. 8.5–8, with עוון בשר, 'the sin of flesh' in 1QS 11.9 and 12.

This Qumran perspective, by its very clustering of these themes into a consistent unity, moves beyond the Old Testament.[24] Thus it is possible that the *yahad* may have prepared the way for Paul to be open to reformulating these emphases based on his encounter with the risen Christ (Gal. 1.15–16). There are, of course, obvious differences between Paul and the *yahad*, the most notable is the centrality of the death and resur-rection of Jesus Christ in his theology. Because Messiah has come, the righteousness of God has already been revealed. For the *yahad*, since they are still waiting for Messiah(s), their radicalized obedience to Torah suggests that the righteousness of God still remains a future goal and intention. Thus Fitzmyer reminds us that this community's emphasis on the mercy and the righteousness of God 'is transitional, because it is not yet the full-blown idea of Pauline justification by *grace through faith*'.[25] For

---

[23] Translations by Wise, Abegg, Cook, *A New Translation*.
[24] For example, righteous צדק, sin תמאה and mercy חסד.
[25] Fitzmyer, 'Paul and the Dead Sea Scrolls', p. 604.

this reason one should also follow his lead in translating משפט as 'judgment' and not as 'justification'.[26] 'Judgment' allows Qumran to influence Paul's thinking without suggesting the closer approximation that 'justification' implies. This same situation of similarity and dissimilarity is evident in the common yet different use of Hab. 2.4 in the *yahad* and in Paul (Rom. 1.17). Although 1 QpHab 8.10 goes beyond the Old Testament by connecting the words of Habakkuk to a person, as does Paul, yet for the apostle πίστις/אמונה is not simply fidelity to a person but it is faith in the risen Christ (Rom. 10.9–10).

These few examples, briefly cited, already suggest a proximity to Paul's theological formulations. There is still, however, another term that Paul uses, ἔργα νόμου ('deeds of the law'), that has been found in the Qumran scrolls. In all likelihood, as we will show below, the Pauline use of this anarthrous phrase, ἔργα νόμου, appears to be a reaction to the *yahad's* (or a similar tradition) use of this terminology. It is important to remember, especially in this context, that neither Paul's relationship to the *yahad* nor to the Torah, from his new perspective as the apostle to the Gentiles, was uncomplicated.

It has been correctly stated that the Pauline phrase ἔργα νόμου has no parallel in the Jewish Bible. Close, but not exact, is the use of the noun מעשה ('deed') in Ex. 18.20: 'teach them the statutes and instructions and make known to them the way they are to go and the deed they are to do'. Referring to similar ideas, Num. 15.39 and Deut. 16.12, 30.8 use alternative terms, מצוות ('commandments') and חוקים ('laws'). However, the precise parallel phrase to Paul's ἔργα νόμου is found in the Qumran texts. In 4QMMT C27 one reads מקצת מעשי חתורה ('some deeds of the law'), in 4QMMT C 30–31 the emphasis falls on the correct practice of these deeds ('in your deed [בעשותך] you may be reckoned as righteous') and in 1QS 5.21 and 6.18 one finds the phrase מעשיו בתורה ('his deeds in the law'). It is not unimportant to recognize that the *yahad* does not use the typical Pharisaic

---

[26] Against, for example, S. Schulz, 'Zur Rechtfertigung aus Gnaden in Qumran und bei Paulus', *ZTK* 56 (1959), pp. 155–85, and Vermes, *Complete Dead Sea Scrolls.*

language, חלקות or מצוות, yet appears to be fully aware of this terminology in creating the clever and polemical turn of phrase, דרשי חלקות, 'seekers of smooth things' (4Q 169.3–4).[27]

How is מעשי התורה to be understood in the scrolls? Baumgarten observes that in 1QS 6.18 'a novice in the community is examined "as to his intelligence uma'asaw batorah" [in his deeds of the torah]. The covenanters are themselves called 'ose ha-torah. It is apparent that the phrase refers to scrupulous observance of the Law and particularly to the study of the Law in accordance with sectarian principles.'[28] The emphasis here is that one should act according to the law, viz. to observe and practice it. This appears to be a sharply different tendency from the pharisaic, rabbinic branch of Second Temple Judaism described by Talmon above.[29] It is to the former, the yahad, or a similar tradition, that Paul is reacting by using their own terminology. Although criticizing the context out of which they practice the law there is no suggestion whatsoever in the Pauline letters that he is, as a result, rejecting the Torah. Once that is recognized, greater attention needs to be given to Paul's particular perspective with regard to the practice of the law, insights that are not to be found in his negative asser-tions but rather in those places where he actually assumes the practice of the law, as, for example, in 1 Thess. 4.1–12.[30] Significant in this regard is the recognition that Paul's polemic against the 'deeds of the law' is frequently found within a broader apologetic context as is the case in Rom. 3.31 ('Do we then overthrow the law by this faith? By no means! On the contrary, we uphold the law') and Rom. 7.12 ('So the law is holy, and the commandment is holy and just and good'). While the 'deeds of the law' are not the basis of righteousness – for Paul only Christ

---

[27] Throughout the scrolls there are other variations of the theme לעשות תורה which require a separate, fuller treatment.

[28] J. M. Baumgarten, Studies in Qumran Law (Leiden: Brill, 1977), pp. 82–3.

[29] It is imperative for an accurate 'mapping' of the law in Second Temple Judaism to recognize that these two 'theologies' of the law are so different that they are, in fact, in fundamental conflict. In addition to the foundational article by Talmon cited in n. 10, see further L. H. Schiffmann, Reclaiming the Dead Sea Scrolls (Philadelphia and Jerusalem: The Jewish Publication Society, 1994), pp. 245–55.

[30] See further Donfried, 'Paul and Qumran'.

is – that does not negate a positive function of the law, properly understood, in the life of those who are 'in Christ'. And for that very reason justification and last judgment are intimately bound to one another in Pauline theology and once they are loosed from one another the thought of Paul is easily converted into a form of gnosticism.

Some Reflections on the 'New Perspective' of Paul[31]

This discussion of the Qumran texts, especially 4QMMT, in relationship to both late Second Temple Judaism and Paul, is imperative to correctly understand the position of the apostle and to what type of Judaism he is reacting. Because of this a few critical words are necessary with regard to Paul O'Callaghan, *Fides Christi: The Justification Debate*,[32] especially the section on the relationship of Paul to Judaism. In an otherwise splendidly erudite book which makes a major contribution to scholarship, O'Callaghan, in this particular discussion, limits himself primarily to the interpretations of E. P. Sanders and James Dunn.[33] The essential argument they make is that Judaism was not primarily a religion of works but rather 'one of mercy and faith in God as Saviour'.[34] In what Sanders terms 'covenantal nomism', the law simply 'maintains one's position in the covenant, but does not earn God's grace as such'.[35] Especially for Dunn the law increasingly became a boundary marker for the Jews as a way to be set apart from the Gentiles. It is against this reading of Judaism, which O'Callaghan accepts, that he interprets

---

[31] I refer here particularly to the 1977 publication of E. P. Sanders, *Paul and Palestinian Judaism. A Comparison of Patterns of Religion* (London: SCM Press, 1977), in which he argues that in ancient Jewish literature salvation comes not through the doing of meritorious works but through belonging to and participating in the covenant people of God. In criticizing Lutheran scholarship's distorted view of Judaism, Sanders refers to his new paradigm as 'covenantal nomism'.

[32] P. O'Callaghan, *Fides Christi: The Justification Debate* (Dublin: Four Courts, 1997).

[33] J. D. G. Dunn, *Romans 1–8* (WBC 38A; Dallas: Word, 1988); *Romans 9–16* (WBC 38B; Dallas: Word, 1988); *Jesus, Paul and the Law: Studies in Mark and Galatians* (London: SPCK, 1990).

[34] O'Callaghan, *Fides Christi*, p. 171.

[35] O'Callaghan, *Fides Christi*, p. 172.

Paul's understanding of justification. The following paragraph is representative of his position:

> In other words, Paul's insistence on justification 'by faith alone', that is without 'works of the law' was an expression of the fact that God was ready to accept Gentiles as his children, with the same privileges as Jews, without requiring them first to 'become' Jews, that is, to adopt a new culture, to observe an exact fulfillment of the *Torah*, to subscribe to ritual laws of purification, circumcision, etc. In the words of James Dunn: 'The Christian doctrine of justification by faith begins as Paul's protest not as an individual sinner against a Jewish legalism, but as Paul's protest on behalf of Gentiles against Jewish exclusivism.'[36]

O'Callaghan is not unaware of the Dead Sea Scrolls, including the unique phrase 'works of the law' in 4QMMT but, unfortunately, he misinterprets these matters by imposing on Qumran the imprecise, if not incorrect, conception of 'covenantal nomism'.[37] There are several problems with this so-called 'new perspective' that need to be mentioned: 1) In the first place, the fact that Sanders section on 'The Dead Sea Scrolls' *follows* his discussion of the 'Tannaitic Literature', thus suggesting that this considerably later material pre-dates the Dead Sea Scrolls. This problematic portrayal of late second-century Judaism is concisely summarized by Joseph Fitzmyer: 'What a picture of first-century "Palestinian Judaism" emerges!'[38] 2) Sanders' 'covenantal nomism' paradigm allows him both to misread the apocalyptic background of the term 'righteousness' (צדקה/ צדק) and to make it virtually synonymous with 'mercy'[39] which is neither the case with the *yahad* or with Paul.[40] 3) The phrase 'works of the law' (ἔργα νόμου /מעשי חתורה) in both Paul and the scrolls is misunderstood both in terms of the thesis of 'covenantal nomism' and 'identity markers'. The citation of Dunn ("'Works of the law" refer not exclusively but particularly to those requirements which

---

[36] O'Callaghan, *Fides Christi*, p. 175.

[37] O'Callaghan, *Fides Christi*, pp. 176–7.

[38] Fitzmyer, 'Paul and the Dead Sea Scrolls', pp. 603–4, n. 7.

[39] Sanders, *Paul and Palestinian Judaism*, pp. 305–12.

[40] A similar criticism can be made of C. M. Pate, *The Reverse of the Curse* (WUNT 2/114; Tübingen: Mohr/Siebeck), p. 125, who seems more influenced by Sanders than by the text of 4QMMT! See also J. D. G. Dunn, '4QMMT and Galatians', *NTS* 43 (1997), pp. 147–53.

bring to sharp focus the distinctiveness of Israel's identity') is a misrepresentation of the situation, as a careful reading of 4Q MMT C32 reveals.[41] Here, as we have pointed out above, the text speaks of your following our 'works of the law' and then concludes, 'in your deed (בעשותך) you may be reckoned as righteous'. The great importance of this text is not only that it provides an exact parallel for the Pauline phrase but that it is used *exactly* in the same context as צדקה (righteousness/uprightness) and uses the identical words of Gen. 15.6 that Paul cites about Abraham in Rom. 4.3, viz. ἐλογίσθη αὐτῷ εἰς δικαιοσύνην ('it was reckoned to him as righteousness').

That O'Callaghan's interpretation of Paul is significantly shaped by the work of Dunn is again evident in this citation: 'Paul himself was protesting... not individual human effort, but the assumption that ethnic origin and identity is a factor in determining the grace of God and its expression.'[42] This is simply not how the *yahad* understood the matter nor apparently Paul. Because of this misunderstanding O'Callaghan, in the midst of some solid insights, has difficulty incorporating the themes of sanctification and obedience within the tension of Paul's theology. Where he and the so-called 'new perspective' of Sanders and Dunn are most vulnerable are precisely in their interpretation of the crucial phrase 'the righteousness of God' which is determinative of Paul's entire theology. If the apostle means by this phrase that God's righteousness/uprightness is manifested to all humanity through the death and resurrection of Jesus Christ and that this results in the vindication and acquittal of sinful persons, then one is dealing with a paradigm substantially different from one that emphasizes ethnic origins, boundaries and identity markers in the thought of Paul.

It is precisely because the Lutheran–Roman Catholic Joint Declaration on the Doctrine of Justification has understood the mind of Paul so well that it has the genuine potential of

---

[41] O'Callaghan, *Fides Christi*, p. 177. Originally, J. D. G. Dunn, 'Works of the Law and the Curse of the Law (Gal. 3.10–14)', in *Jesus, Paul and the Law*, p. 223.

[42] O'Callaghan, *Fides Christi*, p. 185.

transcending some of the one-sided emphases of the Reformation and post-Reformation period. Its final sentence challenges the entire Christian tradition: 'By grace alone, in faith in Christ's saving work and not because of any merit on our part, we are accepted by God and receive the Holy Spirit, who renews our hearts while equipping and calling us to good works.' Grace, as a result of the atoning death of Jesus Christ, must always be the starting point, yet that grace has an effective power to renew the hearts of believers as well as equipping and calling them to do good works. The first without the second tends toward antinomianism; the second without the first is the very legalism that Paul refuted.

15

Paul as Σκηυοποιός and the Use of the Codex in Early Christianity

Paul addresses his co-worker Timothy with these words according to 2 Tim. 4.13: 'When you come, bring the cloak that I left with Carpus at Troas, also the books [τὰ βιβλία] and above all the parchments [τὰς μεμβράνας].' 2 Timothy belongs, together with 1 Timothy and Titus, to a group which scholars refer to as the Pastoral Epistles; many interpreters suggest that we are dealing with pseudonymous literature.[1] Perhaps they were written by students, disciples or co-workers of Paul who wished to have 'Paul' speak to a new situation following his death. Although not from the hand of Paul in their present form, they may well contain genuine Pauline fragments. A leading advocate of the fragment hypothesis, P. N. Harrison, includes 2 Tim. 4.13 as part of a genuine Pauline fragment and we are inclined to agree.[2]

The meaning of τὰ βιβλία is clear: it is a roll, probably made of papyrus. As Finegan has shown, 'the Greek word βίβλινος is an adjective referring to something of βίβλος or βύβλος which is another name for papyrus, although in a few exceptional cases it can refer to books made of leather'.[3] To speak of a book at this

---

[1] For a comprehensive discussion see W. G. Kümmel, *Introduction to the New Testament* (Nashville: Abingdon, 1975), pp. 366–87.

[2] P. N. Harrison, *The Problem of the Pastoral Epistles* (London: Oxford University Press, 1921).

[3] J. Finegan, *Encountering New Testament Manuscripts. A Working Introduction to Textual Criticism* (Grand Rapids: Eerdmans, 1974), p. 19.

point in the Greco-Roman world is to speak of a roll. Undoubtedly the author of 2 Timothy is referring to rolls containing portions of the Old Testament. This is certainly the way the term is used in Luke 4.16–17: 'And he [Jesus] came to Nazareth, where he had been brought up; and he went to the synagogue, as his custom was, on sabbath day. And he stood up to read; and was given to him the book [τὸ βιβλίον] of the prophet Isaiah. He opened the book [τὸ βιβλίον] and found the place where it was written'. The reason Paul requests more than one book is that he wishes to have a significant portion of the Old Testament at his disposal. In view of the fact that Paul asks for several books, it is possible that the first part of this text from 2 Timothy should not be translated 'bring the cloak' (τὸν φαιλόνην), but 'bring the case, or cloth for wrapping'. The Greek word φαιλόνης, which the RSV translates as 'cloak', is a Latin loanword, *paenula*; in this context it might refer to a carrying case for the rolls.[4] If so, it would be a portable form of a book box (*capsa*) designed to hold several rolls.[5]

The major issue in 2 Tim. 4.13 is the meaning of the term 'parchments' (τὰς μεμβράνας). What exactly is it that Paul wishes Timothy to bring him? Before we can answer this question we need to review some matters of technical detail, viz. the difference between papyrus, parchment and related materials, and the relationship between the roll and the codex book.

Let us begin with papyrus. The question posed in Job 8.11, 'Can papyrus grow when there is no marsh?' alerts us to the watery environment of the papyrus plant. The most detailed description of how writing material (*charta*) was made from the papyrus plant is given by Pliny in his *Natural History*.[6] The papyrus is split 'with a needle into very thin strips made as broad as possible, the best quality being in the center of the plant,

    [4] C. K. Barrett, *The Pastoral Epistles* (The New Clarendon Bible; Oxford: Clarendon, 1963), p. 121.
    [5] W. Lock, *The Pastoral Epistles* (ICC; Edinburgh: T&T Clark, 1924), p. 118; against this view see M. Dibelius and H. Conzelmann, *The Pastoral Epistles* (Hermeneia; Philadelphia: Fortress Press, 1972), p. 123.
    [6] 13.21–27. See also the discussion in Finegan, *Encountering New Testament Manuscripts*, pp. 21–7.

and so on in the order of its splitting up'.[7] Next, after having been dipped into muddy Nile water, the fibers were woven on a board, first an upright layer of fiber, then a layer of cross-strips, and then the layers were hammered and pressed together and dried. The new sheet was then trimmed and smoothed with pumice and burnished with rounded polishers made of ivory or shell. The papyrus sheets were then pasted together to make a roll, with never more than twenty sheets to a roll. T. C. Skeat, the Keeper of Manuscripts at the British Museum, has attempted to refute two popular misconceptions concerning papyrus: first, that it was expensive and second, that it was fragile. Not only is the evidence lacking for the first assertion, but the 'lavish manner in which papyrus was often used, with wide margins and large unwritten areas, shows that the cost of the material was never a limiting factor'.[8]

A second group of writing materials in antiquity were composed of leather, parchment or vellum, with parchment being the most popular. All are made from animal skins, mainly such quadrupeds as sheep, goats or calves. Vellum and parchment are virtually indistinguishable terms, since vellum, originally designating a preparation from the skin of calves, is today used as a generic term. The term parchment, from the Latin *pergamena*, was not originally linked with any animal and therefore a convenient general term. According to Pliny,[9] who himself is dependent on the Roman Marcus Varro (c. 116–27 BCE), the invention of parchment took place at Pergamum due to a shortage of papyrus.

The normal Greek term for leather prepared for writing is διφθέρα. The difference between leather and the superior writing form of parchment lies in the manufacturing process. 'After flaying,' writes Skeat, 'the epidermis, with the hair or wool, is removed from the outer side of the pelt, and the flesh from the

---

[7] Pliny, *Nat.*, 13.23.77.

[8] T. C. Skeat, 'Early Christian Book Production: Papyri and Manuscripts', in *The Cambridge History of the Bible*, 3 vol., ed. G. W. H. Lampe (Cambridge: University Press, 1963–70), 2.59.

[9] *Nat.*, 13.21.70.

inner, after soaking in a bath of lime. This is followed, in the case of leather, by tanning; but for parchment the skin, after liming, is washed, placed in a stretching frame, and allowed to dry. It is then shaved on both sides with a heavy iron knife to the required thickness, smoothed and whitened with pumice and chalk, and finally trimmed. The fineness of the resulting product depends upon the extent to which the reduction by shaving is pursued.'[10]

Despite the predominance of papyrus rolls, leather and parchment rolls did exist. While some of the Dead Sea Scrolls were written on papyrus, most were written on leather or parchment. In Persia, for example, we have clear evidence of a marked preference for parchment. This phenomenon has been substantiated by the discovery of a leather bag containing some twenty letters in Egypt in the early 1930s; all were written on parchment.[11]

We noted previously that the Greek term for tanned leather is διφθέρα; however, the term was also used as a reference to parchment. Additionally, the Greek language used the term περγαμηνά for parchment, an obvious reference to Pergamum. In Latin, the term *membrana* became the term for parchment and is taken over into the Greek as μεμβράνα. But its usage in Greek seems clearly connected with the codex, the technical term for a leaf book.[12]

Before returning to our central question with regard to the text in 2 Timothy, let us spend a few moments in discussion of the codex. Important to remember before we proceed is that the dominant form of the book in the first century CE is that of the roll, whether of papyrus or of parchment. What factors, we must ask, lead to the eventual dominance of the codex as the standard form of the book?

The Latin term *caudex* (or *codex*) refers, in the first instance, to the trunk of a tree, and, then, to a chunk of wood split up into tablets.[13] These wooden tablets were probably coated with wax

---

[10] Skeat, 'Early Christian Book Production', p. 62.
[11] Skeat, 'Early Christian Book Production', p. 62.
[12] Finegan, *Encountering New Testament Manuscripts*, pp. 25–6.
[13] See the discussion in Finegan, *Encountering New Testament Manuscripts*, p. 29.

for writing purposes and were then strung together to make a book; a similar procedure of binding together sheets of papyrus or parchment was followed. A codex, then, is a leaf book and in this period the material would consist of wood, parchment or papyrus. Parchment had the particular advantage of not only being substantially thinner than wood and thus allowing for many more leaves, but it also had the advantage over the other two that ink could be erased from parchment and would thus be ideal for first drafts.

Now as we investigate the use of the codex we find that in the pre-Christian period it is virtually nonexistent and yet in the post-Constantinean period it is *the dominant* form of the book. The research of C. H. Roberts has substantiated this dramatic fact. He considered all the non-Christian literature in Egypt and reached these statistical conclusions:

> From the second century we know of 465 rolls and 11 codices; of texts placed on the borderline between the second and third centuries we have 208 rolls and 6 codices; in the third century we find 297 rolls and 60 codices; among texts doubtfully ascribed to third and fourth century 28 rolls and 26 codices; in the fourth century 25 rolls and 71 codices. If we translate these figures into percentages of codices to rolls we get the following results:

Second century	2.31 percent
Second/third century	2.09 percent
Third century	16.08 percent
Third/fourth century	48.14 percent
Fourth century	73.95 percent[14]

Roberts concludes from these figures that 'it is clear that the codex scarcely counted for Greek literature in the second century ... In the pagan world of the second century the codex has barely a foothold.'[15]

When our attention turns to the early Christian literature in Egypt we note some startling differences. Roberts counts 111 biblical manuscripts or fragments of manuscripts in which 62 are

---

[14] C. H. Roberts, 'The Codex', *PBA* 40 (1954), pp. 184–5.
[15] Roberts, 'The Codex', p. 185.

from the Old Testament and 49 from the New. Roberts observes that of

> these 111 texts 99 are written on codices, 12 only on rolls. A closer examin-
> ation makes the contrast even sharper. For of the 12 rolls 5 are
> opisthograph, i. e., the biblical text is written on the back of a roll already
> used for some other purpose; consequently these written private copies or
> school texts are not evidence of a preference for the roll over the codex since
> the scribe had no choice before him. This reduces the number of genuine
> rolls to 7; of these 3 are probably Jewish, 3 more possibly so; the only one
> that is certainly Christian is a roll of the Psalms. No early text of the New
> Testament known to us was written on the recto (i.e. front side) of a roll.[16]

Roberts concludes his detailed evaluation of these texts with the statement that there 'could not be a greater contrast with the pagan book of the second century, and this contrast is the more remarkable when we recall that the country where these early texts were found was where the roll originated, and in which parchment (with which the codex began) was scarce'.[17] It is the Christian movement which elevates the codex to the status of the book. That this major innovation makes a radical break with custom is evident in Augustine's apology for writing a letter in codex form, even though the codex was commonly used for books in his day, and by the comment of Jerome who remarks that as a gentleman and scholar he will write his letters correctly on rolls, even though he writes his books in codices.[18]

We need to refer to one further matter before taking leave of Roberts' research. In a thorough manner he analyzes the use of the term *membrana* in general, and also what Paul meant when he used it in the text in 2 Tim. 4.13. It is concluded that Paul was specifically referring to 'parchment notebooks'. Paul uses the Latin word *membrana* 'because he is referring to a Latin object for which there was no simple equivalent in Greek'.[19]

It is assumed by scholars that parchment notebooks had been used for rough work and note-taking. Quintilian (c. 30–90 CE)[20]

---

[16] Roberts, 'The Codex', pp. 184–5.
[17] Roberts, 'The Codex', p. 186.
[18] Roberts, 'The Codex', p. 176.
[19] Roberts, 'The Codex', p. 174.
[20] *Inst.* 5.3.31.

tells us they were in use in the law courts of his time. These parchment notebooks are, then, the precursors of the codex proper. The earliest evidence concerning the codex per se is from Martial (c. 40–104 CE). In one of his poems he tells that a pocket anthology of his poems is on sale and in view of the fact that he gives the address of the publisher we can reasonably deduct that such an anthology, obviously intended for the convenience of the traveller, was a novelty. Roberts is certain that Martial can only be describing a parchment codex.[21] In addition, Martial composes some poems to accompany a pocket edition of certain standard authors and here again we find that these editions are written on parchment (Latin: *membrana*) pocket editions in codex form of Virgil (*Vergilius in membranis*), Homer, Cicero and Livy and remarks how much such a volume contains. Noteworthy is his recommendation that a small parchment codex of Cicero (*Cicero in membranis*) is a useful traveling companion.

Roberts suggests that these parchment codices were intended for Martial's less wealthy friends and it does appear, indeed, that a parchment codex was a less expensive gift than a papyrus roll.[22] The German scholar T. Birt, in his classic *Das antike Buchwesen*,[23] also suggests that the parchment codex was 'das Buch der ärmeren Klassen'[24] and that it was initially employed for works of literature used in the schoolroom. But despite its apparent low cost and other advantages the parchment codex does not 'catch-on'. The Greco-Roman world was simply not interested in this new form. But Christians obviously were. Why? – and who gave this impulse so that within the next hundred years the codex was on its way toward being the only possible format for the Christian scriptures and eventually the dominant literary form worldwide? T. C. Skeat writes that such

> radical innovations are usually the work of individuals rather than committees – or churches – and we may perhaps imagine the invention as originating with some leading figure in the early Church, who, whatever

---

[21] C. H. Roberts, 'The Ancient Books and the Ending of St Mark', *JTS* 11 (1939), p. 255.
[22] Roberts, 'The Ancient Books', p. 255.
[23] T. Birt, *Das antike Buchwesen in seinem Verhältnis zur Literatur, mit Beiträgen zur Textgeschichte des Theokrit, Catull, Properz, und anderer Autoren* (Berlin: W. Hertz, 1882). [ET: 'the book of the poorer classes.']
[24] Birt, *Das antike Buchwesen*, p. 354.

the ultimate source of his inspiration, succeeded both in devising a distinctive format for Christian manuscripts of the Scriptures, differentiated equally from the parchment roll of Judaism and the papyrus roll of the pagan world, and in imposing its use throughout the Church. Here the reader may reasonably ask whether there is any other evidence pointing to the existence of such a dominating genius at work in the field of earliest Christian literature. The answer is, surprisingly, yes.[25]

However, nowhere in Skeat's essay do we find a clue as to who this mystery person might be.

That the specific impulse of an influential person stood behind this movement toward the use of the codex in primitive Christianity is also argued by C. H. Roberts. He restates his position that the 'codex must have been an imitation of the parchment notebook and this, as we have seen, was of Roman origin and was used in Italy at a time when it was unknown in Egypt and (as far as we know) elsewhere in the East. The first two generations of Christians may be described in general as literate but not literary, and the form in which their writings circulated would have been quite uninfluenced by the practice of the Greco-Roman book trade.'[26] This gap is bridged, suggests Roberts, by the author of the Gospel of Mark who is writing in Rome. He continues: 'The circle in which he moved in Rome – Jewish and gentile traders, small business men, freedmen or slaves – would use waxed tablets or parchment notebooks for their accounts, their correspondence, their legal and official business, and it would be natural that St Mark should use the same format for a work intended to be copied but not to be published as the ancient world understood publication.'[27]

We have two concerns with Roberts' suggestions. First, is it likely that the use of these parchment notebooks or proto-codices is really limited to use in Rome? Is there not enough of a Roman 'diaspora' to account for this practice elsewhere in the Greco-Roman world? Second, and of much greater concern, is the suggestion that the creative mind of Mark lies behind the codex

[25] Skeat, 'Book Production', p. 72.
[26] Roberts, 'Codex', p. 187.
[27] Roberts, 'Codex', pp. 187–8.

development. There are few biblical scholars indeed who would today posit Rome as the location where the Gospel of Mark was written.[28]

Is not the apostle Paul a much more likely candidate? We shall attempt to argue this for a number of reasons, not least of which the information derived from 2 Tim. 4.13 which suggests with reasonable probability that Paul and those around him made use of *membranae*. However, before we proceed to develop this suggestion, we need to ask how Paul was introduced to this usage of the parchment notebook, should Roberts be correct in limiting its initial use to Italy. There are a number of possible ways by which Paul the Roman citizen might have been put in touch with this development. To cite one example: in Acts 18.1–3 we read that after Paul left Athens he went to Corinth and there 'he found a Jew named Aquila, a native of Pontus, lately come from Italy with his wife Priscilla, because Claudius had commanded all the Jews to leave Rome. And he went to see them; and because he was of the same trade he stayed with them, and they worked, for by trade they were tentmakers.' The Greek term here translated 'tentmakers' is σκηνοποιοί. However, 'tentmaker' is not the only possible translation for σκηνοποιός. H. A. W. Meyer,[29] J. Jeremias,[30] Foakes Jackson and Lake[31] and others[32] suggest that the correct translation should be that of 'leatherworker'. In the exegetical tradition of early Christianity such a translation is supported, for example, by Chrysostom and Origen.[33] This text from Acts would show us not only how this proto-codex form could have been introduced to Paul, viz. by Aquila and Priscilla who had just come from Rome, but also how Paul the leather-worker could have quickly learned

---

[28] See the discussion in W. G. Kümmel, *Introduction*, pp. 97–98.

[29] H. A. W. Meyer, *Critical and Exegetical Handbook to the Acts of the Apostles*, 2 vols (Edinburgh: T&T Clark, 1877), 2.131.

[30] J. Jeremias, 'Zöllner und Sünder', *ZNW* 30 (1931), p. 299.

[31] *The Beginnings of Christianity: Part I: the Acts of the Apostles*, 5 vols, ed. F. J. Foakes Jackson and K. Lake (London: Macmillan, 1920–33), 4.223.

[32] For example, W. Michaelis, σκηνοποιός, in *TDNT* 7.393–94; E. Haenchen, *The Acts of the Apostles* (Philadelphia: Fortress Press, 1971), p. 543, n. 3.

[33] T. Zahn, *Die Apostelgeschichte des Lukas* (KNT 5; Leipzig: Deichert, 1921), p. 634. See also the discussion in F. Hock, *The Social Context of Paul's Ministry* (Philadelphia: Fortress Press, 1980), pp. 20–1.

the process of making parchment sheets. Since, as Roberts has indicated, parchment is a 'home-produced ware'[34] it is intriguing to think that Paul might have earned his income in the various cities in which he stayed by leather-working in general and in parchment codex production specifically.[35]

Why would Paul have found these '*membranae*' so useful? In Acts 17.1-3, for example, it is stated that Paul, upon arriving in Thessalonica, found a synagogue of the Jews and 'Paul went in, as was his custom, and for three weeks he argued with them from the scriptures, explaining and proving that it was necessary for the Christ to suffer and to rise from the dead, and saying, "This Jesus whom I proclaim to you, is the Christ."' As is well-known, primitive Christianity was marked by an intense use of the Old Testament scriptures for proving and explaining their conviction that Jesus of Nazareth was the Messiah. To do so one needs an arsenal of Old Testament texts and it is hardly likely that as Paul argues in the synagogue he would roll and unroll many feet of papyrus scrolls to find the relevant texts. The *membrana* is precisely that vehicle which would allow Paul to collect the necessary reference texts which he would require for these discussions. These parchments codices would in essence be testimony books with easy to find proof texts in addition to providing inexpensive and convenient compactness for the travelling missionary since both sides of the page could be written on.

At several points Paul cites traditional formulations, sometimes even using the Jewish formula 'I delivered to you ... what I also received'. This is the case in 1 Cor. 11.23 where he cites the earliest extant words of Jesus concerning the institution of the Lord's Supper, or in 1 Cor. 15.3 when he cites a confession of faith. These kinds of pre-Pauline tradition, together with other

---

[34] Roberts, 'Codex', p. 179.

[35] Hock, *Social Context*, p. 21 states: 'Leatherworking, then, was Paul's trade; the specialized title "tentmaker" reflects a widespread tendency among artisans to use specialized titles, even though they made more products than their titles would suggest.' We would agree with Hock's suggestion about specialization in general but would differ from him in the description of that specialization.

pre-Pauline hymns and confessions (for example, Phil. 2.5–11) might well have been recorded in his *membranae*.

Paul, his co-workers and his secretary (-ies), would have found these parchment notebooks useful for the first-draft writing of his letters, since parchment could be easily erased and revised. Many scholars[36] have noted that the chapter on love in 1 Cor. 13, to cite another example, was very carefully prepared in advance and then inserted at this point in the structure of the letter. Paul would have prepared this in his notebook and then at a later point made use of it in his letter to the Corinthians.

Finally, we would suggest that Paul used the (proto)-codex as a vehicle for his own correspondence. In the first place, for reasons we have already given, it was convenient. Further, rolls at this time were used for literature and it is highly unlikely that Paul thought that his ad hoc letters were literature; rather, they were practical letters dealing with pressing problems. Paul's use of the codex for his correspondence would also explain the ease by which his followers could take several smaller letters and portions thereof and rearrange them into a single, larger one as is the case with what is referred to as 2 Corinthians. Many scholars hold that this letter, as it now stands in the canon, was composed from several Pauline letters.[37] Further, when the Pauline letters were collected by the end of the first century they circulated as one handy codex volume rather than as two cumbersome and inconvenient rolls.[38] This Pauline model, which, on the one hand, meets the needs of the church by easy access to the apostle's writings, and, on the other hand, provides an alternative option to the dominant Jewish roll, a factor hardly to be underestimated in the tension between church and synagogue at the turn of the century,[39] influences and shapes the development of Christian

---

[36] For example, H. Conzelmann, *1 Corinthians: A Commentary on the First Epistle to the Corinthians* (Hermeneia; Philadelphia: Fortress Press, 1975), pp. 219–20.

[37] See the important contribution by G. Bornkamm, 'The History of the Origin of the So-called Second Letter to the Corinthians', *NTS* 8 (1961–2), pp. 258–64.

[38] On this point see C. C. McGown, 'The Earliest Christian Books', *BA* 6 (1943), pp. 21–31.

[39] On this point see P. Katz, 'The Early Christians Use of Codices Instead of Rolls', *JTS* 44 (1945), pp. 63–5.

literature in the succeeding centuries, and, world literature by the fourth century. It is thus quite appropriate to speak of the apostle Paul as the most instrumental factor in the shaping of the book as we know it today, that is, in the form of a codex rather than a roll.

Bibliography

Adinolfi, M., *La prima lettera ai Tessalonicesi nel mondo greco-romano* (BPAA 31, Roma: Editrice 'Antonianum', 1990)

Athanassakis, Apostolos N., *The Homeric Hymns* (Baltimore: The Johns Hopkins University Press, 1976)

Aune, David E., *The New Testament in Its Literary Environment* (LEC 8; Philadelphia: Westminster Press, 1987)

Bailey, John, 'Who Wrote II Thessalonians?' *NTS* 25 (1979), pp. 131–45

Bammel, Ernst, 'Judenverfolgung und Naherwartung. Zur Eschatologie des Ersten Thessalonicherbriefs', *ZTK* 56 (1959), pp. 294–315

Barclay, John M. G., 'Conflict in Thessalonica', *CBQ* 55 (1993), pp. 512–30

Barrett, C. K., 'Acts and Christian Consensus', in *Context* (Festschrift P. Borgen; ed. P. W. Bockman and R. E. Kristiansen; Trondheim: Tapir, 1987), pp. 19–33

—— *The Acts of the Apostles* (ICC; 2 vols; Edinburgh: T&T Clark, 1994)

—— *A Commentary on the First Epistle to the Corinthians* (HNTC; New York: Harper and Row, 1968)

—— *A Commentary on the Second Epistle to the Corinthians* (HNTC; New York: Harper and Row, 1973)

—— *The Pastoral Epistles* (New Clarendon Bible; Oxford: Clarendon Press, 1963)

Barth, Markus, 'Der gute Jude Paulus', in *Richte unsere Füße auf den Weg des Friedens* (Festschrift H. Gollwitzer; ed. Andreas Baudis; *et al.* München: Chr. Kaiser, 1979), pp. 107–37

—— *Justification* (Grand Rapids: Eerdmans, 1971)

Baumert, N., 'ὁμείρομαι in 1 Thess 2,8', *Bib* 68 (1987), pp. 552–63

Baumgarten, J. M., *Studies in Qumran Law* (Leiden: Brill, 1977)

Baur, Ferdinand Christian, *Paul, the Apostle of Jesus Christ; His Life and Work, His Epistles and His Doctrine: A Contribution to a Critical History of Primitive Christianity* (2 vols; London/Edinburgh: Williams and Norgate, 1876)

Becker, Jürgen, 'Die Erwählung der Völker durch das Evangelium', in *Studien zum Text und zur Ethik des Neuen Testaments* (Festschrift H. Greeven; ed. Wolfgang Schrage; Berlin: de Gruyter, 1986), pp. 82–101

Beker, J. Christian, *Paul the Apostle: The Triumph of God in Life and Thought* (Philadelphia: Fortress Press, 1980)

Berger, Klaus, 'Hellenistische Gattungen im Neuen Testament', *ANRW* II.25.2, pp. 1031–432.

Best, Ernest, *A Commentary on the First and Second Epistles to the Thessalonians* (BNTC; London: A and C Black, 1972)

—— 'Paul's Apostolic Authority', *JSNT* 27 (1986), pp. 3–25

Betz, Hans Dieter, *Galatians* (Hermeneia; Philadelphia: Fortress Press, 1979)

Bickmann, Jutta, *Kommunikation gegen den Tod. Studien zur paulinischen Briefpragmatik am Beispiel des Ersten Thessalonicherbriefes* (FB 86; Würzburg: Echter, 1998)

Birt, Theodor, *Das antike Buchwesen in seinem Verhältnis zur Literatur, mit Beiträgen zur Textgeschichte des Theokrit, Catull, Properz, und anderer Autoren* (Berlin: W. Hertz, 1882)

Boers, Hendrikus, 'The Form Critical Study of Paul's Letters. 1 Thessalonians as a Case Study', *NTS* 22 (1975/76), pp. 140–58

Bornkamm, Günther, 'The History of the Origin of the So-called Second Letter to the Corinthians', *NTS* 8 (1961–2), pp. 258–64

—— 'The Letter to the Romans as Paul's Last Will and Testament', in *The Romans Debate: Revised and Expanded Edition*, ed. Karl P. Donfried (Peabody, MA: Hendrickson, 2001), pp. 16–28

—— 'Der Lohngedanke im Neuen Testament', in *Studien zu Antike und Urchristentum* (BEvT; München: Chr. Kaiser Verlag, 1959)

Braun, Herbert, *Gerichtsgedanke und Rechtfertigungslehre bei Paulus* (UNT 19: Leipzig: J. C. Hinrichs'sche Buchhandlung, 1930)

Brocke, Christoph vom, *Thessaloniki – Stadt des Kassander und Gemeinde des Paulus* (WUNT 125; Tübingen: Mohr-Siebeck, 2001)

Brown, Raymond E., *An Introduction to the New Testament* (ABRL; New York: Doubleday, 1997)

—— *The Gospel According to John (I–XII)* (AB 29; Garden City: Doubleday, 1966)

—— Donfried, Karl P. and Reumann, John, *Peter in the New Testament* (Minneapolis: Augsburg, 1973)

Bruce, F. F., *The Acts of the Apostles* (Grand Rapids: Eerdmans, 1951)

—— *1 and 2 Thessalonians* (WBC 45; Waco, TX: Word Books, 1982)

Buber, Martin, 'Imitatio Dei', in *Israel and the World: Essays in a Time of Crisis* (New York: Schocken, 1963), pp. 66–77

Bultmann, Rudolph, 'ΔΙΚΑΙΟΣΥΝΗ ΘΕΟΥ', *JBL 83* (1964), pp. 12–16

—— *Theology of the New Testament* (2 vols; New York: Scribner's, 1951/55)

—— 'Zur Geschichte der Paulus-Forschung', *ThR* 1 (1929), pp. 26–59

Bussmann, Claus, *Themen der paulinischen Missionspredigt auf dem Hintergrund der spätjüdisch-hellenistischen Missionsliteratur* (Europaische Hochschulschriften. Reihe XXIII, Theologie; Bd. 3; Bern: Herbert Lang, 1971), pp. 39–56

Campbell, J. Y., 'The Origin and Meaning of the Christian Use of the Word ΕΚΚΛΗΣΙΑ', *JTS* 49 (1948), pp. 130–42

Campenhausen, H. von, *Ecclesiastical Authority and Spiritual Power* (Stanford: University Press, 1960)

Cerfaux, L., *Christ in the Theology of St Paul* (New York: Herder, 1959)

—— *The Church in the Theology of St Paul* (New York: Herder, 1959)

Chadwick, Henry, '1 Thess. 3.3, σαίνεσθαι', *JTS* 1 (1950), pp. 156–8

Chapa, Juan, 'Is First Thessalonians a Letter of Consolation?' *NTS* 40 (1994), pp. 150–60

Charles, R. H., *The Greek Versions of the Testaments of the Twelve Patriarchs* (Oxford: Clarendon Press, 1908)

—— *The Testaments of the Twelve Patriarchs* (London: Adam and Charles Black, 1908)

Collins, John J., *Apocalypticism in the Dead Sea Scrolls* (London: Routledge, 1997)

Collins, Raymond F., *The Birth of the New Testament: The Origin and Development of the First Christian Generation* (New York: Crossroad, 1993)

—— *Studies on the First Letter to the Thessalonians* (BETL, 66; Leuven, University Press–Peeters, 1984)

—— ed., *The Thessalonian Correspondence* (BETL 87; Leuven: University Press–Peeters, 1990)

Conzelmann, Hans, *Der erste Brief an die Korinther* (Göttingen: Vandenhoeck and Ruprecht, 1969). [ET: *A Commentary on the First Epistle to the Corinthians* (Hermeneia; Philadelphia: Fortress Press, 1975)]

—— *An Outline of the Theology of the New Testament* (New York: Harper, 1969), pp. 155–61

—— 'Paulus und die Weisheit', *NTS* 12 (1965–6), pp. 231–34

—— 'Die Rechtfertigungslehre des Paulus: Theologie oder Anthropologie?' *EvTh 28* (1968), pp. 389–404

Coppens, Josef, ed., *La Notion biblique de Dieu* (BETL 41; Gembloux: J. Duculot, 1976)

—— 'Une diatribe antijuive dans I Thess. II, 13–16', *ETL* 51 (1975), pp. 90–5

Cranfield, C. E. B., *A Critical and Exegetical Commentary on the Epistle to the Romans* (ICC; 2 vols; Edinburgh: T&T Clark, 1975)

—— 'A Study of 1 Thessalonians 2', *IBS* I (1979), pp. 215–26

Crossan, John Dominic, *The Historical Jesus* (San Francisco: Harper, 1991)

Dalbert, P., *Die Theologie der hellenistisch-jüdischen Missionsliteratur unter Ausschluß von Philo und Josephus* (ThF, 4; Hamburg, 1954)

Danker, Frederick W. *Jesus and the New Age* (St Louis: Clayton, 1972)

Davies, W. D., *Jewish and Pauline Studies* (Philadelphia: Fortress Press, 1984)

—— 'Paul and the People of Israel', in *Jewish and Pauline Studies* (Philadelphia: Fortress Press, 1984), pp. 123–52.

—— *Paul and Rabbinic Judaism: Some Rabbinic Elements in Pauline Theology* (Philadelphia: Fortress Press, 1980)

Degenhardt, J. J., ed., *Die Freude an Gott – unsere Kraft* (Festschrift Otto Knoch; Stuttgart: Katholisches Bibelwerk, 1991)

Deissmann, Adolf, *Licht von Osten* (Tübingen: Mohr, 1923). [ET: *Light from the Ancient East* (Grand Rapids: Baker, 1978)]

—— *Die neutestamentliche Formel 'in Christo Jesu'* (Marburg: N. G. Elwert, 1892)

Denis, A. M., 'L'Apôtre Paul, prophète "messianique" des Gentils. Etude thématique de 1 Thes., II, 1–6', *ETL* 33 (1957), pp. 245–318

Devor, Richard C., *The Concept of Judgment in the Epistles of Paul* (PhD diss., Drew University, 1959)

Dibelius, Martin, *Die Briefe des Apostels Paulus. II. Die Neun Kleinen Briefe* (HNT; Tübingen: Mohr, 1913)

—— *An die Thessalonicher I II, An die Philipper* (HNT 11; third ed.; Tübingen: Mohr, 1937)

—— and Hans Conzelmann, *The Pastoral Epistles* (Hermeneia; Philadelphia: Fortress Press, 1972)

Didier, Georges, *Désinteressement du Chrétien. La rétribution dans la morale de Saint Paul* (Théologie 32; Paris: Aubier, 1955)

Dobschütz, E. von, *Die Thessalonicher-Briefe* (KEK X; Göttingen: Vandenhoeck and Ruprecht, [1909] repr. 1974)

Dodd, C. H., *Historical Tradition in the Fourth Gospel* (Cambridge: University Press, 1963)

Donfried, Karl P., 'The Assembly of the Thessalonians. Reflections on the Ecclesiology of the Earliest Christian

Letter', in *Ekklesiologie des Neuen Testaments* (Festschrift Karl Kertelge; ed. R. Kampling and T. Söding; Freiburg, Basel, Wien: Herder, 1996), pp. 390–408

—— 'Augsburg, 1999: By Grace Alone – Some Reflections By A Participant', *Pro Eccl* IX (2000), pp. 5–7

—— 'Chronology, New Testament,' *ABD* 1:1011–22

—— 'The Cults of Thessalonica and the Thessalonian Correspondence', *NTS* 31 (1985), pp. 336–56

—— *The Dynamic Word: New Testament Insights for Contemporary Christians* (San Francisco: Harper and Row, 1981)

—— 'The Epistolary and Rhetorical Context of 1 Thess. 2.1–12', in *The Thessalonian Correspondence: Methodological Discord or Methodological Synthesis?* (ed. Karl P. Donfried and Johannes Beutler; Grand Rapids: Eerdmans, 2000), pp. 31–60

—— 'False Presuppositions in the Study of Romans', in *The Romans Debate* (ed. K. P. Donfried; rev. ed.; Minneapolis: Augsburg, 1991)

—— 'Justification and Last Judgment in Paul', in *La Notion biblique de Dieu*, (ed. J. Coppens; BETL 41; Gembloux: J. Duculot, 1976), pp. 293–313

—— 'The Kingdom of God in Paul', in *The Kingdom of God in 20th. Century Interpretation* (ed. Wendell Willis; Peabody, MA: Hendrickson, 1987)

—— 'Paul and Judaism: 1 Thess. 2.13–16 as a Test Case', *Int* 38 (1984), pp. 242–53

—— 'Paul and Qumran: The Possible Influence of סרך on 1 Thessalonians', in *The Dead Sea Scrolls Fifty Years After Their Discovery* (Jersusalem: The Magnes Press, 2000), pp. 148–56

—— 'Paul as Σκηνοποιός and the Use of the Codex in Early Christianity', in *Christus Bezeugen* (Festschrift für Wolfgang Trilling; ed. Karl Kertelge, Traugott Holtz and Claus-Peter März; Leipzig: St. Benno Verlag, 1990), pp. 249–56

—— *The Romans Debate: Revised and Expanded Edition* (Peabody, MA: Hendrickson, 2001)

—— *The Setting of Second Clement in Early Christianity* (Leiden: E. J. Brill, 1974)

—— 'The Theology of 1 Thessalonians', in *The Theology of the Shorter Pauline Letters* (ed. K. P. Donfried and I. H. Marshall; New Testament Theology; Cambridge: Cambridge University Press, 1993)

—— 'The Theology of 1 Thessalonians as a Reflection of Its Purpose', in *To Touch the Text* (Biblical and Related Studies in Honor of Joseph A. Fitzmyer, S J; ed. Maurya P. Horgan and Paul J. Kobelski; New York: Crossroad, 1989), pp. 243–60

—— '1 Thessalonians, Acts and Early Paul', in *The Thessalonian Correspondence* (ed. R. F. Collins, BETL 87; Leuven: University Press–Peeters, 1990), pp. 3–26

—— '2 Thessalonians and the Church of Thessalonica', in *Origins and Method: Towards a New Understanding of Judaism and Christianity. Essays in Honour of John C. Hurd* (ed. Bradley H. McLean; Sheffield: Sheffield Academic Press, 1993), pp. 128–44

—— 'War Timotheus in Athen? Exegetische Überlegungen zu 1 Thess. 3,1–3', in *Die Freude an Gott – unsere Kraft* (Festschrift für Otto Bernhard Knoch zum 65. Geburtstag; ed. J. J. Degenhardt; Stuttgart: Katholisches Bibelwerk, 1991), pp. 189–96

—— and Beutler, Johannes, *The Thessalonians Debate: Methodological Discord or Methodological Synthesis?* (Grand Rapids: Eerdmans, 2000)

—— and Marshall, I. Howard, *The Theology of the Shorter Pauline Letters* (New Testament Theology; Cambridge: Cambridge University Press, 1993)

Dunn, James D. G., *Jesus, Paul and the Law: studies in Mark and Galatians* (London: SPCK, 1990)

—— 'Prophetic "I" Sayings and the Jesus Tradition: the Importance of Testing Prophetic Utterances within Early Christianity', *NTS* 24 (1977–8), pp. 175–98

—— '4QMMT and Galatians', *NTS* 43 (1997), pp. 147–53

—— *Romans 1–8* (Dallas: Word, 1988)

—— *Romans 9–16* (WBC 38B; Dallas: Word, 1988)

—— 'Works of the Law and the Curse of the Law (Gal. 3.10–14)', in *Jesus, Paul and the Law: Studies in Mark and Galatians* (ed. James D. G. Dunn; London: SPCK, 1990), pp. 215–41.

Eadie, John, *Commentary on the Greek Text of the Epistles of Paul to the Thessalonians* (New York: Macmillan, 1877)

Edson, Charles, 'Cults of Thessalonica', *HTR* 41 (1948), pp. 153–204

Ellingworth, P. and Nida, E. A., *A Translator's Handbook on Paul's Letters to the Thessalonians* (London: United Bible Societies, 1976)

Ellis, E. Earle, *Prophecy and Hermeneutic* (Tübingen: Mohr, 1978)

—— 'The Role of the Christian Prophet in Acts', in *Apostolic History and the Gospel* (ed. W. W. Gasque and R. P. Martin; Exeter: Paternoster Press, 1970), pp. 55–67

Fee, Gordon D., *The First Epistle to the Corinthians* (NICNT; Grand Rapids: Eerdmans, 1987)

Filson, Floyd V., *St Paul's Conception of Recompense* (UNT 21; Leipzig: J. C. Hinrichs'sche Buchhandlung, 1931)

Finegan, Jack, *The Archeology of the New Testament* (Boulder: Westview, 1981)

—— *Encountering New Testament Manuscripts. A Working Introduction to Textual Criticism* (Grand Rapids: Eerdmans, 1974)

—— *Handbook of Biblical Chronology; Principles of Time Reckoning in the Ancient World and Problems of Chronology in the Bible* (rev. ed.; Peabody, MA: Hendrickson Publishers, 1998)

Fitzmyer, Joseph A., *According to Paul: Studies in the Theology of the Apostle* (New York: Paulist Press, 1993)

—— *The Acts of the Apostles: A New Translation with Introduction and Commentary* (AB 31; New York: Doubleday, 1998)

—— *The Dead Sea Scrolls and Christian Origins* (Grand Rapids: Eerdmans, 2000), pp. 249–60

—— *Essays on the Semitic Background of the New Testament* (Missoula, Mont. : Scholars' Press, 1974)

—— *The Gospel According to Luke I–IX* (AB 28; Garden City: Doubleday, 1982).

—— 'Paul and the Dead Sea Scrolls', in *The Dead Sea Scrolls After Fifty Years* (vol. 2; ed. Peter W. Flint and James C. Vanderkam; Leiden: Brill, 1999), pp. 599–621

—— *Paul and His Theology: A Brief Sketch* (Englewood Cliffs, NJ: Prentice Hall, 1989)

—— 'Paul's Jewish Background and the Deeds of the Law', in *According to Paul: Studies in the Theology of the Apostle* (New York: Paulist Press, 1993), pp. 18–35

—— *Romans: A New Translation with Introduction and Commentary* (AB 33; New York: Doubleday, 1993)

Flusser, David, *Jesus* (Jerusalem: Magnes, 1997)

—— *Judaism and the Origins of Christianity* (Jerusalem: Magnes, 1988)

Foakes Jackson, F. J., and Lake, K., ed., *The Beginnings of Christianity* (5 vols; Grand Rapids: Baker, 1966)

Frame, James E., *Epistles of St Paul to the Thessalonians* (ICC; Edinburgh: T&T Clark, 1912)

Fraser, P. M., *Samothrace: The Inscriptions on Stone* (Bollingen Series 60.2.1; New York: Pantheon, 1960)

Fredriksen, Paula, *Jesus of Nazareth, King of the Jews* (New York: Vintage, 2000)

Frend, W. H. C., *Martyrdom and Persecution in the Early Church* (Oxford: Blackwell, 1965)

Fridrichsen, Anton, *The Apostle and His Message* (Uppsala: Almqvist-Wiksells, 1947)

—— 'κῆρυξ', *TDNT* 3.689

Friedrich, Gerhard, '1–2 Thessalonians', in *Die Briefe an die Galater, Epheser, Philipper, Kolosser, Thessalonicher und Philemon* (J. Becker, H. Conzelmann and G. Friedrich; NTD; Göttingen: Vandenhoeck and Ruprecht, 1981)

Funk, Robert W., 'The Apostolic *Parousia*: Form and Significance', in *Christian History and Interpretation: Studies Presented to John Knox* (ed. William R. Farmer, *et. al.*; Cambridge: Cambridge University Press, 1967), pp. 249–68

Furnish, Victor, *II Corinthians* (AB 32A; Garden City: Doubleday, 1985)

García Martínez, Florentino, *The Dead Sea Scrolls Translated* (Leiden: Brill, 1994)

Gärtner, Bertil, *The Temple and the Community in Qumran and the New Testament* (SNTSMS 1; Cambridge: University Press, 1965)

Giblin, Charles H., 'The Heartening Apocalyptic of Second Thessalonians', *TBT* 26 (1988), pp. 350–4

—— '2 Thessalonians 2 Re-Read as Pseudepigraphical: A Revised Reaffirmation of *The Threat to Faith*', in *The Thessalonian Correspondence* (ed. Raymond F. Collins; BETL 87; Leuven: University Press, 1990), pp. 459–69

—— *The Threat to Faith: An Exegetical and Theological Re-Examination of 2 Thessalonians 2* (AnBib 31; Rome: Pontifical Biblical Institute, 1967)

Glover, R., 'Luke the Antiochene and Acts', *NTS* 11 (1964–65), pp. 97–106

Gnilka, Joachim, *Der Philipperbrief* (HTKNT 10,3; Freiburg: Herder, 1968)

Goldstein, Jonathan A., *The Letters of Demosthenes* (New York and London: Columbia University, 1968)

Greenfield, Jonas C. and Stone, Michael E., 'Remarks on the Aramaic Testament of Levi from the Geniza', in M. E. Stone, *Selected Studies in Pseudepigrapha and Apocrypha* (SVTP: Leiden, E. J. Brill, 1991), pp. 228–46

Gundry, Robert H., 'The Hellenization of Dominical Tradition and the Christianization of Jewish Tradition in the Eschatology of 1–2 Thessalonians', *NTS* 33 (1987), pp. 161–78

Hadorn, W., 'Die Abfassung der Thessalonicherbriefe auf der dritten Missionsreise des Paulus', *BFChTh* 24 (1919), pp. 157–284

—— 'Die Abfassung der Thessalonicherbriefe auf der dritten Missionsreise und der Kanons des Marcion,' *ZNW* 19 (1919–20), pp. 67–72

Haenchen, E., *The Acts of the Apostles; A Commentary* (trans. and ed. R. McL. Wilson; Philadelphia: Westminster Press, 1971)

Hafemann, Scott J., *Suffering and the Spirit* (Tübingen: Mohr, 1986)

Hahn, Ferdinand, *Christologische Hoheitstitel* (Göttingen: Vandenhoeck and Ruprecht, 1964)

—— 'Taufe und Rechtfertigung', in *Rechtfertigung: Festschrift für Ernst Käsemann* (ed. J. Friedrich, W. Pöhlmann, P. Stuhlmacher; Tübingen: J. C. B. Mohr, 1976), pp. 104–9

Hamilton, N. Q., *The Holy Spirit and Eschatology in Paul* (SJTOP 6; Edinburgh: Oliver and Boyd, 1957)

Hammond, N. G. L. and Scullard, H. H., ed., *The Oxford Classical Dictionary* (second edition; Oxford: Clarendon Press, 1970)

Harnack, Adolf von, 'ΚΟΠΟΣ', *ZNW* 27 (1928), pp. 1–10

Harrison, P. N., *The Problem of the Pastoral Epistles* (London: Oxford University Press, 1921)

Haufe, Christoph, *Die sittliche Rechtfertigungslehre des Paulus* (Halle: Max Niemeyer, 1957)

Haufe, G., 'Reich Gottes bei Paulus und in der Jesustradition', *NTS* 31 (1985), pp. 467–72

Heidland, H. W., 'ὀμείρομαι', *TDNT* 5.176

Hemberg, Bengt, *Die Kabiren* (Uppsala: Almqvist and Wiksells, 1950)

Hemer, C. J., *The Book of Acts in the Setting of Hellenistic History* (WUNT 49; ed. C. H. Gempf; Tübingen: Mohr Siebeck, 1989)

Hendrix, Holland L., 'Archaeology and Eschatology at Thessalonica', in *The Future of Christianity* (Festschrift Helmut Koester; ed. B. A. Pearson; Minneapolis: Fortress Press, 1991), pp. 107–18

—— 'Thessalonica', *ABD* 6:523–27

—— *Thessalonicans Honor Romans* (ThD diss., Harvard 1984)

Hengel, Martin, *Acts and the History of Earliest Christianity* (Philadelphia: Fortress Press, 1980)

—— *The Pre-Christian Paul* (London: SCM Press, 1991)

—— and Schwemer, Anna Maria, *Paul Between Damascus and Antioch: The Unknown Years* (Louisville: Westminster, 1997)

Henneken, Bartholomäus (*Verkündigung und Prophetie im 1. Thessalonicherbrief* (SBS 29; Stuttgart: Katholisches Bibelwerk, 1969)

Hill, David, *New Testament Prophecy* (London, 1975)

Hock, R. F., *The Social Context of Paul's Ministry: Tentmaking and Apostleship* (Philadelphia: Fortress Press, 1980)

Hogarth, D. G., *Devia Cypria* (London: H. Frowde, 1889)

Holladay, William L., *Jeremiah 1* (Hermeneia; Philadelphia: Fortress Press, 1986)

Holland, Glenn S., *The Traditions that You Received from Us: 2 Thessalonians in the Pauline Tradition* (HUTh 24; Tübingen: Mohr-Siebeck, 1986)

Hollander, H. W. and de Jonge, M., *The Testaments of the Twelve Patriarchs: A Commentary* (SVTP; Leiden: Brill, 1985)

Hollmann, Georg, 'Die Unechtheit des zweiten Thessalonicherbriefs', *ZNW* 5 (1904), pp. 28–38

Holmberg, Bengt, *Paul and Power* (Philadelphia: Fortress Press, 1980)

Holtz, Traugott, *Der erste Brief an die Thessalonicher* (2nd ed; EKK XIII; Zürich/Neukirchen-Vluyn: Benzinger/ Neukirchener Verlag, 1990)

—— 'Traditionen im 1. Thessalonicherbrief', in *Die Mitte des Neuen Testaments* (Festschrift E. Schweizer; ed. U. Luz and H. Weder; Göttingen: Vandenhoeck & Ruprecht, 1983), pp. 55–78

—— 'Zum Selbstverständnis des Apostels Paulus', *TLZ* 91 (1966), pp. 322–30

Horsely, G. H. R. *et al.*, *New Documents Illustrating Early Christianity* (7 vols; North Ryde, NSW: Macquarie University, 1976–94)

Hughes, Frank W., *Early Christian Rhetoric and 2 Thessalonians* (JSNTSup 30; Sheffield: JSOT Press, 1989)

—— 'The Rhetoric of 1 Thessalonians', in *The Thessalonian Correspondence* (ed. Raymond F. Collins; BETL 87; Leuven: University Press–Peeters, 1990), pp. 94–116

—— 'The Social Situations Implied by Rhetoric', in *The Thessalonians Debate: Methodological Discord or Methodological Synthesis?* (ed. Karl P. Donfried and Johannes Beutler; Grand Rapids: Eerdmans, 2000), pp. 241–54

Hurd, John C., 'Paul Ahead of His Time: 1 Thess. 2:13–16', in *Anti-Judaism in Early Christianity. I. Paul and the Gospels* (ed. Peter Richardson; Studies in Christianity and Judaism 2; Waterloo, ON: Wilfrid Laurier University, 1986)

—— 'Thessalonians, First Letter to the', *IDB* 4.900

Hyldahl, N., *Die Paulinische Chronologie* (Leiden: E. J. Brill, 1986)

Jeremias, Joachim, 'Paul and James', *ET* 66 (1954–55), pp. 368–71

—— 'Zöllner und Sünder', *ZNW* 30 (1931), pp. 293–300

Jervell, Jacob, *Die Apostelgeschichte* (KEK 3; Göttingen: Vandenhoeck and Ruprecht, 1998)

—— 'Paulus in der Apostelgeschichte und die Geschichte des Urchristentums', *NTS* 32 (1986), pp. 378–92

—— 'Der unbekannte Paulus', in *Die Paulinische Literatur und Theologie. Skandinavische Beitraege* (ed. S. Pedersen; Aarhus-Goettingen, 1980), pp. 29–40

—— *The Unknown Paul* (Minneapolis: Augsburg Press, 1984)

Jewett, Robert, *A Chronology of Paul's Life* (Philadelphia: Fortress Press, 1979)

—— *Paul's Anthropological Terms* (Leiden: E. J. Brill, 1971)

—— *The Thessalonian Correspondence: Pauline Rhetoric and Millenarian Piety* (FFNT; Philadelphia: Fortress Press, 1986)

Joest, Wilfried, *Gesetz und Freiheit* (Göttingen: Vandenhoeck and Ruprecht, 1956)

Johnson, George, 'Kingdom of God's Sayings in Paul's Letters', in *From Jesus to Paul: Studies in Honour of Francis Wright Beare* (ed. Peter Richardson and John C. Hurd; Waterloo: Wilfrid Laurier University, 1984), pp. 143–56

Johnson, Luke Timothy, *The Acts of the Apostles* (SP 5; Collegeville, MN: Liturgical, 1992)

Joint Declaration on the Doctrine of Justification / The Lutheran World Federation and the Roman Catholic Church (Grand Rapids: Eerdmans, 2000)

de Jonge, M., *The Testaments of the Twelve Patriarchs: A Critical Edition of the Greek Text* (PVTG; Leiden: Brill, 1978)

Judge, E. A., 'The Decrees of Caesar at Thessalonica', *RTR* 30 (1971), pp. 1–7

Jüngel, Eberhard, *Paulus und Jesus* (HUTh 2; Tübingen: J. C. B. Mohr, 1962)

Käsemann, Ernst, *An die Römer* (HNT 8a; Tübingen: J. C. B. Mohr, 1973)

—— *Commentary on Romans* (Grand Rapids: Eerdmans, 1980)

—— *Essays on New Testament Theses* (London: SCM Press, 1964)

—— 'Paulus und Israel', in *Exegetische Versuche und Besinnungen* (2 vols; Göttingen: Vandenhoeck and Ruprecht, 1964), 2.194–97

—— 'Sentences of Holy Law in the New Testament', in *New Testament Questions of Today* (Philadelphia: Fortress Press, 1969), pp. 66–81

Katz, Peter, 'The Early Christians Use of Codices Instead of Rolls', *JTS* 44 (1945), pp. 63–5

Kertelge, Karl, '*Rechtfertigung*' *bei Paulus* (NTAbh 3; Münster: Verlag Aschendorf, 1966)

Klauck, H. J., *Die antike Briefliteratur und das Neue Testament* (Paderborn: Schöningh, 1998)

Klein, Günter, 'Gottes Gerechtigkeit als Thema der neuesten Paulus-Forschung', *VF 12* (1967), pp. 1–11

Knauf, E. A., 'Zum Ethnarchen des Aretas 2 Kor 11,32', *ZNW* 74 (1983), pp. 145–7

Knox, John, *Chapters in a Life of Paul* (ed. D. A. Hare; rev. ed.; Macon, Ga.: Mercer University, 1987)

Koeberlein, Ernst, *Caligula und die aegyptischen Kulte* (BKP 3; Meisenheim am Glan: A. Hain, 1962)

Koester, Helmut, 'Archäologie und Paulus in Thessalonike', in *Religious Propaganda and Missionary Competition in the New Testament World. Essays Honoring Dieter Georgi* (ed. L. Bormann, K. Del Tredici and A. Standhartinger; NovTSup 74; Leiden: Brill, 1994), pp. 393–424

—— 'From Paul's Eschatology to the Apocalyptic Schemata of 2 Thessalonians', in *The Thessalonian Correspondence* (ed. R. F. Collins, BETL 87; Leuven: University Press–Peeters, 1990), pp. 441–58

—— *History and Literature of Early Christianity* (2 vols; Philadelphia: Fortress Press, 1982)

—— 'I Thessalonians – Experiment in Christian Writing', in

Continuity and Discontinuity in Church History (Festschrift G. H. Williams; SHCT 19; Leiden: Brill, 1979), pp. 33–44

Kraus, W., *Das Volk Gottes. Zur Grundlegung der Ekklesiologie bei Paulus* (WUNT 85; Tübingen: Mohr, 1996)

Krodel, G., *Acts* (ACNT; Minneapolis: Augsburg, 1986)

Kühl, E., *Rechtfertigung auf Grund Glaubens und Gericht nach den Werken bei Paulus* (Königsberg, 1904)

Kümmel, W. G., 'Das Problem der Entwicklung in der Theologie der Paulus', *NTS* 18 (1972), pp. 457–8

Küng, Hans, 'Katholische Besinnung auf Luthers Rechtfertigungslehre heute', in *Theologie im Wandel* (TThR I; München: Erich Wewel Verlag, 1967), pp. 449–68

Lake, Kirsopp, *The Earlier Epistles of St Paul* (London: Rivingtons, 1911)

Lambrecht, Jan, 'Thanksgivings in 1 Thessalonians 1–3', in *The Thessalonians Debate: Methodological Discord or Methodological Synthesis?* (ed. Karl P. Donfried and Johannes Beutler; Grand Rapids: Eerdmans, 2000), pp. 135–62

Lapide, Pinchas and Stuhlmacher, Peter, *Paulus – Rabbi und Apostel* (Stuttgart/München: Calwer/Kösel, 1981)

Larsson, E., 'Paul: Law and Salvation', in *NTS* 31 (1985), pp. 425–36

Légasse, Simon, *Les Épîtres de Paul aux Thessaloniciens* (LD Commentaires 7; Paris: Cerf, 1999)

Lehmann, Phyllis Williams, *The Pedimental Sculptures of the Hieron in Samothrace* (Locust Valley, New York: J. J. Augustin, 1962)

—— *Samothrace: The Heiron* (Bollingen Series 60.3; Princeton: Princeton University, 1969)

—— and Spittle, Denys, *Samothrace: The Temenos* (Bollingen Series 60.5; Princeton: Princeton University, 1982)

Lewis, Naphtali, *Samothrace: The Ancient Literary Sources* (Bollingen Series 60.1; New York: Pantheon, 1958)

Licht, J., *Megilat Ha-Serakhim: The Rule Scroll: A Scroll from the Wilderness of Judea 1QS, 1Qsa, 1QSb: Text, Introduction and Commentary* (Jerusalem: Bialik, 1965) [in modern Hebrew]

Liddell, Henry George and Scott, Robert, *A Greek-English Lexicon* (Oxford: Clarendon Press, 1994)

Liechtenhan, R., 'Die Ueberwindung des Leides bei Paulus und in der zeitgenössischen Stoa', *ZTK* 3 (1922), pp. 368–99

Lietzmann, Hans, *An die Korinther I/II* (HNT 9; Tübingen: J. C. B. Mohr, 1959)

Lifshitz, B. and Schiby, J., 'Une Synagogue samaritaine à Thessalonique', *RB* 75 (1968), pp. 368–78

Lightfoot, J. B., *Biblical Essays* (London: MacMillan, 1893)

—— *Saint Paul's Epistle to the Philippians* (London: Macmillan, 1891)

Lipsius, Richard Adelbert, 'Über Zweck und Veranlassung des ersten Thessalonicherbrief', *ThStKr* 27 (1854), pp. 905–34

Lock, W., *The Pastoral Epistles* (ICC; Edinburgh: T&T Clark, 1924)

Lohmeyer, Ernst, *Die Briefe an die Philipper, an die Kolosser und an Philemon* (MeyerK: Göttingen: Vandenhoeck and Ruprecht, 1964)

Louw, Johannes P. and Nida, Eugene A., *Greek-English Lexicon of the New Testament based on Semantic Domains* (New York: United Bible Societies, 1988)

Luck, Ulrich, 'Der Jakobusbrief und die Theologie des Paulus', *TGl* 61 (1971), pp. 161–79

Lüdemann, Gerd, *Das frühe Christentum nach den Traditionen der Apostelgeschichte* (Göttingen: Vandenhoeck and Ruprecht, 1987)

—— 'The Hope of the Early Paul: From the Foundation-Preaching at Thessalonika to 1 Cor 15:51–57', *PRSt* 7 (1980), pp. 196–7

—— *Paulus, der Heidenapostel* (2 vols; Göttingen: Vandenhoeck and Ruprecht, 1980). [ET: *Paul, Apostle to the Gentiles: Studies in Chronology* (Philadelphia: Fortress Press, 1984)]

—— *Paulus und das Judentum* (Munich: Chr. Kaiser, 1983)

Lütgert, W., 'Die Volkommenen im Philipperbrief und die Enthusiasten in Thessalonich', *BFChTh* 13 (1909), pp. 547–654

Lyonnet, Stanislas, 'Gratuité de la justification et gratuité du salut', in *Studiorum Paulinorum Congressus Internationalis*

Catholicus 1961; (2 vols; AnBib 17–18; Rome: Pontifical Biblical Institute, 1963), 1.95–100

—— 'Justification, jugement, rédemption, principalement dans l'épitre aux Romains', *RechBib* 5 (1960), pp. 166–84

Lyons, George, *Pauline Autobiography: Toward a New Understanding* (SBLDS 73; Atlanta: Scholars Press, 1985)

MacMullen, Ramsay, *Enemies of the Roman Order: Treason, Unrest, and Alienation in the Empire* (Cambridge, MA: Harvard University Press, 1966)

—— *Paganism in the Roman Empire* (New Haven: Yale University, 1981)

Malherbe, Abraham J., 'Exhortation in First Thessalonians', *NovT* 25 (1983), pp. 238–56

—— ' "Gentle as a Nurse": The Cynic Background to 1 Thess ii', *NovT* 12 (1970), pp. 203–17

—— *The Letter to the Thessalonians: A New Translation with Introduction and Commentary* (AB 32B; New York: Doubleday, 2000)

—— *Paul and the Popular Philosophers* (Minneapolis: Fortress Press, 1989)

—— *Paul and the Thessalonians. The Philosophic Tradition of Pastoral Care* (2nd ed.; Philadelphia: Fortress Press, 1988)

Marshall, I. Howard, *The Gospel of Luke* (NIGTC; Grand Rapids: Eerdmans, 1978)

—— *The Pastoral Epistles* (ICC; Edinburgh: T&T Clark, 1999)

—— *1 and 2 Thessalonians* (NCB; Grand Rapids: Eerdmans, 1983)

Martin, D. Michael, *1, 2 Thessalonians* (NAC 33; Broadman and Holman, 1995)

Martin, Ralph P., *Reconciliation* (Atlanta: John Knox Press, 1981)

Marxsen, W., 'Auslegung von 1 Thess 4,13–18', *ZTK* 66 [1969], pp. 22–37

—— *Der erste Brief des Paulus an die Thessalonicher* (ZBK.NT 11.1; Zürich: Theologischer Verlag, 1979)

Mattern, Lieselotte, *Das Verständnis des Gerichtes bei Paulus* (ATANT 47; Zürich: Zwingli, 1966)

McGown, C. C., 'The Earliest Christian Books', *BA* 6 (1943), pp. 21–31

McKenzie, John L., *Second Isaiah* (AB 20; Garden City: Doubleday, 1973)

Menken, M. J. J., *2 Thessalonians* (New Testament Readings; London and New York: Routledge, 1994)

Merk, Otto, '1 Thessalonians 2:1–12: An Exegetical-Theological Study', in *The Thessalonians Debate: Methodological Discord or Methodological Synthesis?* (ed. Karl P. Donfried and Johannes Beutler; Grand Rapids: Eerdmans, 2000), pp. 89–113

Merklein, Helmut, 'Die Ekklesia Gottes: der Kirchenbegriff bei Paulus und in Jerusalem', in *Studien zu Jesus und Paulus* (WUNT 43; Tübingen: Mohr, 1987), pp. 296–318

—— 'Der Theologe als Prophet: zur Funktion prophetischen Redens im theologischen Diskurs', *NTS* 38 (1992), pp. 402–29

Meyer, H. A. W., *Critical and Exegetical Handbook to the Acts of the Apostles* (2 vols; Edinburgh: T&T Clark, 1877)

Meyers, J. M. and Freed, J. D., 'Is Paul Among the Prophets', *Int* 20 (1966), pp. 40–53

Michel, Otto, *Der Brief an die Römer* (Meyer K; Göttingen: Vandenhoeck and Ruprecht, 1963)

—— 'Fragen zu I Thessalonicher 2,14–16: Anti-jüdische Polemik bei Paulus', in *Antijudaismus im Neuen Testament? Exegetische und systematische Beiträge* (ed. W. Eckert, et al.; ACJD 1; München, 1967), pp. 50–9

Michaelis, W., σκηνοποιός, in *TDNT* 7.393–94

Milligan, George, *St Paul's Epistles to the Thessalonians* (New York: Macmillan, n.d.)

Minear, Paul S., *The Obedience of Faith* (SBT 19; London: SCM Press, 1971)

Moessner, David P., 'Paul in Acts: Preacher of Eschatological Repentance to Israel', *NTS* 34 (1988), pp. 96–104

Montague, George T., *Growth in Christ* (Fribourg: Regina Mundi, 1961)

Moule, C. F. D., 'The Judgment Theme in the Sacraments', in *The Background of the New Testament and Its Eschatology* (ed.

W. D. Davies and D. Daube; Cambridge: University Press, 1964), pp. 464–81

Müller, Christian, *Gottes Gerechtigkeit und Gottes Volk* (FRLANT 86; Göttingen: Vandenhoeck and Ruprecht, 1964)

Munck, Johannes, '1 Thes 1, 9–10 and the Missionary Preaching of Paul. Exegesis and Hermeneutic Reflexions', *NTS* 9 (1963), pp. 86–110

Murphy-O'Connor, Jerome, 'The Corinth that Saint Paul Saw', *BA* 47 (1984), pp. 147–59

—— 'Paul and Gallio', *JBL* 112 (1993), pp. 315–17

—— *Paul on Preaching* (London and New York: Sheed and Ward, 1964)

Neil, William, *The Epistle of Paul to the Thessalonians* (Naperville: Allenson, 1957)

Neirynck, F., 'Paul and the Sayings of Jesus', in *L'Apôtre Paul: personnalité, style et conception du ministère* (BETL 73; ed. A. Vanhoye; Leuven, University Press–Peeters, 1986), pp. 265–321

Nilsson, Martin P., *The Dionysiac Mysteries of the Hellenistic Age* (Lund: Gleerup, 1957)

Nodet, Étienne and Taylor, Justin, *The Origins of Christianity: An Exploration* (Collegeville: The Liturgical Press, 1998)

Oberlinner, Lorenz, *Die Pastoralbriefe* (HTKNT XI/2; Freiburg: Herder, 1995)

O'Callaghan, Paul, *Fides Christi: The Justification Debate* (Dublin: Four Courts, 1997)

Oepke, Albrecht, *Die Briefe an die Thessalonicher* (NTD 8; reprint of 1933 edition; Göttingen: Vandenhoeck and Ruprecht, 1970)

Ogg, G., *The Chronology of the Life of Paul* (London: Epworth Press, 1968)

Okeke, G. E., '1 Thess. ii. 13–16: The Fate of the Unbelieving Jews', *NTS* 27 (1980), pp. 127–36

Otto, Walter F., *Dionysus: Myth and Cult* (Bloomington: Indiana University Press, 1965)

Pate, C. Marvin, *The Reverse of the Curse* (WUNT 2/114; Tübingen: Mohr/Siebeck, 2000)

Patte, Daniel, *Paul's Faith and the Power of the Gospel* (Philadelphia: Fortress Press, 1983)

Pearson, Birger A., '1 Thessalonians 2:13–16: A Deutero-Pauline Interpolation', *HTR* 64 (1971), pp. 79–94

Penna, R., 'Les Juifs à Rome au temps de l'Apôtre Paul', *NTS* 28 (1982), pp. 321–47

Perkins, Pheme, '1 Thessalonians and Hellenistic Religious Practices', in *To Touch the Text* (Festschrift J.A. Fitzmyer; ed. M. P. Horgan and P. J. Kobelski; New York: Crossroad, 1989), pp. 325–34

Pesch, R., *Die Entdeckung des ältesten Paulus-Briefes* (Freiburg: Herder, 1984)

Pixner, Bargil, 'Jerusalem's Essene Gateway – Where the Community Lived in Jesus' Time', *BAR* 23 (1997), pp. 22–66

—— *With Jesus through Galilee According to the Fifth Gospel* (Rosh Pina, Israel: Corazin, 1992)

—— *With Jesus in Jerusalem: His First and Last Days in Judea* (Rosh Pina, Israel: Corazin, 1996)

Plooij, D., *De Chronologie van het Leven van Paulus* (Leiden: 1918)

Plutta-Messerschmidt, Elke, *Gerechtigkeit Gottes bei Paulus* (Tübingen: J. C. B. Mohr, 1973)

Pobee, J. S., *Persecution and Martyrdom in the Theology of Paul* (JSNTSup 6; Sheffield: JSOT Press, 1985)

Popkes, Wiard, *Paränese und Neues Testament* (SBS 168; Stuttgart: Katholisches Bibelwerk, 1996)

Qimron, Elisha, *The Hebrew of the Dead Sea Scrolls* (Atlanta: Scholars Press, 1986)

Räisänen, Heikki, 'Paul's Conversion and the Development of His View of the Law', *NTS* 33 (1987), pp. 404–19

—— *Paul and the Law* (WUNT 29; Tübingen, 1983)

Reicke, Bo, 'Thessalonicherbriefe', *RGG* 6.851–53

Reinmuth, Eckhart, 'Der erste Brief an die Thessalonicher', in *Die Briefe an die Philipper, Thesslonicher und an Philemon*

(N. Walter, E. Reinmuth and P. Lampe; NTD 8/2; Göttingen: Vandenhoeck and Ruprecht, 1998)

Reumann, John, *Righteousness in the New Testament* (Philadelphia: Fortress Press, 1982)

Richard, Earl J., *First and Second Thesslonians* (SP 11; Collegeville, MN: Liturgical, 1995)

Riesner, Rainer, *Die Frühzeit des Apostels Paulus. Studien zur Chronologie, Missionsstrategie und Theologie* (WUNT 71; Tübingen: Mohr, 1994). [ET: *Paul's Early Period: Chronology, Mission Strategy, Theology* (Grand Rapids: Eerdmans, 1998)]

Rigaux, B., *Saint Paul. Les Épîtres aux Thessaloniciens* (EtB; Paris-Gembloux: Gabalda-Duculot, 1956)

Roberts, C. H., 'The Ancient Books and the Ending of St. Mark', *JTS* 11 (1939), p. 255

—— 'The Codex', *PBA* 40 (1954), pp. 184–5

Roetzel, Calvin J., *Judgement in the Community* (Leiden: Brill, 1972)

Roloff, Jürgen, *Die Apostelgeschichte* (NTD; Göttingen: Vandenhoeck and Ruprecht, 1981)

—— *Die Kirche im Neuen Testament* (GNT 10; Göttingen: Vandenhoeck and Ruprecht, 1993)

Rost, L., 'ἐκκλησία', *TDNT* 3.529

Sanders, E. P., *Paul, the Law, and the Jewish People* (Philadelphia: Fortress Press, 1983)

—— *Paul and Palestinian Judaism: A Comparison of Patterns of Religion* (Philadelphia: Fortress Press, 1977)

Sanders, J. T., 'The Salvation of the Jews in Luke-Acts', in *Luke-Acts: New Perspectives from the Society of Biblical Literature Seminar* (ed. Charles Talbert; New York: Crossroad, 1984), pp. 104–28

Schade, Hans-Heinrich, *Apokalyptische Christologie bei Paulus* (GTA 18; Göttingen: Vandenhoeck and Ruprecht, 1981)

Schelkle, Karl Hermann, 'Lohn und Strafe nach dem Neuen Testament', *BibLeb* 10 (1969), pp. 89–95

Schenke, Hans-Martin und Fischer, Karl Martin, *Einleitung in die Schriften des Neuen Testaments* (Berlin: Evangelische Verlagsanstalt, 1978)

Schiffmann, Lawrence H., *Reclaiming the Dead Sea Scrolls* (Philadelphia and Jerusalem: The Jewish Publication Society, 1994)

Schippers, R., 'The Pre-Synoptic Tradition in I Thessalonians II 13–16', *NovT* 8 (1966), pp. 223–34

Schlueter, Carol J., *Filling up the Measure: Polemical Hyperbole in 1 Thessalonians 2.14–16* (JSNTSup 98; Sheffield: JSOT Press, 1994)

Schmidt, Daryl, '1 Thess. 2:13–16: Linguistic Evidence for an Interpolation', *JBL* 102 (1983), pp. 269–79

Schmithals, W., *Die Briefe des Paulus in ihrer ursprünglichen Form* (ZWKB, Zürich: Theologischer Verlag, 1984)

—— 'The Historical Situation of the Thessalonian Epistles', in *Paul and the Gnostics* (Nashville: Abingdon, 1972), pp. 128–318

Schnackenburg, Rudolf, *Der Brief an die Epheser* (EKK; Neukirchen-Vluyn: Neukirchener, 1982)

Schnelle, Udo, 'Der erste Thessalonicherbrief und die Entstehung der paulinischen Anthropologie', *NTS* 32 (1986), pp. 207–24

—— *Gerechtigkeit und Christusgegenwart* (GTA 24; Göttingen: Vandenhoeck and Ruprecht, 1983)

Schoeps, H. J., *Aus frühchristlicher Zeit: Religionsgeschichtliche Untersuchungen* (Tübingen, 1950)

—— *Paul: The Theology of the Apostle in the Light of Jewish Religious History* (Philadelphia: Westminster, 1961)

Schoon-Janßen, J., *Umstrittene 'Apologien' in den Paulusbriefen. Studien zur rhetorischen Situation des 1. Thessalonicherbriefes, des Galaterbriefes und des Philipperbriefes* (GTA 45; Göttingen: Vandenhoeck and Ruprecht 1991)

Schrage, Wolfgang, *Der erste Brief an die Korinther* (EKK VII 1/2; Zürich: Benzinger, 1991/1995)

Schrenk, G., *Urchristliche Missionspredigt im 1. Jahrhundert*, in *Studien zu Paulus* (Zürich: Zwingli, 1954)

Schubert, P., *Form and Function of the Pauline Thanksgivings* (BZNW 20; Berlin: Alfred Töpelmann, 1939)

Schulz, Siegfried, 'Der frühe und der späte Paulus', *ThZ* 41 (1985), pp. 228–36

—— *Neutestamentliche Ethik* (Zürich: Theologischer Verlag, 1987)

—— 'Zur Rechtfertigung aus Gnaden in Qumran und bei Paulus', *ZTK* 56 (1959), pp. 155–85

Schuster, Hermann, 'Rechtfertigung und Gericht bei Paulus', in *Stat Crux Dum Volvitur Orbis* (Festschrift H. Lilje; ed. Georg Hoffmann and K. H. Rengstorf; Berlin: Lutherisches Verlagshaus, 1959), pp. 57–67

Schweitzer, Albert, *The Mysticism of the Apostle Paul* (New York: Holt, 1931)

Selwyn, E. G., *The First Epistle of St Peter* (London: Macmillan, 1961)

Sherwin-White, A. N., *Roman Society and Roman Law in the New Testament* (Oxford: Oxford University Press, 1963)

Shires, Henry M., *The Eschatology of Paul in the Light of Modern Scholarship* (Philadelphia: Westminster Press, 1966)

Skeat, T. C., 'Early Christian Book Production: Papyri and Manuscripts', in *The Cambridge History of the Bible* (3 vols; ed. G. W. H. Lampe; Cambridge: University Press, 1963–70), 2.54–79

Slingerland, D., 'Acts 18:1–17 and Lüdemann's Pauline Chronology', *JBL* 109 (1990), pp. 686–90

Smith, Abraham, *Comfort One Another: Reconstructing the Rhetoric and Audience of 1 Thessalonians* (Literary Currents in Biblical Interpretation; Louisville: Westminster/John Knox, 1995)

—— 'The Social and Ethical Implications of the Pauline Rhetoric in I Thessalonians' (Unpub. PhD diss.; Vanderbilt University, 1989)

Snodgrass, K. R., 'Justification by Grace – to the Doers: An Analysis of the Place of Romans 2 in the Theology of Paul', *NTS* 32 (1986), pp. 72–93

Steck, Odil Hannes, *Israel und das gewaltsame Geschick der Propheten* (WMANT 23; Neukirchen-Vluyn: Neukirchener, 1967)

Stegemann, W., 'Anlaß und Hintergrund der Abfassung von 1 Th 2,1–12', *Theologische Brosamen für Lothar Steiger* (ed. G. Freund and E. Stegemann; DBAT 5; Heidelberg: Wiss. Theol. Seminar, 1985), pp. 397–416

Stendahl, Krister, 'The Apostle Paul and the Introspective Conscience of the West', *HTR 29* (1963), pp. 199–215

—— 'Justification and the Last Judgment', *LW 8* (1961), pp. 1–7

—— 'Kirche, Im Urchristentum', *RGG* 3.1297–304

Still, Todd D., *Conflict at Thessalonica: A Pauline Church and its Neighbours* (JSNTSup 183; Sheffield: Sheffield Academic Press, 1999)

Stone, Michael E., 'The Hebrew Testament of Naphtali', *JJS* 47 (1996), pp. 311–21

—— 'The Parabolic Use of Natural Order in Judaism of the Second Temple Age', in Michael E. Stone, *Selected Studies in Pseudepigrapha and Apocrypha* (Leiden: Brill, 1991), pp. 457–67

—— and Greenfield, Jonas C., 'The Third and Fourth Manuscripts of *Aramaic Levi Document* From Qumran (4QLevicaram and 4QLevidaram)', *Le Muséon* 109 (1996), pp. 246–59

Stoops, Robert F. Jr, 'The Social Context of Acts 19:23–41', *JBL* 108 (1989), pp. 73–91

Stowers, Stanley, *Letter Writing in Greco-Roman Antiquity* (Philadelphia: Westminster Press, 1986)

Strobel, August, 'Lukas der Antiochener', *ZNW* 49 (1958), pp. 131–4

Stuhlmacher, Peter, *Gottes Gerechtigkeit bei Paulus* (FRLANT 87; Göttingen, Vandenhoeck and Ruprecht, 1965)

—— *Das paulinische Evangelium*, I (Göttingen: Vandenhoeck and Ruprecht, 1968)

Suggs, M. J., 'Concerning the Date of Paul's Macedonian Ministry', *NovT* 4 (1960), pp. 60–8

Suhl, A., *Paulus und seine Briefe: Ein Beitrag zum paulinischen Chronologie* (Gütersloh: Mohn, 1975)

Synofzik, Ernst, *Die Gerichts – und Vergeltungsaussagen bei Paulus: Eine traditionsgeschichtliche Untersuchung* (GTA 8; Gottingen: Vandenhoeck and Ruprecht, 1977)

Talmon, Shemaryahu, 'The Community of the Renewed Covenant', in *The Community of the Renewed Covenant: The*

Notre Dame Symposium on the Dead Sea Scrolls (Christianity and Judaism in Antiquity Series, 10; ed. Eugene Ulrich and James VanderKam; Notre Dame, Indiana: University of Notre Dame, 1994), pp. 3–24

Tasker, R. V. G., *The Biblical Doctrine of the Wrath of God* (London: Tyndale Press, 1957)

Thomas, Johannes, 'παρακαλέω', *EDNT* 3.23–27

Trilling, W., *Untersuchungen zum zweiten Thessalonicherbrief* (EThSt 27; Leipzig: St Benno, 1972)

—— *Der Zweite Brief an die Thessalonicher* (EKK XIV; Zürich, Einsiedeln and Köln, Neukirchen: Benziger and Neukirchener Verlag: 1980)

Trocmé, Etienne, 'The Jews as Seen by Paul and Luke', in *To See Ourselves as Others See Us* (ed. J. Neusner and E. S. Frerichs; Chico, CA: Scholars Press, 1985), pp. 145–61

Vander Stichele, Caroline, 'The Concept of Tradition and 1 and 2 Thessalonians', in *The Thessalonian Correspondence* (ed. R. F. Collins, BETL 87; Leuven: University Press–Peeters, 1990), pp. 499–504

Vermes, Geza, *The Complete Dead Sea Scrolls in English* (New York: Penguin, 1997)

—— *The Dead Sea Scrolls in English* (New York: Penguin, 1995)

Vickers, Michael, 'Towards Reconstruction of the Town Planning of Roman Thessaloniki', in *Ancient Macedonia I: Papers Read at the First International Symposium Held in Thessaloniki, 26–29 August 1968* (ed. B. Laourdas and C. I. Makaronas; 2 vols; Thessaloniki: Institute for Balkan Studies, 1970), 1.239–51

Vielhauer, Philipp, 'On the "Paulinism" of Acts', in *Studies in Luke-Acts* (Festschrift Paul Schubert; ed. Leander E. Keck and J. Louis Martyn; Nashville: Abingdon, 1966), pp. 33–50

Viviano, Benedict T., 'The Kingdom of God in the Qumran Literature', in *The Kingdom of God in 20th Century Interpretation* (ed. W. Willis; Peabody, MA: Hendrickson, 1987), pp. 97–107

Vos, J. S., *Traditionsgeschichtliche Untersuchungen zur Paulinischen Pneumatologie* (Assen: van Gorcum, 1973)

Walker, William O., 'Acts and the Pauline Corpus Reconsidered', *JSNT* 24 (1985), pp. 3–23

Walter, Nikolaus, 'Paulus und die urchristliche Tradition', *NTS* 31 (1985), pp. 498–522

Wanamaker, C.A., *The Epistle to the Thessalonians. A Commentary on the Greek Text* (NIGTC; Grand Rapids: Eerdmans, Exeter, UK: Paternoster Press, 1990)

—— 'Epistolary vs. Rhetorical Analysis: Is a Synthesis Possible', in *The Thessalonians Debate: Methodological Discord or Methodological Synthesis?* (ed. Karl P. Donfried and Johannes Beutler; Grand Rapids: Eerdmans, 2000), pp. 255–86

Weinfeld, Moshe, *The Organizational Pattern and the Penal Code of the Qumran Sect* (NTOA; Göttingen: Vandenhoeck and Ruprecht, 1986)

Wetter, G. P., *Der Vergeltungsgedanke bei Paulus* (Göttingen: Vandenhoeck und Ruprecht, 1912)

White, John L., 'Ancient Greek Letters', in *Graeco-Roman Literature and the New Testament* (ed. David E. Aune; SBLSBS 21; Atlanta: Scholars Press, 1988)

—— *The Form and Function of the Body of the Greek Letter: A Study of the Letter-Body in the Non-Literary Papyri and in Paul the Apostle* (2nd ed. corrected; SBLDS 2; Missoula: Scholars Press, 1972)

Wicks, Jared, ed., *Catholic Scholars Dialogue with Luther* (Chicago: Loyola Press, 1970)

Wilckens, Ulrich, *Die Missionsreden der Apostelgeschichte* (WMANT 5; Neukirchen-Vluyn: Neukirchener Verlag, 1963)

—— 'Zur Entwicklung des paulinischen Gesetzesverständnis', *NTS* 28 (1982), pp. 154–90

Wilson, S. G., 'From Jesus to Paul: The Contours and Consequences of a Debate', in *From Jesus to Paul* (Festschrift F. W. Beare; ed. Peter Richardson and John C. Hurd; Waterloo: Wilfrid Laurier University, 1984), pp. 1–21

Wise, Michael O., Abegg, Martin G. Jr and Cook, Edward M., ed., *The Dead Sea Scrolls: A New Translation* (San Francisco: Harper, 1996)

Witt, Rex, 'The Egyptian Cults in Ancient Macedonia', in *Ancient Macedonia II: Papers Read at the Second International Symposium Held in Thessaloniki, 19–24 August 1973* (ed. B. Laourdas and C. I. Makaronas; 2 vols; Thessaloniki: Institute for Balkan Studies, 1977), 1.324–33

Wrede, Wilhelm, *Die Echtheit des zweiten Thessalonicherbriefs untersucht* (TU 9/2; Leipzig: Hinrichs, 1903)

Wuellner, Wilhelm, 'Greek Rhetoric and Pauline Argumentation', in *Early Christian Literature and the Classical Intellectual Tradition* (Festschrift Robert M. Grant; ed. William R. Schoedel and Robert L. Wilken; ThH 54; Paris: Beauchesne, 1979), pp. 177–88

Zahn, Th., *Die Apostelgeschichte des Lukas* (KNT 5; Leipzig: Deichert, 1921)

—— *Introduction to the New Testament* (New York: Scribner's, 1917)

Ziesler, J. A., *The Meaning of Righteousness in Paul* (SNTSMS 20; Cambridge: University Press, 1972)

Index of Modern Authors

Index of Ancient Texts

**Other Books by
Karl Paul Donfried**

Peter in the New Testament
(with Raymond E. Brown and John Reumann)

The Setting of Second Clement in Early Christianity

The Romans Debate

Mary in the New Testament
(with Raymond E. Brown, Joseph Fitzmyer and John Reuman)

*The Dynamic Word: New Testament Insights for
Contemporary Christians*

The Theology of the Shorter Pauline Letters
(with I. Howard Marshall)

Judaism and Christianity in Rome in the First Century
(with Peter Richardson)

*The Thessalonians Debate: Methodological Discord or
Methodological Synthesis?*
(with Johannes Beutler)